Local Institutional Development:
An Analytical Sourcebook
With Cases

Local Institutional Development:

An Analytical Sourcebook With Cases

Norman Uphoff
for the
Rural Development Committee
Cornell University

Kumarian Press

Cover design by

Maxine Fabian

Uphoff, Norman Thomas.
  Local institutional development.

  (Kumarian Press library of management for development)
  Bibliography: p.
  1. Developing countries—Economic conditions.   2. Rural
development—Developing countries.   3. Agricultural development projects—Developing countries.   4. Natural
resources—Developing countries—Management. 5. Medical
care—Developing countries.   I. Cornell University.
Rural Development Committee.   II. Title. III. Series.
HC59.7.U64   1986   302.3′ 5   86-15288
ISBN 0-931816-45-9
ISBN 0-931816-38-6 (pbk.)

CONTENTS

Chapter Three—LOCAL INSTITUTIONAL DEVELOPMENT FOR RURAL INFRASTRUCTURE

Chapter Four—LOCAL INSTITUTIONAL DEVELOPMENT FOR PRIMARY HEALTH CARE

Chapter Five—LOCAL INSTITUTIONAL DEVELOPMENT FOR AGRICULTURE

Chapter Six—LOCAL INSTITUTIONAL DEVELOPMENT FOR NONAGRICULTURAL ENTERPRISE

Chapter Seven—STRATEGIES FOR SUPPORTING LOCAL
INSTITUTIONAL DEVELOPMENT

Chapter Eight—MOBILIZING AND MANAGING ECONOMIC
RESOURCES FOR LOCAL
INSTITUTIONAL DEVELOPMENT

ANNEXES ON LOCAL INSTITUTIONAL DEVELOPMENT EXPERIENCE

PREFACE

This volume consolidates the efforts of a working group on Local Institutional Development (LID) sponsored by the Rural Development Committee in the Center for International Studies at Cornell University. The work was funded by the Office of Rural and Institutional Development of the U.S. Agency for International Development's Bureau for Science and Technology during 1983-84. The group met regularly, with my faculty colleagues, Milton J. Esman (Government), William F. Whyte (Organization Theory), and Rada Dyson-Hudson (Anthropology), sharing in the leadership of discussions.

Most of the members of the working group were graduate students in various departments at Cornell, with Gregory Schmidt (Government), Rebecca Miles Doan (Rural Sociology), and Gerard Finin (Regional Planning) serving in turn as coordinators for the group. Other members were: Harihar Acharya (Anthropology), Chris Brown (Government), Arturo Corpuz (Regional Planning), Peter Doan (Regional Planning), David Douglin (Agricultural Economics), Johanna Looye (Regional Planning), Ruth Meinzen-Dick (Rural Sociology), Nancy St. Julien (Regional Planning), Katy Van Dusen (Vegetable Crops), Suzanne Wallen (Regional Planning), and Ruth Yabes (Regional Planning).

The group undertook a wide-ranging review of the literature on local institutional development during the summer and fall of 1983, with group analyses of experience and concepts throughout the fall of 1983 and spring of 1984. Drafting of a series of eight reports took most of 1984 and led to a series of monographs written by myself with inputs from various other members of the working group.* These have now been further edited and integrated to provide what we are calling "an analytical sourcebook" on local institutional development, buttressed by case synopses from many sectors and from all areas of the world.

---

*Those who worked with me on the respective chapters were: Harihar Acharya, Peter Doan, David Douglin, Ruth Meinzen-Dick and Nancy St. Julien (Chapter 2), Greg Schmidt, Arturo Corpuz and Ruth Yabes (Chapter 3), Rebecca Doan and Jerry Finin (Chapter 4), Katy Van Dusen and David Douglin (Chapter 5), Johanna Looye (Chapter 6), Jerry Finin and Suzanne Wallen (Chapter 7), and Rebecca Doan, Greg Schmidt and Chris Brown (Chapter 8). Jerry Finin gave much appreciated assistance in completing the written product.

Faculty and graduate student colleagues who contributed in various ways to our work though they were not able to be as actively involved as were working group members included:

Jonathan Carr (Business Administration), Roy Colle (Communication Arts), Walt Coward (Rural Sociology), Peter Ide (Business Administration), Kevin LeMorvan (Rural Sociology), Charles Kafumba (International Development), Waqar Malik (Extension Education), Kathryn March (Anthropology), Ed Martin (Agricultural Economics), Porus Olpadwala (Regional Planning), Dan Sisler (Agricultural Economics), Catherine Tardiff (Rural Sociology), Bob Yoder (Agricultural Engineering), and Larry Zuidema (International Agriculture).

We had the benefit of many comments from consultants who participated in a workshop at Cornell in April 1984 to review our analysis, and we wish to thank them for their suggestions:

Harry Blair (Political Science, Bucknell University), Don Chauls (Education, Management Sciences for Health), John Field (Political Science, Tufts School of Nutrition), Dwight King (Political Science, Northern Illinois University), Cheryl Lassen (Rural Sociology, Partnership for Productivity), David Leonard (Political Science, University of California, Berkeley), Douglas Pickett (Economics, USAID), Susan Poats (Anthropology, Farming Systems Support Project, University of Florida), Lucrecio Rebugio (Social Forestry, University of the Philippines), and John W. Thomas (Economics, Harvard Institute for International Development).

The work benefited throughout from the inputs of Dr. Douglas J. Merrey, Senior Social Science Advisor in the Office of Rural and Institutional Development, USAID. This work had the support of Dr. Ruth Zagorin, Dr. Norman Nicholson, Mr. Jerry French and Dr. Eric Chetwynd who have provided leadership on this subject within USAID. Production of this study depended greatly on the word processing skills and endurance of Jane Kellogg, and was assisted by Debi Ostrander, Virginia Hicks, Rosalind Grigsby, Ellen Klinko, Rosanne Paradiso and Elisabeth Thorn of the Center for International Studies, Cornell University.

Norman Uphoff, for the
Working Group on Local
Institutional Development

CHAPTER ONE

Analyzing Options for Local Institutional Development

1.1 INTRODUCTION

In recent years international donor agencies have come to recognize how crucial *institutional development* is for overall development success. Indeed, USAID has identified it as one of the four leading elements of its assistance strategy, and the World Bank has concluded from its project experience that the neglect of institutional development has often diminished the productivity of its investments.[1]

The majority of investments in institutional development made thus far, however, have been focused at the national level. This is understandable in that these are the most visible institutions and the ones that donors deal with first and most easily. Still, it is unfortunate to the extent that *local* institutions—those closest to the intended beneficiaries and those which shape project outcomes most specifically—are allocated so few resources and are treated almost as afterthoughts.[2]

---

[1]USAID's policy paper on institutional development states: "Effective public and private institutions are essential for providing a country the self-sustaining capacity to solve critical development problems . . . It is therefore A.I.D. policy to help recipient countries establish and strengthen public and private institutions in support of mutually agreed, priority development objectives" (USAID, 1983:1-2). World Bank experience in this regard is assessed in a staff paper (1980).

[2]A documented example of such neglect of local institutions is seen in a study for the World Bank on developing village water systems (Saunders and Warford, 1976). Only a few pages are devoted to local institutions even though those pages (142-145) give strong evidence of local institutions' value. The Bank's own review of experience with village water supply projects (1976) reached the same conclusion about the value of local institutions, but likewise passed quickly over ways that local participation in planning, construction, and management could improve utilization, maintenance, and financial operation (pages 63-65).

Local institutions were scarcely considered in the Bank's analysis of managerial and institutional aspects of development in its 1983 *World Development Report*. An example of USAID neglect would be the study of small farmer cropping systems research in Central America

Local institutions as enumerated in Section 1.3 are not sufficient in themselves for promoting development. National institutions are needed for the development and dissemination of improved technologies and for the mobilization and management of resources. Local institutions, however, can significantly contribute to these tasks and others. USAID presently states as a matter of policy:

> . . . investments in national public institutions must be balanced both by the establish-ment of decentralized institutions at regional and local levels and by encouragement to the private sector. Balanced assistance of this sort is essential if excessive central control is not to inhibit private and local initiative. (USAID, 1983:4)

Yet one finds little explicit analysis of what kinds of local institutional development are most appropriate, for what tasks, and how they can best be supported. For comparative and cumulative work to be done on the subject, there need to be some consistent categories for analysis that are theoretically informed and empirically relevant. This analytical sourcebook, the product of several years of research and critical consideration of local institutional development (LID) by faculty and graduate student members of the Rural Development Committee at Cornell University, assisted by a grant from USAID, undertakes to provide such a systematic treatment of LID. It seeks to balance analytical and action-oriented concerns in a way that academics and practitioners can both become more engaged in LID work and can con-tribute to each other's success.

1.2 ACTIVITY AREAS FOR LOCAL INSTITUTIONAL DEVELOPMENT

What kinds and combinations of local institutions are likely to be most appropriate to support different kinds of rural development activities? This was the question we began with. Surely local institutions are not equally necessary or useful for all tasks. Therefore, we started with a framework for differentiating the kinds of activities that might require appropriate local institutional development.[3] Five main activity areas for rural development stand out as major focuses of local, national, and international concern. Not coincidentally they correspond to the distinctions economists make between *inputs* and *outputs* of production. The activity areas, dealt with in Chapters Two through Six in terms of their respective LID requirements, are the following:

(1980) which deals instructively with national and international institutions but ignores local institutions and their role in farming systems development. USAID now has a policy statement (1984) which explicitly endorses the development of the local institutional capacities such as described in Sections 1.3 and 1.4 below.

[3]The following framework, first prepared for USAID's Office of Multi-Sectoral Develop-ment in 1982 to assist in formulating a rural development strategy statement for the Bureau of Science and Technology, is elaborated in Uphoff (1984).

(a) natural resource management;
(b) rural infrastructure;
(c) human resource development;
(d) agricultural development; and
(e) nonagricultural enterprise.

The first three activity areas listed encompass the economic factors of production referred to respectively as *land, capital,* and *labor,* though the development processes that sustain, create, or enhance these "inputs" are more complex than such a classification implies. Each of these three areas includes a varied set of activities providing "outputs" that in turn become "inputs" for production processes in the areas of agricultural development and nonagricultural enterprise. These two areas divide activities according to whether *primary commodities* (food or fiber) are produced or whether they furnish *secondary products* (goods) or *tertiary products* (services). Most of the interactions among these activity areas are indicated in Figure 1.1. It would be even more complex if all of the connections within as well as between the areas were sketched in.[4]

Figure 1.1: ACTIVITY AREAS IN RURAL DEVELOPMENT

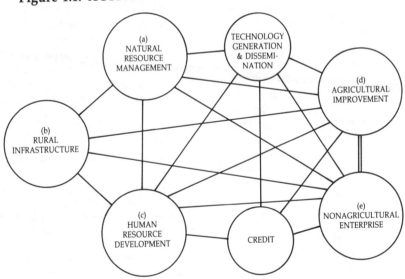

LID tasks will differ according to the area of activity. The institutional requirements for controlling access to common property such as rangeland,

---

[4]Two additional "cross-sectoral" activity areas, *credit,* and *technology generation and dissemination,* are shown here but are not treated separately in the chapters that follow, though each is supportive of the other areas. LID analysis could readily be extended to deal with these as supporting activity areas.

for example, are not the same as those that ensure proper operation and maintenance of an irrigation system after design and construction work are completed. Systematic treatment of LID variations between and within sectors is long overdue, and much can be learned from such work. Both natural resource management and rural infrastructure, to continue the comparison, confront problems of "collective action" when it comes to creating and maintaining "public goods." At the same time, within both areas there are some significant differences in LID tasks such as between range management and social forestry or between rural roads and rural electrification. Thus, LID should not been seen as an abstract process. In addition to dealing with local institutional development as a general goal and process for government, private, and donor agencies, thought should be given to LID in the different activity areas and indeed for specific activities within those areas as delineated in Chapters Two through Six.

1.3 ALTERNATIVE LOCAL INSTITUTIONAL CHANNELS

Local institutions range from *public sector* to *private sector* channels of activity, with an *intermediate sector* of membership organizations that have both public and private characteristics, as analyzed in Esman and Uphoff (1984). The major categories of local institutions can be classified as follows:

(a) **Local administration** (LA)—local agencies and staff of central government ministries, accountable to bureaucratic superiors;

(b) **Local government** (LG)—elected or appointed bodies such as village councils or panchayats, having authority to deal with development and regulatory tasks and accountable to local residents, in contrast to LA;

(c) **Membership organizations** (MOs)—local self-help associations whose members may seek to handle;
  (i) *multiple tasks*, e.g. local development associations or village development committees,
  (ii) *specific tasks*, e.g. water users' associations managing irrigation or health committees overseeing village programs, or
  (iii) *needs* of members who have some particular characteristic or interest in common, e.g. mothers' clubs, caste associations, or tenant unions.[5]

(d) **Cooperatives**—kinds of local organizations that pool members' economic resources for their benefit, e.g. marketing associations, credit unions, consumer societies, or producer co-ops;[6]

(e) **Service organizations** (SOs)—local organizations formed

---

[5]Membership in local organizations can range from being inclusive (as in *i* above) to being exclusive (as in *iii*). Leonard (1982) analyzes when "exclusive" local organizations or co-ops may be more desirable than "inclusive" local organizations.

[6]Tendler's study of Bolivian cooperatives (1983) shows that co-ops can benefit persons in the community who are not members of the cooperative. But co-ops are generally established for members' benefits and not as philanthropies like SOs.

primarily to help persons other than members though members may benefit from them. Examples are religious or charitable associations, service clubs, Red Cross or Red Crescent societies, and *sociedades de beneficiencia* which run rural hospitals in a number of Latin American countries;

(f) **Private businesses** (PBs)—either independent operations or branches of extra-local enterprises engaged in manufacturing, services and/or trade.

Each of these six categories is distinct and offers different advantages and disadvantages for supporting certain kinds of rural development.[7] They correspond to a continuum ranging from the public to the private sectors as shown in Figure 1.2. A broad category of *local organizations* (LOs) covers the middle range of MOs, co-ops, and SOs, as analyzed in Esman and Uphoff (1984).

Figure 1.2: CONTINUUM OF LOCAL INSTITUTIONS BY SECTOR

PUBLIC SECTOR		*VOLUNTARY SECTOR*		*PRIVATE SECTOR*	
Local Admini- stration (LA)	Local Govern- ment (LG)	Member Organi- zations (MOs)	Coop- era- tives (Co-ops)	Service Organi- zations (SOs)	Private Busi- nesses (PBs)
Bureau- cratic Institu- tions	Polit- ical Institu- tions	Local Organizations (based on the principle of membership direction and control; these can become institutions)			Profit- Oriented Institu- tions

Local administration and *local government* are set apart from other local institutions in that they have the force of law and the resources of the state behind them. They differ in that LA personnel are responsible to higher levels of decision making, whereas LG representatives and staff are accountable, at least in principle, to "constituents" but are not themselves "members" of the local government. When LGs have little financial or operational autonomy, they function for all practical purposes as LA units. Together, LA and LG comprise the "public" end of the institutional continuum at the local level.

At the "private" end, we find *local service organizations* and *private businesses*. Both produce benefits for persons outside their organization, but these persons are regarded either as clients or customers rather than

---

[7]Local political organizations, such as branches of political parties, are sometimes active in development efforts but usually they are not. We have not considered them here as local institutions for promotion since external agencies are expected to avoid getting involved in domestic politics.

as members and thus have no right to determine the activities of the organization. This makes them "private" institutions even though they may
receive some public funds through subsidies or contracts and may be subject to some public regulation.[8]

Local membership organizations as well as *cooperatives* come into
being to serve the interests of their members. Though LOs share certain
characteristics with both the public and the private sectors, there are also
some significant differences.[9] The calculus of action in this "third sector"
is collective rather than individual, so in this respect LOs operate more
like public institutions than private ones. Yet they need to proceed largely
by consensus and persuasion because no state authority backs up their
decisions. LOs resemble private organizations in that they can be more
flexible and adaptive than government agencies, but they are more oriented to public benefits than are private, for-profit enterprises.

Co-ops represent a diverse category of LOs of special interest because
they offer possibilities for increasing the productivity of economic activity.
Unfortunately, though there are some notable exceptions, the performance
of cooperatives has often been below expectations, and their record for
helping poorer sectors of the community is not very good (Fals Borda, 1976;
Lele, 1981). Special attention to co-ops is warranted to establish when,
where, and how they may be productive.

1.4 EXISTING INSTITUTIONS

When planners or managers remark that "local institutions" are very
weak, they are usually referring to the so-called "modern" institutions that
have been assigned specific developmental tasks by the government.
Localities vary in the extent and vitality of their so-called "traditional"
(indigenous, informal) institutions, evolved and supported by rural people
to deal with diverse problems—economic, social, cultural, religious,
political, etc. Some such institutions almost always exist though they may be
hard to find or to work with. Pre-existing institutions often parallel those
described in Section 1.3 and can be quite modern in many respects.[10] Certain

---

[8]A U.S. Commission on Private Philanthropy and Public Needs described what it called "a
third sector," operating between business and government (Douglas, 1983). However, we
would not lump self-help membership organizations, as the Commission did, together with all
nonprofit, philanthropic, and charitable organizations (collectively designated as PVOs, private voluntary organizations). We find more analytical coherence in Leonard's classification
(1982) which groups "philanthropy" and "marketization" as alternative forms of "private" activity for meeting the needs of the rural poor. We likewise group SOs and PBs together in the
"private" sector because both clients and customers have an analogous relationship, which is
different from that of "members."

[9]Esman and Uphoff (1984) analyze in detail the broad and diverse segment of the local institutional continuum within which LOs fall. See also Berger and Neuhaus (1977) on the value of
such institutions as buffers between the public and private sectors.

[10]An example would be "burial societies" in Botswana (Brown, 1982).

administrative roles, such as that of tax collector or registrar of lands, may have existed for hundreds of years and been incorporated into contemporary local administration (LA). Traditional chiefs or village headmen, sometimes acting in conjunction with local councils of elders, may function as indigenous LG institutions.[11] There are many kinds of traditional LOs—age cohorts, women's secret societies, craftsmen's guilds, to mention a few examples—and indigenous cooperatives such as rotating credit associations or labor exchanges.[12] Traditional manufacturing and commercial enterprises can be found in most rural areas and often constitute an "informal sector" providing goods and services. One can commonly find indigenous practitioners as private health providers (Pillsbury, 1979). Moreover, there are many kinds of traditional philanthropic organizations and roles, some of which take the form of what are called "patron-client" networks. Some examples of pre-existing service organizations in the area of forest management are given in Chapter Two.

Governments and donor efforts to develop local institutional capabilities should be cognizant of such existing institutions and should work cooperatively with them where possible recognizing that these roles and organizations are familiar and accepted because they have been meeting some local needs. It has often proved difficult for governments and donor agencies to link up with such institutions in the past, however, and knowledge on how to do this effectively is limited.[13] There is a real danger that outside intervention will destroy or warp these institutions' operations in ways that undermine their present capacities (March and Taqqu, 1986). Accordingly the capacities and complementarities of such institutions for cooperation with new activities should be carefully considered, and we would not recommend the cooptation of pre-existing institutions as a general strategy.

Some combination of building on what exists and carefully fostering something new is likely to be the preferable course of action. It is advisable for "modern" institutions to imitate familiar and accepted patterns of responsibility, communication, resource mobilization, etc. as much as possible. Often there will be opportunities for them to collaborate with existing institutions. In our review of LID experience in the literature, we did not find existing institutions particularly unwilling to engage in new development activities so long as the activities were ones which were beneficial and appreciated by members and so long as decisions were not imposed from outside.

---

[11]The *panchayat* systems in India and Nepal, while imitating traditional models of local government and using familiar terminology, should be regarded as introduced rather than indigenous institutions.

[12]See, for example, the study of Liberian cooperatives by Seibel and Massing (1974).

[13]Such institutions like the civil-religious hierarchies in the Andean communities in Peru are very complex, with irrigation operation and maintenance connected to sacred rituals (Isbell, 1978). Some linkages are possible however as shown by innovative work with indigenous healers in Ghana (Warren et al., 1981).

1.5 WHAT IS AN INSTITUTION?

What constitutes an "institution" is a subject of continuing debate among social scientists. The following formulations reflect some degree of consensus in the literature and apply to what governments, donor agencies, and private voluntary organizations can do to support LID. Some institutional manifestations are indigenous or diffuse and thus are difficult to address in terms of technical or financial assistance, so we are focusing on organizational structures or channels which have been, or could be, more readily institutionalized.

The terms *institution* and *organization* are commonly used interchangeably and this contributes to ambiguity and confusion. Three categories are commonly recognized: (a) organizations that are not institutions, (b) institutions that are not organizations, and (c) organizations that are institutions (or vice versa, institutions that are organizations). We are concerned here with the last category.

The three categories can be illustrated with examples from the legal realm. A new firm of lawyers would represent the first category, an organization that is not (yet?) an institution. "The law" is an institution that is not an organization and exemplifies the second. Courts, which are both organizations and institutions, fall in the last category.[14]

To elaborate how these concepts overlap and diverge, we need basic definitions. Organizations are structures of recognized and accepted roles. The structures that result from interactions of roles can be complex or simple. The more complex an organization is the more varied its capabilities. Organizations may operate on a formal or informal basis. The latter means there is no legal or otherwise explicitly prescribed basis for the roles or for the authority and other resources associated with them.

Not all organizations are "institutions," as noted above. To the extent that an organization has acquired special status and legitimacy for having satisfied people's needs and for having met their normative expectations over time, one can say that an organization has become "institutionalized." This formulation matches Huntington's observation that

> institutions are stable, valued, recurring patterns of behavior. Organizations and procedures vary in their degree of institutionalization. . . . Institutionalization is the process by which organizations and procedures acquire value and stability. (1965:378)

Roles and practices, and also systems of relations (referred to as "organized

---

[14]These distinctions fit Frank Knight's suggestion that there are two kinds of institutions corresponding to (b) and (c) above. The first kind, according to Knight, "may be said to be created by the 'invisible hand' . . . deliberate action hardly figures." The other type of institution is "deliberately made." The respective examples Knight gave were language and the Federal Reserve System. Cited in Ruttan (1978:328).

systems" by Crozier and Friedberg, 1980), can likewise acquire institutional status through valued performance over time.

In general, institutions, whether organizations or not, are *complexes of norms and behaviors that persist over time by serving collectively valued purposes*. Institutions can be concrete and specific like a nation's central bank or quite diffuse and general such as the institution of money. Some kinds of institutions have an organizational form with roles and structures, whereas others exist as pervasive influences on behavior.[15]

One approach to the study of institutions has focused on the *rules* that shape behavior rather than on *roles*, which accomplish the same thing. Analysis dealing with rules has been shaped most strongly by the work of John R. Commons, who contributed to what is now called "institutional economics."[16] Examining rules provides many insights into the processes and consequences of institutionalization. But it directs attention and action toward diffuse, even abstract institutional forms which are not embodied in an organizational structure. These can be extremely difficult to address and deal with in development efforts. So without denying the existence or importance of rule-based institutions, we have chosen to concentrate on institutions having organizational structure, or on organizations that have potential to become institutionalized. The institution of academic freedom is vital for the operation and productivity of a university, but our concern here is with more tangible institutions such as universities.

Both role-oriented and rule-oriented approaches to institutional analysis encompass consideration of people's values and social norms. Institutions are inextricably bound up with normative considerations, which is why they cannot be constructed mechanically like a hydroelectric dam or a trunk road. Selznick (1957) suggested that to "institutionalize" is to infuse with value beyond the technical requirements of the task at hand. This suggests that an institution is an organization (or a role, a rule, procedure, a practice, a system of relations) that is valued by persons over and above the direct and immediate benefits they derive from it.

One way of thinking about the extent to which an organization qualifies as an "institution" is to ask whether, if it were to disappear, people in the community, not just members or direct beneficiaries, would want it back and to what extent people would act or sacrifice to preserve the institution in

---

[15]In distinguishing between "organizations" and "organized systems," Crozier and Friedberg (1980) identify the latter as being more diffuse and less formal patterns of interaction. To use Knight's metaphor, the latter are institutions created by the "invisible hand." Young (1982) in analyzing natural resource management makes the same distinction when he contrasts "explicit organizations" and "social institutions." Montgomery (1984) has treated organizations and institutions as we do, as overlapping categories, as does also Hufschmidt (1985).

[16]See the excellent literature reviews on "institutions" by Runge (1983) and E. Ostrom (1985) which cover the concepts of Commons, Rawls, Riker, Ruttan and others in this social science tradition.

question. Whether an organization has become institutionalized depends on people's evaluations of it—whether it is seen as having acquired value beyond direct instrumental considerations.

In some discussions, "institutions" are regarded negatively, as lethargic, aloof, ossified. This suggests that such organizations have acquired enough power and status that they do not have to be responsive to people's needs. However, if they lose the legitimacy they have been accorded by members of the public, they will also decline as institutions. An institution cannot operate indefinitely without providing benefits—economic, social, political, ethical—that justify its continued existence. To the extent it enjoys institutional status in people's minds, it will have more stability and capability for dealing with common problems over time than a less valued and less supported organization would have.

"Institutionalization" should be conceived as a matter of degree, even though things get classified in common use as either being or not being "institutions." For exposition's sake, we will treat institutions as a nominal category. In practice, transforming an organization into an institution takes time (Uphoff and Ilchman, 1972). We should thus be interested both in the extent of institutionalization and in strategies of institutional development as dealt with in applied social science (Esman, 1972).[17]

1.6 WHAT IS LOCAL?

Our task, like that of agencies wishing to support rural development, would be easier if there were only one "local" level. The local level is most often equated with the *community level*, but many kinds of collective action are better undertaken at a level below the community—at the group or neighborhood level—and others may be better handled by several communities together. Moreover, what is called a "community" may provide no substantial social basis for collective action. Rather it may be only a geographic entity labelled as a village or community by outsiders for their own convenience.[18] Community institutions are thus only one kind of local institution, not always the preferred kind and not always a feasible kind.

Delimiting what is "local" turns out to be almost as complicated as determining what is an institution. "Local" has different meanings

---

[17]Though we have used the term "institution building" in the past and have contributed to the IB literature, we prefer to use the term "institutional development." It designates a process that is less amenable to "blueprint" approaches and one that requires considerable innovation in its implementation.

[18]Field research for the Rural Development Committee has documented how often "communities" are ineffective or nonexistent as units for natural resource management. See Roe and Fortmann (1982) on water supply and range management in Botswana, Blustain (1982) on soil conservation in Jamaica, and Abeyratne (1982) on irrigation water management in Sri Lanka.

depending on whether it is regarded from the perspective of an outside agency or from the vantage point of rural people themselves. Many mistakes in development assistance derive from too gross an understanding of this apparently simple term.

Viewed from above, what is referred to as "the local level" has at least three levels—numbered 6, 7, and 8, in Figure 1.3. Above and below these levels one is no longer dealing with what should be described as "local." Households and individuals are quite different units of decision making and activity as they are smaller and not confronted with the same kind of

Figure 1.3: LEVELS OF DECISION MAKING AND ACTIVITY

1. International Level
↕
2. National Level
↕
3. Regional (State or Provincial) Level
↕
4. District Level
↕
5. Sub-District Level
(e.g. *taluk* in India or *thana* in Bangladesh)

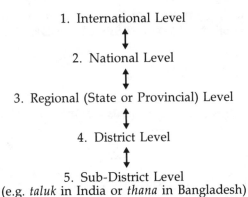

6. LOCALITY LEVEL
(a set of communities having cooperative/commercial relations;
this level may be the same as the sub-district level
where the sub-district center is a market town)
↕
7. COMMUNITY LEVEL
(a relatively self-contained, socio-economic-residential unit)
↕
8. GROUP LEVEL
(a self-identified set of persons having some common interest;
may be a small residential group like a hamlet, or neighborhood, an
occupational group, or some ethnic, caste, age, sex, or other grouping)

LOCAL LEVELS

↕
9. Household Level
↕
10. Individual Level

problems of "collective action" as are evident at the group, community, and locality levels (this latter term is used in Mosher, 1969). At higher levels, which are no longer local, qualitative differences arise because state authority and very large units of decision making and activity are involved.

When viewed from above, these make up a nested hierarchical set of levels of decision making and activity, though from the perspective of rural people choosing whether or not to invest some effort in common enterprises with others, the reality is not so neat. An individual's primary identification is usually with his or her family and relations. But even the common category of "household" is not as fixed and predictable as presumed in most writings and surveys.

Figure 1.4: SETS OF PERSONS FOR JOINT DECISION MAKING AND ACTION, SEEN FROM PERSPECTIVE OF THE INDIVIDUAL

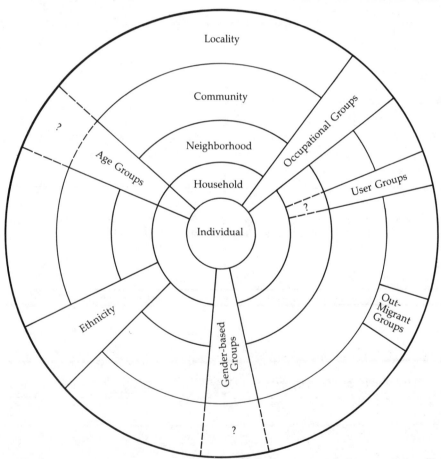

Individuals generally identify with a number of categories of persons beyond the household whom they look to for cooperation and assistance ("reference groups" or "action sets" in the language of sociologists). Joint action with them is thought to be relatively easy and productive because of some common identity and some existing familiarity and trust among individuals. From below, "levels" are seen concentrically rather than hierarchically, in a manner described by Bennett (1983:14-15) and suggested in Figure 1.4.

The uppermost limit of "local" is likely to be the area served by a rural market town as defined by Johnson (1970), (see also Mosher, 1969, and Owens and Shaw, 1972). This will generally correspond to a "locality"—a grouping of communities that have trading and other cooperative links with one another, where people have some possibility of personal acquaintance, and usually some experience of working together.

In some places, this socio-economic reality matches the administrative sub-district, in which case the designation "local" would extend to that level. More often a sub-district covers several such areas and thus should not be regarded as "local" according to our criteria. Occasionally a district is small enough that it may function as "local" level but usually not.

The household is also regarded as outside the "local" continuum. Although there may be differences of interest and opinion within a household, it represents a socio-economic unit with enough role definition that whether there will be collective action is not generally questioned. The question is usually what can be done, often in very complex survival strategies, to sustain the members, especially in poorer households (Sisler and Colman, 1979).

From the group level upwards, activity is more problematic and relatively more effort has to be invested in forming and maintaining institutional connections. There are substantial recurrent problems at the levels of the group, the community, and the locality (multiple communities) revolving around the difficulties of initiating and sustaining collective action.

Determining what is or is not "local" is sometimes ambiguous and drawing a firm boundary line is not important in itself. What is important is to see that people's perceptions of common interest and orientations toward collective action will change once the unit of potential action includes a significant number of "strangers." There can be disagreements and differences within smaller units. Indeed, some of the bitterest conflicts occur in small groups, even households. But the basis for decision making and mobilization of resources is much different where an established identity exists—in smaller groups—than in larger groups lacking that sense of identity.

Elsewhere we have identified four basic categories of organizational activity—decision making, resource mobilization and management, communication, and conflict management (Uphoff, Meinzen-Dick and

St. Julien, 1985). To the extent that these activities occur, formally or informally, in simple or complex ways, one can say that organization exists at
that level. Such activities are seldom absent at the household level but they
become problematic at the group level and above.

The challenge is to link development efforts at "higher" levels to the
needs and capabilities of individuals and households. To get to and from
these lowest levels, the path of communication and resource flows must
pass through one or more of the levels identified as "local." An example from
Kenya of such a network of intermediary institutions is shown in Annex
One (Figures A1.1 and A1.2). With unusual specificity, the respective diagrams map the actual or potential linkages between center and community
from the perspective of the center and of the community.

1.7 COLLECTIVE ACTION AND PUBLIC GOODS

Institutions at any level involve more than purely individual efforts.
They embody some kind of "collective action" in which the interests,
resources, ideas, and ideals of many persons are brought together.
Institutions serve as channels for collective action that are reinforced by
diffused benefits, legitimation, and shared expectations. There can also be
penalties imposed for persons who violate institutional obligations. The
growing literature on collective action following issues raised by Olson
(1965) is helpful for understanding problems of local institutional
development, though some qualifications often need to be made in the
analysis to fit local problems and circumtances.[19]

Similarly the benefits from institutions tend to be "public goods," things
of value to persons besides those immediately engaged in the activity,
having what economists call positive "externalities." By the nature of
institutions, it is difficult to require all beneficiaries to contribute to the cost
and maintenance of the institution, so many of the analytical problems
addressed in the economics and organization theory literature on public
goods are relevant.[20] Together, collective action and public choice concerns
have contributed to what is called "public choice" theory. It too has
relevance for assessing institutional development—both strategy and
design—though it also has some limitations as a source of conclusions for
policy decisions (Ingram and Scaff, 1984).

The widespread concern one finds in much of the literature about the
incentives individuals have to be *free riders* suggests the illogic of most
collective action that would create public goods (Olson, 1965; G. Hardin,
1968; R. Hardin, 1971). According to such analysis, the more difficult it is for

---

[19]Good examples of this literature would be Russell (1979), Russell and Nicholson (1981),
and R. Hardin (1982).
[20]For example, Buchanan (1968) and Ostrom and Ostrom (1977).

an organization to require all who benefit from its goods and services to contribute a fair share toward creating them, the less likely it is that the organization will come into being or will survive.

Excluding noncontributors from getting benefits is a problem particularly for the middle sector of local institutions, for local membership organizations and cooperatives, as is recovering costs for organizational maintenance. Businesses need not worry about external benefits so long as they can recoup enough costs to earn an acceptable profit, and agencies of government, both central and local, are in a position to enforce some payment or compliance. To be sure, private enterprises may be concerned about, and possibly deterred by, providing uncompensated benefits to others, and government institutions in general confront the basic problem of collective action—how to mobilize sufficient resources to cover costs and attain goals—even if free riding does not jeopardize particular activities. Issues of externalities arising from and affecting the possibilities of collective action are widespread.

In practice one observes more collective action in the real world than might be predicted from the literature, which regards free-ridership as a ubiquitous deterrent to collective undertakings. Actually individuals' decisions about whether or not to join and contribute to an organization are not as independent of one another as assumed in the literature (Kimber, 1981; Runge, 1984). The widespread existence of organizations in the real world testifies to the interdependence and net benefits of people's decisions to cooperate. This does not mean that free-ridership is no problem but rather that it is not as pervasive or overriding as presumed. The process of "institutionalization" creates constraints on free riding so that public goods can be provided by common effort.

Our analysis has distinguished three kinds of collective action problems having quite different implications for local institutional development. It makes a difference, first, whether or not collective action is needed to create the common good, and second, whether or not the group can exclude from benefits those who did not help to create the common good.

(1) Where the problem of collective action is using or protecting an existing resource, such as with social forestry or range management, any noncooperating individual can benefit at the expense of others. The task of regulating behavior may require severe sanctions, such as LA can introduce, though this also requires detailed and continuous information such as membership organizations may be better able to mobilize. Social sanctions through local organization may or may not be strong enough to deter abuse of common property.[21] In practice we

_____

[21]Even G. Hardin (1968) notes that such local control by users is the best way to deal with

find many local institutions able to carry out regulation as seen in Chapter Two. One should recognize that the incentives and sanctions to be channeled through local institutions are different for this than in the other two collective action situations.

(2) Where people need to contribute resources as a condition for creating the benefit in question, it may be possible to restrict access to that benefit by organizational means. A marketing cooperative, for example, may handle the produce of members only, who have helped create the facilities and services that get a better price through collective action. In this situation, the institution can deal with free-ridership directly. In a number of agricultural development contexts, such linking of contributions to benefits is possible provided that the local institutions involved are designed accordingly.

(3) The free-rider problem is particularly serious where creation of the public good depends on collective action, and preventing noncontributors from benefiting is difficult or undesirable, if not impossible. Examples would be a farm-to-market road, a disease eradication program, or public schooling. These situations seem to occur more often in the rural infrastructure or human resource development areas, though one can introduce excludability with rural electrification or fee-for-service clinics, as seen in Chapters Three and Four. The role of local government or local administration is likely to be greater where serious problems of collecting for external benefits arise.

Here we only introduce such considerations, indicating some of the implications of such distinctions for LID options. We will address these issues more fully in Section 2.4 and in other sector-specific treatments of LID where relevant.

1.8 ASSESSING COMPARATIVE ADVANTAGE FOR LOCAL INSTITUTIONS

The economic principle of comparative advantage is a useful one in making resource allocation decisions, and it can give some guidance in assessing alternatives for institutional development. Such considerations apply at two levels:

(1) When are local institutions, generally speaking, likely to be more effective or efficient in promoting and sustaining certain kinds of rural development activities, or when are these better left to national institutions? Is there reason to think, for example, that

---

"the tragedy of the commons." Runge's analysis of "the assurance problem" (1981 and 1984) deals with the possibilities for self-management of "common property." Such property is not simply "open access," as predictions of "tragedy" presume, but is governed by certain shared norms of use.

water supply is more appropriate for local institutions to provide than power supply? Or why might trunk roads best remain the responsibility of national institutions, with feeder roads under the aegis of local institutions?

(2) If some local advantage is identified, what kind of local institution (from among the categories described in Section 1.3) would probably be most suitable and why? For forest management, is it better to give responsibility to some local government body or to local agents of the Forestry Ministry? Are cooperatives a feasible vehicle for providing primary health care?

Sometimes the questions should be posed so as to differentiate among kinds of rural development activities to be promoted:

(3) Is one type of local institution more appropriate than another for achieving certain objectives? User associations are generally effective for tasks of irrigation water management, but will they be equally useful for managing rangelands? Which activities of agricultural production and distribution might be better performed by private businesses than by cooperatives?

These are the kind of questions we deal with in Chapters Two through Six, trying to clarify which kinds and combinations of local institutions enumerated in Section 1.3 seem to mesh well or to fit poorly with the different tasks of rural development mapped out previously in Section 1.2.

In seeking answers, we have found a number of concepts and distinctions helpful, though not all are equally relevant to all activity areas.

(1) Differences in the *distribution* of benefits and costs of the activity are important influences on comparative advantage. As elaborated in Section 2.3.2, local institutions are more sustainable where benefits are immediate, tangible, locally concentrated and matched to costs. For example, watershed management turns out to have quite a different profile of benefits and costs from that for either irrigation water management or social forestry (even though watershed management deals with both water and trees as resources). Accordingly different kinds of institutional strategies are needed even within the area of natural resource management.

(2) Activity areas involve different basic *processes*, which affect the comparative advantage of various kinds of local institutions. Natural resource management, for example, revolves around the balancing of utilization and conservation, whereas rural infrastructure depends on the generic activities of design, construction, operation, and maintenance. Agricultural production may be better done by private (household or corporate) producers, but the provision of inputs and the handling of outputs, which is important for modern agriculture, can possibly be better left to other institutional arrangements.

(3) The *interdependence* that an activity establishes among local people

as managers, users, or producers, requiring cooperation or accommodation, will affect local institutional advantages. In agriculture,
irrigated rice production, for example, requires close coordination
of operations not just for water use but also for land preparation,
variety selection, planting, field operations, and harvesting. Even as
individual an activity as bird scaring is best done in concert with
other farmers. Millet farmers working under rainfed conditions, on
the other hand, are much more on their own in all operations and
are less in need of local institutions.[22]

The significance of interdependence and of horizontal and vertical linkages
is most evident in the area of agriculture and this is treated most explicitly in
Chapter Five. The implications of different core processes come through
most clearly with reference to rural infrastructure and are taken up in Chapter Three, though they are discussed in other activity area chapters. Because
the effects of benefits vis-a-vis costs are most evident in the natural resource
area, this subject is taken up analytically in Chapter Two.

Comparative advantage is not static and can change over time. As a
population becomes more educated, for example, there is relatively more capability at local levels for operating complex institutions. On the other hand,
if with more education there is greater outmigration to urban areas, rural
communities may lose a large number of their most talented and energetic
members so that a consequence of education could be less local capability
for managing many tasks of rural development. In areas with less education,
central institutions might have an advantage for certain kinds of work, but
for other tasks local institutions could be preferable channels.[23] Literacy as a
factor affecting local institutions is addressed in Section 5.6 as are the influences of gender discrimination, land tenure differences, and migration on
local institutional performance.

Factors like literacy that bear on the capacity and appropriateness of
different institutional arrangements are fairly common across rural development activities, though some factors are more evident or dramatic in a

---

[22]To be sure, there can be interdependence and need for cooperation under rainfed conditions, as discussed in Chapter Five. Bird scaring is obviously important also to millet
growers—maybe very important. Getting land prepared for planting and then actually planting right after the first rains can make a big difference in yield. So group action through labor
exchange may be found in rainfed agricultural communities, as Vincent (1971) documents in
Uganda. She also shows that such cooperation can be inegalitarian and even exploitative.

[23]How much education is needed for successful local institutions depends partly on what requirements are set for their operation by the central government. Cooperatives in Northern
Nigeria were previously required to make fourteen complex reports regularly, which placed a
premium on having literate officers and personnel, when several simplified documents would
have sufficed (King, 1981). Local administration can be made less effective by requiring excessive paperwork. In one Indian state, Reddy (1982:103) found agricultural officers having to
spend 19 to 44 percent of their time just writing reports; district agricultural officers were supposed to make 125 reports each year. The monthly workload of extension staff in Kenya was
such that Chambers (1974:66) estimated that meeting all prescribed paperwork would take
474(!) percent of available staff time.

certain area. Rather than discuss each factor as it can influence activity in each sector, we have introduced different analytical and prescriptive considerations in the respective sectoral chapters so as to avoid repetition. Readers are advised to keep in mind that the discussion in Chapters Two through Six, though focusing in turn on the five main activity areas, is presented so that it has some general relevance for local institutional development across most sectors.

1.9 PROMOTING LOCAL INSTITUTIONAL DEVELOPMENT

Once LID objectives have been determined for specific situations on the basis of analysis, there remain the problems of achieving them in practice. Usually programs are designed and implemented with staff, responsibilities, sequences, budgets, etc. laid out in some detail in advance, based on what has been done elsewhere or what experts think will succeed in this instance. Some planning is certainly needed for LID as for other development efforts, but it is advisable to proceed inductively, experimentally, and flexibly, rather than following a kind of "blueprint" (D. Korten, 1980; Johnston and Clark, 1982; Rondinelli, 1983). A "learning process" approach is more likely to contribute to the creation of local capacities for mobilizing and managing resources, as discussed in Chapters Seven and Eight. There we also consider three alternative modes for support of local institutional development efforts—assistance, facilitation, and promotion, which reflect differences in the extent of local initiative and institutional capability.

The kinds and combinations of local institutions to be supported will vary from sector to sector and from place to place. But there are some generalizations about LID that appear valid cross-sectorally and cross-nationally. These have been drawn together in the concluding chapters, Seven and Eight, addressing matters like training and leadership development and forging networks of local institutions having horizontal and vertical linkages. There is no point in summarizing these strategic elements of LID here. Rather they will be taken up after considerations formulated in sectoral terms have been presented.

The analysis is supplemented throughout with empirical case references amplified in the annexes. These demonstrate the concreteness and relevance of the concepts and categories introduced. There are no formulas for local institutional development, but the structural and operational elements of LID can be better understood. LID efforts will benefit from the principles and ideas to be extracted from diverse experiences as well as from the encouragement and examples they provide.

CHAPTER TWO

Local Institutional Development For Natural Resource Management

2.1 ACTIVITIES IN NATURAL RESOURCE MANAGEMENT

Local institutions of various types and in various combinations are required for the sustainable utilization and maintenance of soil, water, forest, and other primary assets vital for lasting development.[1] The basic natural resources to be managed are water and soil in conjunction with the plant and animal populations they support (often referred to as biomass). The system of vegetation associated with a particular soil-water-climate combination represents the biomass of primary concern in natural resource management.

Water may be regarded as "first among equals" in that soil and biomass become inert without it. Fortunately water is a renewable resource so long as soil, biomass, and water are managed together in a stable, mutually supportive system. *Soil*, on the other hand, is renewable only in the very long run through natural processes involving weather, water, plant, and geological interactions. Nonetheless, soil can be maintained and even improved through management practices such as manuring, crop rotation, and physical control (e.g., terracing or contouring). Thus, some activities can maintain the soil as well as the water supply.

The *biomass* forms of special interest are trees, grasses, and crops (most of which are neither trees nor grasses). These biomass forms are renewable as long as water and suitable soils are available, within tolerable climatic ranges. Soil is seldom managed by itself but usually in conjunction with some regime of trees, grasses, or crops. In fact, most natural resource

---

[1]In this analysis, we are dealing with renewable natural resources since they are most significantly linked with agricultural and rural development. We will not be addressing management and exploitation of nonrenewable resources such as mineral resources.

management, even if focused on just one resource such as soil, must involve the other resources as well.

There are five main kinds of natural resource management (NRM). Each has different local institutional requirements because of the ways in which resources and user/managers interact.

1. **Forest management** involves the utilization of tree and related plant and animal populations in ways that perpetuate the forest ecosystem. Forest products such as fuel, fodder, and building materials (timber and thatch) are important inputs in agriculture and domestic economies. If forest resources are handled properly, both the quantity and quality of soil and water will also be maintained. LDC governments and donor agencies are increasingly interested in what is called *social forestry*, where forest resources are managed by rural people through their community local institutions. It is this approach to forest management that we are treating here.

2. **Rangeland management,** which focuses on grasses, is practiced where rainfall constraints favor livestock raising and where crop production is only minor and low yielding. The characteristics of grasses present decision makers with different time horizons for natural resource management. The local institutions in these sparsely populated areas have structures and dynamics and present special challenges to any program seeking to assist people in range areas (Dyson-Hudson and Dyson-Hudson, 1980).

3. **Irrigation water management** involves the acquisition and distribution of water for agriculture. This type of management has more direct links to production than do other NRM activities, but it shares crucial characteristics with them such as the need to regulate access to common property. Water management institutional issues confront ubiquitous tensions built into any irrigation system between upstream and downstream cultivators.

4. **Watershed management** aims at the maintenance of the water cycle through activities of forest and soil management.[2] Preventing soil erosion and preserving the biomass will reduce the likelihood of climatic changes that may destabilize the ecosystem such as reduced rainfall. Forest and grazing resources of a watershed area can be utilized so long as these activities do not disturb the water cycle.

5. **Soil conservation** could practically be called "cropland management" since it usually arises as a problem where crops other than trees and grasses continually extract soil nutrients and disturb the soil's structure. As noted already, good forest and rangeland management includes soil conservation. The means for controlling erosion, restoring soil nutrients, and maintaining soil structure may

---

[2]We are using the term "watershed" to refer to the catchment area, usually forested and hilly, where rainfall is collected and carried to the lowlands by streams and rivers. We are not using it with the "continental divide" meaning.

be regarded as highly technical matters but these require a strong local institutional base.[3]

Natural resource management contributes directly to the profitability and sustainability of both agricultural and nonagricultural enterprises, and poor management can have detrimental consequences for rural infrastructure and human health. Thus, NRM and the local institutions supporting it must be considered together not in isolation.

2.2 LOCAL INSTITUTIONAL OPTIONS

The principal organizational options for mobilizing local efforts and responsibility for natural resource management are those described previously in section 1.3.

- *local administration,* agencies of government operating in a regulatory mode, setting policies and enforcing them by technical (and often political) criteria;
- *local governments,* responsible to the community but functioning within the state's formal-legal framework;
- *membership organizations,* often called *user groups,*dealing with resource and with associated productive activities in functionally specific ways to serve members' needs; when operating by pooling members' economic resources, called *cooperatives;*
- *service organizations,* working on a not-for-profit basis to protect or regulate natural resource use; and
- *private businesses,* utilizing resources according to calculations of profitability over time and according to established business practices.

An additional option, corresponding to the category of nonorganizational institutions analyzed in Section 1.5 is:

- *use-management,* carried out by individuals and households according to community norms and personal understandings of the limits and possibilities of resource exploitation (Roe and Fortmann, 1982).

This mode of resource management is underestimated and largely ignored because it has no formal-legal existence. Since it is diffuse and has no authority structure to be activated, governments and donor agencies find it difficult to invoke this method though they can try to enhance or revitalize it by exhorting or educating rural communities. We note it here so that its role in NRM is not forgotten. It is important as a complement of any organizational mode of LID for natural resource management.

Each of the organized modes offers advantages and disadvantages that

---

[3]This has been seen in the U.S. experience with soil conservation programs, documented by Morgan (1965). Examples from Jamaica are written up in Blustain (1982) and (1983). That soil cannot be managed apart from the growing of crops is seen from the conflicts that arose in the U.S. between the Soil Conservation Service and the various state agricultural extension services, both of which sought to get farmers to draw up complete farm plans.

need to be weighed in specific contexts for specific NRM objectives. *Local administration* may be more favorable for achieving technically prescribed management levels and practices but it has certain limitations. Efforts to protect the forests in Nepal through only the work of the Forestry Department, for example, have proved largely unsuccessful, whereas working in conjunction with local government bodies (panchayats) and membership groups (under the Small Farmer Development Programme) has produced more beneficial results described briefly in Annex Two.[4]

. The role for government agencies or branches of local administration such as the Agriculture or Forestry Ministry is greatest when there is conflict between users of a single resource who come from different localities or when there is a perceived lack of congruence between the costs and benefits of resource use. We see this in soil conservation (where benefits may be much deferred while costs are immediate) or in watershed management (downstream communities get most of the benefit from upstream communities' efforts), as discussed in Section 2.3.2.

Local administration may be a more appropriate channel where the preferred management practices are quite technical or complex. However, government staff commonly lack the detailed information on local resources and problems needed to be efficient or effective in implementing NRM programs. Such staff may also be unfavorably associated with restrictive government policies and thereby lack legitimacy in the eyes of the local people. Such legitimacy is necessary in order to gain local cooperation in carrying out NRM tasks at low cost (Temple, 1972).

The community management option is attractive because of the fact that local residents have both the most stake in, and the most information about, natural resources. However, there may not be any coherent community capacity to discharge management responsibilities or stronger communities may take advantage of weaker neighboring communities (Acharya, 1984). Also, it is sometimes difficult to determine exactly who constitutes "the community" responsible for a given resource.

When there is a multiplicity of potentially conflicting uses of a resource in a single locality, elected *local government* is in the best position to work out satisfactory solutions if two conditions are met. First, LG jurisdiction must be recognized by all parties. This may not be the case with large-scale commercial users of natural resources who can circumvent local decisions by going to higher governmental levels. Second, the interests of local elites should not dominate decision making; otherwise NRM decisions will not be equitable, and they may not even be effective if they are seen as unfair and thus as not binding on all community members.

---

[4]The cases given in Annexes are intended to give readers concrete illustrations of experience and lessons that have informed our analysis.

User groups are likely to be smaller management units, more homogeneous and with fewer problems of managing the organization itself. They are likely, however, to lack the legitimacy and authority that LA or LG would have when it comes to resolving conflicts vis-a-vis competing users who are not group members. Also, such groups are sometimes inclined to follow more extractive practices than advisable from a larger community or national perspective.

The utility of user groups for NRM depends very much on the nature of the resource, the users involved, and the correspondence between costs and benefits analyzed in the next section. Irrigation groups are more effective as a rule than groups for soil conservation, and membership organizations, while seldom appropriate for managing large watersheds, may be able to protect smaller forests. User groups are more viable for NRM when membership is homogeneous and concentrated.

Local *service organizations* are less often involved in natural resource management activities than LG or LA. However, we find in India, for example, a variety of nongovernmental organizations involved in community forestry activity.[5] Acharya (1984:44–47) has documented some "traditional" local service organizations involved in managing *guthi* and sacred forests in Nepal.

Private businesses have incentives to undertake management practices that will produce more benefit than cost. In situations where resources are being managed for industrial use or for energy utilization, such as on large plantations, private companies may be more efficient in economic terms due to the need for getting returns from intensive inputs over a relatively short time horizon (Palin, 1983). However, the benefits and costs considered by private operators are internal ones; and externalities, which are particularly important in NRM, are not taken into account in decision making. Downstream water users or downhill agriculturalists may suffer serious losses from purely profit-oriented management upstream or uphill. Also, the way in which future benefits are "discounted" gives a strong here-and-now bias to calculations, assigning too little value to the productive needs and possibilities of future generations.

As suggested above, *user-management* can be viewed as a complement to organizationally directed NRM. The herder who limits grazing in forest areas so that seedlings can grow undisturbed or the farmer who fills up gulleys in his field as soon as they appear is taking individual actions but is likely to be responding to cultural and social norms. Under such a system,

---

[5]These include the Ranchi Consortium for Community Forestry, the Silent Valley Movement, the Friends of Tree Club, and Himalaya Seva Sangh, which are involved in popularizing the need for preserving trees (Basu, 1983). These organizations exist to serve their members in addition to other people in the community, but to the extent they engage in information sharing and consciousness raising about the importance of NRM, they go beyond local membership organizations basically oriented to self-help.

individual action contributes to collective benefit where there is clear socio-cultural definition of the community of interest. The swidden system of shifting cultivation, for example, relies on unstated agreements among resource users on the length of fallow periods to prevent soil exhaustion (Grandstaff, 1978; Brush, 1983). Such responsibility is the least expensive and the most effective kind of NRM if the practices are technically correct. Unfortunately this management mode is not very amenable to creation by policies though it can definitely be undermined by government actions. Also, it is quite vulnerable when community norms and social structures come under outside pressure, for example, from the spread of commercialization or from population growth greatly increasing pressures on the land.

Much has been written about the "tragedy of the commons," where each individual resource user gains more than he loses by increasing his use of that resource, but if all increase their use the resource will be depleted and lost (G. Hardin, 1968). The contradiction between individual and collective interests has been presented most graphically for range management describing the temptation of herders to overgraze pastureland, but the same logic applies to forest use or any common property.

There is currently some re-thinking of the "tragedy of the commons" logic, which assumes an independence of decision making that is not empirically warranted and ignores the extent to which institutions have been devised precisely to coordinate expectations and behavior in resource-maintaining ways (Runge, 1981 and 1984). The existence of "common property" has implications for any local institutional development, but since these implications are particularly important to local institutions' capacity to manage natural resources, we consider this subject in detail in Section 2.4. User-management by individuals can be seen as a complement or an alternative to the kind of formal institutions we are focusing on in this study. However, traditional local organizations and roles such as described in Section 1.4 stand behind most use-management arrangements and apportion sanctions and rewards. So more is involved in use-management than just shared norms among users.

It is unfortunate that local institutional means and alternatives are so frequently overlooked in favor of focusing on technical packages and options. A study on developing "fragile lands" in the humid tropical lowlands and steep slopes of the Latin American region, for example, done by a consulting firm that has provided significant leadership in the LID area, passed over the subject of local institutions with only brief mention of their importance (Bremer et al., 1984:21, 60). The report's recommendations for institutional development deal with national institutions not with the local possibilities and requirements reviewed here.

2.3 INTERACTIONS OF RESOURCE
AND USER CHARACTERISTICS

The management of natural resources for agriculture is institutionally complex due to the diverse ways in which a resource may be used. For example, though water is involved in both irrigation water management and watershed management, different arrangements are appropriate for each because of the different ways users relate to the resource and to each other within space and over time. An understanding of such differences is essential for evaluating and promoting LID for natural resource management.

2.3.1 "Boundedness" of Resources and Users

What kinds of local institutions will be effective and sustainable for natural resource management depends on the nature of the resource to be managed and on the composition of the community of resource users, in particular whether indeed they constitute an identifiable community. To the extent that the resources and the relevant set of users are "bounded," that is, delimited and identifiable, the management tasks will be easier and more amenable to local institutional responsibility.

**Figure 2.1: RESOURCE MANAGEMENT SITUATIONS,
ACCORDING TO NATURE OF THE RESOURCE
AND THE USER-MANAGERS**

NATURAL RESOURCE IS:

USER-MANAGERS ARE:	Known and predictable	Little known and unpredictable
Identifiable and coherent group	(I) Irrigation water management	(II) Coastal fishing (done by fisher-man groups)
Lacking group identity and structure	(III) Forest management	(IV) Rangeland management

As shown in Figure 2.1, there are important differences among natural resources in terms of the "boundedness" of users and resources (though changes in technology can affect this). One should examine the extent to which: (a) resource user-managers constitute an identifiable and delimited set of persons, and (b) they have some established and effective authority structure whose legitimacy is recognized and accepted. If there is in effect a community of user-managers, both criteria are satisfied. But in many NRM situations, the user-managers are an ill-defined set of persons not a group or community and with no existing mechanisms for making or enforcing decisions.

Similarly one should consider the extent to which the user-managers know and can predict with confidence: (a) the amount and quality of the resource to be managed, and (b) its availability at a certain time and place. When the amount and availability of a resource are known for certain, the possibilities of effective management are greatly increased and more routinized institutions are possible.

When there is less knowledge and predictability, institutions are useful to reduce the resulting risk but they must operate differently, usually oriented more toward insurance and welfare functions than to optimizing productivity. Institutions can be said to deal with two kinds of risk and uncertainty: (a) arising from vagaries and variability in the natural environment, and (b) arising from the behavior of others—what others do and how that will affect one's own well-being. Local institutions need to deal with both kinds of problems faced by rural people (Runge, 1984).

The different characteristics of users and resources combine to present different contexts for natural resource management, ranging from known resources managed by a definite set of users to a situation where both the resource and the users are varying. These combinations, shown in Figure 2.1, approximate different kinds of resource management situations.

Not all irrigation situations have the characteristics of (I), but the group of users and the resource itself are likely to be more identifiable and definite than for most other natural resources. The distinctions made here shed light on the different LID problems faced with water management, social forestry, and rangeland management because they vary along these dimensions. Soil conservation resembles (I) but has different cost and benefit patterns as discussed below. Watershed management has characteristics of (II), (III) and (IV) and is therefore more complex analytically and also operationally more difficult. To the extent that the resource and the users are well known and identifiable, local institutions become more viable. Conversely when the resource is more uncertain and the set of users ill defined, higher level institutions have a greater role to play in NRM.

Where the resource and the users are more definite, local membership organizations of resource users are particularly appropriate. It is no accident that the best examples of user associations for NRM are found in the area of irrigation water management.[6] Though there are year-to-year fluctuations

---

[6]In our study of local organizations worldwide, we fould that water user associations had

in water supply, the technology of irrigation can compensate for such variability, and adjustments in supply can be made among a fixed set of water users known to each other. Thus, user groups can be more effective for irrigation because users are geographically delimited and the resource can be distributed with some precision.

Rangeland management, on the other hand, has characteristics that make user groups less effective. Herders have great mobility and can seek alternate grazing sources, and the users for a particular rangeland resource (usually unfenced) are more difficult to identify. Though user groups are usually needed as part of the LID complex for range management, some higher level, authoritative decision-making institution is desirable to deal with membership and resource ambiguities.

With forest management, the resource is geographically fixed and bounded, but the persons having access to it are not as limited or limitable as with irrigation water. User associations are harder to form and maintain on a voluntary basis. An authoritative and inclusive body such as local government becomes more effective in the situation where the resource is more bounded than the set of users. Possibly local agents of the national government will be needed to balance and control claims to use such a resource. We will consider such institutional alternatives for each NRM area specifically in Section 2.5.

2.3.2 Distribution of Costs and Benefits

The assessment of costs and benefits from natural resource management will vary according to the time span and the geographical area involved. Also affecting assessment are the degree to which the costs and benefits are tangible and perceptible, and the extent to which both costs and benefits are borne by the same persons. Such considerations affect the feasibility of LID alternatives. We have identified four dimensions along which NRM costs and benefits can vary with respect to the users (or potential users) involved.

1. Temporal Dimension
   (a) Benefits accrue immediately or very soon, or
   (b) Benefits accrue after a long time.
2. Spatial Dimension
   (a) Benefits accrue locally, or
   (b) Benefits accrue remotely.
3. Tangibility
   (a) Benefits are quite evident, or
   (b) Benefits are relatively hard to identify.
4. Distribution

---

somewhat higher performance scores on average than other kinds of LOs (Esman and Uphoff, 1984). Examples of indigenous water user associations are given in Annex Two.

(a) Benefits accrue to the same persons who bear the costs of management, or
(b) Benefits accrue to different persons from those who bear the costs of management.

This analysis presumes that managing natural resources always has some cost, either direct investment of labor and funds or abstaining from some present use to preserve the resource over time. Local institutions will be most effective in natural resource management where NRM benefits accrue:

- quickly (1a),
- locally (2a),
- visibly (3a), and
- to those who bear the cost (4a).

In such circumstances it clearly pays for individuals and groups to take responsibility for a resource. The opposite circumstances could make LID for natural resource management almost impossible—where benefits are:

- delayed (1b),
- remote (2b),
- hard to identify (3b), and
- do not accrue to the investor of effort, money, or foregone use (4b).

One reason why irrigation water management is more readily handled through membership organizations than is soil conservation, for example, is that the benefits are immediate as well as local. Further, the farmer who invests in soil conservation may not readily see the benefits—the benefits of stopping runoff and flooding commonly accrue to others not just at lower elevations but in future generations. To be sure, if land tenure is secure and the farmer is confident that those future generations will be his own children and grandchildren, investment in soil conservation or tree planting will be more attractive and local residents will be more amenable to taking responsibility for NRM and the local institutions supporting it.

There can be significant differences within a resource management category. Gully erosion is more likely to elicit collective action to prevent it, for example, than is sheet erosion, which can go unnoticed and unchecked. Villagers may undertake forest management when they find they no longer have trees suitable for building materials, whereas the increasing increments of time required to gather adequate firewood may not be marked enough to elicit community action.

The lack of coincidence between benefits and costs is often a major factor affecting social forestry. In many countries, women do the firewood gathering but men make all decisions about planting trees. Unless women are included in influential roles in the local government bodies or any local organizations dealing with forestry, the costs of women's labor will not be fully considered (Hoskins, 1979). Also, in parts of Malawi where men settle after marriage into their wife's village, the rights of tree ownership remain

with the women and their families, although the planting of trees is traditionally assigned to males. This introduces a further asymmetry between
benefits and costs that inhibits local responsibility for social forestry
(Kafumba, 1983).

We find more vigorous and successful local institutions dealing with irrigation partly because good water management produces quick and
evident benefits to those who undertake those activities. In contrast watershed management has quite the opposite profile of benefits even though
both sets of activities nominally deal with the same natural resource, water.
Because the benefits of watershed management are more remote in time and
space, there is usually need for a government role if such management is to
be undertaken strenuously. Benefit and cost profiles, which vary according
to the resource, thus condition the applicability of LID options.

2.3.3 Characteristics of the Resource

The nature of the resource being managed will affect how desirable certain institutional options are. We highlight the effects of three different
characteristics: resource renewability, seasonality, and public perception of
the resource.

Renewability. The less renewable a resource is the more risk there is that
poor management will have drastic consequences, and the more reason one
can offer for some form of central government involvement. The length of
time required for a natural resource to be renewed varies greatly. Grasses on
a range may revive after a few weeks of rain, while forest vegetation can
take from 20 to 100 years depending on the species. Indeed, tropical
rainforests may take 400 years to become fully mature (Guppy, 1984), and
the pool of genetic material they represent may not be renewable or
replicable once destroyed (Oldfield, 1981). Soils take even longer for renewal, and in some cases if severely eroded, they may become nonrenewable,
especially if the loss of biomass affects the water cycle.

Forest maintenance requires institutional arrangements with a long
time horizon and sustained commitment. This may not be assurable with
certain local institutions if the imperceptibility of deterioration and an asymmetry between benefits and costs make such institutions less promising for
NRM. Range management, in contrast, can be left to local institutions with
less risk. To be sure, careful balancing between utilization and conservation
is needed for range management since over-grazing can lead to soil degradation, which substantially lengthens the cycle of regrowth. This concern
may justify a central institutional role or a role for LA in preference to other
local institutions. But within some limits, responsibility for range management can be more readily devolved to user groups or local governments,
taking care to align the distribution of costs and benefits as much as possible
to give proper NRM incentives at the local level.

Seasonality. Seasonality is another factor of great importance for NRM. The flow of local institutional activity is generally affected by variations in the agricultural seasons as documented by Fortmann (1985). To the extent that activities need to be carried out year round at the same level, or need to be continued during the time of peak demand for agricultural labor, the role of LA, or possibly that of central institutions, will be enhanced.[7]

Whatever kinds of local institutions are charged with NRM responsibilities, under conditions of high seasonality they will need to operate with more flexibility and informality than usually seen in government operations. In Botswana, for example, it was found quite unreasonable to expect user groups set up for maintenance and operation of small catchment dams to function on a year-round basis when seasonal fluctuations in water availability made the need for, and supply of, the dams' water highly variable (Roe and Fortmann, 1982). Other research in the Philippines and Indonesia has found governments too often expecting irrigation water user associations to operate the same way in the wet season when water is abundant as in the dry season when it is scarce (Robinson, 1982; Duewel, 1982). If LA and LG institutions find it too difficult to adapt to seasonal variations, their functions should be handled by membership organizations, cooperatives, or private businesses which can be more flexible. Central institutions, on the other hand, are likely to be less viable where seasonality is great because they are more attuned to budget or calendar years than to cropping or herding cycles.

Perceptions of Resources. Apart from their physical characteristics, how resources are perceived by users is an important consideration. How users regard the "renewability" of a resource, for example, will affect their willingness to invest in its maintenance. In particular, it is important to consider whether potential managers of a resource perceive it as a "public" or as a "private" resource, to be managed for collective or for individual benefit.

The usual norm is that if individuals or groups (or the state) have invested in improving a resource, whether land, water, or forest, they have established a right to the benefits thereof, whereas any unimproved resource should be accessible to others. If legal norms regulating resource use have been introduced by a government, a property claim can be made through cash and paper transactions. These are not visible to the public, in contrast to labor and other investments, which can be seen. In most African

---

[7] A social forestry project in the Tahou Department of central Niger, for example, found that during the time when its activities required the most involvement from villagers, they had to be busy attending their own fields. Given the unpredictability of when and where the rains would fall, when they did begin, everyone rushed to get field crops planted. They were thus unwilling or unable to assist the Forestry Department personnel in planting operations, which had to be started at this very time if the seedlings were to become established. It was thus impossible under these circumstances to make the project as "participatory" as intended (Brechin and West, 1982:84).

countries surface water in ponds or from rivers is seen as accessible to any-body, whereas groundwater is regarded as the property of whoever pumps it up. The legitimacy of local groups' controlling access to water will be af-fected by such beliefs. If groups are unable to exclude anybody from using a resource, they have little incentive to invest in its development or protection.

The development of private enterprises at the local level depends in part on whether local people accord legitimacy to formal-legal rights of ownership. Some private ownership is recognized in virtually all societies, but businesses as such may not be an effective vehicle for natural resource management unless there are widely shared perceptions that private own-ers have a right to exclude others from access to that resource.

2.3.4 Characteristics of the Users

In addition to whether or not users are a definite set of persons and have some recognized authority structure, discussed in Section 2.3.1, other characteristics are also important to consider.

Interdependence. To the extent that resource users are dependent upon one another for their livelihood and even survival, the incentives for making local institutions operate successfully are greater. For example, farmers managing irrigation water need to consider the decisions, interests, and ac-tions of each other to a much greater degree than persons who live and work in watershed areas. This consideration adds to the reasons given earlier why local institutions for irrigation water management are usually stronger than those for watershed management.

Interdependence is more evident to rangeland user-managers than to their counterparts in forest resources, perhaps because the availability and adequacy of water for herds and humans is so dominant a concern. Spoiling or exhausting a water point has dire consequences for others, and there are various means of retaliation that can deter irresponsible behavior more readily than one can check abuse of forests.

Certain techniques of natural resource management may create or re-quire interdependence. For example, in soil conservation, if bench terraces are constructed on a hillside, there must be cooperation in constructing toe drains and waterways to carry away the runoff. Otherwise one farmer will be dumping water onto another farmer's field and increasing the erosion there. The use of grass stripping or strip cropping, on the other hand, retards runoff more evenly and can be used independently of what others do. Thus, local institutional action by LA, LG or membership organizations may be more appropriate for terrace methods of soil conservation but individual ef-forts suffice for grass stripping.

Interdependence can be created by organizational design to establish incentives for more efficient or equitable institutional performance. In the Philippines some indigenous irrigation organizations give their officers plots of land at the tail end of the command area as compensation for their services. As the productivity of these plots depends on the amount of water reaching them, officers have incentive to ensure sufficient flow through the system (See Annex Two). Traditional irrigation systems in Sri Lanka used a similar incentive system according to Leach (1961).

Homogeneity. The tasks of local institutions in natural resource management are greatly simplified when users are homogeneous since decisions can be more uniform. The most significant kind of heterogeneity arises from multiple uses of the resource. Range management projects, for example, commonly run into problems when some of the land is (or can be) used for crop production. This was seen in a Burkina Faso project where pastoralist and agricultural families were to be members of a single local organization (Gooch, 1979). Similarly when the water in irrigation projects must serve competing or conflicting purposes, membership organizations are less likely to be successful.

There is no assurance that local governments will be able to allocate and regulate the resource in an optimal way when internal conflicts exist. The incentive for one set of users to predominate when scarce, valued resources are at stake is great. This may mean that local administration, representing the central government, must be active to preserve a balance of interests. LG can provide a legitimate forum for bargaining, turning zero-sum conflicts into positive-sum situations through accommodations and side-payments where possible, e.g., making adjustments in water allocation schedules and compensating for forgone shares of water.

Conflict over natural resource use is less likely when users see themselves as unified by kinship, occupation or on some other basis. Where socio-economic identities are varied, LA or LG may be more effective than membership organizations in reaching decisions if there is deadlock or in enforcing compromise solutions if there is disagreement. One limitation to LA and LG involvement is that compliance with decisions and regulations can be difficult to achieve through coercive means. Processes of consultation and consensus may therefore be needed even (or especially) where heterogeneity makes natural resource management a complicated undertaking. User involvement in discussing, planning, and implementing NRM is possible through various kinds of channels. Where heterogeneity is substantial, actually having an established process for consultation may be more important than which channel has formal responsibility.

Tradition. One should not presume that resource users living in traditional social settings are necessarily able and willing to manage forests, soil, and water productively, equitably, and without conflict. We did find in our literature review, however, that in communities where traditional roles and norms are relatively intact, the capacity of local institutions of all kinds to manage natural resources appears greater (e.g., Acharya, 1984; Siy, 1982; Coppee, 1980). Diminished capacity at the local level to sustain resource productivity often goes along with the decline in traditional institutions such as those operated by chiefs and councils of elders (Roe and Fortmann, 1982).

Opinions differ on how strong and useful such institutions are in the contemporary world. One can find traditional roles resilient in some places and atrophied in others. Where they exist and are not biased markedly in favor of privileged interests, traditional institutions should be engaged if such cooptation will not itself detract from their effectiveness. To introduce modern institutions that compete with traditional ones is usually unlikely to be successful. Local institutional development should build as much as possible on existing roles and relationships that support NRM as discussed in Section 7.3.1. To the degree that these relationships can regulate the use of forest, soil, and water resources, they are themselves natural resources of some value.

2.4 "COMMON PROPERTY" CONSIDERATIONS

Local institutional development for natural resource management must often deal with issues arising from common ownership of property. When resources are privately owned, their management is left to individuals who can themselves weigh the benefits and costs of exploitation, now and in the future, and act accordingly. On the other hand, when forest, water, and other resources are held in common, individuals have incentives to exploit the resource for private gain at co-holders' expense. This has come to be known as "the tragedy of the commons."[8]

Privatization of resources is often recommended to avert overuse, but this solution can introduce its own problems according to the nature of the resource—for example, when rangeland becomes uneven because of variable rainfall. If a herder has access only to a fixed area, his herd will starve in a year of insufficient rainfall as he cannot move it to other more fortunate areas. The mobility of pastoralists is a strategy dictated by the vagaries of weather in a resource-scarce and vulnerable environment.

Where individual decisions would culminate in undesirable outcomes, some form of collective action is needed. The question is whether it will be voluntary or coerced, and whether it can be generated within the community of users or must be imposed from outside the community. The assumptions about collective action by Olson (1965) suggest that the "free

---

[8]G. Hardin (1968) described a situation where herders are grazing cattle on common pastureland. If an individual increases his herd, this reduces the total amount of forage available. But each herder's loss when divided among all herders including the individual who added to the burden on the commons is small, perhaps imperceptible, and much less than the benefit he derives from grazing more cattle. So he has an incentive—as do all other herders—to increase the size of herds until the commons are destroyed by over-grazing. As Sandford (1983:118–127) points out, however, this is a deductive, not an empirical account of collective behavior.

rider" problem makes voluntary cooperation unlikely. Individuals who are able to get the benefits of group action without bearing any of the costs of creating this "good" are likely to do so in keeping with their "rational" self-interest. According to Olson, free ridership can be limited only if the group is so small that any individuals taking advantage of others can be readily observed and controlled by social sanctions, or if the benefits of group action can be withheld from non-contributors.

Resource users themselves have been thought to be incapable of managing common natural resources because the same "rational" behavior that gives rise to the tragedy of the commons also leads to free riding, which undermines the cooperation among users that could avert the "tragedy." Why should one bear the costs of maintaining an institution for resource management if one can gain the benefits therefrom without paying for them? If one's neighbors protect the village forest, this creates more firewood for one to take surreptitiously.

The most common response to such problems is for the state to introduce into such a situation its agents, whose decisions regulating resource use are backed by coercion if necessary to ensure compliance. Such coercion must have at least the tacit consent of the majority of users to be effective, but the source and control of coercion rests with persons who are external to the community of users. Such a strategy of NRM can rely on local administration for resource management.

Yet we find that government agency options for natural resource management are of limited effectiveness by themselves. Officials face difficulties in mobilizing the information and legitimacy needed for efficient enforcement and cannot readily mobilize social supports and sanctions which affect resource-using behavior most directly. The private ownership option appears to have advantages where it matches the costs and benefits of resource management in the same person. But this may not be possible because of the spatial and temporal distribution of costs or benefits.[9]

Private management of forests, for example, may lead to overcutting if current market prices for fuel and timber are attractive, contributing to soil erosion and attendant environmental deterioration elsewhere.[10] Soil conservation measures may lag because the value that affected land would have to future generations is underestimated. Privatization of rangeland was seen in Botswana as a solution to its degradation, yet the implementation of this policy proved to have undesirable equity effects without demonstrable

---

[9]Perhaps this is why overgrazing is reported also under private ownership regimes. Gilles and Jamtgaard (1981:131–133) and Sandford (1983:119–120) find no consistent evidence that overgrazing is a worse problem on common than on private rangelands.

[10]Fife (1977) suggests two situations in which private ownership would lead to resource abuse: if low risk investment alternatives encourage a rapid exploitation of the resource to earn profits to invest in them, or if holdings were too small to provide an adequate standard of living, and users feel forced to run the risk of resource deterioration.

ecological benefits compared to communal management practices (Dekure and Dyson-Hudson, 1983).

There is now in the literature considerable rethinking of the "tragedy of the commons" thesis. Empirically there is more collective action than one would predict according to Olson (1965) and others in the "rational actor" tradition of deductive analysis. Such theories are inconsistent with their own premise of rationality, since anyone who decides to free-ride is unjustifiably assuming that he is the only rational actor, i.e., that the others who are to create the collective good which he expects to enjoy are not likewise "rational" (Kimber, 1981).

Such an assumption is not only arrogant; it is itself irrational. If one assumes, more reasonably, that others are as "rational" as oneself, one's utility is maximized by making contributions in good faith to creating the collective good to be produced, so long as one values the good itself more than the cost of contributing one's required or expected share. As long as enough others do the same, it pays to be cooperative (Popkin, 1981).

Such behavior is consistent with the general maximizing strategy of cooperation which Axelrod (1984) has derived from computerized game-theoretic research. Runge suggests, with specific regard to natural resource management, that cooperation can be reinforced by dealing with "the assurance problem" through establishment and maintenance of institutions, which coordinate people's expectations of what others will do. Experimental evidence shows that the level of voluntary contributions is far from zero even in large groups (Runge, 1984:172–175).[11]

In more recent work, R. Hardin emphasizes the role of sanctions and conventions in controlling individual behavior. These usually derive from the norms and roles associated with institutions. An analysis by Blomquist and Ostrom (1986) on how institutions can control environmental crises suggests that collective action to stem the deterioration of a resource can be triggered by a combination of information and discussion. Critical components of such a strategy are (a) the ability to identify all users and (b) to establish clear boundaries within which management will occur.[12] Other conditions for maintaining effective collective action are the possibility of ongoing discussion among users about the common problem and about

---

[11]Kimber notes with evident irony that rational self-interest in joining organizations is not based only on discrete individual benefits. "There is surely something absurd in the idea that . . . the Council for the Protection of Rural England is really organized, not to protect rural England, but to provide wine and cheese parties for its members' (1981:196). If members join for selective rather than collective benefits, why do not organizations undertake to provide only the former?

[12]That the analysis by Blomquist and Ostrom independently focused on the same variables analyzed in Section 2.3.1 suggests the utility of cross-national as well as cross-resource analyses of natural resource management. Their analysis was prompted by the study of a water use conflict in Southern California, while our concern with "boundaries" came from comparing experience in irrigation management in Sri Lanka with range management in Botswana.

alternative courses of action plus effective monitoring of participants' behavior so as to reduce incentives to free-ride.

Such findings and rethinking concerning collective action suggest that there is more of a role for membership organizations in NRM than indicated by previous theory. Some development of government agencies' local capacity is invariably important to complement voluntary efforts. But there appears to be considerable potential for institutions such as local government and user groups, provided that they have responsibilities consistent with the kind of analysis concerning "boundedness" and distribution of costs and benefits discussed in Sections 2.3.1 and 2.3.2

In some situations and for some resources, it will make sense for private local institutions to take on certain NRM responsibilities. Experimentation with this mode of LID is appropriate where resource management problems are evident and an analysis of incentives and constraints points to privatization. There appears to be some confusion in many minds over the difference between private property and "common property," as if the latter meant that all potential users have unrestricted access to the resource. This is not true. There are well-known if not necessarily formal rules governing access in most common property situations (Runge, 1981; Gilles and Jamtgaard, 1981; Sandford, 1983).[13] These lead to institutionalized use-management, which is nonorganizational or quasi-organizational following the distinction between organizations and institutions elaborated in Section 1.5 above. A strategy of institutional development of practical necessity will focus on developing organizations with explicit roles and rules. But to acquire the legitimation needed for institutional effectiveness, some foundation in nonorganizational institutions for resource management is important.

2.5 IMPLICATIONS FOR LOCAL INSTITUTIONAL DEVELOPMENT

When planning support of local institutional development in the natural resource management area, the preceding lines of analysis give guidance by assessing how factors such as "boundedness" and the distribution of benefits and costs of resource management can affect the viability of different kinds of local institutions. Such considerations contribute to preferring different local institutional arrangements for the respective NRM tasks.

---

[13]Such traditional rules are documented in a study of local forest and pasture management in Nepal by one of our working group members (Acharya, 1984). These rules have informally become part of the management strategy of "modern" local institutions like panchayats and user groups. Netting (1976) offers an intriguing study of the management of common pastures dating back to at least the 13th century without deterioration of the resource base.

2.5.1 Irrigation Water Management

Our discussion of local institutions for managing irrigation water can be relatively brief since they are probably the most common and best documented.[14] Water user associations built around a common interest in acquiring and sharing water, in maintaining the system, and resolving conflicts appear quite feasible. Many observers of irrigation management have been impressed with the efficiency and stability of indigenous local organizations such as the *subaks* on the island of Bali in Indonesia (Geertz, 1967; Birkelbach, 1973) and the *zanjeras* in the Ilocos region of the Philippines (Lewis, 1971; Siy, 1982). Less well-known are similar organizations in Latin America, e.g., in Peru (Mitchell, 1976; Isbell, 1978) and Ecuador (Cornick, 1983). Contemporary analogues have been introduced in the Philippines by the National Irrigation Administration (F. Korten, 1982; Bagadion and F. Korten, 1985) and in Sri Lanka by the Agrarian Research and Training Institute (Uphoff, 1985 and 1986).

Irrigation management invariably confronts the problem that farmers upstream have locational advantage over those who are downstream and this creates at least the potential for continual conflict. Water users at the head of the channel or at the head of the system are in a better position to acquire water than those at the tail end and are less dependent on proper maintenance of the channel or system. However, this problem of conflicting interests can also give impetus to users to organize and cooperate to assure getting at least some water for all and to prevent violence. The same farmers along a channel who have conflicting interests over the supply they receive if water is scarce also have a common interest in guaranteeing that supply or in expanding it. Thus, the centrifugal forces of competition over water can be countervailed by centripetal pulls toward cooperation.

One problem for membership organizations operating as channels for irrigation management is that the water may be used for other purposes besides irrigation. Often a water source is used also for domestic water supply, usually by women, though their needs and interests are seldom represented in what are commonly all-male "water users associations."[15] Where other users are also dependent on the water supply, e.g., operators of water-driven mills, river transporters, or fishermen, conflicts may make local organizations of irrigators less effective.

In such a situation, local government institutions with broader jurisdiction become more viable, though if the competing users reside outside the community, local government may itself be unable to resolve the conflicts. Local administrative agencies will then become more relevant if they have

---

[14]Also, a more extended state-of-the-art analysis has been done on farmer organization and participation for water management by Uphoff (1986a).

[15]The term, "water user association," widely used by donor agencies to designate local irrigation organizations, is often a misnomer because it ignores nonirrigation water uses.

the necessary authority to deal with the problems.[16] For local administration to handle irrigation management tasks, some degree of decentralization of authority is needed. This is taken up analytically in Section 7.5.3.

Local government can be a preferred LID option where virtually all households within its jurisdiction are involved directly in irrigated agriculture. Then water management can legitimately and effectively be dealt with as a concern of the whole community. One advantage of the LG alternative is that conflicts between agricultural and domestic users of water can be better resolved than through membership organizations of irrigators provided that women's interests are effectively represented in LG deliberations. Irrigation water management at the local level is most often handled through user groups. But there are good examples of traditional local government institutions handling irrigation management in Indonesia (Duewel, 1984), Mexico (Lees, 1973), and Northern Pakistan (Bhatty, 1979; see Annex Two). Under certain conditions, LG is a feasible local institutional alternative.

The best comparative study of the development of local institutions for water management is by Maass and Anderson (1978). For hundreds of years effective local government systems in Spain have handled water management. Well-established water courts enforce an elaborately evolved water law with widespread understanding and participation. The evolution of these local institutions occurred over centuries and was backed by timely and strong support from higher levels of government. In the U.S. irrigation management is handled by user associations rather than by local government bodies, but the associations were given legal recognition and sanctions, so they could operate effectively in a quasi-governmental manner.

Only if the size of irrigated holdings is quite large do private sector institutions become particularly useful for water management. With small holdings, there is great interdependence among water users for acquisition, allocation, distribution, and maintenance, making public sector or membership institutions tenable.

Widespread experience supports relying on user groups or local government institutions for irrigation management though they can usefully be backed by technical and financial resources provided through local administrative staff of a Department of Irrigation. Even (or especially) large-scale irrigation cannot be managed by national institutions without strong local institutional capabilities. Moreover, it is simply beyond the capacity of national administration to play much of a role in small-scale irrigation systems

---

[16]In a Chilean community reported in Annex Two, mining interests outside the local government jurisdiction were reducing the water supply and thus undercutting the irrigation associations managing water. The fact that control over the associations and over irrigation had been preempted by the national irrigation bureaucracy meant that local solutions and accommodations could not be worked out (Lynch, 1978).

where user associations or local governments are clearly the more effective institutions for management (F. Korten, 1982; Coward, 1984).

2.5.2 Social Forestry

The term *social forestry* has been introduced to distinguish a new approach to the management of trees, which is different from the technically and commercially directed development that previously prevailed. The commercial development dealt only with trees on a large scale, in monocrop operations, without involvement of the people who lived in and around the forests. In social forestry, trees are to be managed in association with other plants and animals, often in small or fragmented areas. Multiple uses not necessarily for market sales are emphasized, and management is done largely by the people living nearby and primarily for their benefit. This is quite a departure from conventional bureaucratic approaches, which have sometimes appeared to regard people as enemies rather than as partners in forest management.

Forest management in the past has too often been undertaken through national institutions (forestry departments or corporations) with no more local institutional development than assigning a few technicians and many forest guards to look after the trees. The case literature, however, is virtually unanimous on the need for associating local people closely with any forest management effort, and there is considerable agreement on the most promising local institutional arrangements.

In contrast to irrigation management, where user associations are generally preferred over local governments, in forest management the preference is reversed. This is not surprising because users of forest resources are an ambiguous group even when the resources themselves are readily identifiable and delimitable. Persons in the immediate area draw on forests for fuelwood, animal fodder, construction materials, minor forest products, and recreation, but outsiders too may use them for these purposes as well as for grazing and commercial exploitation.

One cannot confidently rely on membership organizations to enlist all users, with their conflicting objectives, into a single voluntary association. More authoritative institutions are usually required to regulate outside as well as local resource use and to mobilize people's time and funds for improving the forest resource base. Because benefits from investments are more deferred than in irrigation management, some compulsion may be needed for protecting and upgrading forests.

These considerations make local government usually the preferred local institution for forest management, often in combination with some re-oriented units of local administration which can provide appropriate technical guidance. Although LGs are often dominated by richer elements of the community, they are more likely than central government agencies to produce a consensus on a resource management regime that is broadly acceptable as fair and binding. The broader the participation in decision making and the less biased the resulting decisions the more likely they are to receive voluntary compliance.

Forestry management more than other forms of natural resource management requires what West (1983) calls "collective adoption," i.e., it depends on the cooperation of the poorer strata in rural areas as well as the richer ones. The rural poor, who are less likely to join organizations, can undercut most management schemes. They are also very sensitive to equity considerations and are unlikely to comply voluntarily with schemes they regard as unfair. Of course, the rich may also seek to circumvent resource regulations for the sake of short-run benefits.[17]

We already referred to experience with forest management in Nepal, where the government took away local responsibility in 1957. One of the keys to enlisting local governments' acceptance of responsibility after 1977 when the forest law was again changed was that panchayat LG be given clear responsibility for the resources and that all or most of the immediate benefits from improved management accrue to the community. This question of "who benefits" has to be resolved satisfactorily if rural people are expected to take responsibility for managing trees productively over time.[18]

This matches the conclusion of a World Bank study on social forestry in Pakistan. Locally elected bodies at the village level can provide effective institutional support for small social forestry schemes provided that the government's forest land is allocated to the elected bodies (Cernea, 1980). This was also found to be effective in a USAID-supported reforestation project in Senegal (Annex Two). An analysis of Sri Lankan experience similarly concluded that for effective environmental management, responsibility should be given to formal village-based institutions with proper governmental backing (Moore and Wickramasinghe, 1978).

One reason why rural people may require relatively unqualified control over forest resources before they will commit their time and effort to forest management is that the benefits from planting and protecting trees, compared to other activities, are relatively long term. To the extent that forest use rights are limited or ambiguous the prospects that rural people will actually realize benefits are accordingly diminished.

Simply assigning certain responsibilities to LG within administratively conceived and implemented social forestry programs is not the answer.

---

[17]We found case studies from Nepal (Acharya, 1984) and Peru (Durham, 1977) where it was the rich rather than the poor who were responsible for destruction of forest resources.

[18]In Niger, the government enacted a National Forestry Code which named 15 "protected" species that rural people would not be allowed to cut without government permission. Understandably, rural people in Niger have been reluctant to participate in programs to plant "protected" species in windbreaks and woodlots (Thompson, 1982). Readers can imagine the difficulties a peasant would have in meeting a forestry official to get a license to cut a protected tree, with no assurance of getting the approval even if the tree were on his own land.

There needs to be an effective sharing of responsibility, with the community having control over forested land and its benefits. If forests are thereby preserved, soil erosion reduced, and the water cycle protected, there are obvious national gains. Such an arrangement was the key to the success of the Chautara experiment in Nepal that helped to reverse that country's forest policy (Annex Two). Social forestry activities in the Indian state of Gujerat have been funded by the World Bank, but Spears (1982) reports that the community components of the program could not be sustained for lack of effective devolution to local government bodies.[19]

If other local institutions are too weak and unpromising to build a social forestry program on the basis of collective action, local administration becomes the main channel for activity in programs directed to households, which we would classify as "sub-local" institutions (Section 1.6). Cernea (1980) has suggested that household woodlots will have advantages over community woodlots

> where capacity of the village for collective action is meager; where the interdependence required by community schemes cannot be immediately elicited and not everyone can be counted on to contribute his share of the work; and/or where community woodlots are ill-suited in the local ecological context to serve as a vehicle for reforestation powered by local people.

These analytical and prescriptive observations match ours exactly.

We note that *cooperatives* do not figure very often among local institutional options for social forestry. One might think that pooling private forest holdings and then exploiting and preserving them jointly would offer some advantages. But we found only three references to cooperative social forestry—in Guatemala (Barnes, et al., 1980:43-44), in the Northwest Frontier Province of Pakistan (Cernea, 1980:31), and in Gujerat State of India (Gadgil, 1983:124-125).

Easily the best example of social forestry carried out by local institutions was in South Korea, where Village Forest Associations have responsibility for over 2 million acres of local forests. These associations, which have features both of local government and membership organization, were started by central government initiative after 1961, but they built on pre-existing informal forest management groups at the village level. Although sometimes coercive at the start, they have reportedly become genuinely popular programs (Annex Two).

The forms of local institutions for forestry management may change

---

[19]The program, which was implemented through the district forestry department, had three components: (1) farm forestry by individual households, (2) community woodlots under the panchayats, and (3) string plantations along roadsides, planted and maintained by the department. The first and third components fared satisfactorily, but the second was a failure with only 7 percent of the target achieved. Given the history of constraints on panchayats, most villagers did not expect any benefits from the panchayat forests and thus these received no local support.

and evolve. One of the most noted successes grew out of the Chipko movement in India, which mobilized tribal people in the state of Uttar Pradesh to protect their forest resources (Annex Two). What started as a cooperative to gain income for poor people became for a time a political movement, where people clung bodily to trees threatened with cutting by outside commercial interests. After such dramatic efforts had forced the government to accept a policy of forest conservation, Chipko took up its own guarding and planting of forest areas, completing a progression from economics, to politics, to ecology. Because the area's population is so homogeneous, membership organization operates practically like a local government.

The differences in local institutional possibilities and profiles between forestry and irrigation management are instructive for both areas of activity. LID for social forestry has not received much systematic attention in the literature. However, because the participation of local people in managing forest resources is so crucial to success, LID is of great urgency.

2.5.3 Range Management

Managing rangeland differs from other NRM activities in several ways. First, the resource user-managers, mostly pastoralists, represent a mobile, unbounded population, the opposite of fixed canal irrigation water users. Second, the resource itself is highly variable in time and space (Sandford, 1983:33–36, 49–51). Third, the land tenure institutions tend toward common property because of climatic variation. These differences have important implications for LID.

The fact that user-managers of rangeland resources are highly mobile does not mean they have little social organization. There is clear consensus in the literature that most pastoralist societies have strong social organization at the lower levels, though little hierarchical structure of authority (Hoben, 1976; Horowitz, 1979; Dyson-Hudson and Dyson-Hudson, 1980).

In traditional range management there was much consultation among the interested parties seeking accommodation and consensus since zero-sum decision making could lead to one party's demise. However, because many decisions had to be made without opportunity for regular deliberations, traditional systems often had strong executive roles that were accorded considerable authority. For example, in earlier times in Botswana, there was in each locality a grazing superintendent (*modisa*) who represented the paramount chief for allocating grazing rights and handling disputes (Wynne, 1981).

It appears that traditional authority structures are generally in decline in pastoralist societies though they retain considerable residual influence. Unfortunately for LID there is no assurance that modern institutions will inherit any lapsed traditional authority. The total amount of authority available for regulating range use can decline when chiefly or other indigenous roles lose their potency (Roe and Fortmann, 1982; Brown et al., 1982).

Most reviews of range management experience suggest that adjusting modern local institutions to traditional roles and practices is advisable. Where the latter remain important in pastoralist communities, they can lend legitimacy to the modern institutions. Indeed, without such legitimacy from the public concerned, they will not operate as "institutions"—only as organizations with which people cooperate (or not) as they see fit.

The most crucial resource in range management is water. Most pastoral activity occurs in marginal, arid and semi-arid environments where mobility is induced by the inherent variability of water. Though persons living in such environments may seek to produce some arable crops, they cannot survive on crops alone.

The land ownership pattern in these areas naturally responds to these ecological and climatic variations. Private ownership of land is rare, except in oases or other prized locations, because there is no value in land itself unless it has water, and rainfall is unpredictable. Thus, communal ownership of land is the most common tenure form in arid and semi-arid areas; however, livestock is usually owned by individuals or households.

Analytically there are four alternative situations in which LID for range management might be undertaken:

Figure 2.2: ALTERNATIVE RANGE MANAGEMENT SITUATIONS

	LIVESTOCK OWNERSHIP	
PASTURE OWNERSHIP	Private	Communal
Private	(I) U.S. ranches, often promoted by LDC govts. favoring sedentarization	(II) Uncommon, could occur with cooperative steer fattening
Communal	(III) Most common situation in pastoral areas of LDCs	(IV) Current Mongolian collectives; Chinese ranching communes; Israeli kibbutzim

Range management tasks are simplest in (I) because costs and benefits are "internalized" and can be compared over time. Little local institutional development is required because the household is carrying out all NRM activities on its own. But this form of land and livestock tenure is feasible only where individuals can privately own large enough areas of land that they have opportunities for mobility of their herds. This institutional form has been advocated as a means of controlling "overgrazing" and of averting "the tragedy of the commons." The evidence that private ownership leads to better range management, however, is not conclusive, and giving some individuals or households exclusive rights to large land areas raises very controversial issues of equity.

The most frequent situation, private stock grazed on common land, is ecologically motivated. Overstocking and abuse of rangeland resources can and does occur, but there is increasing evidence that "the tragedy of the commons" (not restricted to range management but best exemplified in range areas) is exaggerated (Runge, 1981; Sandford, 1983).[20] Herders in the highlands of Bolivia had definite controls on grazing (Annex Two) as did the Sherpa in Nepal. Until the government preempted their community responsibilities for resource management, the Sherpa annually appointed "guardians" to enforce rules governing grazing and collect fines (Fuerer-Haimendorf, 1972). The issue for local institutional development is often how best to manage a combination of public land and private livestock. In traditional range management systems, pastoralists keep their ownership of herds separate and control land as common property. This makes decentralized exploitation of available resources easier and, given the importance of attention to animal health, private ownership of livestock encourages more careful husbandry.

The situation of communal livestock and private grazing land (II) is possible but highly unusual. Where it occurs, the private owners of land can limit access to pasture through mechanisms such as pricing. The purely communal situation (IV) is similar to (I) because costs and benefits are all internalized. The difference is that many more persons are involved in decision making. In our literature review, we found collective pooling of livestock grazing on common land only where national policies dictated this. Even in Mongolia there is decentralized allocation of land to units within the collective which then operate quite similarly to groups of households within traditional pastoral systems (Humphrey, 1978).

Because of the relative unboundedness of rangeland resources, there is a larger role for local administration than in water or forest management provided that it can be both mobile and flexible, the two essential requirements for any range management strategy. Unfortunately these are not common features of most administrative institutions. One would have to achieve considerable bureaucratic reorientation for this to occur.

To allow for mobility and flexibility of decision making in any range management strategy, the household, or more commonly an informal group of households, will have to be the basic operational unit. The services of the local administration should be directed to supporting the productivity and

---

[20]Indeed, the concept of "overgrazing" is itself now questioned (Gillis and Jamtgaard, 1981). Sandford (1983) in his review of the literature finds little empirical support for claims about "desertification" or about "stocking rates" exceeding the "carrying capacity" of rangeland areas.

security of this unit. It is helpful to have some channels of communication among households and groups to negotiate over resource access and movement of livestock, but such arrangements are best kept informal and not rigorously institutionalized. Efforts to create larger permanent organizations to manage rangeland resources "can lead to a unit which [is] too small to cope with environmental fluctuations, and too large to cope with social coordination" (N. Dyson-Hudson, 1985:91). This is seen in the Kenya case in Annex Two.

One form of membership organization that can be useful in range environments deals with the provision of water, which is essential for exploiting either grazing or agricultural possibilities. One difficulty in organizing local efforts to provide water is that any new rights may be at variance with traditional rights. This was discovered in Botswana when the Ministry of Agriculture delegated management responsibility for the small catchment dams it was building to groups of users. Such groups lacked clear authority to regulate their use by nonmembers (Annex Two).

There have been numerous experiments with group ranches, which represent a local organization or cooperative LID option. By and large, these ranches have not been very successful; for example, in Kenya (Doherty, 1979), Tanzania (Hoben, 1976), Botswana (Odell and Odell, 1980) or Burkina Faso (Gooch, 1979). The reasons for their failure appear to be many but chief among them are: (1) the bureaucratic way in which they have been carried out; (2) underlying antagonism between the government and the pastoralists as the former sought to change the latter's way of life; and (3) the misleading concept of "carrying capacity," which has guided much of the planning and implementation. The introduction of rather formal organizations to do what can be managed by pastoralists themselves on an informal basis is an inappropriate mode of LID.

Market mechanisms have been suggested for regulating herd size (Range Management Center, 1981). But pastoral economies are usually semi-monetized at most, and there are security as well as status values inherent in livestock. It is not surprising therefore that our literature review did not find price incentives for herders to be a reliable basis for resource management.

In summary the role of government and its local administration appears significant in range management, though it cannot be effective if authority is exercised coercively (Hoben, 1976). Mobility and self-sufficiency are essential features of pastoralism, and thus government agencies will have to be highly mobile and accommodating. For example, LA will need to find ways to make its veterinary, marketing, and other services more accessible than at present (D. Sandford, 1981). Forms of local organization that are consistent with traditional modes of inter-household cooperation can facilitate government interaction with herders and their families. Working with and through membership organizations is an area in which some experimentation is going on (Wall, 1983), and it may become more effective if appropriate approaches can be developed. So far, state interventions have a poor record, and much more systematic work remains to be done before a reliable LID knowledge base for range management can be said to exist.

2.5.4 Watershed Management

This requires protection or restoration of forest resources in conjunction with better water and soil management practices in hilly areas that capture rainfall. LID tasks and choices are complicated by the multiplicity of resources involved but also by other factors. Watersheds are typically less densely populated because they cannot support any significant agriculture, and sparse population makes institutional development and maintenance more difficult. Since raising livestock is often important in watershed management, some of the LID considerations for range management apply. The population in watershed areas is often culturally and economically outside the national mainstream having been pushed out of the more productive lowland areas at some time in the past. Not surprisingly one of the few specific studies we found of local watershed management institutions dealt with a marginal "tribal" area in the Indian state of Gujerat (Jayaraman, 1980).

Local institutional development alternatives are limited in such areas. Both local administration and local government are likely to be weak in what have become "peripheral" areas. Other modern forms of organization may not be much stronger though indigenous organizations can be quite effective. The household is the basic unit of decision making and activity. Gaining cooperation from the population as a whole to preserve forest resources and maintain the water-gathering capacity of a watershed requires some institutional structures. Given the weakness of outside institutions, the best course is often to devise arrangements for management responsibilities with "traditional" local institutions based on religious or cultural identities where these exist.

Conservation efforts are more likely to succeed if combined with other activities like supply of production inputs, development of transportation facilities, or provision of social services. This was seen in the Northern Agricultural Development Project in Thailand, financed by the World Bank (Spears, 1982), and the Damodar Valley Corporation efforts at watershed management in India (Jaiswal et al., 1985). For such an approach to yield the intended results, however, there needs to be considerable local-level coordination, as documented in the watershed development efforts in the Machakos District of Kenya (Annex Two), and this in turn requires a greater

degree of LID. The Damodar experience just referred to demonstrated limited results until a more participatory approach was taken in conjunction with
the panchayat local government.[21]

The earlier approach to watershed development was similar to that in
forestry, concentrating efforts on formal tree plantations. This approach, if it
strengthened any local institution, emphasized the role of LA and bypassed
or ignored LG and membership organizations. The thinking now is to promote agroforestry within sustainable limits or to rely more on natural
regeneration (Spears, 1982). The first of these alternatives requires much
more in the way of LID than does the plantation method while the latter requires much less though cooperation from area residents is required for
either to succeed.

Reducing livestock pressure on watershed vegetation is often an important part of the management strategy. Two approaches may be used. Efforts
to increase the marketing of livestock, as done in Kenya during the 1960s,
can be undertaken through private businesses. The second method, introducing livestock exchange programs to get farmers to trade in surplus
animals for improved breeds as done in the Kandi Watershed Project in
India (Spears, 1982), requires the involvement of government agencies, possibly with LG or membership organization support.

It makes sense for administrative agencies working in watershed programs to work closely with local governments where they exist. A recent
watershed management project in Indonesia was planned in an area where
LA was strong enough to have sustained large-scale conservation efforts.
However, the project was based on a newly created Regional Watershed
Authority set up by the central government at a "supra-local" level and accountable to higher authorities rather than to local communities. It has
encountered many difficulties in coordinating work and eliciting cooperation (B. Dwight King, personal communication). Similarly joint catchment
area committees set up as part of the Erosion Control Programme in the Indian state of Gujerat faced many problems. Though the committees
included LG representatives, they could not be very effective because of the
reluctance of officials working for separate agencies to coordinate their
respective programs or to delegate budget authority to panchayat local governments (Annex Two).

Membership organizations are less important for watershed management than for other NRM areas unless some subsidy is provided by
government. Watershed management offers weaker incentives to resource
users for collective action for the following reasons:

---

[21]A small PVO program in the area, working with and through a cooperative to get farmers
to reshape fields and change cropping, showed some substantial progress. However, the "catalyst" agent (Section 7.3.2) made the mistake of taking on the leadership role in the cooperative
rather than developing local leadership, and this became a bottleneck in LID as well as in improving watershed management (Jaiswal et al., 1985:433–434, 437–439).

- the community of users is only geographically defined and usually does not have any group identity or operative authority structure;
- benefits are deferred and generally accrue to persons who do not bear the costs of watershed management (i.e., to downstream populations);
- changes in the condition of resources are hard to recognize or measure, so the need for making investments and the return therefrom is generally ambiguous; and
- there is little perceived interdependence among the resource users.

Where such circumstances do not apply, the possibilities for building watershed management around LG bodies or membership organizations will be more encouraging.

We found little discussion of local institutions in the watershed management literature. This could be because the conditions are not often favorable for much local institutional responsibility in watershed management. In probably the most thorough analysis of planning and implementation for watershed management, Hufschmidt (1985) suggests several "organizational institutions" needed for this category of NRM: planning and management agencies (both public and private); extension services; and credit agencies—national institutions possibly with local branches functioning as agencies of local administration.[22]

In an analysis of water resources management in Thailand covering all aspects of irrigated agricultural production and including watershed management, Hufschmidt lists thirty-eight government agencies that have responsibilities and also three categories of local institutions—water user associations, farmer cooperatives, and farm suppliers and merchants (private businesses). The latter are shown to have a role only in irrigation and agriculture activities, while watershed management is left entirely to the central government's Royal Forest Department and the Forest Industry Organization, a state enterprise (Bower and Hufschmidt, 1984). Hufschmidt may be right that national institutions are the ones most commonly utilized. But there should be scope for involving or establishing other kinds of local institutions for watershed management, ones that build on the interests and talents of communities in the watersheds themselves rather than rely only on outside personnel and on external perceptions of "the problem."

Our analysis indicates that getting local institutions to take a major and active role in watershed management will be difficult, but not that it is impossible. Most experience in watershed management indicates that people's cooperation cannot be effectively commanded or compelled from outside.

---

[22]Hufschmidt distinguishes, as we did in Chapter One, between "nonorganizational" and "organizational" institutions. In the first category, he lists land tenure systems, legal codes, economic policies, and informal arrangements as needed for each kind of management activity. Planning and management agencies, extension services, and credit agencies he puts in the latter category. He does not consider local government or other local institutions in his analytical framework.

Watershed management usually must be attempted in areas where resources of all kinds are very thinly stretched. Some consolation may be taken in the finding of the World Bank's forestry advisor based on experience in Nepal, that response from farmers has been better in the more remote areas where there has traditionally been more reliance on indigenous local institutions and less central government capacity for direction (Spears, 1982). This is a situation in which LID may not be easy but it is relatively more promising.[23]

2.5.5 Soil Conservation

Although soil conservation NRM has several of the characteristics of watershed management just listed (benefits deferred and accruing to others, changes in resource condition often hard to recognize, less perceived interdependence among users), it differs in an important respect. The persons who should be involved—the users of land in danger of losing its fertility—are readily known and identified because the resource of land is so tangible and so demarcatable. Whether soil needs special management practices might be unclear, but who is responsible for the soil can be determined (partly because owners of land risk losing it if they deny their responsibility for it). Where land is rented out or there are irregular land tenure arrangements, such as the "family land" in Jamaica (Blustain, 1982a), there may be disagreements about responsibility. But property rights for agricultural land are usually much better defined than for water, forests, or rangeland.

The value of an organization to its members is affected by their dependence on one another and whether it helps them gain access to benefits. In the Jamaican project (Annex Two), neither condition applied. Individual farmers could apply for and receive a grant to construct bench terraces on their own fields. But the committees had no role in reviewing farm plans worked out directly with project staff or in screening applications. There could and should have been coordination in laying out and constructing the terraces since the runoff from one farmer's field could accelerate erosion on farmers' fields below him. But the grants were given out by project staff on an individual basis in keeping with the local traditions of "patronage" from the government. As the committees served no technical or organizational purpose, they did not "take root" (Blustain, 1982).

Given the technology chosen for this project—bench terracing—there was good reason for collective action to coordinate the disposal of rainwater runoff. Had the project promoted planting of grass strips to retard runoff instead of building more costly bench terraces, the technical need for farmer

---

[23]Spears' conclusion is consistent with our finding based on statistical analysis of 150 local organization cases worldwide, that LO performance is not adversely affected, and possibly even positively correlated, with unfavorable environments such as mountainous terrain and poor infrastructure (Esman and Uphoff, 1984:106–112).

committees would have been less but they might still have been promoted for the sake of more efficient communication among farmers and with the government and for creating community consciousness supporting soil conservation. To further organizational capacity, the project should have provided that grants at least be reviewed if not controlled by the committees.

This underscores the need for any membership organization to be viewed by members as necessary and beneficial. Such legitimacy is, of course, a requirement for gaining compliance with soil conservation and resource management practices generally. The introduction of bench terraces in the Uluguru Land Use Scheme in Tanzania was a failure because it provided no demonstrable benefit to farmers or to the community as a whole. Indeed, the technology introduced was itself destructive of soil structure and fertility given the soil conditions of the region. So noncooperation by farmers was a kind of soil conservation. In fact, in parts of the region farmers were using an indigenous form of ladder terracing which provided quick benefits, showing that farmers would adopt suitable conservation measures (Temple, 1972). Certainly the technology must be appropriate and advantageous at the micro-level to have a beneficial impact at the macro-level. No institutions, local or national, can be expected to succeed otherwise.

National institutions must certainly take some initiative in soil conservation efforts, if only to compensate those who must bear present costs for the sake of beneficiaries in downhill or downstream areas or in future generations. The frequently gradual nature of deterioration also means that it is difficult to get soil conservation efforts started unless or until erosion problems become serious, at which point they may be hard to control and reverse. Implementing new technologies and channeling subsidies will usually require some local institutional arrangements in order to get the job done.

For soil conservation as for other kinds of natural resource management, LID is therefore important. The question is what kinds and combinations of local institutions, operating at which levels (group, community, locality) will be most supportive of NRM objectives? As analyzed in this chapter, the specific characteristics of the resource as well as of the resource user-managers will affect the appropriateness of different local institutions.

Often we find central governments carrying practically all of the burden of NRM planning and implementation. The predominant role of national institutions is often predicated on the weakness or inadequacy of local institutions. Yet the lack of strong local institutions is often directly related to the central government's preemption of functions and of financial resources. So a major issue is how to redress the current imbalance in institutional capacity where the center has created a larger burden for itself by its preeminence. This issue is not restricted to the area of natural resource management and is addressed in Chapter Eight on a cross-sectoral basis.

CHAPTER THREE

Local Institutional Development for Rural Infrastructure

3.1 ACTIVITIES IN RURAL INFRASTRUCTURE

The productivity, well-being, and security of rural people is greatly affected by the adequacy of the infrastructure that exists in their communities and that links them to district, provincial, and national centers of administration and commerce. Infrastructure includes all physical facilities that provide services to agriculture or nonagricultural enterprise or that benefit the population directly. Transportation, power, water supply, and communication facilities are valuable for both categories, while other infrastructure such as post offices or recreation facilities will provide general benefits. Certain facilities support tasks of natural resource management (e.g. irrigation and drainage structures or forest roads) while others aid in human resource development (e.g. schools and health clinics).

Five categories of rural infrastructure can be provided through some combination of public and private institutions at various levels. Not all are of equal relevance to local institutions, but we list them to indicate the boundaries of this activity area.

1. **Transportation** for moving persons and materials quickly, cheaply, and reliably.
   a. There are basically three *modes* of transportation: (a) by *land*, (b) by *water*, and (c) by *air*. The first is by far the most important for rural development, though the others may be crucial for remote or mountainous areas.
   b. In each mode, there needs to be some basic investment in (a) *structures* that permit (or facilitate, speed, cheapen) movement of persons and goods, with secondary investment in (b) *vehicles*

or other transport means to utilize the roads, waterways, or airstrips, e.g., trucks, barges, airplanes.

2. **Power** from inanimate sources which permit (or make more efficient) agricultural production activities, nonagricultural enterprises, and improvements in the quality of life in rural areas.

   a. The most versatile is *electricity*, which can be generated in various ways. For ecological as well as other reasons, *biogas* is of increasing interest in rural development as the residue can provide fertilizer for agricultural production.

   b. Whether power *generation* is centralized or decentralized affects which if any local institutions are relevant. Moreover, local institutions may have a comparative advantage in the *distribution* of power more than in its generation. This is often seen with rural electrification cooperatives, which may buy power from regional or national (public or private) institutions.

3. **Water supply.** The use for which the supply is created affects which local institutions will be most relevant, as does the *technology* employed for obtaining it and the *distribution system* involved.

   a. *Domestic water supply* for potable water has greater local institutional requirements than water for *livestock*, for example, because water quality is more important.

   b. Water used only for *irrigation* presents simpler tasks for local management, suitable for membership organizations of users, than does water with *multiple uses* where many different and conflicting interests must be reconciled, necessitating a role for local government or possibly representatives of the national government.

4. **Communication.** While there is a great deal of communication at the local level, there is relatively little infrastructure that is strictly "local." Radio transmitters, television relays, telephone or telegraph wires are almost always part of national systems. The local institutional development implications of communication infrastructure are therefore fewer. An exception would be the use of local listening groups to make radio more effective in rural areas (Berrigan, 1979; Crowley et al., 1981).

5. **Service and other facilities.** These are often dependent on local institutions for provision and/or maintenance: schools, clinics, community centers, libraries, post offices, marketplaces, sanitation facilities, etc. *Housing* also can be provided through one or more local institutional channels.

For practical reasons, we concentrate on three types of rural infrastructure—roads and bridges, electrification, and domestic water supply, bearing in mind that all can have multiple uses. LID implications of the irrigation aspects of water supply have already been considered in Chapter Two and are not treated here.

The services provided by physical infrastructure are commonly, but not always, classifiable as "public goods," as discussed in Section 3.3. For some

combination of physical, financial, or social reasons, it is impossible, uneconomical, or undesirable for services to be provided only to certain persons
individually on a market-price basis. When this situation applies, the institutional options are narrowed because private channels of service provision
are not viable. Some kinds of membership organizations may be effective
where public goods are involved, but such possibilities need to be assessed
carefully.

3.2 LOCAL INSTITUTIONAL OPTIONS

Many of the goods and services provided by infrastructure can be created by individuals and households, such as constructing a path or digging a
well, or even installing a diesel electric generator provided they have sufficient resources. However, such a generator may be quite uneconomical; the
well may not provide as much water or be as reliable as if a deeper one were
installed with more investment; and many hand-made paths do not add up
to an all-weather road suitable for movement of many goods and persons.
So while individuals and households can provide for themselves some of
the benefits of infrastructure, collective action to create and maintain them
is needed for substantial development.

Many kinds of infrastructure have been created by traditional local
institutions—communal irrigation systems, village roads, wells, capped
springs, etc. We are concerned here with the larger scale and more technologically advanced forms of infrastructure that may be established and
maintained by local or national institutions.

Because infrastructure is essentially area-based and most often provides public goods, LA and LG institutions have some inherent advantages
compared to LOs or private enterprises. The latter two channels lack the
authoritative basis for requiring users to pay for goods or services received.
Nevertheless, LOs and private enterprises can make important contributions to certain kinds or phases of infrastructure development. Moreover,
although our analysis addresses institutional alternatives, in practice the
best solution is to have several institutions working together.

Where infrastructure provides public goods from which users cannot
be excluded, or for which they cannot be made to pay, private businesses
have difficulty operating profitably, and thus are not viable. Infrastructure
such as rural electrification, however, has products that can be marketed,
making private enterprises feasible. Further, private providers may be an
important part of the mix of local institutions involved with rural infrastructure by meeting specific needs such as making spare parts for water supply
equipment (USAID, 1982).

Most of the infrastructure found in rural areas can be attributed to
national government agencies, often but not always having locally based
staff and operations. Despite its many weaknesses and inefficiencies, LA

contributions to design and construction are often vital even if other institutions take over responsibilities for operation and maintenance. Agency staff can be found working under very difficult conditions to get roads, wells, and other facilities established. Unfortunately LA, like other local institutions, is better at creating infrastructure than at maintaining it for a variety of reasons.[1]

While it has limitations, local government usually appears to be the most promising base for developing and maintaining rural infrastructure, especially if it can be supplemented by some form of local organization. To meet particular local needs, LG can engage certain specialized staff to ensure performance of routine operations. For example, in irrigation overseer roles have been created to supervise the operation and management (O&M) of water distribution systems. Local government, with its legal authority and its more assured (if not fully adequate) financial base, has a comparative advantage for such continuous activities. Indeed, we find such roles have sometimes been incorporated by local governments for current irrigation O&M.[2]

One of the conditions for an effective LG role in infrastructure is that it have a predictable resource base. While the amount of financial resources available will affect LG's decision making about construction, the stability of resource flows will be crucial for operation and maintenance, which are essential for deriving benefits from any infrastructure. This is stressed by Garzon (1981) in his comparative analysis of rural public works experience. He found the performance of Local Development Associations in North Yemen, which receive an assured portion of the *zaqat* tax (Annex Eight), better than that of local governments in Tunisia and Pakistan, which built infrastructure with temporary Food for Work funds.

Membership organizations or cooperatives can oversee continuous operations, but as a rule, they appear better at one-time activities where resources of money or labor are mobilized for a specific task. The handling of funds and supervising of personnel for O&M requires day-in, day-out effort and great responsibility. While LGs may fluctuate in their capability according to the commitment and skill of their officers and personnel, membership organizations are likely to have even greater variation. MOs may have highly effective leadership for some years, but it is hard to sustain this over long periods. Certain membership organizations have, in numerous situations, discharged O&M tasks quite satisfactorily, but this does not

---

[1]A study of Kenyan rural water supply experience, for example, found LA not equipped to operate and maintain the systems due to the large areas to be covered, the lack of transportation to visit these areas, and unreliable supplies of fuel and parts. Also, often the engineers were expatriates with short-term tenure who were not prepared for working in close collaboration with communities (Dworkin, 1980a).

[2]Examples of traditional watermaster roles now serving more modern functions would be the *ulu-ulu* in Indonesia (Duewel, 1982) and the *chowkidar* in Pakistan (Bhatty, 1979).

change our generalization about the comparative advantage of local government. That the best examples of O&M by membership organizations are found with irrigation water supply suggests, first that if a service is highly valued by members, they will sustain O&M activities, but also that considerable management capability can be mobilized if the demand for a service is strong.[3]

Membership organizations and cooperatives are more subject to the constraints that "free riding" presents than are other local institutions operating in rural infrastructure. Where the benefits that members produce by their resource contributions can be enjoyed by others who contribute nothing, this may be a deterrent to the organization's providing the service. This, however, is a conditional not an absolute statement since the net benefits to members may be sufficient to justify their effort even if others appear to gain unfairly.[4]

We found more of a role for MOs and cooperatives in rural infrastructure than would be predicted on the basis of social science theorizing about "the logic of collective action" (Olson, 1965). Even if such organizations do not create the infrastructure themselves, they may be enlisted to assess, collect, and account for fees, as reported in Tanzania and Tunisia (Dworkin, 1980b; Bigelow and Chiles, 1980). In Bolivia, Tendler (1983) found that cooperatives established for other purposes also undertook some rural infrastructure investments, which benefited the whole community not just members. User associations are often successful in mobilizing local resources to expand infrastructure (USAID, 1982).

We did not find "alternative organizations," those composed only of poorer members of the community (Leonard and Marshall, 1982), frequently involved in infrastructure. There are some examples such as an organization of untouchables in an Indian village who collected funds and built and maintained a well. But to the extent that the membership covered the whole community, their organization would constitute a local organization or even local government more than an "alternative organization."

Local service organizations, as a special category for providing rural infrastructure, were not very common in our reading of the case literature. This may reflect our concentration on roads, electrification, and water supply. We know that there are private service organizations that invest in providing public facilities such as community centers and market stalls, and

---

[3]In the Chattis Mauja area of Nepal, four thousand farmers living in a locality with fifty-four villages manage an irrigation system that is 150 years old and serves 7,500 acres through a complex membership organization described in Annex Eight. The farmers hire their own technical supervisors to oversee O&M work. Over 60,000 man-days of labor are mobilized annually from members for maintenance. All this is done by a largely illiterate membership without any inputs from government (LA). So one can see the possibilities for local management of even fairly complex tasks if the incentive and responsibility are clear.

[4]These questions and some of the relevant literature are considered in Sections 1.7 and 2.4

local religious organizations often provide amenities like drinking water or resthouses for travellers.

These examples underscore our observation that while different institutional channels have certain comparative advantages, it is likely that some combination will contribute to more effective provision of even a single form of infrastructure like bridges or potable water. It is also important to see how institutions operating at different local levels can fit together.[5] In the Baglung bridge case, the overall planning by a district panchayat was based on proposals emanating from the village panchayats below it. Once a bridge was approved, actual construction was assigned to a special committee (MO) made up of persons who had the keenest interest in having a safe, reliable crossing at the particular point (Annex Three). The Malawi self-help water scheme, given the nature of decision making and operation needed for the supply and distribution system, had committees at several levels working with LA staff of the Department of Community Development (Annex Three).

The preferred local institutional arrangement for rural infrastructure often appears to be a combination of local government and local organizations. Imboden's review (1977) of rural drinking water projects concludes that: "A water committee and strong local authority facilitate the execution of water projects." This is seen in the water supply cases from Peru and India reported in Annex Three, though in the Malawi case, it was a combination of LA and LO that accomplished a remarkably quick and inexpensive spread of water facilities. The similarly impressive case of bridge building in the Baglung district of Nepal relied on LOs with LG sponsorship having minimal but crucial inputs from central government.

Many factors affect the value of local institutional alternatives. Most electricity generation, for example, requires a larger scale of operation than does biogas, but the technology used makes some difference. Biogas digesters constructed for a single household require little LID, whereas electricity generators cannot be efficient at that level. One usually looks to community or locality institutions to handle electricity distribution and/or generation because of the interdependence among users created by technical and economic considerations. Where large biogas digesters are preferable because of investment costs or supply requirements, group or

---

[5]Our discussion here of "levels" follows the analytical distinctions made in Chapter One. We identified three different "local" levels—the *locality*, which is a set of communities having some tradition of cooperation, perhaps because they have had previous economic, social, and other interaction focused on a market town; the *community*, which is a residential entity made up of households living in close proximity; and the *group* made up of households or individuals cooperating at a level "below" the community. Above the "local" level, one can have sub-district and district levels, which are defined essentially in administrative terms. These are not units of actual or potential collective action by rural people and thus are not regarded as "local" in our LID analysis.

community institutions become necessary.[6] While the technologies for electricity and biogas are variable and not fixed, as are efficiency considerations, the level of institutional development will usually be higher for electricity as a rural energy source. Similar considerations are found with domestic water supply using gravity versus lift (pump) systems.

Rural infrastructure activities differ from those in other areas of rural development because generally the services of infrastructure are public goods. This makes their provision through private sector channels less feasible if not impossible. Membership organizations are confronted by the free rider problem when undertaking to provide public goods. This inhibition can be overcome through the exercise of authority by LG or LA requiring all beneficiaries (and sometimes also nonbeneficiaries) to pay a share of the cost of providing services.

3.3 "PUBLIC GOODS" CONSIDERATIONS

Their ability to deal with the free rider problem gives LG and LA an advantage over both membership organizations and private enterprises for undertaking rural infrastructure. Equating public goods with public sector channels of provision, however, is too simple. The services of infrastructure should not be categorized as all public goods. Rather one should examine to what extent and in what ways the goods and services produced are "public," to get a better idea of what are indeed the best institutional options.

The two main characteristics of public goods are *excludability* and *jointness of use or consumption* (Ostrom and Ostrom, 1977). To the extent that goods are indivisible or users cannot be kept from using them, and to the extent that one person's use of them does not diminish or preclude another's use, they are public. But these factors are often matters of degree, and excludability and jointness are not simple characteristics. Each has physical, economic, and social aspects which establish different kinds and degrees of "publicness" observed in the examples of rural infrastructure considered here. These differences in turn have implications for local institutional development.

Excludability for a good may be impossible in physical terms if the good is indivisible, like a weather forecast, and anyone can enjoy it. Excludability is impractical if the cost and difficulty of collecting payment for a good are so great that the benefits of collection are negligible even if it is physically possible. Or there may be moral or practical reasons for making the good available to all. Exclusion from polio vaccination, for instance, may be

---

[6]Although the technology of biogas generation does not create interdependence among users (except sometimes in terms of supply of material for digestion), the adoption of this technology seems to have some characteristics of "collective adoption" discussed by West (1983). This is seen from the instructive case study of biogas development in China by Sheridan (1981:29-50).

socially unacceptable on equity or moral grounds, or externalities may make exclusion undesirable such as when spraying to control mosquitoes. So excludability is a complex consideration.

Three aspects of jointness also help make a good "public." Physically, a good may be consumed by many persons without being diminished, such as use of a road or an abundant water supply. Exclusion is difficult where, once the facility exists, there does not appear to be any cost to others from some individuals' free riding. Yet from an economic perspective, creation of the facility may require such a large aggregation of resources that it will not come into being unless many people contribute. It is possible that not everyone needs to contribute—only enough persons to surpass some threshold for the good to exist.[7] Additionally one's own benefits may depend at least in part on others enjoying them too, as with raising the literacy level of a community or reducing communicable diseases.

These variables can be summarized in a set of questions. First, regarding excludability, one should ask:

- Is exclusion *physically possible*? Is the good divisible so it can be given or withheld according to whether or not a person contributed to its creation?
- Is exclusion *economically efficient*? Is it cost-effective to collect payment from all users?
- Is exclusion *socially desirable* or even possible? Are there ethical or practical considerations which restrict the scope for exclusion?

The less excludability there is on one or more of these grounds the less basis there is for private enterprise and possibly for membership organizations to undertake investment in the particular infrastructure and the larger the role for LG or LA.

Regarding jointness of consumption or use, one can ask:

- Is there *physical jointness*? Does the good exhibit qualities of nonsubtractibility?
- Is there *economic jointness*? Are there normative considerations that make others' benefit from the good enhance one's own self-respect and sense of well-being?
- Is there *social jointness*? Are there externalities that make others' benefit from the good add to one's own benefit from it?

The more jointness that exists the more "public" is the good and the more reason there is for LA or LG to be responsible for the infrastructure providing it.

We note these characteristics to be able to point out differences among

---

[7]This is analogous on the "production" side of public goods to *indivisibility* on the "consumption" side of public goods.

the kinds of infrastructure we are considering. Roads, for example, are generally rather low in excludability while high in jointness. People could be required to pay a user fee, but monitoring use is difficult, and the net revenue when costs of collection are deducted may be small. The amount of capital (or invested labor) required to build a road is very great relative to the individual's benefit so collective investment is almost always necessary to create it.

Roads are rarely constructed by private enterprises unless a plantation or mining operation justifies this financially. Usually roads are built by governments, local or national, with local organizations occasionally undertaking road-building activities where their membership is fairly inclusive and the need for roads is great.

Bridges differ from roads in that excludability is definitely greater. Use is more easily monitored and denominated (in terms of crossings) and this makes collection easier. The capital costs of construction are usually greater than for any equivalent length of road. Except where technical requirements are very high, bridges are suitable to local government or even local organizations. Private bridges are not very common but private ferries (which serve the same function) are.[8]

Electricity, in contrast, ranks high on excludability and less high on jointness. Specific amounts of power can be provided and charged for, and only those hooked up to the distribution system have access making collection fairly easy.[9] What may keep electricity infrastructure from being privately provided is the large initial capital cost required especially if an extensive distribution network must be built.

Often the law restricts electricity generation and/or distribution to public bodies on the ground that private business should not profiteer from what is regarded as a public utility. It is regulated so that a wider service can be provided than would result from profit-maximizing investment decisions. If the most lucrative service can be skimmed off by private investors, even government agencies may find it financially unfeasible to extend service to more marginal areas.

What is important for LID considerations is that rural electrification can be undertaken more readily than other forms of infrastructure by any of the alternative channels. Businesses are well suited to provide electrical power, possibly subject to some public sector regulation. In the United States, cooperatives have been important local institutions for rural electrification

---

[8]The main difference between bridges and ferries is in the amount of capital required. The two components of transport infrastructure cost are *structures* and the *vehicles* to use them (Section 3.1). Ferries are relatively cheap in that there are no structures needed apart from docks and most of the cost is in the vehicles.

[9]To be sure, unauthorized "taps" can be made and may be difficult to control or remove. Despite their having authority and enforcement powers, public agencies often find it difficult to collect from all users because of political considerations, whereas private providers can more easily cut off free riders.

having brought power to about 90 percent of American farm families between the mid-1930s and the mid-1950s.

Domestic water supply shares the characteristic of excludability with electrical power, and charging for water is physically and economically possible. (Actually the unit-value of water, except in situations of scarcity, is such that costs of collection may cut into profit potentials.) Community norms and expectations, however, come into play modifying the relevance of the physical and fiscal features otherwise used to define public goods. It is often regarded as unethical to charge for water, though private providers in scarcity situations (often persons from outside the community) may sell water, possibly at a high price. Where this occurs, nonprivate local institutions are likely to invest in facilities to make water more widely available at lower cost.

Jointness is usually less with water than with roads though more than for electricity. These contrasts between water and electricity suggest why domestic water supply is commonly provided through LA or particularly LG. LOs or co-ops, as in the case of roads, can undertake this responsibility if LA or LG do not and if their members can agree on the importance of meeting such a need. Which institutions can appropriately undertake to provide water often depends on the technical possibilities and the economic cost of acquiring and distributing it. The lower the threshold of investment the more likely membership or private institutions will invest in this infrastructure. If the cost becomes low enough, water will be secured by household or individual investments in small-scale infrastructure.

This discussion demonstrates how the characteristics of excludability and jointness are important concepts but not neatly deterministic ones for identifying which are public goods and which are not. One cannot deduce easily which infrastructure goods and services are more appropriately provided through public sector than other institutions.

Ostrom and Ostrom (1977) have delineated four kinds of goods according to whether or not characteristics of exclusion and jointness exist.

(1) **Private goods**: exclusion feasible and use is not joint, e.g. automobiles, haircuts, books, shoes, bread, etc.
(2) **Common pool resources**: exclusion unfeasible and use is not joint, e.g. common pasture for grazing, fish in ocean, water pumped from groundwater basin (the most common situation for natural resources management analyzed in Chapter Two).
(3) **Toll goods**: exclusion feasible, and use is joint, e.g., theatres, telephone service, toll roads, electric power, etc.
(4) **Public goods**: exclusion unfeasible and use is joint, e.g., peace and security, mosquito abatement, air pollution control, etc.

To some extent all infrastructure by definition presents some jointness of consumption or use. However, excludability is more a continuum than a category, and just because excludability is technically possible does not mean it is economically efficient or socially desirable. Such considerations point to the need to look upon the whole continuum of local institutions as possible channels for rural infrastructure development with some institutional modes more commonly suitable than others for providing certain kinds of infrastructure.

3.4 PHASES OF RURAL INFRASTRUCTURE DEVELOPMENT

The different kinds of infrastructure have in common a set of activities having somewhat different local institutional requirements:

- *design* of facilities and supporting activities;
- their *construction*;
- their *operation*, and
- their *maintenance*.

These are generally conceived as constituting a fixed sequence in infrastructure development. However, in practice one may find maintenance concurrent with operation, and redesign, rehabilitation, or repair occurring whenever they are needed. For simplicity's sake, we discuss these four activities as *phases* of infrastructure development though they do not present themselves so discretely or sequentially in the real world. Our concern is with the comparative advantage that local or national institutions may have in each phase, and with which local institutions, if any, seem to have some comparative advantage.

3.4.1 DESIGN

Design is usually regarded as a highly technical process in which local people are not likely to play much of a role. This is particularly true when the technology involved is quite complex, for example, with the installation of a large hydroelectric generating facility or an advanced telecommunications network. Highly trained staff from national agencies might work with their local technical counterparts (LA) in design as well as construction activities for such cases, but not with other local institutions.

One should not underestimate the technical understanding of at least some rural residents, however, and at least consultation on designs may be appropriate if properly organized through LG or LOs. We know of three documented cases—in the Philippines, in Nepal and in Mexico—where farmers told engineers who were planning dams across rivers reaching high seasonal crests that the designs being drawn for that location would not stand up. In all three cases the engineers insisted that their calculations were correct and the designs adequate, and in all three cases the dams washed out (Korten, 1980; Shrestha, 1980; Cernea, 1984). If farmers can be correct about such technical matters as dam design, they should be able to contribute useful information about other projects as well. In Peru the location and design of spring-fed gravity water supply systems being built by CARE was facilitated by local people's knowledge of hydrological conditions contributed through their local institutions (Haratani et al., 1981). Similar experience is reported from Nepal where water supply through local management has been provided in sixty-eight hill communities with over 11,000 population (Williamson, 1983). The fact that simple technology was used so that systems were inexpensive to build and required no expenditure on fuel, made them more comprehensible and more attractive to rural residents. The kind and complexity of technology employed in rural infrastructure will affect the feasibility and usefulness of local involvement in design.

In the design process, there is a danger of overspecification when laying out the projects. Moving into rural areas with standardized designs, which may not address the perceived needs of the intended beneficiaries and thus will not enlist the local commitment and resources needed for operation and maintenance, is a recipe for failure. This was seen in a Tunisian rural water supply project where significant local participation was not included in design (or in implementation, operation, or maintenance). At the time of evaluation, three-fourths of the systems were not producing potable water as intended (Bigelow and Chiles, 1980).

On the other hand, a basic design may be successful if presented and adapted through a process of consultation that enlists active local participation in all stages as seen in the Malawi self-help water supply program. Ultimate responsibility for designs remained with the Department of Community Development but special committees (functionally specific membership organizations) operating under the aegis of traditional chiefs (indigenous LA) mobilized both managerial talent and local labor. Only when local institutions are quite advanced, with their own technical staff, can full responsibility for design be delegated to them. Such a capacity is reported for some local governments in Brazil, which have taken over design and other functions in connection with a World Bank project for construction of rural roads (Beenhakker et al., 1984).

There is increasing evidence that local involvement in design as well as construction of rural infrastructure contributes both to better design and to better subsequent performance. This is most clearly seen with domestic water supply (World Bank, 1976; USAID 1982; Williamson, 1983). With regard to rural roads, there is an expanding number of sources suggesting that design decisions and choice of technology are more appropriate when made at the lower levels.[10] There is also more incentive for communities to

---

[10]An evaluation by USAID (1982a:7) found that "where road selection was centralized, there was a tendency to specify uneconomically high design standards and to over emphasize primary roads at the expense of rural roads." Tendler (1979) concluded from her study that more appropriate design resulted from road decisions made at lower levels.

take responsibility in the construction phase if they have had significant involvement in design (Edmonds, 1980).

3.4.2 Construction

The role of local institutions in construction is affected by the technological requirements of the task. Building large-scale, complex infrastructure is not particularly suited to LG or LOs or even to LA. Farm-to-market roads are more readily undertaken by local institutions than are inter-city highways as the former have less exacting standards and can draw on techniques already known by rural people. Any errors in construction or alignment are not so serious and are more easily corrected. The same would be true of installing a diesel generator for electricity compared to building a hydroelectric dam. To be sure, the larger and more highly technical infrastructure is also less likely to be of predominant benefit to the rural community where it is located (or passes through), so this consideration also tilts the assignment of such infrastructure responsibilities toward regional or national institutions.

In some less-developed nations where major infrastructure investments remain to be made such as completing a national road network or setting up an inter-city electricity grid, local institutions may have less substantial roles. Conversely in countries where major infrastructure is already in place, building feeder roads or making extensions of the electricity grid to communities is more clearly suited to local institutions.

At the same time, it should be considered that where the budgets and personnel of national institutions are preoccupied with large-scale investments, the only way localities and communities will get the smaller scale infrastructure they need for transportation, water, power, communication, etc. will be through self-help investments. Some modicum of technical assistance to local institutions for establishing such infrastructure should be very cost-effective if the demand from below for new services is great and local resources can accordingly be mobilized.

When undertaking construction, local institutions and particularly LOs and co-ops can more readily take responsibility to the extent the work can be done on an incremental basis rather than having to be done all at once. If there is a tight construction schedule that cannot adjust to the peaks and troughs of labor demand in the agricultural sector, local institutions will be hard-pressed to carry out their obligations.

The village subsidy (*subsidi desa*) program in Indonesia was organized to plan and construct local infrastructure in a decentralized manner through local governments. Unfortunately the disbursement of central funds was often delayed. Money that could only be used productively during the slack agricultural season frequently did not reach the villages in time to be used, which greatly hampered the pace and extent of construction (Annex Three).

A more productive approach to working with local institutions has been documented in Nepal with Chinese-aided highway construction. Though this was a major national infrastructure project, much of the work was broken into small tasks which local organizations, even informal traditional groups, could undertake on a contractual basis. The minimum size of a contract was 25,000 rupees, compared with the 250,000 rupees minimum set for most other donor-assisted highway projects.[11] What could have been viewed by villagers as an "alien" public works project became a "local" project. Moreover, capability for performing maintenance and repairs was created, which the government could utilize. That this highway was completed within budget and ahead of schedule and that it is one of the best in technical terms (CEDA, 1973) indicates that this method of disaggregating and delegating construction to local groups need not be slower or substandard.

To the extent that construction relies on local materials and familiar technologies, the role of local government, private enterprises, and other local institutions can be greater. The staff of local administration can more easily have access to government resources and personnel though local contractors can also tap expertise and technology from outside the locality.

A study of rural drinking water projects by Imboden (1977) supports the involvement of local institutions. He found that projects using local materials and skills rather than imported ones have a greater chance of success measured in number of persons served, percent of schemes actually operating, frequency of breakdowns, and nature and use of the facilities. Experience in Peru supports this with the observation that: "Imported materials tend to become the limiting element in development projects and produce rigidities in project design and implementation" (Haratani et al., 1981).

One of the reasons for the success of the remarkable bridge building in Baglung district of Nepal was the use of local materials and techniques. Yet it should be noted that the construction technology was made feasible by the government's contribution of steel cables, which were much superior to any local materials available. This case indicates the kind of local capacity for infrastructure construction that may be enlisted through organizations like the Baglung bridge committees.[12] Similar abilities to construct drinking

---

[11]The methodology of construction differed in many ways from the standard approach. Rather than hire individuals to work for daily wages as members of massive labor gangs, payment was made to community groups on a piece-rate basis according to a contract negotiated in advance. Payment was made in public to minimize extortion of "commissions" from workers. There was one supervisor for every two kilometers rather than one for every seven or eight as on other projects so technical advice was easily available. Supervisors spent most of their time walking on foot rather than riding in vehicles so as to be more accessible.

[12]These committees are "organizations" rather than "institutions" because they have not continued in existence. Although there were plans eventually to construct twice as many bridges, once the sixty-two priority bridges were finished, the push behind this program dissi-

water systems have been demonstrated by largely illiterate communities in Nepal and in Malawi.

3.4.3 Operation

The tasks of operation and maintenance are not the same, though they are usually grouped together in language and practice as "O&M." We will focus on operation in this section though some references to maintenance will be made as well. The latter will receive separate consideration in Section 3.4.4. O&M tasks are often conceded by central government agencies to be "suited" to local institutions. These are often made local responsibilities even when such institutions do not have the needed financial base or qualified personnel.

Such delegation is done partly in recognition of the great limitations upon central agencies in staffing and supervising activities in a large number of dispersed locations. Keeping roads and bridges in repair, combating impurities in village water supply systems, and keeping diesel generators in working condition and operating are commonly recognized as difficult tasks for any institution, national or local, working in rural areas.

The central government attitude is also motivated by a desire to get rural communities to take responsibility for recurrent costs, which are increasingly a burden on national budgets, as discussed in Chapter Eight. There is much less reluctance at the center to have operation (and maintenance) handled by "locals" than to share design and construction tasks with them.

It must be said that one of the literature's most frequent conclusions is that the extent of willingness and ability of local institutions to discharge O&M responsibilities depends in large part on their having been involved in design and construction activities (e.g., World Bank, 1975). So simply handing over O&M responsibility to local institutions as in a "turnkey project" is not very promising. It should be further said that a study of experience with community-level water systems found that the supply was reliable in every case where users covered all O&M from their own resources (USAID, 1982).

For operation as well as maintenance, local government may have some advantages over membership organizations and co-ops because of the nature of the task. Such organizations are often better at episodic activity in response to definitely felt needs than at routine efforts day-in, day-out. A more "professionalized" capacity is commonly needed for tasks like O&M. On the other hand if the activity is valued enough by members, they can

---

pated. We do not know whether the bridges have continued to be adequately maintained by local effort. This would be a good test of the proposition that local participation in planning and construction leads to better maintenance. The village panchayats (LG), which acted as sponsors of the committees and which qualify more as "institutions," should be able to carry out maintenance as needed.

arrange to carry it out even by hiring persons to act on their behalf if necessary. This is common in traditional irrigation systems as noted above and can be done under contemporary leadership as need arises.[13]

Where operation (or maintenance) is a solitary activity rather than a collective one, free riding may be more common. Absence or an unsatisfactory level of effort within work groups is fairly visible and easy to control when the whole community is involved. Various requirements or penalties can be imposed to discourage free riding.[14] Many operation (and maintenance) activities, however, are of a different sort. It is difficult, for example, to get members of a co-op to check regularly to see that the drains under a road are clear so that water does not back up and flow over the road and damage it. If this is everybody's responsibility it is likely to be nobody's responsibility. As a rule, one can say that membership organizations are less likely than LA or LG to handle O&M activities effectively, even if national governments might welcome such organizations' assumption of responsibility.

The critical variable appears to be how much the community understands and values the benefits provided by the infrastructure in question. This is why local participation in design and construction is important, first in ensuring that the infrastructure is needed and supported, and second in giving people a sense of ownership and responsibility for the facility (Coward, 1983). In Nepal one can find quite sophisticated membership organizations operating and maintaining irrigation systems in the mountains (Martin and Yoder, 1983). In the Philippines the zanjeras have carried out extensive O&M responsibilities in addition to design and construction for many years. (Siy, 1982). In Honduras we found a case where agricultural cooperatives have done a good job of maintaining access roads in their areas (Hamilton et al., 1981).

In the Honduras example members depend on the roads for sale of the crops they produce. Thus, members can see evident payoffs from good

---

[13]Wade (1982) describes how two Indian villages not getting enough water for their crops from the main irrigation system formed an organization to operate and maintain their portion of the command area. The organization hired several dozen water guards (at twice the minimum agricultural wage) to distribute all available water fairly and to patrol upstream channels to be sure members would get as much water as they were legally entitled to. All members were charged a set fee (100 rupees) per acre, and there was a surcharge to form a contingency fund for bribing officials if water supply was threatened. Significantly one of these villages had long been riven by extreme factionalism, but it was agreed that disputes within either village would be referred to the headman of the other village for arbitration. Such institutional innovation was prompted by the need for water. Similar hiring of special personnel is documented elsewhere in India by Meinzen-Dick (1984; see Annex Eight).

[14]The zanjeras in the Philippines have strict and regular attendance checks during work sessions with specified fines set for absences or delinquencies (Siy, 1982:49-52). For cleaning and repairing channels in a community irrigation system in northern Thailand, a careful system of supervision and control is used. Identification cards are given out to all group members at the beginning of the day and collected at the end of the day to check on who has completed his share of the work (Abha, 1979).

operation and maintenance. Also there are no good alternatives to local management of infrastructure. National institutions are not effective at this local level, so people know that if they do not handle O&M nobody else will. The central government could take over these responsibilities and with enough expenditure might discharge them better. But when resources are limited one seeks to optimize not maximize performance. The principle of comparative advantage proposes that all parties concentrate on doing what they can do best or avoid what they do worst in order to contribute to the greatest total benefit. Central government operation of infrastructure facilities at the local level seldom uses scarce financial and management resources to best advantage.

3.4.4 Maintenance

A number of the considerations affecting local institutions' role in maintenance are similar to those for construction. However, some factors bearing on maintenance deserve separate discussion. Maintenance ranges from continuous (routine) activities to periodic (ad hoc or planned) ones. The former are often undertaken as "preventive maintenance," which is important but commonly neglected.[15] The latter can involve repair, rehabilitation or, if the deterioration is substantial, reconstruction, which may amount to deferred maintenance.

Some kinds of infrastructure such as water supply, electricity, and bridges need fairly continuous attention because any failure disrupts the working of the system and its provision of a crucial good or service. Other kinds like roads and irrigation systems are more subject to gradual deterioration and thus more amenable to periodic maintenance. Those infrastructures needing routine servicing must have institutional support whether national or local.

Three conditions appear to govern how well institutions of any kind will carry out maintenance responsibilities, ranging from preventive maintenance to repair:

(a) how **perceptible** is the deterioration of function and the need for restoring or preserving adequate service;
(b) how **clearly fixed** is responsibility for dealing with deterioration; and
(c) how **empowered** are those affected by the deterioration.

We can contrast roads and rural electricity supply in these regards with bridges and water supply appearing to occupy an intermediate position:

---

[15]Preventive maintenance is a problem for all kinds of institutions. A USAID study (1982) suggests that the lack of preventive maintenance is the major cause of failure of water supply systems in LDCs.

(a) Road deterioration is usually quite incremental, compared to interruption or reduction of electricity supply. While vehicles can usually operate on a deteriorated road, electrical appliances may be damaged by reductions or fluctuations in the current and will stop entirely when the supply is cut off.

(b) Responsibility for a road may rest with a highway or public works department, but maintenance delays can be blamed on different people at different levels. When an electricity generator fails, responsibility is more easily pinned on one person—the supervising engineer or technician—as the problem usually comes down to a single piece of equipment.

(c) Further, it is likely that the persons served by electricity are on the average more influential than those using a road (unless it is a thoroughfare used frequently by a cabinet minister or other high official). If businessmen find their equipment stopped or damaged by a power failure, they are usually in a better position than are road users to demand quick repair and to penalize the person who let this happen.

If the need for maintenance is easily measured or specified, if responsibility can be fixed on one person or a few persons, and if those inconvenienced or injured by the lack of maintenance are influential, it is more likely that local institutions can be charged with maintenance responsibilities.

This is not to say that national institutions handle such tasks well when it is hard to show precise maintenance needs, when responsibility is diffused, or when the persons affected are politically weak. Bureaucratic norms and structures are not known for their ability to overcome ambiguity and inertia. But local institutions are more likely to default on maintenance responsibilities when they are faced with such situations. One compensating consideration is that when infrastructure deteriorates, those most directly affected by this are more likely to report on it and better able to make demands for maintenance or repair if the institution responsible for improvement is accessible, as is more true of local than of national institutions. The contribution of decentralized administration to improving maintenance of rural roads has been documented in Thailand when public works LA was strengthened there (USAID, 1980a).

It would be convenient if we could conclude from the literature that local institutions are ideally suited to carry out all maintenance activities. Unfortunately the record on maintenance is largely unsatisfactory for all institutions, national as well as local. A key factor governing how well local institutions can discharge maintenance responsibilities is the intensity of demand for the benefits of the particular infrastructure. The examples cited of local O&M of irrigation systems indicate that if infrastructure services are important to local users, they can usually find ways to make one or more local institutions manage maintenance functions effectively.

One key to good maintenance performance is for local institutions to select certain persons to receive special training and compensation for carrying out maintenance activities. Such responsibilities have been effectively taken on by local water supply committees in Malawi and Nepal where communities select and pay para-technicians for maintaining their systems (Liebenow, 1981; Williamson, 1983).

3.5 CHARACTERISTICS OF THE USERS

Whether local institutions have a comparative advantage in infrastructure development, and which kinds of institutions if any may be most appropriate, will depend not only on the phase of infrastructure development and management but on the people concerned, their incentives, and their characteristics. The literature is not very specific or systematic on these questions but some suggestions can be made.

3.5.1 Benefits

Unless it is clear that rural residents derive recognizable benefit from the infrastructure in question, assigning local institutions a role in its creation and maintenance is not particularly advisable. Comparing a national trunk highway with farm-to-market roads, for example, it is clear that quite apart from any differences in the technical expertise and the amount of investment involved, local institutions should be more willing as well as able to assume responsibilities for the latter category of roads.

Which local institutions might best be responsible also depends on the benefits people can derive from the infrastructure. If its operation can be made profitable, private businesses are possible channels for infrastructure development. However, where benefits of infrastructure are indivisible or nonexcludable, this works against using private, for-profit institutional mechanisms. Local service organizations are often feasible, though they tend to be involved more in community facilities like market stalls, libraries, or recreation grounds than with the kinds of infrastructure considered here.

Membership organizations and co-ops do not effectively manage infrastructure unless its operation is crucial to their performance, e.g., feeder roads for marketing agricultural produce or piped water supply to free up members' labor for more productive activities. If community members do not all have a perceived stake (or an equal stake) in the infrastructure, local responsibility is more likely to be effective if given to LG or LA, which can draw on governmental authority to mobilize resources or regulate behavior. Even where such authority exists formally, it will not be effective unless there is sufficient general appreciation of the infrastructure on the part of the public to sustain ongoing local responsibility. If such appreciation is lacking, responsibility for the infrastructure is better vested at higher levels.

This factor of "benefit" is well illustrated with regard to domestic water supply. While water is needed by the whole community, women in particular are most engaged in drawing and carrying water when no convenient source is available.[16] The intensity of their involvement in water activities means that water development through local institutions is feasible so long as women have an active role in those institutions (local government, membership organizations or whatever). An experiment in Angola found a decrease in breakdowns and in repair time for village water supply systems when women were involved in their maintenance and repair (FAO, 1983). Similarly an AID study in Peru concluded that it was particularly important to garner the support and cooperation of women in local institutions when they are the most direct beneficiaries of water projects (Haratani, et al., 1981). Who is participating in local institutions will thus affect how well these institutions can carry out infrastructure tasks.

3.5.2 Community Need

It could be argued that local responsibilities for investment and management of infrastructure are likely to be performed better where the communities are more advanced in terms of economic development and education. While having a larger pool of economic resources and trained personnel to draw from is an advantage, it also appears there are offsetting factors in less advantaged communities to the extent that infrastructure facilities are more needed there.

An analysis of water supply experience cross-nationally concluded that villages chosen according to criteria of greatest need (a "worst-first" strategy) have no less chance of success than ones chosen on the basis of their evident material and personnel capacities to install and maintain facilities (Imboden, 1977). An evaluation of an AID-supported water supply project in Tunisia found that community participation was "greatest in the driest area, Kairouan, where the need for water is most critical" (Bigelow and Chiles, 1980:9). The government had installed pumps without providing resources for fuel to operate them so users themselves set up local organizations to collect fees to cover costs of fuel supply and maintenance. This, however, does not mean that local organizations will always emerge in such cases or that

---

[16]In Africa women contribute 90 percent of the hours devoted to procuring water according to one estimate (FAO, 1983).

this is a good way for outside agencies to operate, ignoring operation requirements.

A comparative study of patterns of investment in fifty-four villages in Thailand found a negative correlation between level of economic development and the extent of community action to create community facilities (AIR, 1973). This is not surprising as the more advanced communities already had most of the basic infrastructure needed, and resources were accordingly invested more often in creating private rather than public goods. The relevant implication for our analysis is that the less advanced Thai communities were able and willing to mobilize resources for infrastructure and other common investments. That they have capacity to manage resources for such investments is seen in the study by Calavan (1984).

One might argue that local institutional development for rural infrastructure would be more likely to succeed where the need for common facilities was greatest. But this would be restating the converse of Say's law that "supply creates its own demand." Demand doesn't necessarily create its own supply. Rather one can note that there does not seem to be a comparative advantage for infrastructure LID where economic and educational conditions are more advanced. The factor of need can countervail the greater sufficiency of resources.[17] The factor of literacy as it relates to LID is examined in Section 5.6.1.

3.5.3 Homogeneity

One of the concerns most often raised in opposition to devolving responsibility for rural development to local institutions is that the burdens and benefits will not be fairly shared. Unless there is relative homogeneity within a community, local elites can monopolize benefits for themselves and impose costs on others. Since socio-economic heterogeneity is the rule rather than the exception, this would suggest not developing rural infrastructure through local institutions, at least not if one is concerned with equitable outcomes.

This problem is frequently pointed out in the literature. We would cite just two examples. A study of an AID-supported water project in Ethiopia found that not only did the rural poor contribute most of the labor to dig the trenches and lay the pipe but once it was finished they had to pay for the water, which they had previously gotten elsewhere free. The new water supply was cleaner and more convenient but the out-of-pocket costs were a real burden on the poor (Uphoff, Cohen, and Goldsmith, 1979:274). In his

---

[17]In our analysis of performance by 150 local organizations worldwide, we found that LO performance was not necessarily higher where levels of per capita income or literacy were higher (Esman and Uphoff, 1984). Our review of literature for this LID analysis did not produce evidence contradicting that finding.

study of rural works in Bangladesh, Garzon says that the local labor requirement there had the regressive effect of taxing the poor for projects that
might not benefit them. "Under the conditions of inequality, 'voluntary'
labor is in fact usually forced, and produces only alienation and even subversion" (1981:18-19).[18]

There are measures that can be taken to reduce the biasing effects of
stratification on infrastructure provided through local institutions. Rural
electrification projects in Ecuador, which emphasized forward linkages to
agricultural processing and nonagricultural enterprises, generated employment for the poorer sections of the communities whereas parallel projects in
the Philippines that promoted household connections (consumption rather
than productive uses) did not have this effect (Tendler, 1979a). Electrification projects in Bolivia some years later included a credit component, which
made it possible for larger numbers of poorer households to hook up to the
rural systems there. Such a provision kept the benefits of the infrastructure
from being monopolized by richer households. One way in which local
elites commonly gain at the expense of non-elites is by cutting back on the
quantity of benefits produced in order to increase their quality. If project
design can curtail such revisions, the effects of stratification can be reduced
(Leonard, 1982).[19]

To the extent that quantity is more important than quality, relevant
infrastructure is more feasible for local institutional agents to manage. This
is not only because elite diversion of benefits may be less but because less
exacting standards may be applied. Where socio-economic heterogeneity is
a major problem, it appears that service organizations dedicated to serving
the poor will be more effective than local government or cooperatives.

"Alternative organizations," homogeneous membership organizations

---

[18]The bias in LG expenditure patterns when rural elites are in control can be seen from a
study in Nepal, where all household heads in a panchayat (locality) were interviewed. Actual
LG expenditures clearly reflected landlord rather than tenant preferences (Sainju et al.,
1973:72, 86).

	Tenant Priorities	Landlord Priorities	Local Govt. Expenditure
Irrigation	58%	33%	8%
Roads & transportation	31	41	50
Education	6	18	28
Health	3	7	10
Administration	–	–	10

[19]Current thinking about rural water supply concludes that public health as well as other
benefits are greater simply by insuring a larger quantity of water to households without great
regard for quality. Even if high water quality is achieved at the source, the chances of contami-
nation in carrying and storage containers are so great that purity cannot be maintained in most
rural households. On the other hand, simply having a convenient and large volume of water
available increases the washing of hands, clothes, food, and utensils, which makes a direct
contribution to health. Usually the more effort put into achieving water quality the less is the
quantity that reaches households.

that draw on poorer sections of the community (Section 7.3.3), could in principle provide infrastructure services for members but in practice we seldom find them doing so. Capital costs for most infrastructure are substantial and benefits tend to be indivisible or nonexcludable as we know. So such "private" provision of infrastructure makes little sense unless it is very small-scale, e.g., a tubewell for drinking water but not a road or bridge or electrical distribution system. Although there is the risk that local government will be dominated by elite groups in heterogeneous communities, it often remains the most promising channel for rural infrastructure development. Where heterogeneity makes distortion of benefits easier, LID efforts should proceed with knowledge of this danger and seek to promote LG accountability to all sections of the community.[20]

3.6 IMPLEMENTATION PROCESS

While some major rural infrastructure such as highways and hydroelectricity generation and distribution can be developed directly by national institutions, creating and maintaining a thorough and adequate network of roads, bridges, water and electricity supply, communication, and community facilities in rural areas requires a similar network of local institutions. Which institutions are most appropriate for which kinds of infrastructure will vary according to the kind of considerations discussed already. Our main conclusion is that a mix of public, private, and voluntary institutions is to be sought rather than to assign responsibility to just one channel for each activity.

Thus, establishing rural infrastructure should go hand in hand with creating or strengthening local institutions to build and manage the infrastructure. Local knowledge and resources are important for the design and construction phases just as local inputs and commitment are needed for operation and maintenance. The alternative of centrally operated and maintained infrastructure can apply at most to core infrastructure like the examples given above—trunk highways and hydroelectricity. Given the growing "fiscal crisis" in developing countries, preserving, let alone extending, infrastructure networks will be possible only if localities, communities, and groups accept increased responsibility.

It is not our task to formulate strategies of infrastructure development for LDCs but rather to consider LID strategies that could support such development. How such development is undertaken will condition the chances of success in getting sustained benefits from infrastructure in rural areas.

---

[20]Some methods for controlling financial abuses or leadership domination have been discussed in Esman and Uphoff (1984: Ch. 7).

3.6.1 Decentralization

Decentralization of responsibility is a first condition of LID as local institutions cannot be expected to take root and thrive unless they have both tasks to perform and matching powers to carry out those tasks. This subject is discussed in more detail in Section 7.3.3 but we note it here because it is so necessary for rural infrastructure development.

Central government policy is important in this regard. In the case of rural electrification for example, the Philippine government has limited its own role to power generation leaving institutional "space" for local governments, cooperatives, and private enterprises to engage in electricity distribution. Some Latin American countries, on the other hand, have passed laws restricting distribution to central government agencies. Just recently the Indian government being faced with severe power shortages in rural areas has lifted its ban on the private sale of electricity. (Companies could generate electricity for themselves if they did not want to depend on the state power grid but they could not sell any surplus, which discouraged private investment in generating capacity.) This shift in policy should permit the development of various local institutions, particularly private ones, to spread the benefits of electrification.

There is a view in many LDCs that only the state administration can provide public utilities efficiently and fairly but this is not supported by the evidence. One of the few systematic evaluations of the consequences of devolving responsibility for rural electrification to local bodies in the Indian state of Rajasthan has been done by Hadden (1974). When authority for deciding which villages would be hooked up to the state electricity distribution grid was devolved from the State Electricity Board to panchayats, the board's own standards of productivity and efficiency were better met, and illegitimate influence by politicians was reduced (Annex Three).

Decentralization is certainly open to abuses and inefficiencies, but central institutions are at least as vulnerable, often on a grander scale. Corrupt practices can be more easily covered up from superiors (who seldom get to the field) than from persons "on the ground" who live with the consequences of malfeasance or mistakes. Where local institutions are empowered to take action against misconduct, the chances of proper performance are increased. If local institutions are made responsible for decisions and operations, however, they can benefit from having some oversight from higher levels, which can serve to reduce local temptations for misusing positions of trust. Hence, decentralization does not imply complete abandonment of responsibility to local institutions.

The objection is sometimes raised that a decentralized approach will affect the speed of implementation, as less technically competent persons are involved and more persons' concurrence must be gained. In fact, the pace of implementation through central institutions is usually quite slow for rural infrastructure, given personnel and decision-making bottlenecks. The worst situation is to have nominal decentralization with approval of design, expenditure, staff assignments, etc. still retained at the center.

If a reasonable degree of effective decentralization is provided, the pace of work can be brisk. The Basic Village Services project in Egypt supported by USAID was designed to provide funds to local councils for improving water supply, roads, sewerage, etc. It was feared that this would be a slow-moving project because of the country's 869 local governments, 480 would be involved. In fact, the rate of work and fund disbursement have been so satisfactory that this is one of the few projects in Egypt to exceed its implementation schedule, disbursing over $200 million in three years for rural infrastructure (Annex Three).

This Egyptian project has been implemented, it should be stressed, in many disaggregated increments. One requirement for decentralized planning and management of rural infrastructure is that the size of tasks be kept manageable at the local level. This recommendation, mentioned in Section 3.4.2, is a product of road-building experience in Nepal. This does not mean that the amount of investment is small. A large number of small undertakings can match in scale a few large ones and will have better distributional effects.

The inclination of donors to "move money" in large chunks can be quite disruptive of local institutional development as seen in the case of the Provincial Development Administration Project in the Philippines. This USAID-supported project developed with some difficulty a decentralized capacity for planning, constructing, and maintaining rural roads, but this capability was subsequently undermined by another donor's project which overtaxed the capacity of the local institutions. It assigned all project funds to just four provinces instead of ten as proposed from the Philippine side. The result was that the scale of design and construction work was too great to be handled subnationally and much responsibility was resumed centrally.

3.6.2 Learning Process

The scale of program that can be supported through local institutions needs to be determined experimentally. This is one of the principles of a "learning process" approach to development, treated in Section 7.1.2. One of the most instructive current efforts to develop community infrastructure is found in Pakistan with the Orangi Pilot Project (for the peri-urban poor if not exactly the rural poor). This project, directed by Akhter Hameed Khan who pioneered the participatory rural development work at Comilla, applies a "learning process" approach quite explicitly. Through experimentation, which included some false starts and failures, the project has been able to develop technical and organizational methodologies that permit construction of sanitation facilities at 25 percent of the government's cost. Also important, the people benefited are willing and able to cover all capital and maintenance costs themselves (Annex Three).

National programs that evolve with appropriate experimentation such as the Malawi self-help water scheme can indeed reach large numbers of people at low cost once appropriate technical and organizational strategies have been devised. The Malawi scheme has, in ten years' time, brought permanent piped water to over 500,000 persons in rural areas at a cost of about $4 per person. The subsidi desa program in Indonesia, mentioned in Section 3.4.2, has also had a significant impact on rural infrastructure though it has probably not been as efficient in the use of resources. (Both experiences are reviewed in Annex Three.)

When considering local institutional development for rural infrastructure, it should be kept in mind that the allocation of responsibilities may shift over time. In the case of rural electrification, for instance, cooperatives may often be appropriate in the first stages where autogeneration from diesel generators is involved. However, once the distribution networks are linked to a regional grid, the co-ops may be much less viable. That a particular institution's functions might diminish is not in itself undesirable, as a local agency of government could be more effective and efficient in managing this form of infrastructure once the system develops beyond scattered local generation points.

Similarly local governments that undertake road construction may at some point reasonably hand over maintenance responsibilities to the local division of the public works ministry (LA) if the latter has the equipment and staff to do the work more reliably and efficiently. Conversely roads built by a public works ministry might be turned over to local governments for maintenance if the latter have been helped to develop appropriate capacities. Such responsibilities should not be shifted by decisions at higher levels without consulting the local institutions concerned. This can cause confusion and lead to poor performance, as happened with rural water supply in Kenya (Tiffen, 1983). To the extent possible, changes should proceed experimentally in increments and in manageable geographic areas to build experience, which informs and directs subsequent policy.

The essential point is that the infrastructure not be conceived and created independently of the institutions, national or local, that will be responsible for its different stages—particularly the continuing ones of O&M. Previously concerns with infrastructure focused mostly on its inadequacy in terms of quantity. As the amount has gradually increased, attention needs to shift to quality, especially when the deterioration of much infrastructure for lack of central capacity and motivation becomes more evident.

In introducing the subject of local institutional development in Section 1.1, we cited water supply as an area where experts had documented how critical local institutions are for utilization and maintenance, yet those institutions were considered by a major donor only in passing. With the kind of attention now being focused on the subject, local institutional development for rural infrastructure should receive greater priority in the planning and investment of national governments and donor agencies.

CHAPTER FOUR

Local Institutional Development for Primary Health Care

4.1 ACTIVITIES IN HUMAN RESOURCE DEVELOPMENT

Among the activity areas for rural development, human resource development (HRD) is crucial for providing the energy and talent needed to transform economic and social conditions for the benefit of those who have been bypassed. Human resource development is usually pursued in four program areas of activity: health, education, nutrition, and family planning. Helping human populations become more productive and fulfilled entails more than sectoral programs in these four areas. Influences such as culture, motivation, security, and even what Hirschman (1984) calls "social energy" come into play. Because such diffuse factors are difficult to deal with in government or donor-assisted projects, however, HRD efforts usually appear within the four sectors of health, education, nutrition, and population.

The four areas are themselves complex, and we cannot do justice here to the respective local institutional requirements of each. We will address local institutional development for *primary health care* because it is such a basic requirement for human resource development and because it presents many of the institutional issues that arise in other areas of HRD especially as health programs move beyond curative services into preventive programs.

The main elements of primary health care as defined by the American Public Health Association include efforts to:

- motivate community members to take care of their own health needs and to encourage them to help identify and solve their problems;
- build or strengthen community institutions to carry out rural programs, using local resources to reduce operating costs;
- train new cadres of paraprofessionals and community health workers;
- integrate the delivery of health services; and
- strengthen the institutional capacity of governments to support rural programs (APHA, 1982:14).

In recent years primary health care (PHC) has received significant attention from both national and international agencies. Yet despite the great need and opportunity to improve rural health conditions, political and administrative factors continue to pose real obstacles to effective implementation of PHC (Bossert and Parker, 1982). First, there is often fierce competition over the scarce financial resources allocated for health care, which often comprise only 3 to 5 percent of the total national budget. Resistance to PHC by bureaucracies or professional associations is not easily overcome. Further, broad-based participatory PHC efforts may be seen by central governments as potentially threatening, and this perception may in practice overshadow public pronouncements about the desirability of establishing such a program.

These difficulties make all the more relevant the central question for local institutional development strategy: What kinds and combinations of local institutions are most likely to be effective for PHC and how can appropriate capacities be supported from outside the community? We are assuming some level of government interest and we recognize that strong national government support can contribute much to PHC. Yet there are cases where programs have operated with strong local support and central government acquiescence. Some PHC programs have avoided opposition from health professionals by initially developing local institutions to address health needs without the use of paraprofessionals. A review of local institutional options can offer insights into how political and administrative constraints could be approached in various settings.

Although the 1978 conference of the World Health Organization at Alma Ata strongly endorsed a primary health care strategy and described the need for local institutions for PHC (WHO, 1978), it did not indicate how external agencies and government ministries might best attempt to introduce the requisite changes and adaptations in institutions at "local" levels as defined in Section 1.6. Even the recent health sector strategy statement of USAID, which is built around primary health care, gives little attention to the local institutions needed to make effective the national policies and institutions as well as the health technology and research that the statement addresses in specific forms (USAID, 1983a).

PHC strategies assume a high level of community involvement in planning and managing the curative and preventive aspects of such programs (World Bank, 1981). In the PHC programs undertaken to date, one can see various exploratory steps taken by national ministries of health, nutrition, rural development, social affairs and others beginning to work with local institutions. If these efforts are to evolve into more than a series of scattered pilot projects, however, central authorities will need to transform national health systems that operate now as centrally concentrated and directed hierarchies into more dispersed, responsive organizations with responsibilities shared among many persons, including patients, in a variety of roles (WHO,

1981). Such a transformation requires a major elaboration and strengthening of local institutions.

PHC presents a special LID challenge for another reason. Health care, especially in rural areas, comes from various sources including often existing indigenous health care providers.[1] More than in other areas of rural development activity, these existing roles and institutions can be viewed as both an opportunity and an added complication in efforts to improve rural health conditions. In any event, attention must be given to the issues associated with developing new institutions versus strengthening or modifying those presently in operation. This subject, addressed generally in Section 7.3.1, warrants specific discussion with regard to PHC in Section 4.3 below.

Rural health generally involves a combination of traditional and modern roles as part of national and local systems, with a mixture of public and private institutional support. While primary health care operates mostly at the community level, its effectiveness depends on linkages to and support from a more complicated system that operates at several levels and can handle referrals, provide supervision, carry out research and evaluation, etc. PHC undertakes to provide a wide range of simple and cost-effective health services, concerned not only with illness but with disease prevention and improvement of the public's general well-being.[2] Such a mandate is obviously broad and touches upon aspects of rural development treated in other chapters as well as on other sectors of HRD.

4.2 LOCAL INSTITUTIONAL OPTIONS

When donor agencies, national governments, private voluntary organizations or rural communities (or some combination of them) decide to promote or strengthen a primary health care system, one of the main issues is to choose among local institutional options. The alternatives are those identified in Section 1.3, with some specification.

- *Local administration* (LA) is the local offices and staff of the Ministry of Health.
- *Local government* (LG), *membership organizations* (MOs), and *cooperatives*, have less defined roles in health than in other sections but they offer important institutional options.
- *Service organizations* (SOs), charitable, religious, or fraternal

---

[1]We use the terms "indigenous" and "traditional" interchangeably. For a discussion that suggests a distinction, see Pillsbury (1979).

[2]USAID's health sector strategy statement says: "Primary health care emphasizes increased access to basic and affordable health-related services, community participation, reliance on paraprofessional workers, adequate referral and support facilities and systems, and intersectoral coordination, as opposed to hospital services dependent on high technology and specialized manpower and available to only a small proportion of the population." (USAID, 1983a:1)

organizations often operate clinics and hospitals on a not-for-profit basis.

- *Private providers*, doctors, midwives, pharmacists, and others who operate as individuals on a fee-for-service basis may include Western or indigenous health practitioners (the latter are discussed in the next section).

The fact that a Ministry of Health is promoting primary health care does not necessarily mean that government agencies (LA) must be the lead actors in its PHC scheme. It may work with or work through any of the kinds of local institutions listed here. Similarly a private voluntary organization (PVO) undertaking PHC could seek the active involvement of local government rather than work only with local charitable organizations. Even if LG has in the past had only perfunctory responsibility for health care services, it might be able to make a significant contribution to fostering primary health care in the community.

This delineation of local institutional options should not be seen as presenting the institutions as "alternatives" to one another. In most PHC situations, it will be advisable to work through some combination of local institutions that constitute a network of channels to undertake planning, mobilize resources, communicate needs, etc. The contrasts among options are presented here to show comparative advantages and disadvantages for each. However, under appropriate circumstances all have positive contributions to make.

4.2.1 Local Administration

Government agencies almost always have some role in primary health care programs. Their mandate is to give free or subsidized care as part of the government's commitment to assist the public. Of particular relevance, government staff can be posted in areas where private providers would not find practicing sufficiently profitable or personally attractive (though the levels of qualification and motivation for government staff found under these conditions may be less than desired).

Most government systems can be characterized in terms of service attenuation the farther one goes from the capital city where the most modern facilities are available in national-level hospitals. At regional or provincial levels, there are smaller hospitals with less specialization and equipment and below that clinics serving market towns and possibly villages. The staff at all levels are employees of, and accountable to, the Ministry of Health (MOH).

Rural clinics are in general charged with serving as the front line for curative care, referring difficult cases to higher levels of specialization. They also may be involved in preventive and educational programs aimed at improving the health status of the community, such as through infant food supplementation or health classes. Even with the best of efforts, however, such facilities are seldom adequate in serving the rural populations, if only because few developing countries have enough resources to provide strong support to clinics and staff in a sufficiently large number of locations (Bryant, 1969).

Primary health care strategies attempt to compensate for the lack of more intensive rural health care by expanding outreach efforts to include those who need them most. PHC emphasizes implementing community-based measures with widespread benefits involving the broader participation of rural people. Paraprofessionals, commonly called village health workers (VHWs), most frequently recruited from the community in which they reside to augment government services, can help to spread information and give access to the under-served (Esman et al., 1980).

However, government agencies involved in primary health care need to do more than add a greater number of minimally trained staff members to serve as "low rungs on the ladder." The role of government agencies in PHC changes from being a basic service *provider* to being an *enabler* of communities. This means that local administration needs to be reconceived and reoriented to work as part of a *support system* for village-based health care.[3]

4.2.2 Local Government

Previously local governments have not had a large, formal role in health care services. In some cases they have assisted in the provision of clinic or office space through donation of land or construction of facilities. But the view has been that they lack the expertise and staff to handle such technical tasks as health involves. A largely unexplored role for LG in primary health care is in assisting with organizational tasks that make technical services more effective and efficient.

A good example of such a role is seen in the Pikine project in Senegal where once health committees had been established in neighborhoods by project staff, a general assembly of representatives from all the committees was formed with its own elected Executive Board operating under the aegis of the local government. Similarly in Burma the Village People's Councils, which constitute the local government, are responsible for selecting and overseeing the work of volunteer community health workers. They also mobilize funds for the resupply of essential drugs and have substantial authority over how funds are allocated. The majority of volunteers in this nationwide program continue to perform their tasks several years after their initial training. (Both cases are described in Annex Four.)

Local governments are also frequently in a position to support primary health care by undertaking sanitation measures such as improving and

---

[3]Reorientation for a bureaucracy is considered in Section 7.5.4.

inspecting markets and constructing latrines. Such a role should be integrated into practically any primary health care program.

4.2.3 Membership Organizations

There have been many attempts in PHC programs to form village health committees to work in conjunction with government agencies. Too often these committees have been conceived and implemented as part of a prescribed "blueprint" which placed more emphasis on simply having a VHC than on matching its functioning to perceived needs of the community and supporting village health workers. It is common to find that where VHCs were formed, they selected persons for VHW training, helped build local health facilities, and then atrophied. This is reported from Cameroon and the Sine Saloum project in Senegal, though in the latter case once a less bureaucratic approach was taken, VHCs revived (Annex Four).

The American Public Health Association found that in fifty-two PHC projects assisted by USAID, only a few had VHCs that functioned on a continuing basis (APHA,1982). However, in a number of cases VHCs have successfully supported health workers. The Pikine project in Senegal, for instance, achieved active local participation buttressed by horizontal and vertical linkages among VHC groups through their larger Association for Health Promotion. In some regions of Panama, VHCs have continued to be effective even after national political and bureaucratic support was withdrawn (LaForgia, 1985).

Local organizations identified in the APHA study as examples of useful contributors to primary health care are quite diverse. For example, LOs may range from the village development committees in Tanzania (which have worked better on health than on agriculture), to the mothers' clubs in Indonesia, which have responsibility for various health programs (APHA, 1982). The federations of village health committees established in Panama in the early 1970's worked closely with the Ministry of Health to resolve problems. The federations linked experienced health committees with recently organized committees and raised funds to pay transportation costs so that health officials could regularly visit distant communities (Annex Four).

It may be more effective to work with and through existing local organizations rather than to set up new ones, but there is not enough systematic evidence to prove the point one way or the other. Three-quarters of the projects APHA reviewed created special health committees and only one-quarter worked through existing groups. In either case it is apparent that, more than in some other aspects of rural development, membership organizations in the health area need outside support and supervision.

4.2.4 Cooperatives

Cooperatives are not as common a form of local institution for providing primary health care as might be expected. One very pragmatic consideration favoring cooperatives may be that in certain countries they are the only legally sanctioned forms of peasant organization. They may by law have special status with respect to taxes and subsidies that give them advantages not available to other local institutions (Tendler, 1981:48). For example, one form of cooperative action could be pooling patients' purchasing power to prepay medical costs—to get the benefit of scale economies, to give health consumers some influence on the care they receive, and to have assurance of protection in time of need.

In Nepal one government resettlement program decided to establish a local health post but had no budget for drugs. To obtain funds for this, it required that anyone who wanted land in the settlement had to "volunteer" to join an insurance scheme. To no one's surprise, there were many members. As both the health post and its insurance scheme were well managed, in succeeding years there was little difficulty getting people to pay their annual premium. Subsequently the Ministry of Health opened its own health post, which offered free drugs—whenever it had drugs, which was not frequently. Despite the shortcomings of the MOH health post, it destroyed the cooperative because people preferred to hope they would be sick only when free drugs were available rather than pay the costs of an assured system (Don Chauls, personal communication).

A worldwide review by the APHA (1982a) found documented cases of prepayment arrangements in fifteen Third World countries. Some of those with personal prepayment by members had functioned for a decade or more with some highly satisfactory results in terms of low-cost access to health services. Yet renewal and premium collection rates were often low, and any scheme that requires monetized payment often runs into difficulties where cash incomes are low.

One way to deal with this problem of low cash incomes is through production-based cooperative health programs. The Chinese commune system has been the largest and best-known undertaking of its kind, but community or regional schemes have been documented in Bangladesh, Benin, Colombia, Ethiopia, India, and Indonesia. The Mallur Milk Cooperative in India, for example, finances clinical services from a one-cent surcharge on each liter of milk it collects and sells (APHA, 1982a:25-26). Such cooperatives are usually not set up initially for health purposes but as agricultural co-ops to which health activities were subsequently added.[4]

One kind of cooperative institution relevant to PHC is the communal

---

[4]A historical example worth citing is from rural Japan, where communities began forming mutual aid societies around the middle of the 19th century and contracted with physicians at predetermined annual rates of compensation. "One rural district reported over a hundred mutual aid societies, with the largest having a membership of 330 households. Agricultural cooperatives began health-related work around 1920, and by 1940, over a million rural households belonged to cooperative-based prepayment schemes." (APHA, 1982a:26)

pharmacy, with examples including the Bajada medical cooperative in the Philippines, the *chaquicocha* in Peru, and the co-ops under the *Santé Rurale* project in Mali (APHA, 1982a). Such pharmacies are often started with locally mobilized capital and use volunteers for sales, inventory maintenance, and restocking. By pooling purchasing power, people can buy drugs in bulk for cheaper prices or can ensure supplies in areas that private sellers ignore.

One of the more innovative uses of a cooperative mode of organization in the health sector is the initiative by the Kottar Social Service Society in south India (Annex Seven). KSSS leaders are decentralizing their Community Health Development Project until each village is able to function autonomously as a health cooperative registered with the government and entitled to its financial support. It is still too early to know how this strategy will fare but it could offer important lessons for cooperatives' potential in PHC efforts.

4.2.5 Service Organizations

Rural health care is an area where local service organizations are likely to be active. There is now an apparent trend among SOs that operate hospitals or clinics to develop broader, community-based PHC programs with emphasis on preventive measures. Such organizations often operate where governments do not have effective services. Their presence in a region may span several decades giving them stability and legitimacy not usually found in efforts of more recent vintage. Moreover, many SOs have extensive linkages both within and outside the areas they serve which enable them to carry out innovative PHC programs with leeway for learning through organizational experimentation.

A good example of this type of SO transition is the Project Esperança in Brazil (Annex Four). Originated as an Amazon River-based hospital boat activity where U.S. surgeons performed dramatic operations on children, the project today focuses on primary health care serving some 30,000 subsistence farmers and fishermen in a remote area. Seventeen rural health aides work on a full-time basis with the suppport of fifty-six part-time health promoters. Another example of a local service organization developing a PHC system is the Kottar Social Service Society, mentioned above. While KSSS itself operates at the sub-district level, it has been developing independent, village-based institutions in some 124 communities in southern India.

4.2.6 Private Providers

As noted already health is one sector where private, for-profit institutions are widely established in rural areas. By some definitions of

PHC, such care is already being provided by private practitioners. However, to the extent that one includes health education and preventive activities as essential elements of primary health care, the present role of private providers is less than adequate. In several PHC schemes, village health workers have been allowed to operate on a fee-for-service basis while in some other projects, individual health workers receive a percentage of a set fee. Often, health workers are responsible for maintaining supplies of medicine for villagers by operating a revolving fund, prescribing, selling and restocking basic drugs and keeping any profits as their own compensation (APHA, 1982a). This poses the danger, of course, of creating an incentive for prescribing drugs whether needed and effective or not.

Within the category of private providers, one may find "vaccinators," individuals (often self-trained) who for a fee will give an injection of some kind for almost any ailment. Unfortunately such practices often influence rural peoples' perception of appropriate health care. These perceptions, in turn, can create considerable difficulties for VHWs and other better trained health care providers (Don Chauls, personal communication).

Several PHC programs have experimented with providing drugs and contraceptives through private business channels. Probably the best known example is the Community Family Planning Services program in Thailand. The philanthrophic organization that manages this program has been very effective in getting contraceptives to the rural population by supplying them to village storekeepers who sell them for a modest profit (Annex Four). Another innovation backed by UNICEF involves trying to sell through village stores oral rehydration packets which can stave off the life-threatening effects of severe diarrhea in young children. In Bangladesh these private channels are also being used to sell "birth kits," a bar of soap and sterile razor blades for cutting the umbilical cord. Such a strategy is now referred to as "social marketing" (Fox and Kotter, 1980).

While development of such private channels by themselves will not create a primary health care system, these examples suggest how the private sector can serve as an important conduit for delivering goods and services in ways that relieve village health workers of some tasks allowing them more time to concentrate on other responsibilities. Moreover, private practitioners can and very commonly do provide a large share of the curative health care that is part of PHC.

4.2.7 Coordination

Because primary health care cuts across sectors like agriculture (nutrition), public works (sanitation), and education, there are significant problems of coordination that complicate questions of institutional design. Private providers for example, while quite flexible and efficient in providing services or medicines, are in no position to coordinate others besides themselves. Market mechanisms have a role in PHC, but they cannot be used by themselves to determine the level and pattern of services.

Government personnel operating at the local level seem to have the authority for coordination, but they are themselves usually partisans in the inter-department battles that go on. An Indonesian government report on experience with PHC concludes:

> Cross-sectoral cooperation is a beautiful concept. In many instances, however, each of the sectors is interested only in their own program. . . . They may still feel that a better result might be achieved with their own individual conventional approach.

> It is interesting to note that the efficacy with which coordination is achieved is inversely proportional to the level of administration [at which coordination is attempted]. It means that the coordination mechanism works more smoothly at the village level than at higher levels of administration. (Republic of Indonesia, 1978)

There appear to be few cases of really successful coordination anywhere on which to base generalizations, but this suggests that there probably needs to be some significant role for local government, perhaps through specialized health committees, following the pattern often observed for rural infrastructure.[5]

4.3 INDIGENOUS HEALTH PRACTITIONERS

Efforts to introduce supportive local institutions must recognize that some health services are almost always already being provided, often in so-called traditional modes. "Indigenous health practitioners are there already" suggested one study for USAID in its subtitle (Pillsbury, 1979). In Indonesia it is estimated that traditional birth attendants help to deliver more than 75 percent of the babies born in rural areas (Republic of Indonesia, 1978:25), while in Egypt an estimated 10,000 traditional midwives (*dayas*), although they function illegally, help deliver at least 80 percent of newborns in addition to their larger role in the community (Assaad and El Katsha, 1981:7). Traditional practitioners can be well organized, as seen in the case of the Association of Ghanaian Psychic and

---

[5]Coordination in Burma's PHC program is effective primarily because the multi-sectoral local government (the Village People's Council) and the district government unit (the Township People's Council) play such major roles from the outset. Both these Councils have considerable authority, a fact which makes health personnel responsive and respectful. The sequence of the flow of information in beginning PHC activities in a township is important. First, the Township Medical Officer (TMO) meets with the TPC and describes the system to them. Second, each VPC's representative on the TPC informs the other members of his VPC. Only as a third step is there any interaction between the VPC and the local Rural Health Centre (local administration), with the latter coming to the VPC to clarify uncertainties, answer questions, provide schedules, etc. This initiating role of the TPC and VPC are factors in their continuing to perceive PHC as *their* program, and continuing to exercise effective coordination between health projects and other activities (Don Chauls, personal communication).

Traditional Healers (Annex Four), and even powerful, as seen with *ayurvedic* physicians in India and Sri Lanka.[6]

Generally speaking indigenous health practitioners qualify as institutions that are not organizations, to follow the distinction made in Section 1.5. They operate in individual roles but not as structured sets of roles that could be regarded as organizations. Since these roles are widely accepted and are accorded high legitimacy within the community, they have institutional qualities.

Some of the roles such as that of traditional birth attendant are almost always reserved for women. Other roles such as setting broken bones or making herbal medicines can be filled by either men or women. Many times the health-related role is but one function of a larger role embedded in religious or cultural traditions (March and Taqqu, 1986). The range and degree of specialization among these existing health institutions will vary greatly from place to place. What does not vary is the fact that these practitioners are often the predominant means of health care for the rural poor (Pillsbury, 1979).

All PHC programs face the issue of what kind of institutional arrangement or accommodation to seek with the existing system. Alternatives range from working exclusively with and through those who are already established in a community as health care providers on the one hand to the other extreme of trying to start anew by banning indigenous practitioners and permitting only newly trained personnel to be consulted. Still other options include dividing various health-related functions between indigenous practitioners and PHC workers so as to establish mutually exclusive spheres of competence, or organizing PHC activities in such a way that they can support indigenous healers by reinforcing those services which are effective. The latter relationship could include such support as providing sterile supplies to traditional birth attendants.

Presumably the most frequent users of primary health care services will be women, both for themselves and for their children. It is therefore not surprising that government and external agencies have made particular efforts to enlist women who are indigenous practitioners in PHC activities since they know well the health problems facing their communities. Moreover, they are likely to be highly trusted by the local population.

One foreseeable problem with this approach is that women health practitioners may often be part of informal women's associations that come into action in times of daily difficulty or distress. Assistance is not motivated by some sort of contractual arrangement but rests more on an interpersonal ethic of mutual obligation (March and Taqqu, 1986:35). If PHC programs

---

[6]In India, there are 108 colleges teaching ayurvedic or other traditional health systems at the large undergraduate level and twenty-two post-graduate departments. There are some 10,000 registered traditional practitioners in Sri Lanka alone (Nemec, 1980:4).

are to avoid diminishing the effectiveness and possibly destroying the fabric of solidarity within informal associations, external agencies must be sensitive to the undesirable effects that "integration" into a PHC system may have.[7]

Moreover, when mandatory fees or other forms of remuneration from nontraditional sources are made part of newly expanded roles, effectiveness can be seriously undermined. For example, in the first phase of the Sine Saloum Rural Health Project in Senegal, many traditional birth attendants received three months of training to supplement their practical experience. After training was completed, they were formally incorporated into the PHC program, which operated on a fee-for-service basis. Since this required cash for payment, the number of women who requested assistance from these attendants during childbirth decreased dramatically (Hall, 1981:38).

In many situations the delicate nature of these valuable and beneficial informal social relationships, often essentially a tacit compact, argues against working with indigenous practitioners. But whether a role or association is formal or informal is not always clear. To assume that all informal roles and associations will lose their effectiveness if they receive outside assistance is to underestimate the resourcefulness, the flexibility, and even the aspirations of rural people. There are several approaches for deciding whether or how to engage indigenous practitioners in PHC activities.

First, the extent to which an informal association is "active" or "reactive" should be considered as this will affect its viability as a vehicle for new services. March and Taqqu (1986) define an active informal association as one which has relatively explicit objectives coupled with resource capabilities to pursue those objectives. Such associations contrast with reactive ones, which perform more defensive or ad hoc activities and which are usually less formal. Active associations are more likely to be amenable to an expansion or extension of their functions provided these benefit their members.

A second strategy is to examine the development initiative itself to see how closely the procedures, roles, and values involved might mimic those of existing roles or institutions. For example, in activities where money has not been exchanged before, as well as in communities where money is not readily available or very familiar, there is more chance of getting medicines

---

[7]March and Taqqu write: "The local midwife/healer cannot simply be turned into a neighborhood paramedic and pharmaceutical agent within the planned expansion of a Western medical organization system. Instead of thinking of these midwives and healers as ill-trained and poorly remunerated quasi-doctors who only need more scientific training in order to bring the medicine of their communities into the 20th century, we must learn to respect not only their herbs but also their position within an informal associational network of clientele. Their relative autonomy and legitimacy must be preserved. More centralized health delivery systems cannot subsume or fully rationalize the midwife's role if they expect to derive continuing benefits from traditional practitioners." (1986:92)

distributed as intended if their provision through traditional birth attendants can be handled on a gift or barter basis rather than for cash payment
only. If the drugs must be paid for, some other local institutional arrangement would be more appropriate.

A third and more general strategy, discussed at greater length in Chapter Seven, is to follow a "learning process" approach, planning and
implementing a program in an incremental, participatory, experimental
manner, adapting it in ways suggested by experience. With such an
approach, the extent to which traditional roles and relationships can be
modified without damaging them can be ascertained empirically.

This discussion does not presume that indigenous practitioners are
always effective or even always ethical. It does assume that before trying to
construct or strengthen any local institutional framework in support of
PHC, the effectiveness of existing health care providers be considered and
that, where practicable, such established capacities be drawn into the
emerging institutional structure.

4.4 ISSUES IN PRIMARY HEALTH CARE

A number of issues bear on the appropriateness of different local
institutions for supporting PHC such as differences in the way members
of the public perceive costs and benefits of various aspects of a PHC
program or the extent to which a service can be provided as a private
good. Here, we will address some of the most important issues affecting
LID alternatives.

4.4.1 Ensuring Access

The need for good health is universal, though those in poorer
circumstances who are not well nourished and have neither the means nor
the information to practice good hygiene, will be at greater risk than others.
In any rural population, there are certain groups that may be considered
particularly "vulnerable"—women during and after pregnancy, the young,
the malnourished, the overworked. Local institutional development in the
health care area needs to assure their access to PHC services.

In principle government agencies should be the most effective
organizations for providing PHC services to those people in greatest need.
However, in practice this is not always the case because LA is weakest at the
socio-economic periphery. If local government is controlled by more
privileged elements, they may take little interest in ensuring broad access to
services provided through LG. Similarly private practitioners have less
incentive to serve the poor. Membership organizations including co-ops
that have poor members will be more sensitive to this issue of assuring

access, as will service organizations (religious or charitable) where they exist.

The location of a health facility such as a clinic or health post affects who has access to its services, especially in areas with high levels of social stratification or where difficult terrain makes some areas remote. But even a highly accessible facility will be of little use if community members are uncertain about when personnel can be found there or whether necessary supplies are available. PHC programs will gain credibility in the community's eyes when users know that their trip will not be wasted. We must recognize that sometimes when a service is located in remote areas so as to be more accessible, its supplies and staffing become less reliable. Where such a constraint occurs, decisions on location need to optimize accessibility and reliability in order to facilitate institutionalization, whatever type of channel is used for PHC.

In many localities conducting mobile clinics is an excellent way to increase geographical accessibility while simultaneously reducing social distance, especially when health workers walk or use public transportation to the location rather than arrive by government or private vehicle. To the extent possible, prior notification of an impending trip can increase effectiveness of such visits. The Burmese PHC system has found that the best way to increase accessibility was simply to close down its rural health centers in rural towns (localities) three days per week to give the staff sufficient time to supervise community health workers in the villages and to conduct mobile clinics.

Accessibility of PHC services needs to be considered in terms of time as well as distance. Many rural areas experience significant seasonal variation. As Chambers and his associates (1981) have documented, malnutrition, morbidity, and mortality commonly peak during the rainy season at the same time that rural health services are likely to be operating least effectively because of logistical and staffing problems. The demand for medications goes up just when keeping them in stock in rural dispensaries is most difficult. Supervision of staff is likely to slacken, and health personnel themselves are more likely to become sick or take leave. Simply getting to health services, even ones located in villages, can be arduous for rural people during these months.[8]

The implications of seasonality for LID are not clear-cut though they need to be considered. If it becomes unprofitable to provide services during the difficult months, private channels lose their value when they are needed most and LA or possibly LG will have to be relied on more. On the other hand, these alternative channels may be immobilized also during the same

---

[8]Chambers (1979) reminds us that while the rainy season generally presents the most health problems, in some areas like northern India, it is the hot dry season that creates the most severe health and nutrition stresses.

period. One of the reasons why the PCDA in Thailand turned to private shopkeepers to handle the distribution of contraceptives was because government supplies were interrupted during the rainy season, while the private sector tended to be more dependable and more accessible to villagers year-round (Annex Four).

In the development of local institutions, whether government agencies, local government, or other forms, the involvement of women in the management of PHC services is likely to make the services more accepted and effective. In countries as different as Bangladesh and Samoa, networks of women's committees have been integrated into health programs to good effect (Fonaroff, 1982).

The gender of health workers can affect accessibility because of socio-cultural norms within a society. It is frequently presumed that women can carry out a wider range of PHC functions and are therefore preferable as VHWs. Yet in some societies, women may not travel as freely as men either within communities (e.g. for emergencies) or outside their communities (for training). Men, on the other hand, may be unacceptable for a wide range of tasks including attending births. One innovation to lessen gender-related problems can be selection of husband-wife teams for training as reported from Guatemala's PHC program (Colburn, 1981:24).

Such considerations as the gender of personnel or the location of facilities are not unique to any particular kind of local institution. Rather, these considerations bear on the institutionalization process—the acceptability of services and the acceptance of local responsibilities—so that the benefits of PHC can be extended and sustained through channels enjoying moral and material support. These channels, as discussed in Section 4.5, should be integrated into a network of service and education providers so as to create a system for primary health care.

4.4.2 Recurrent Costs

A feature of rural health programs generally is that recurrent costs far outweigh initial or capital costs and can become a significant financial burden for any government. One reason why most governments have at least some interest in local institutional development in the health sector is to mobilize additional resources for covering some of the ongoing expenses of providing health services. We treat LID issues of financial resource mobilization in Chapter Eight, but address them here since they are so important for PHC.

The subject of recurrent costs is one of the few PHC issues that has been analyzed with a broad and systematic data base thanks to the American Public Health Association (1982a). Methods of community financing and their success have been reviewed for over 100 projects and programs worldwide. Some examples of community self-sufficiency or near self-sufficiency were impressive but could not be generalized for lack of adequate documentation (a problem we confronted often in this LID study). We cite here the conclusions of the APHA study:

> The most common forms of community support are voluntary labor and direct personal payments, and both have limited utility. Voluntary labor is useful chiefly for one-time construction costs, while direct personal payments place the financing burden on the sick and limit access to persons who can afford to pay. Community financing, at best, is just one element of a balanced financing approach. It has not paid for supervision, logistical support, or referral linkages and can be effective only if these services are financed from other sources. (APHA, 1982a:41)

What can be most readily financed through community institutions are: construction and maintenance of physical facilities; provision of community health workers (paraprofessionals); and local currency costs of basic drugs. "These decisions generally reflect national budgetary restraints, not communities' willingness and ability to pay. Community financing would be more viable if planners started by studying demand" (APHA, 1982a:42).

For local institutions to achieve sustained financial capacity to support health programs, there need to be major community mobilization efforts. Yet in order for such efforts to become institutionalized, technical and managerial support is necessary to set up systems for financial accounting and accountability. The utility of the "goldfish bowl" approach, whereby the location and public visibility of funds is never in doubt, is critical to sustain the capacity for ongoing mobilization. Back-up resources from outside—for example, revolving funds—are frequently desirable to cover temporary deficits.

Another potentially important connection between meeting recurrent costs and LID is that continuing (or at least periodic) engagement of local residents in dealing with recurrent cost issues for their institutions is an excellent means of sustaining involvement. For this reason, in LID terms it may be more desirable for the institution to have responsibility for recurrent cost items like VHW remuneration and drug resupply rather than a major capital cost item like building construction. If the community builds a structure at the beginning of the project, villagers may then feel that it is also up to the government to do the rest—and involvement may suffer (Don Chauls, personal communication).

One difficult LID issue in this area is the fact that, to the extent PHC relies on local financing, higher-income communities will generally get more and better health care (Golladay, 1980). One way to compensate for this is to have the central government apply differential rates for subsidizing or supporting local programs according to the economic levels and potential of each area. This strategy could create undesirable "dependency" relationships, with poorer communities having an incentive to remain in the "poor" category, though this does not appear a necessary consequence as much depends on the structure of incentives.[9]

The alternative—leaving the financing of PHC entirely up to each community—can lead to unequal (possibly quite unequal) health opportunities. Some effort to compensate for inequalities in the level of available resources seems appropriate, though this may lock the government into financing at least some portion of recurrent costs. While we see no fully satisfactory solution to this problem, it should not be allowed to become an obstacle to devolving PHC responsibilities to a stronger and broader set of local institutions. Delaying LID only perpetuates overall dependency on central resources and continues the inadequacy of rural health services.

4.4.3 Preventive vs. Curative Programs

One frequent issue in primary health care is the extent to which PHC programs should persist in emphasizing public health and preventive activities when the rural people to be served would give more weight to curative efforts. An example of this preference is seen in the rural health program using paraprofessionals in one of the more inaccessible corners of Guatemala (Annex Four). In its training of village health workers, the program stressed prevention of disease, but the communities were more interested in having medical services, for which the paraprofessional had limited qualification. Where PHC programs are able to develop effective approaches to health education, preferences for curative tasks may be superseded by a strong interest in preventive tasks as documented in the Panama PHC program (La Forgia, 1985).

Where primary health care programs are turned over to participatory local institutions, particularly LGs or membership organizations, preventive activities may be downplayed, at least initially. On the other hand, since one of the comparative advantages of LG or membership organizations is likely to be in organizing preventive activities, it is especially important to provide for this role as early as possible. This reinforces the earlier conclusion that government or service organization staff, through local clinics and other facilities, must play an active role if the aims of primary health care are to be advanced.

One strategy in response to this situation may be to use curative services as an enticement or a *quid pro quo* for getting rural people to accept

---

[9]In South Korea, after two years of giving 35,000 villages the same level of material assistance, the Saemaul movement classified all villages into three categories: most responsive (self-standing), typical (self-helping) and least responsive (basic). Greatest assistance was given to the middle category, with enough to the first and third to provide some encouragement. The message to the latter category was to become more self-helping. In 1973, about one-third of the villagers were in the latter, but before long this number was negligible, and two-thirds had "graduated" into the top (self-standing) category, accepting reclassification partly because of pride and partly because there were still benefits to be received from the program (Lee, 1981:152-153). See Annex Seven.

and participate in preventive activities. In the early stages of the Esperança project in Brazil, adults who wanted to be treated in its clinics were required to have all the members of their families immunized. Sometimes some of the funds raised or allocated for curative care may be allocated for preventive measures. The Kottar Social Service Society in India has made the right to participate in decision making about expenditures from the primary health care fund contingent on mothers' regularly attending health education classes (John Field, personal communication).

In practice, the choice between preventive and curative activities need not be "either-or." One suggestion has been made to phase PHC work starting with a curative program and then introducing preventive measures once rapport and confidence have been built up. This would probably mean starting by working through government agencies and then bringing in other local institutions later on to add a participatory dimension to the program.

Another option would be to proceed in a more integrated manner. Where mobilizing resources and getting community cooperation is easier for curative activities, these may be used concurrently as a springboard for other less immediately popular efforts. Participation would be encouraged from the outset by such an approach, for example, in mobilizing funds for drug resupply or in making decisions about who should have fees for service waived because of inability to pay.

While it may be true that curative services can often be effective with only minimal participation from beneficiaries, their effectiveness can usually be improved through local assistance in scheduling, follow-up, and material contributions. Community participation in curative efforts can provide a basis of organization and experience when tackling important preventive activities, which require widespread understanding and active support.

It may be more feasible to start with a preventive focus if PHC programs move away from the common notion that the newly trained health workers are to "deliver" health care while they are "teaching" villagers about health requirements, and instead work to foster a climate of greater consciousness about the sources of ill health in the community. Such an approach was taken in Sierra Leone where after a decade of trying to improve village health through a mobile clinic, a church-affiliated hospital terminated this program for lack of results and tried a preventive program based on group discussions and community participation. For the first several years, curative care in the community continued to be provided by indigenous practitioners. Only later were certain community members given responsibility for handling curative drugs (Annex Four).

One observation of a PHC program in Burma suggests that those programs which spend more time on curative services are also likely to spend more time on preventive and promotive efforts due in part to their greater involvement with villagers.[10] Village health workers in the course of their daily work have opportunities for informing and motivating people, whether part of a formal training program or not. For instance, one of the best times to discuss preventive efforts may be when a health worker treats a sick child. In the process of treating the child, there is often time to explain how to prevent a recurrence. Effective use of such opportunities depends on the orientation and skills of the health workers.

4.4.4 Perceptions of Costs and Benefits

Primary health care encompasses a wide variety of activities intended not just to cure illness but to prevent disease or, put positively, to increase vitality and well-being. Which institutions are most appropriate for undertaking which aspects of a PHC program will depend in part on the relation of perceived costs and benefits. Four categories can be distinguished according to whether individuals see the costs of participating in a particular activity as low or high, and whether they see the benefits of that activity as clearly resulting from the cost. See Figure 4.1.

Figure 4.1: RELATIONS BETWEEN COST AND BENEFIT OF HEALTH MEASURES

	CONNECTION PERCEIVED BETWEEN INCURRED COST AND RESULTING BENEFIT	
LEVEL OF COST INVOLVED	Clear	Not Clear
Low	(I) Mosquito nets	(II) Contraceptives
High	(III) Hospitalization	(IV) Public sanitation

The first circumstance (I) represents something that can be fairly readily handled through private market institutions such as village shops, or through membership organizations like cooperatives. The second (II) may also be handled through private channels, but some subsidy would be needed to attain a satisfactory level of participation. If the connection becomes quite remote in people's minds, public sector institutions become the only alternative, assuming that sufficient social benefit is agreed upon. The third situation (III) is amenable to private institutions, but there would

---

[10]This observation was made by Don Chauls at a LID workshop at Cornell in April 1984. As a consultant for Management Sciences for Health, Chauls helped establish a PHC program in Nepal (funded by USAID) and has studied PHC in numerous other countries.

need to be some subsidization for lower income groups if there is to be equitable distribution of participation.

The likelihood that people will seek a particular health service reflects their perception of some clear benefit or minimal cost. As the benefit becomes ambiguous or uncertain and/or as the cost rises, people become less likely to participate in that service without some special inducements or sanctions. The combination of ambiguous benefits and high costs (IV), illustrated by investment in public sanitation, will not be handled by market means and requires public or collective action.

Somewhat less costly, but not less difficult, examples of the fourth situation would be building public latrines that people will use or keeping animals segregated from the human population. Because such activities require a great deal of cooperation from individuals, they pose difficulties of organization that compound the inhibition of low perceived net benefit.

An intermediate example would be improving public health through disinfecting a village's water supply. This should show clearer, quicker results with less cost and little interdependence of action. There would have to be some cooperation to the extent that persons used only the protected water source and kept it uncontaminated. Local government and membership organizations would likely have to be involved in such an effort even if it were initiated by local administration.

These examples raise the issue of "public" versus "private" goods, discussed in Section 3.3 and in the next section. The first situation in the matrix exemplifies a "private" good. However, the distinction made here turns particularly on the size and perceptibility of net benefits as incentives, not simply on the difference between public and private goods.

Perceptions, quite obviously, are subject to change over time for many different reasons. In planning primary health care, one is best advised, at least at the outset, to accept existing perceptions and allocate local institutional responsibilities for different PHC elements accordingly. This should help to gain initial cooperation and not to risk alienating those whose cooperation is desired (Flavier, 1978).

4.4.5 Public vs. Private Goods and Services

The nature of the goods and services provided or supported by PHC programs will have implications for the local institutions best undertaking their provision. *Public goods* are those which in practice are not subject to *exclusion* and are subject to *jointness* of consumption or use (Section 3.3). Such goods cannot be readily divided into units that can be sold or cannot be "owned" so as to exclude others from use and benefit. Further, the use of such goods does not appreciably diminish them. Examples of public goods include eradication of diseases like malaria or smallpox.

Within the realm of public goods, there is a further distinction to be made between activities that entail a degree of interdependence, requiring collective action, and activities where there is little interdependence. With malaria eradication, for example, all homes and adjoining areas must be sprayed for the effort to be successful. With smallpox eradication, on the other hand, each person gains the benefit by being vaccinated, regardless of whether others also get the vaccination. (True, if everyone participates and the virus is eliminated, vaccination may no longer be necessary, which is a collective benefit.)

Private goods can be sold to individuals or groups up to a level where they judge the benefit to be no greater than the additional cost. Curative health care such as treatment by means of antibiotics is an example of this.[11] Market mechanisms can usually indicate a level of user fees that will cover the costs of provision, though there is no guarantee that all who need care will get it. In principle, any of the institutional channels can provide private goods, though private enterprises cannot purvey public goods (at least not without subsidy from public sources). In practice, public institutions tend to stay away from providing private goods through market mechanisms though this would often be sensible.

In many health systems, government agencies have chosen to make private goods for curative health care available free of charge to all individuals, making them "public" goods in the sense of being provided by the public sector. But that does not change their nature as having divisible and excludable benefits. In the Philippines, for example, not only curative health care but also some preventive measures such as family planning services are given free to all who come to government clinics. In Thailand, on the other hand, the Lampang project gave responsibility for determining the fees to be paid by each household to village health committees (Coombs, 1980).

Where a high degree of social and economic inequality exists, PHC programs providing goods and services through private enterprises risk excluding poorer households from their benefits. Even so, regardless of the type of local institution serving as a channel for PHC, there are few if any private goods that could not be sold to the recipients, especially if there were some subsidization to encourage utilization. Subsidization can introduce problems of underuse, to be sure, such as households storing free drugs in case of future illness or perceptions that the drug is of little value because it is given free of charge.

In such analysis, there is a useful middle category of *mixed goods*—those subject to some degree of exclusion but which retain characteristics of jointness. Family planning services are an example of a mixed good in the

---

[11]To the extent that the disease is communicable, there would be a public goods aspect in its control, however. If people do not take steps to reduce and contain the spread of such a disease, there would be a public interest in requiring or subsidizing care or in imposing a quarantine if the disease is not curable.

health field. They can be given to some families but not others, yet one family's use of the counseling and services does not preclude others' use (unless there are definite constraints on staff time and supplies). How much of a public benefit there is from family planning can vary. To the degree that population is pressing upon scarce natural resources, family planning can be viewed as something of a public good. Where resources are relatively ample, it can be seen as a more private good. In a broader sense, however, to the extent that people are able to have the number of children they desire when they desire, and opportunities are thereby improved for education, employment, and health, most notably for women, family planning can be viewed as a public good. Potable water, another mixed good, varies similarly depending on the context of water availability.

Insofar as PHC activities are private goods, self-help membership organizations and private sector institutions are more viable options. Equity preferences can be accommodated through a variety of means including subsidization mechanisms and sliding fee scales. Public goods, usually exemplified by activities aimed at preventing health problems, call for greater involvement of local administration and local government. Since the demand for public goods may not be strongly articulated, especially in the early stages of a PHC program, and costs are not easily applied to users, collaborative efforts between LA and LG can significantly improve PHC performance levels.

4.5 ESTABLISHING LOCAL INSTITUTIONAL NETWORKS

The provision of adequate primary health care requires the functioning and cooperation of a number of local institutions. The hierarchical structure of government health agencies needs to be extended downward to provide care and education at the locality and/or community level (Section 1.6). The level at which clinics and other facilities are located depends on the size of communities in the area and on the financial and personnel capacity of the government. To recapitulate earlier discussion, some appropriate role for private health care providers, both modern and traditional, should be worked out in consultation with them to take advantage of what they can do well. What division of labor there will be between public and private sectors for the distribution of medicines, contraceptives, and other supplies needs to be determined by discussions and experimentation. The objectives of economy, reliability, accessibility, and equity need to be balanced in arriving at a suitable arrangement.

What is not as clear is the role that other kinds of local institutions should play—local government, membership (user) organizations, cooperatives, and charitable organizations (the not-for-profit private sector). This depends on the capacities of each and how well the more conventional public and private channels can perform PHC functions.

As primary health care programs have evolved, two particular innovations have usually been part of the PHC support system—an *organization* and a *role*—the village health committee (VHC) and the village health worker (VHW). Neither is an institution at the outset but both can become "institutionalized" to the extent they acquire legitimacy on the basis of their performance. VHCs can be either membership organizations or adjuncts of local government; VHWs can operate under the aegis of LA, LG, membership organizations, cooperatives, or service organizations. As suggested above, they might even function as private providers on a fee-for-service basis if their services were highly enough valued and not prohibitively expensive.

4.5.1 The Need for an Institutional Base

Primary health care programs often place VHWs in the unusual role of being both a direct service provider and a "catalyst" for community organization (see Section 7.3.2). Given the almost universal interest in curative aspects of PHC, it is assumed that those who provide medicines will gradually gain legitimacy and be able to expand into areas of sanitation, nutrition, and health education. Yet the performance of VHW's preventive and curative activities is very much dependent on the institutional base from which they operate.

The objective of primary health care is not so much to institutionalize a health worker role as to develop several complementary institutional capabilities to deal with the range of curative and preventive needs. While a government agency or regional service organization may serve as the "lead agency" in initiating PHC and in providing subsequent technical support, health workers require intensive connections with the community, which are more likely to come from institutions that are directly accountable to rural populations such as membership organizations or local government.

In a number of PHC cases reviewed, VHWs were given technical training and then returned to the communities to work with newly formed village health committees and to coordinate with other local institutions. Equal investment was not made by program authorities in the development of VHCs or other local institutions. Instead, VHWs were expected to carry that load as well as to handle more "technical" tasks. Two examples point up this key difference.

In Project Esperança in Brazil, the service organization that served as the lead agency in introducing the PHC approach not only gave extensive training to health workers but also made an explicit effort to assure that a local institutional base existed from which they could work. The project accomplished this in large part through perseverance over several years. Even when many of the original VHCs did not last more than a few months,

Esperança Foundation, recognizing the importance of having a local institutional base, made ongoing investments in training new VHC representatives to replace ineffective ones. Support included paying transportation expenses and developing a practical curriculum with subjects like simplified financial management and how to build up community confidence in VHWs.

The VHCs now oversee day-to-day administrative matters including the hours that health posts are open and the charges for various services. Esperança continues to provide in-service training and technical supervision for heath workers. Linkages have been established with the Ministry of Health to provide medicinal supplies. In many locations local government revenues provide remuneration for VHWs. Crucial to this development is the fact that the VHC rather than the VHW is responsible for managing the various linkages with other institutions and it is backed by the Foundation, a service organization operating at the regional level (Annex Four).

In sharp contrast is the Sine Saloum project in Senegal. Its village health workers were envisioned as being direct service providers while simultaneously working as catalysts for transformation of the health situation. Although village management committees were created to oversee financial matters, they were limited in this domain and were not expected to play a promotional or mobilization role (Hall, 1981:21). As a result the VHWs were very much on their own, especially when the level of support planned by the Ministry of Health personnel did not materialize. The project subsequently lost effectiveness when many VHWs left to find other forms of employment (Annex Four). The requirement for a solid local-level institutional base was overlooked. In this case project managers were trying to institutionalize a *role* without attention to institutionalizing a viable grassroots *organization*.

Fortunately many of the above inadequacies have subsequently been addressed by MOH and AID staff. With greater focus on LID, the Sine Saloum project appears to be reviving. One of the most interesting changes has been the project's effort to organize a women's committee for each village health-hut. This is intended to give women a greater voice by creating parallel community organization, a structure that is traditional to villages in the region (Bloom, 1984).

4.5.2 Use of Paraprofessionals

One way of reducing the cost of health services and of increasing their accessibility is to refashion the roles of service providers, especially to introduce new paraprofessional roles in primary health care (Esman et al., 1980). Simply recruiting and training persons from the community is not the answer, however. Though their salaries are less than those of more qualified professionals, their performance can be of negligible value, quite apart from their level of technical competence, unless two conditions are met.

First, as stated previously, there has to be effective periodic if not continuous supervision and back-up from higher levels (district or region), usually from a government agency but possibly from a nongovernmental (church or charitable) organization. It is necessary for supervision to be sensitive to the position of the health worker as well as to the community itself. Both the amount and the way supervision is handled will have far-reaching consequences for a program's viability. The intent of supervision is not only to monitor technical performance of the VHW and to ensure that he or she is actually working at assigned tasks but also to provide him or her with the status needed in the community's eyes to be accepted and respected. Otherwise, a local person is commonly "a prophet without honor." Supervision can facilitate the growth of local problem-solving capacity by giving the VHW confidence as well as consultation in reaching solutions.

Second, there has to be accountability to the community. This can be achieved through its local government or some membership organization. Outside officials, for the sake of getting a program started, have themselves often selected someone from the area to serve as VHW or have let local influentials do the selecting (Colburn, 1981; Hall, 1981; Taylor, 1981). There has too seldom been a real group in the community to whom the paraprofessional felt responsible or that felt committed to working with the VHW after initial training was completed. Yet such a relationship, as noted in the Brazil and Senegal cases cited above, is critical for success. Use of paraprofessionals without some concomitant local institutional development is not an effective strategy even if it is superficially attractive on budgetary grounds.

Another important subject involves the amount of time that paraprofessionals devote to their work. While it is not possible to draw reliable conclusions concerning the advantages and disadvantages of full-time versus part-time paraprofessionals, the issue does relate rather directly to financial resource mobilization capabilities. Where a sufficient and reliable means of funding is not available, it is unlikely that paraprofessionals will be able to work effectively on a full-time basis. Rather, local institutions in such circumstances are more likely to maintain ongoing activities if part-time paraprofessionals work voluntarily or for a small stipend. Several cases in Annex Four detail the problems associated with paraprofessional health workers expecting one level of remuneration and receiving something less, all with discouraging results.

4.5.3 Comparative Advantages of Local Institutions

Even if a PHC support network can involve the whole range of local institutions, not all are equally useful for all PHC tasks. A network should take advantage of what each channel can do best.

Government agencies are by their nature better suited to routine, repetitive tasks like health inspection or mosquito spraying, which need regularity. This strength may have a converse weakness in inflexibility and inertia. PHC programs require regular support and supervision, and government agencies can be reasonably effective in this if sufficient staff are available for the task with offices and transport facilities at appropriate sub-district or district levels. Government agencies also have an advantage in being better able to mobilize and provide a higher level of technical skill than village-based institutions. They can also increase the status and legitimacy of health workers and committees at the village level (Colburn, 1981).

One limitation is that the orientation and methods of operation of government staff are commonly rather bureaucratic or technocratic, assuming a posture of superiority that discourages local responsibility and initiative. Such attitudes are quite inappropriate for PHC. For this reason it may be desirable for government agencies to work through intermediaries who operate in more responsive and respectful ways. Private voluntary organizations have been nominated for playing such a role on behalf of the government to develop more supportive linkages with the public and with nongovernmental bodies (Steinmo, 1982). However, it may be possible for government agencies to employ, train, and deploy staff who will work in a new manner themselves (Section 7.5.4).

Local government has rarely been found taking the lead role in initiating PHC, yet it does appear to offer a viable local institutional base for nontechnical support and management. This is particularly true where alternative forms of health care are not readily accessible and where an absence of government or private providers has created a clear "demand" for health care. In these situations LG may be preferable since virtually all households will have an interest in PHC. LG can work with VHWs in determining arrangements regarding when and where services are to be provided and it can serve as the institutional base to which VHWs are accountable.

In any situation where LG exists and has some authority to manage public facilities, it can support PHC by introducing or enforcing protective measures associated with public sanitation. Municipal governments commonly oversee public markets. Through provision of infrastructure including waste disposal and running water, the sanitary conditions in markets and in communities can generally be improved.

Where LG raises funds through various taxes and user fees, among other methods, it will be able to make financial allocations to PHC for specific services, e.g. health education for young children or funds for VHW travel for training programs. Additionally LG can oversee the activities of government agencies or private organizations and can hold them more accountable to the public, an important contribution to PHC institutionalization.

Membership organizations can play various roles in PHC. For normative and practical reasons, health-related organizations are more likely to be "inclusive" than "exclusive" as defined by Leonard (1982). Humanitarian considerations usually rule out not providing curative medical care to certain persons, and the "public goods" nature of many preventive measures makes excluding certain members of the community self-defeating.

The caution some have stated about supporting inclusive membership organizations, fearing that the benefits might be monopolized by richer or more powerful members, does not apply as much for PHC as it would, say, for an agricultural input supply cooperative. Not all of the goods and services for PHC are joint in a way that makes them "public." Many PHC goods and services have the characteristics of divisibility and excludability so they can be given to some and not others. Moreover, some of the drugs and vaccines can be diverted to private gain.[12] However, compared with agricultural credit, forest resources, and other similar goods and services, PHC does not provide many things that elite groups would like to accumulate. While elites surely want health practitioners' services to be available when they are ill, educational or preventive activities are not worth "capturing," and although one could get more than one immunization or parasite purgative, each is painful or at least inconvenient enough that additional ones are of little incremental value.

These considerations work in favor of inclusive organizations and indeed suggest that PHC tasks can be devolved to local institutions with more confidence that benefits will reach the poor than in other activity areas. One danger to be kept in mind for PHC is that local elites, if in control of the programs, could revise them to upgrade the quality of services at the expense of quantity (Leonard, 1982:9). This would apply to local government responsibility for PHC as much as to membership organizations and should be guarded against.

Because inclusive organizations with large memberships are operationally difficult to manage, supporting the daily workings of a village-based PHC program is often more feasible through a smaller elected village health committee. If constituted through procedures that are well understood and accepted by the community, VHCs can perform many management functions in the health area more effectively than can "mass" organizations. However, retaining larger mass organizations still appears desirable in many instances when important decisions or activities (especially preventive) with broad effect are required.

---

[12]These questions of divisibility and divertibility as they affect human resource development generally are analyzed in Uphoff (1980).

Apart from having clear procedures, it is necessary for VHCs to have clear roles that will keep them active and keep members' morale high. Assigning VHCs responsibility for financial management and for overseeing the work of VHWs is common, but more tasks can be undertaken according to the level of competence and enthusiasm of members.[13] As noted in Section 4.2.3, the record of VHCs is uneven. The mode in which they are established is particularly important as learned the hard way in the Cameroons where some of the first experimentation with VHCs was undertaken (Annex Four).

One kind of exclusive membership organization found useful for PHC is women's associations, often called mothers' clubs. They have produced some impressive results in programs ranging from rural lunchrooms for poorly fed children in Honduras to carrying out comprehensive programs of community improvement in South Korea (Ickis, 1975; Kincaid et al., 1976; F. Korten and Young, 1978). The success of such organizations has depended primarily on the quality of local leadership that comes forward; on whether it can convert a sense of common interest into collective action.

Service organizations have a long history of involvement in health care, particularly operating hospitals. They have in recent years been quite active in refocusing their efforts toward community medicine. In general they appear to have been better at providing private goods such as curative medicine than at promoting public goods like mosquito control. For the latter, some involvement with membership organizations is useful to gain community cooperation. An example of successful linking of service and membership organizations comes from Zaire where a rural hospital in Bandungu province, by working through VHCs to improve public sanitation, was able to reduce ascaris infestation from 70 percent to less than 15 percent within one month (Fountain, 1973).

One strength of service organizations is that they are usually less constrained by the jurisdictional limits and rivalries that characterize most government agencies. This is a particular advantage in dealing with communities where administrative boundaries are incongruent with the social boundaries of kinship or ethnicity. Service organizations can work with people as individuals according to their convenience.

---

[13]One of the most encouraging reports on VHCs is from Uganda, where political and ethnic strife have disrupted almost all medical services in the country (Dodge and Wiebe, 1985). In Teso a mission doctor found his clinic-based efforts beginning in 1980 of little use, so he got the chiefs in the area to form committees to support and extend PHC. Many of the VHWs initially selected were unsatisfactory and all but two of the VHCs were "bogus, created for my benefit only" (Stockley, 1985:223). The effective VHWs were those "backed strongly by their committees where their committees had wide community support . . . gradually a number of good committees emerged, and by January 1984 viable PHC programmes had been established in six of the twelve villages in which they had been initiated, plus in four other subcounties." *Ibid.*

The types of service organizations that can be of assistance to PHC net-works can include non-health-related groups such as Rotary or Lions Clubs or their equivalents. Youth groups such as *Anak Bukid*, Boy Scouts and Girl Scouts also have potential to become involved with such activities as motivational campaigns for oral rehydration therapy, immunization, and so forth. In Latin America a wide variety of service (social activist) organiza-tions have emerged in recent years. Their members are generally better educated individuals dedicated to working at the grassroots level by assist-ing capacity-building activities in different areas including health (Hirschman, 1984).

Another advantage of some service organizations, those which are church-affiliated, is that they can work through ecclesiastical channels of communication that enjoy a legitimacy seldom matched by secular institu-tions. That many religiously supported mission hospitals have become such strong "institutions" in very difficult and unpromising locations is due in large part to the combined legitimacy of serving both health needs and reli-gious faith.

Private practitioners and *private enterprises,* as we have said, should be considered explicitly as part of any PHC system. Many of their advantages have already been discussed. Where there is a demand for goods and ser-vices and also purchasing power among the public, these private roles and organizations (institutions to the extent they enjoy legitimacy) can provide those goods and services more quickly and responsively than government agencies or even most service organizations.

Private channels can be particularly useful in the sale of contraceptive devices and in dissemination of family planning information where there is demand for these. This was found in the PDCA case in Thailand. Similarly village shops have been used to help control goiter in inland areas through sale of iodized salt. In a two-year field evaluation of three nutrition inter-vention strategies to control vitamin A deficiency in the Philippines—a public health and household gardening approach, distribution of vitamin A capsules through official channels, and sale of fortified MSG (a popular food additive) in small village stores—only the last resulted in a significant reduction in the clinical signs of xerophthalmia (Solon et al., 1979).

A village doctor or storekeeper may have the added advantage of being more flexible than a bureaucracy in providing short-term credit. With few exceptions, the location and setting of private practitioners and enterprises is more convenient, familiar, and congenial than are public sector facilities. This reduces the transaction costs, social as well as economic, of getting goods and services for improving health.

These considerations argue for a definite and often larger role for the private sector in primary health care efforts. There is no evidence, however, that PHC can be brought within the reach of the rural majority simply through private channels operating on a fee-for-service basis. This reinforces the concern we have stated that planning for primary health care focus on establishing networks of local support institutions.[14]

4.5.4 Systems and Stages of Health Care Development

The scope and complexity of primary health care requires that agencies support more than a single institutional channel. Developing a network of complementary local institutions will require more time and patience than introducing any one kind of institution. But the effectiveness of any one ultimately rests on the set of other institutions it can interact with horizontally (at the same level) and vertically (above and below.)

Primary health care represents a departure from the traditional concepts of "providing" services and medicines. It involves a greater degree of self-help and self-reliance than in previous formulations of what role rural populations are to play. They are to become participants in their own health improvement rather than only patients. For this to happen, local institutional development is crucial.

The appropriateness of different institutions will be a function of the level of health knowledge and awareness in the community as well as of the evolution of institutional capacities for providing basic services. The contributions that self-help membership organizations can make to PHC, for example, may well relate to how much attention or education has been devoted to health issues in the past.

Improvements in health and nutritional status as well as acceptance of practices that make these improvements more likely depend on community standards and common activities and on individual knowledge and motivation. Changing these is not simply a matter of individual persuasion. While health is an intensely personal matter, people's practices are influenced by what others are thinking, saying, and doing. For any significant and widespread change to occur, people need opportunities to talk among themselves about health problems and possible remedies.

Such discussions do not occur readily in visits to government or private clinics. There need to be congenial forums for discussion, perhaps organized

---

[14]An example of this type of local institutional network is found in Nepal's Community Health Leader Project. The Ministry of Health Training Unit initiated activities with technical and financial assistance from AID, an AID contractor, and WHO. The project trains staff of the Health Post (LA) to get the Panchayat (LG) to set up a Village Health Committee to support the activities of the community health leaders. Other foreign donors and PVOs as well as indigenous SOs (Nepal Red Cross and Women's Organization) are also involved in experimenting with project variations and in implementing the basic project or variations in different parts of the country. In at least one instance, the VHC was expected to have representatives from village membership organizations (the farmers' groups of the SFDP described in Annex Five). Finally, assistance was also being sought from district-level SOs (youth groups, Lions' Club) to help in the villages on a voluntary basis (Chauls and Rajbhandari, 1980; also Donald Chauls, personal communication).

by a health educator or VHW, where health professionals and paraprofessionals can participate and a process of attitude and behavior change can be nurtured. This is more critical to improvements in PHC ultimately than are facilities, drugs, and service providers. This realization is one reason why mothers' clubs are so often looked to in PHC programs, not just to encourage participation in specific services but to create a climate of opinion that supports a change in practices.

In most rural areas there will be some indigenous private sector sources of health care, as noted already, and commonly also some government sources, however thinly and unreliably provided. The best health care and education may be available from church-related institutions in those areas where government agencies and private practitioners, at least those practicing modern medicine, are not inclined to work.

Where other institutional channels are weak or not available, *self-help efforts* through membership organizations make a great deal of sense. They can introduce and support public health measures, construct facilities, raise money to attract medical practitioners, etc. They may be particularly effective when supported by service organizations such as the church-sponsored Kottar Social Service Society in India.

As rural people gain more knowledge, motivation, and material means to deal with their health problems, they should be able to reduce their most basic needs for medical services. Yet, their use of health services may well increase as they seek care for a greater percentage of their problems. As incomes and educational levels rise, it is often the case that more private doctors will seek to locate and practice in rural areas, and the spread of government health services is also likely to be greater. But for many parts of the world this extension of health services may be generations away.

One can anticipate that the role of paraprofessional health workers is likely to change as are local institutional arrangements in latter periods of rural development. Membership organizations for health improvement may no longer support part-time VHWs, for instance, and instead may prefer to support a community health clinic with full-time professional staff, though providing more advanced or specialized care does not preclude retaining community organizations for health. Eventually LA and private practitioners may replace self-help collective action for health. This may represent a natural evolution where persons prefer not to bear the organizational maintenance costs of MOs or cooperatives, leaving health matters entirely to the public and private sectors if these can provide adequate services at the local level. A strategic perspective on LID for primary health care must be dynamic. It will periodically reexamine the set of institutional channels to see how effectively and broadly the system of local institutions is progressing from inadequate services with narrowly curative measures to more satisfactory and comprehensive activities promoting wellness in ways that are responsive to the needs of all local residents.

CHAPTER FIVE

Local Institutional Development for Agriculture

5.1 ACTIVITIES IN AGRICULTURAL DEVELOPMENT

Agricultural development basically involves improvements or increases in three categories: *technology, resources,* and *institutions.* Identifying or devising appropriate new technologies and then getting them effectively disseminated is extremely difficult. Mobilizing and managing the money, manpower, and other material inputs needed to take advantage of technological opportunities is not much easier. Given the effort required to deal with issues of technology and resources, it is not surprising that the additional attention and energy necessary to foster supportive institutional arrangements are often lacking.

Institutional development must often seem like an extra burden or obstacle in agricultural development programs, yet it is as essential to such programs as either technology or resources. Most of what effort has been put into institutional development for agriculture to date has been devoted to establishing or strengthening national institutions.[1] Here we are concerned with the development of institutional capacities for supporting agricultural development at local levels. The process can be summarized analytically as follows:

(1) Agriculture requires converting *natural resources,* including plants and animals, into useful products through the application of *human*

---

[1]An important exception has been the many programs or projects to set up "cooperatives" in developing countries. But the way these have been introduced has been too often ill conceived and mismanaged, producing caricatures of co-ops with little value and little longevity (e.g., Hamer, 1981; for review of experience, see Bennett, 1983). The "community development movement" also engaged in local institution-building, but seldom with an agricultural capability, one of the reasons for its decline (Holdcroft, 1978; Blair, 1982). Even some of the current work on "farming systems" is surprisingly preoccupied with national-level institutions (e.g., USAID, 1980). Reasons for including local institutions in farming systems work are elaborated in Whyte and Boynton (1983).

resources, which are made more productive by the use of *capital*—
infrastructure, equipment, credit, etc.

(2) Local institutional development for agriculture is more complicated than for natural resource management, rural infrastructure, or primary health care, because two different kinds of local
institutions are involved: (i) *supporting institutions*, and (ii) *units
of production*.

(3) The activities of agriculture fall into three sets: (i) acquiring or preparing *inputs*; (ii) turning them into *products* through labor and
management efforts; and (iii) putting *outputs* to best advantage, as
analyzed in Table 5.1.

(4) Over and above these activities, there needs to be support for agriculture in the form of favorable *policies* and *investments* from
institutions at the national and regional levels, e.g. in research, extension and infrastructure.

(5) The complexity of agriculture comes in part from the variety of
units and institutions which are involved and from the difficulties
of achieving a good "fit" among the sets of institutions. *Supporting
institutions* (2.i. above) represent the crucial link in getting effective
and broad-spread agricultural development.

**Figure 5.1: LEVELS AND FUNCTIONS FOR
AGRICULTURAL DEVELOPMENT**

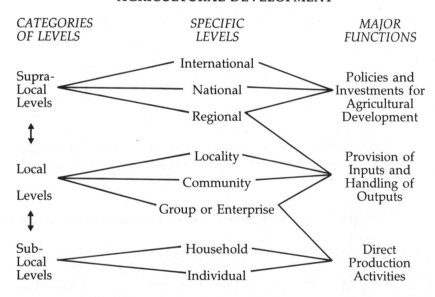

Activities are focused at different levels which range from the individual to the international arenas of decision making and activities, as discussed
in Section 1.6. In Figure 5.1, we show in somewhat abbreviated form the

levels at which activities concerning agriculture may be undertaken and the major functions to be considered when thinking through appropriate LID for improving agriculture. Table 5.1 identifies more specifically the input, production, and output activities described in (3) above.

Table 5.1: An Analysis of Agricultural Activities

I. *INPUT ACTIVITIES*—commonly mediated by local institutions.

   A. MATERIAL INPUTS
   1. Seeds and seedlings: purchased, exchanged, preserved
   2. Nutrients: chemical fertilizer is usually channeled through local institutions; other sources of nutrients, e.g., animal manure, green manure or compost, more often provided by households
   3. Chemicals: herbicides, insecticides, fungicides
   4. Traction: oxen or buffalo power, tractor power
   5. Implements: plough, hoe, shovel, machete, etc.
   6. Animal feed: fodder usually provided by households; other feed often purchased
   7. Veterinary medicines

   B. CAPITAL INPUTS
   1. Short-term (production) credit, for crop season
   2. Medium-term credits, for equipment or other purchases
   3. Long-term credit, most often for land purchases

   C. GENERALIZED INPUTS—usually managed by national institutions.
   1. Land access: land tenure systems, rental or share-crop arrangements, etc.
   2. Technology: information about new products, practices, or techniques, commonly developed through research and conveyed through extension system; may use communications or education systems
   3. Policy: price relations, subsidies, etc.

   D. INDIRECT INPUTS—considered in Chapters Two, Three and Four respectively.
   1. Natural resource management: protection and provision of soils, water, forest, and other natural resources
   2. Rural infrastructure: roads, water supply, housing, etc.
   3. Human resource development: education, literacy, health, etc.

II. *PRODUCTION ACTIVITIES*—usually carried out by individual or group enterprises; may involve some exchange of labor or inputs like traction power but seldom a real pooling of resources with producers undertaking joint risk.

   A. LABOR—work activities.
   1. For annual crops:
      a. Land preparation, fencing, etc.

        b.   Planting, including possibly nursery work
        c.   Thinning and weeding
        d.   Fertilizing
        e.   Plant protection, pest and disease control, bird scaring, etc.
        f.   Water management (where irrigation is possible)
        g.   Harvesting
        h.   Seed selection (re-starts cycle of production)

    2. For perennial crops, same as under 1, except:
        a.   Less frequent land preparation and planting
        b.   Possibly grafting and/or pruning

    3. For animals:
        a.   Feeding, includes grazing as well as bringing fodder
        b.   Housing
        c.   Disease control
        d.   Milking, shearing, slaughtering, etc.
        e.   Breeding

B. MANAGEMENT—decision-making activities.
    1. Procure or ensure inputs (listed in section I.)
    2. Mobilize, coordinate, supervise labor inputs (section II.A.)
    3. Determine amount, kind and duration of production
    4. Ensure balance between inputs and outputs so as to achieve a value of outputs greater than that of inputs

III. *OUTPUT ACTIVITIES*—commonly mediated by local institutions.

  A. STORAGE—post-harvest and/or post-processing.

  B. PROCESSING—manually and/or by machine.

  C. TRANSPORTATION—for processing, storage and/or sale.

  D. MARKETING—wholesale and/or retail.

Production is carried on by *individuals*, by *households* and by *groups* or *enterprises*, the three lowest levels shown in Figure 5.1, with households being the most common locus of production activity. The provision of inputs and handling of outputs, in contrast, ranges from the group or enterprise level through the *community* level up to the *locality* and often the *regional* level.

    This schematization indicates that no input or output activities come directly from the national level to production units. All need to be mediated through intervening institutions, many at local levels. The figure also points out how various less proximate supports come from regional or higher levels and are not really local in nature. A great range of levels are thus involved in

---

Note: "Nonagricultural" enterprise, treated in Chapter Six, is generally considered to begin at the point where produce is sold to a nonhousehold enterprise. This classification is conceptually somewhat inconsistent, equating sector with kind of unit, but the boundary between what is "agriculture" and what is not will be invariably somewhat ambiguous.

agricultural development, and if structures and capabilities are lacking at any one level, the whole system will function less satisfactorily.

Hunter (1980) has summarized the four main problems confronted by governments and donors in agricultural development as:

(1) the **large number of farmers** who will make their own decisions about how to run their own farms; in addition there is a large non-farm-owning rural population who survive by pursuing a wide variety of other activities, many of which affect agricultural possibilities;

(2) the **large variations** in physical, social and political environments between communities and localities;

(3) the **great variety of facilities, activities and institutions** involved in agriculture; and

(3) the **difficulties in coordination and organization** of a complex series of ministries, extension services, marketing boards, corporations, authorities, cooperatives, local governments, etc.

In light of these requirements, it may be tempting to try to manage this far-flung, demanding task from above. But the very magnitude and complexity of the task, and the limitations on achieving coordination at field level through higher level exercises of authority make increasing local capacity for planning and implementation part of the solution rather than just another part of the problem (Rondinelli, 1984:74-88, 136-140).

Local institutions can help to reach large numbers of small producers in scattered and remote locations, achieving economies of time in communicating with producers, and economies of scale in handling the inputs and outputs involved in an improved agriculture. Moreover, such institutions can augment external resources and management with funds, labor, information and other local inputs. Local institutions are useful for adapting programs and activities to the variety of conditions encountered in the rural sector, so as to use scarce human and material resources to best advantage. Perhaps most important for dealing with the variety of facilities and activities involved in agricultural development, local institutions can relieve some of the burdens on higher level administrators and technicians by undertaking more planning and coordination from below.

The conventional model of bureaucracy presents inherent contradictions when it tries to achieve coordination of activities across departmental lines. Coordination requires *horizontal* communication with a view to accommodation and adjustment. This contrasts with the *vertical* patterns of communication in bureaucracy, which aspire to command and control. Within a bureaucratic structure, subordinates are accountable only to their administrative superiors and will have little interest in taking risks or incurring inconveniences that benefit clients unless the latter are organized or powerful enough politically to influence superiors to discipline any poor performance of subordinates. To the extent that the staff of any organization are accountable to clients (such as customers of enterprises or voters within a local government jurisdiction), coordination should be more attainable since customers, users, and voters will be able to assess bureaucratic performance better than administrative superiors ever can.

What is frequently being termed "the fiscal crisis" in underdeveloped countries will become, if anything, more severe in future years (Howell, 1985). Even in the event that central government personnel have enough commitment, knowledge, and talent to pursue a transformation of the agricultural sector, they are unlikely to have the material means. Accordingly the role and capability of local institutions will have to increase if agricultural development is to be achieved in the years ahead. The concomitant "energy crisis" facing LDCs, even if it abates somewhat in its financial dimensions, will continue in physical terms and is likely to reinforce a tendency to move away from large-scale, capital-intensive patterns of investment, toward the kind of dispersed, labor-oriented development efforts more appropriate to management by local institutions.

5.2 LOCAL INSTITUTIONAL OPTIONS

Local institutional development for agriculture as we have said covers both production units and supporting institutions, though we are focusing here on the latter. *Production units* usually take one of three organizational forms, but especially the first:

  (a) **private** operations, usually household enterprises, though in more modern agriculture they may operate as corporations;
  (b) **cooperative** enterprises where individuals pool productive resources and share both risk and output, with decisions made on the basis of one-person, one-vote rather than in proportion to resources contributed; and
  (c) **state-owned** enterprises, operating according to public laws and with public resources.

Household enterprises are not "local institutions" as we have defined the term. LID does not seek to develop households as institutions but rather to assist them by government and donor efforts which strengthen supporting institutions. The other two kinds of production units can be considered local institutions but we will not deal with them except in passing. We find few production enterprises that are true cooperatives in the sense that all inputs including land are pooled and production is shared accordingly.[2] Cooperative enterprises that provide inputs for members' own

---

[2]A study of farmer organizations in the communal (tribal) areas of Zimbabwe found that "production groups" were the most common form of agricultural organization (35 percent). Yet even here, the pooling of resources included only labor, implements, and draft power, not

production activities operate as *supporting institutions* rather than as production units. State enterprises in agriculture will not be analyzed because they are seldom productive for reasons we need not elaborate.[3]

In our discussion we are considering *households* as the operative production units. Agriculture, as we know, entails considerable risk—from weather, pests, disease, fluctuating prices or labor supply. Cooperative or collective enterprise could offset such risks. But by and large, rural households prefer to keep their respective production activities separate and to deal with risk through other institutional mechanisms such as mutual aid, labor exchange, credit or marketing cooperatives, or state agencies.

Among the *supporting institutions* for agriculture dealing with inputs and outputs, there are multiple possibilities which include both modern and traditional institutions. One finds examples of traditional institutions in certain communities of Peru and Bolivia where elaborate crop rotation schemes are still managed by traditional local authorities who determine what crops will be planted, the work schedule for farm cycles, and the length of cropping and fallow periods (Brush, 1983). Whether such decision-making roles should be considered as a traditional form of local administration or local government depends on whether the persons in those roles are accountable mostly to government authorities or to members of the community. The traditional authorities in Peru and Bolivia operate more as local government, whereas the role of village headman (*lurah*) in Indonesia functions more as an arm of local administration. There are many kinds of indigenous cooperatives. Seibel and Massing (1974) document sixteen different kinds of rotating savings and credit associations in Liberia alone, and of course there are innumerable traditional businesses dealing with agriculture, often in the roles of traders or middlemen.

In thinking about local institutional development for agriculture, all of these channels for moving resources and information upward, downward, and horizontally should be considered. We focus here on the more modern institutions since they are more amenable to support and strengthening from outside the locality. But having cooperative relations among the various local institutions, traditional and modern, should enhance both local and outside efforts to improve agriculture. The kind of complex network of

---

land, and each member received the produce only from his or her own fields (Bratton, 1983). A review of mutual aid work groups by Ralston et al. (1983:106-107) supports this generalization that cooperative production is unusual.

[3]State farms in Ghana, for example, were spectacularly unprofitable (Miracle and Seidman, 1968). Experience in other countries has been similar if not so extreme. Some group farming has been moderately successful (Wong, 1979; Sasaki, 1985), but the state is seldom a good manager of agricultural production. Collective agriculture in China has been largely rejected by the leadership there because the incentives it gave for investment and for hard and careful work were not sufficiently strong. Even when production from a common plot is divided in proportion to labor inputs, this is seldom satisfactory because the quality of labor inputs, which has a crucial bearing on output, cannot be taken adequately into account and rewarded.

local institutions affecting agricultural development that can exist is suggested by the structure diagrammed for rural Botswana in Figure 5.2[4]

Figure 5.2: BOTSWANA EXAMPLES OF LOCAL INSTITUTIONS AFFECTING AGRICULTURE

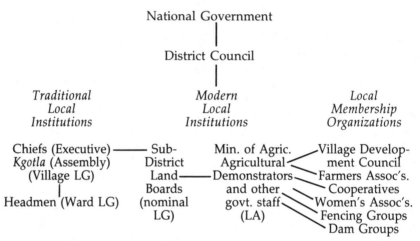

Source: Adapted from Willett (1981).

Each country's configuration of local institutions will be different, of course. In Botswana, the District Council is called "local government" but it is not really a local institution because it operates at too high a level. Because production and commercialization are so limited in rural areas, there is little private activity connected with the provision of inputs and handling of outputs; thus, government agencies cover these functions. This may change in the future though in unfavorable environments like most of Botswana, it will be some time before the level of income and sales will support a significant network of private suppliers and buyers. Private commercial organizations may play a more important role elsewhere.

None of these channels is suggested as an exclusive option. Our review of literature for this study confirmed our earlier conclusion, based on analysis of Asian experience, that agricultural development proceeds better when there are *multiple channels* that link rural communities to regional and national centers of trade, technical assistance, and policy (Uphoff and Esman,

---

[4]On this complex of institutions, roles and organizations, see also Brown et al. (1982) and Kloppenburg (1983). There are a number of service organizations at the local level such as Red Cross Societies and Social Service Committees but they are not shown as most are not involved in agricultural work. That SOs can be involved in agricultural work is seen in Section 5.2.5.

1974). Private businesses, like government agencies, are an important kind of channel but not the only one to be developed. As a rule, local institutions function better when operating in association with one another as part of a *network* of agricultural support institutions.

5.2.1 Local Administration

Any efforts to encourage or accelerate agricultural development will have some prominent role for the staff of various government agencies working at the local level. This does not mean however that they can or should try to "administer" such development. It is one thing to administer agricultural credit or manage crop purchase schemes where there can be reasonable control over the factors involved, but agriculture itself is in the hands of thousands, even millions, of producers subject to so many fluctuations of weather, disease, market prices, etc., that it remains beyond the reach of "bureaucratic" or "technocratic" approaches to development.[5] Local personnel of the central or state government are providing technical, economic, or organizational support to producers and are not engaged in agriculture as such. The question is how can local administration best make a contribution as part of a system of local institutions furthering agriculture.

The most common role for LA is to provide advice and demonstration of new technologies to raise production. To be useful and accepted, these must be truly appropriate and productive. If the most innovative agricultural research and experimentation is being done under government auspices, LA is usually in the best position to disseminate this, especially if a technology is not "embodied" in a tangible form that permits private distributors to make a profit selling it. For example, to promote raising fish in rice paddies, LA would be the most appropriate channel. To the extent that the advantages of an innovation are insufficiently known to make it commercially viable, LA may need to play a role in popularizing it. But it should be paving the way for private businesses to handle the task rather than have LA maintain responsibility for dissemination.

In assessing when LA has an advantage for disseminating new technology, one should bear in mind that government staff are not the only, or always the best, means of dissemination. There is a great deal of horizontal diffusion of technology among farmers whenever something truly beneficial is introduced. This can be done on an individual basis through noninstitutionalized channels of communication such as through local shops or tea-stalls or through organizations such as the seed-exchange societies formed among farmers in rural Japan during the early years of that country's agricultural modernization (Aqua, 1983). Private suppliers of

---

[5]This problem was aptly phrased in an editorial in the *Economic Weekly* of Bombay which said: "The clue to the failure of rural development [in India] lies in this, that it cannot be administered, it must be organized." (Cited in Huntington, 1968:395.)

.......)logy are often some of the most active purveyors of new techniques or products.[6]

When the inputs needed for improved production are scarce and some rationing system is desirable to spread them most fairly and productively, LA is more likely than private distributors to be able to handle this in keeping with policy objectives being more directly subject to state authority. Cooperatives or other membership organizations can be enlisted in this, but whether or not they can avoid corruption depends on their traditions and on the degree of local stratification, which could lead to elite domination and manipulation. Whenever there are shortages any local institution is liable to distorting influences.

If use of inputs such as seed or fertilizer is thought to be productive and to benefit not just producers but also the public at large, arguments can be made to subsidize them. LA will probably be the channel of choice for such purposes, though subsidized distribution can be handled through private agencies or through MOs and cooperatives with the same caveats about possible corruption applying as mentioned above. Subsidies create incentives for corrupt practices to which no form of local institution can be assuredly immune. In deciding among channels, their respective histories should be considered to see which is most disposed by precedent to retain reasonable standards of conduct. Also, if subsidies—or shortages—are substantial, new "precedents" may emerge.

Extension advice as a service rather than a good is less visibly liable to maldistribution through corruption though its distribution can be similarly unequal. A detailed study of extension services in western Kenya by Leonard (1977) found that a "progressive" farmer was forty-two times more likely to get an extension visit than was a "traditional" farmer. Extension can be provided through private sector channels as seen from the successful work on commercial crops like cotton and tobacco in a number of countries. However, most extension work will be done through agents who are part of the LA cadre.

The problems of getting good extension advice to farmers through local administration channels are many, quite apart from how it gets distributed to farmers. The problems are so common that they need no documentation.

- Extension workers often receive little useful information from their agency to transmit, or there is little information available that could improve the farming system.

---

[6]In several cases of diffusion of agricultural technology, farmers stole and spread new varieties that they saw as particularly advantageous—high-yielding wheat seeds from Punjab Agricultural University plots in India and a better variety of potato (*Renacimiento*) from experimenters' fields in Peru (personal communications from Mohinder S. Mudahar and William F. Whyte). So the role of institutions in technology diffusion should not be exaggerated. On this, see Nicholson (1984), but also Goodell (1984).

- Being posted in the hinterland, extension workers are often isolated and ignored, thereby becoming demoralized.
- They tend to avoid taking responsibility because they are outside the decision-making process and initiative is not encouraged or rewarded.
- They are often burdened with many tasks besides agricultural extension work and they have many bureaucratic duties to fulfill.[7]
- They work in an atmosphere of uncertainty, not knowing how long they will be posted in that area, and thus feeling little identity with it.
- The conditions of work are generally difficult and the facilities for transportation and communication inadequate.

Because performance of extension services is usually far below their potential, judgments about their utility should be made in terms of what could reasonably be achieved with some reforms and reorientation, rather than in terms of present activity. For example, Roling and Jiggins (1982) suggest that the effectiveness of extension agents could be improved by not having them play "regulatory" roles in addition to their more important "advisory" roles. If extension agents are monitoring and enforcing soil conservation measures, for example, farmers are less likely to listen to them on improving production practices (Temple, 1972).

One approach that has been introduced to increase LA effectiveness has been the "training and visit" (T&V) system supported by the World Bank (Benor and Harrison, 1977; Cernea et al., 1983). It seeks to ensure and standardize the performance of extension cadre through fortnightly training sessions. Simple standard messages are given to extension agents to take to a series of "contact farmers," whom they are to meet fortnightly and who in turn are supposed to carry the messages to other farmers.

This methodology, when it works, is most effective when there is:

(a) an unutilized but productive technology readily diffusable;
(b) a degree of supervision over farmers' production;
(c) a uniform pattern of farming, preferably monocropping; and
(d) relative homogeneity among farmers (Howell, 1982).

These conditions are unlikely to apply in very many areas and this limits the applicability of the approach.

One additional problem with the T&V approach is that it has focused so heavily on messages and on meetings that it has seldom tackled the local institutional development requirements for productive linkage with the farming community, particularly effective organization among farmers. Legitimacy needs to be built up not just for the activity but for the channel

---

[7]Examples and data on this were given in footnote 23 in Chapter One. Reducing such bureaucratic demands on time would be an important contribution to LID for the extension service in most countries.

through which activity occurs so that both the channel and the activity become institutionalized.

Studies have suggested that even when messages get to a contact farmer, they do not go much farther. Contact farmers have usually been chosen by the extension agent or are elected only perfunctorily by a set of farmers who have been brought together by the agent and do not constitute a real group with any sense of solidarity and mutual responsibility. The contact farmer is not socially accountable to such a quasi-group. Thus, the transmission of messages commonly breaks down at this lowest but crucial level for lack of local organizational underpinning for LA activities.[8]

The orientation of the LA organization and staff is important when trying to judge its potential for work with farmers. As a rule LA works more frequently and congenially with more advantaged farmers. Indeed, Tendler (1982) has suggested that Departments of Agriculture and rural banks derive bureaucratic power from their ability to provide subsidized inputs to local elites, so they are likely to resist reorientation of their services toward less privileged groups. On the other hand, in cases such as reported in Botswana by Willett (1981), one finds some extension agents working quite actively on behalf of small farmers and rural women. In the majority of cases, it appears that there needs to be some amount of bureaucratic reorientation (Section 7.5.4) if LA staff are to become productively engaged with typical farmers in need of technical assistance.

The activities of marketing and processing are further discussed below when considering the role of cooperatives and private businesses. We note here that, of the various support activities, marketing and processing do not appear particularly suited to government agencies. Maintaining price stability is about the only thing such agencies can accomplish by their intervention. Seldom do they act as an intermediary between farmers and the commercial or export market in ways that increase farmers' production and benefits. Only the monopoly power of government buying and processing agencies keeps them from looking as uneconomic as they actually are (Bates, 1981). In Jamaica state marketing corporations contributed to a decline in output of certain crops rather than to an increase as intended when they were set up (Annex Five).

---

[8]A study of T&V in Thailand found that so much of the program's effort was concentrated on getting messages "out" (or "down") that there was little attention paid to the information that farmers could, and in principle were supposed to, contribute to a two-way flow back to the researchers and planners (Compton, 1982). A study analyzing the operation of T&V in a major project in Sri Lanka concluded that the percentage of farmers in regular contact with the contact farmers was not sufficient to make the program effective (Gunawardana and Chandrasiri, 1981). Another study of a T&V program in Sri Lanka found only about one-quarter of the contact farmers actually elected by a group, but found a high correlation between their being elected and their being "suitable" contact farmers according to six objective criteria like knowledge, attending meetings, etc. (Hindori and van Renselaar, 1982).

There is no question that the technical and policy requirements of agricultural development will establish a substantial LA role in every country, but this needs to be evolved in conjunction with other institutional channels. One of the considerations when weighing LID alternatives is the fact that once a government undertakes certain functions, it usually pre-empts other channels, private or voluntary, from entering that area of activity. A decision to use LA staff and to enhance LA capabilities for a task is not an independent choice. It has implications for whether or not other local institutions can and will expand their capacity. Accordingly the challenge is to work out a network of different channels, which will enhance each other's effectiveness in their respective tasks.

5.2.2 Local Government

LG institutions play less of a role in agricultural development than might be expected. In our review of experience, we found few instances where they had much substantial direct responsibility in the area of agriculture. For example, although the legislation that established panchayat local government in India in 1957 envisioned an active role in agriculture for these bodies, this has not materialized (Nicholson, 1973). The reasons for this are worth considering. From the vantage point of a local government, the technical requirements for agricultural improvement may appear to be beyond LG competence, and LA agencies may encourage such a perception to keep control over decision making about agriculture. This is apparent in India where the bureaucracy has kept a tight hold on agricultural functions (Haragopal, 1980; Reddy, 1982). Still, this does not seem a sufficient explanation because the panchayats could have played a larger role if their leadership had been more assertive.[9]

A more theoretically interesting reason may be that most agricultural production is private and its benefits are private rather than public goods.[10] Even though village panchayats in India are notoriously dominated by larger and more prosperous farmers who could use their authority to promote agricultural innovations of special interest to themselves, LGs appear to have undertaken mostly activities of a public goods nature like roads or water supply that are ostensibly more broadly beneficial and thus less controversial. Richer farmers can "legitimately" pursue their agricultural interests through membership organizations like cooperatives as is regularly

---

[9]One detailed study of Indian local administration and politics found that areas of higher productivity and agricultural growth had more political pressures for performance, coming mostly from the panchayat system (Bjorkman, 1979:219). Even then, the panchayats tended to be more involved in lobbying and planning efforts than in service provision for agriculture.

[10]"Public goods" have been discussed in Section 3.3. That local governments may feel constrained to provide "public goods" was proposed by Nicholson (1973).

done.[11] Since local government bodies are established to benefit all the persons within their jurisdiction, those activities which are useful to any and all community members will maintain or enhance LG legitimacy. According to this reasoning, a health clinic or a school is a more appropriate undertaking for a local government than an irrigation channel or a fertilizer program.[12]

A separate explanation based on bureaucratic considerations is that local governments invariably come under the jurisdiction of some other ministry than the Ministry of Agriculture. A Ministry of Interior, of Local Administration, or of Home Affairs may steer local governments away from agriculture because of concerns about bureaucratic "turf." Similarly a Ministry of Agriculture may not like to have its staff assist in local government programs. Where such problems of territoriality exist, they would need to be overcome before LID efforts could succeed in strengthening local government capacity to work directly on agricultural development.

If local governments provide infrastructure as discussed in Chapter Three or play an active role in forest or rangeland management as suggested in Chapter Two, these are valuable indirect contributions to agricultural development (see Section I.D. of Table 5.1). The question is usually, What other local institutions will play primary roles? While we conclude that in general the direct role of local government in agricultural development is limited, we found cases where LG institutions made substantial contributions to agriculture. Usually these were institutions "descended" from traditional local government roles such as those mentioned above from Bolivia and Peru and documented by Isbell (1978). A common factor in these instances is that practically the whole community is engaged in agricultural activity and landholdings are relatively equal, so almost all members of the community have a similar stake in increasing or guaranteeing production. Management of irrigation systems in Pakistan and Indonesia through community institutions fits both of these conditions (Bhatty, 1979; Coward, 1983). Such conditions—links of local government to traditional roles and

---

[11]A detailed demonstration of such control is found in Blue and Junghare (1975) in their study of agricultural yields associated with farmers' access to fertilizer through cooperatives in India. Some farmers getting no fertilizer from the co-op had very good production while others received large amounts of fertilizer but did not have commensurate output. Closer examination showed that the first group was purchasing fertilizer on the black market rather than from the cooperative, being willing and able to pay a higher price for good quality fertilizer that arrived on time. The latter group were officials of the co-op who were taking as much fertilizer as they could get to distribute as payoff to members who had supported their election and who constituted a third group of farmers—those who had better yields than predicted based on their official receipt of fertilizer. A fourth group were farmers who received no fertilizer because they were not allied with the co-op officers.

[12]Ralston et al. (1983:36-38) cite a number of studies from Peru, Kenya, Tanzania, Zambia, Zimbabwe, and elsewhere, where community self-help groups as well as local governments have engaged in activities to build schools, dispensaries, water supply, etc. but not to promote agriculture (e.g. Bratton, 1980). They attribute this pattern to low rural demand for agricultural improvement rather than to the "public choice" explanation suggested here, which I think is more valid.

little economic differentiation of the population—are not likely to be found very widely, however.

Local government under the guidance of vigorous and agriculturally oriented leadership can play a key role in promoting agricultural development. An example is seen in a retrospective study of agricultural development in northern Nigeria (Annex Five). In those areas where policies supportive of agriculture were carried out through the Native Authorities (LG), comparative success in agricultural development without much infusion of central government funds was achieved (Tiffen, 1980). Obviously where local governments are willing and able, with sufficient taxing powers and personnel, to play a larger role in agriculture, this deserves support.

5.2.3 Membership Organizations

Voluntary associations can perform a wide variety of functions to facilitate agricultural development (Oxby, 1983). Membership organizations (MOs) operate like limited-liability companies, but instead of seeking to make a profit, they are formed to serve their members, who hope to benefit from getting better, cheaper, or more reliable goods and services. We distinguish such organizations from cooperatives (Section 5.2.4) which are a special and important kind of local organization that involves the pooling of resources and risks. Generally no pooling of resources is involved in MOs except when an organization negotiates for greater purchasing power or seeks higher selling prices for the group's commodities. Together MOs and co-ops constitute an "intermediary sector" between what are known as the "public" and the "private" sectors as was sketched in Figure 1.1.

Probably the best-known membership organizations serving agriculture are the Farmers' Associations in Taiwan, which have contributed substantially to the advancement of productivity there (Annex Five). The Associations provide farmer-members with extension advice, production inputs, credit, processing, marketing, banking, and other services. Such comprehensive organizations, of course, represent the culmination of a sustained program of developing local institutions. The Japanese colonial administration, which governed Taiwan before World War II, had already started farmer associations decades earlier.

Multi-functional organizations are more likely to develop under environmental conditions where water supplies are good, where tasks and outputs are predictable, and where the level of resources generated can facilitate such an evolution.[13] In environments where soil and rainfall are poor such as Botswana, one is likely to find more specialized, single-function organizations. The vitality of self-help efforts in Botswana has encouraged the

---

[13]This consideration of environmental conditions is analyzed in Section 5.5.

government there to embark on a "group development" program (Kloppenburg, 1983). Some Farmers' Associations and Farmers' Committees in Botswana are in principle multi-purpose but usually they concentrate on a few needed functions. Single-purpose groups are legion in that country. They manage small catchment dams for agricultural and livestock production; they sink and operate wells for irrigating gardens; they rent or purchase tractors for plowing; they construct stock dipping tanks to control cattle ticks; they build drift fences to protect planted fields against cattle damage; they start up poultry or horticultural production (these are mostly women's groups), and so forth.[14] What these membership organizations have in common is that they all enhance or protect the private production of their members. Some goods or services may be sold to nonmembers such as water from a livestock dam or tick-dipping services. This contributes to MO revenue or to MO effectiveness (in the latter example, ticks spread unless all herders control them). These groups also evolve and change functions as new opportunities are recognized, adding activities or forming new organizations to meet these needs.[15]

The functions of local organizations in agriculture can go beyond self-help measures to engage in tasks of technological modernization thus attracting the attention of scientists and administrators (Goodell, 1984). It is not yet common for MOs to hire their own extension staff, but the example of the Taiwanese Farmers' Associations has encouraged planners to see this as possible for other organizations. The Malaysian government sought to introduce the Taiwanese model of organization in the 1970s but without much success because the roles and tasks were being transferred wholesale without modification or experimentation. Subsequently with some bureaucratic reorganization and a less mechanistic approach, farmer organizations were introduced in that country with more promise of effectiveness (Mohamed, 1981).

If technical staff are hired and directed by farmers associations, such extension agents can be held accountable to their clientele, ensuring that knowledge is put at members' disposal with appropriate adaptations to specific field conditions. Also, more energetic follow-up is possible. Another function can be lobbying representatives of the national government to get

---

[14]The structure and performance of these various kinds of associations as well as of parallel traditional institutions are analyzed in Willett (1981) and Brown (1983). Drift fence groups are described in Annex Five as representative of such local initiative in Botswana. Dam groups have been analyzed in detail in Roe and Fortmann (1982) and are discussed in Annex Two.

[15]Such dynamism of self-help groups, called *mwethya* in the Machakos district of Kenya, is documented by Tiffen (1983). She gives an example of a mutual aid society among women engaged in agriculture. This MO used its agricultural earnings to buy sewing machines for members, becoming an informal cooperative to make money by sewing school uniforms. The profits from this were then devoted to establishing a nursery school, so the MO ended up as a service organization with an agricultural base.

more and better services for agriculture or holding local government officials accountable to their constituencies. In the northern Nigerian case
referred to above, villages have been able to secure a greater share of development services through the efforts of the Native Authority (LG) and of
rural interest groups.[16] In Nepal where farmer groups have been organized
under the Small Farmer Development Program, these groups have been
able to curb the local power structure in some places by gaining influence
within the local government (Annex Five).

Perhaps the greatest strength of MOs is their flexibility, which facilitates their identifying needs and mobilizing efforts to meet them. MOs can
retract as readily as they rise or change their form (as the example from
Kenya in footnote 15 indicates). Such flexibility means that these kinds of
groups may not be easily institutionalized. MO contributions, however,
namely the extent to which they can facilitate resource mobilization and
two-way communication, are more important than whether or not they become proper "institutions." Their purpose may be served by a succession of
organizations over time no one of which necessarily lasts a very long time.

5.2.4 Cooperatives

Various kinds of cooperatives can be associated with agricultural improvement. As indicated in Section 5.1, we are not including here the
category of *producer cooperative* since this is a unit of production parallel to
the household, private company, or state enterprise. The resources that
members can pool in cooperatives for economic gain are: (1) *money*, (2) *labor*,
(3) *purchasing power*, and (4) *products*. These are associated with the following kinds of cooperatives:

(1) *Credit unions or savings and loan associations.* These pay interest on
members' savings and provide loans to members. They are not exclusively involved in agriculture but are important for agriculture
where banking institutions are not available and moneylenders
are extractive.

(2) *Labor cooperatives.* These are not as common as formal cooperatives,
but informal ones are fairly common in less commercialized settings
such as in Africa (Seibel and Massing, 1974) or in the Latin American Andes as discussed already.

(3) *Consumer cooperatives or buying clubs.* These can lower prices by
group purchasing of commodities or services. When the goods or

---

[16]"Gombe NA has always vigorously defended expenditure on the villages, protesting
strongly in 1950 when its projects for rural development were excised from the plan. In 1967
Rural Development was the only section of the 1962-68 Plan in which expenditure targets had
actually been exceeded (less than 50 percent of the remainder of Plan projects had been completed). There is a contrast here with Bornu, a centralized emirate, where over (half of its)
Development Plan for 1962-68 was allocated to Public Buildings and Urban Development,
mainly for the capital." (Tiffen, 1980:31)

services are directly involved in agricultural production, two kinds of cooperatives can be classified separately:

(a) *Input supply cooperatives.* The purpose of these co-ops is to get lower priced or better quality agricultural inputs. These are important worldwide for agricultural producers, and

(b) *Marketing cooperatives.* These try to provide more favorable prices for members by grading, processing and/or transporting products in common, or by storing and selling when the price is most advantageous. They are found frequently around the world, giving incentives to members to use new technology and increase production because of more favorable returns to labor.

The last two are the most common kinds of co-ops for agricultural development. Cooperatives can vary considerably in form. The following distinctions can apply to other kinds of local organizations but are particularly relevant for cooperatives:

(1) *Functions.* Co-ops can range from *single-function*, covering just one of the resources noted above, to *multiple-function*, dealing with several of them. Multi-purpose cooperative societies are fairly common in South Asia, handling credit, agricultural inputs, and marketing, as well as consumer goods in some cases.

(2) *Structure.* Co-ops can be *simple* organizations operating independently, or they can be federated into *larger, more complex* organizations linking base-level primary societies into two, three, four, or more tiers of organization.

(3) *Objectives.* Co-ops can be *purely economic*, with the material advantage of their members as the only goal, or they can have broader *socio-political goals* as well, viewing the co-op as a means for achieving social change and even wielding political influence.[17]

(4) *Membership.* Co-ops can be *exclusive,* restricting membership (e.g. permitting only small farmers to join) or they can be *inclusive*, allowing anybody who contributes a specified share (of money, labor, or material goods) to become a member.

(5) *Initiative.* Co-ops can be started by their *members* alone, or at *government* or *PVO* instigation. Those in the former category have generally been more successful but no strict delineation is possible because a co-op started by its members may become coopted by the government through economic or legal strings; conversely one set up by government may become quite independently run by its members.

Almost all of these combinations can occur. For example, a marketing cooperative may have been started by its members or at government

---

[17]If there are no economic objectives, it would not be a cooperative. Dobrin in his study of Kenyan cooperatives notes two contending views—that cooperatives are "essentially economic tools," i.e., business organizations, or "essentially social organizations which serve a need more basic than an economic one" (1970:108-109).

initiative; it may move on to perform other functions or may continue to focus only on one task; it may have just economic goals or not; its membership may be exclusive or open to anyone.

The most important variable observed in cooperatives is:

(6) *Accountability.* To whom is the cooperative accountable? Are its decisions made mostly in the interests of its members, or are they shaped in response to government objectives and policies? Do officers look mostly "downward" to members or "upward" to officials? Do members see the cooperative as belonging to themselves or to the government?

In some organizations called "cooperatives"

- the functions are not ones which members understand and appreciate,
- the structure is complex and lower levels of organization are controlled by personnel at higher levels (rather than vice versa),
- the objectives are broader or narrower than members want,
- membership is so open that there is no sense of mutual responsibility (the co-op is in effect a public utility),
- the organization was not the members' idea in the first place, and
- it operates in response to government interests and directions.

Such organizations are essentially public sector organizations (LA) rather than cooperatives. A substantial proportion of co-ops in developing countries are "cooperatives" in name only. Others operate only partially along cooperative lines, constrained by standardized models of organization and by government controls.

If cooperatives always operated as they are intended to, they would be ideal contributors to agricultural development. Unfortunately actual experience is quite mixed. King says of the cooperatives he studied in northern Nigeria:

> The institution created in the villages was insubstantial and dependent on government patronage. If credit or the rewards of leadership were removed, it would collapse immediately. The sophisticated organization described in the rule books would not provide a framework for the rural population to mobilize their own resources and undertake activities immediately useful to them. Rather, the existence of the sophisticated legally registered cooperative, dependent on government credit and authoritarian leadership, inhibited the formation of small simple self-sufficient groups which could be responsible to local needs and might form the basis of genuine village institutional development. (King, 1983:278)

A review of World Bank project experience suggests that co-ops have a high mortality rate within three to eight years of their inception when their initial momentum has passed and the complexities of accounting and management are confronted (Cernea, 1982a). There are, however, some impressive cooperatives that have survived many years and contributed both to increased production and to members' welfare. Examples would include the AMUL dairy cooperative in India (Korten, 1980; Paul, 1982:15-36), the Sukuma cotton growers' cooperative in Tanzania (Lang et al., 1969) and the

Portland-Blue Mountain Coffee Cooperative Society in Jamaica (Gow et al., 1979). A recent study of a number of Bolivian cooperatives found much more basis for approval than the author had expected (Tendler, 1983).

It has been suggested that co-ops do better if they limit themselves to a single function (Tendler, 1976), but this may be a matter of phasing. Esman and Uphoff (1984) found on the basis of quantitative case study analysis that, other things being equal, having multiple functions is associated on average with greater success in performing all of them. This does not mean, however, that co-ops or other local organizations should start with multiple tasks. Rather they do better starting with one or a few activities moving to take on more only when their members feel a definite need for this and feel capable of managing them.

Cooperatives often experience difficulties in competing with private marketing or supply companies because of their financial structure (Turtianen and Von Pischke, 1982). Whereas private firms have a clear incentive to re-invest earnings to build up capital and become technologically more advanced, co-op members may prefer to distribute profits because they perceive less personal advantage from the accumulated book value of assets. Also, cooperatives must maintain satisfactory relations with many different sets of actors: their members, the government, their employees, their customers (where nonmembers also do business with them). If any of these become dissatisfied, the organization can be undermined.

One problem faced almost universally, though not always succumbed to, is corruption. Few things are more deadly for a co-op than this since loss of members' confidence and support will kill it quickly. One should not exonerate those responsible for corruption, but it is often partly a consequence of the way the co-ops have been set up. Fieldwork on coffee cooperatives in the Bukusu area of western Kenya concluded that the observably pervasive corruption could be traced to the way they had been established by colonial authorities (Hamer, 1981). A foreign structure was imposed on a society that was not well acquainted with cash let alone with formal-legal organizations. There was no attempt to incorporate traditional roles or sanctions. The externally constructed system was incomprehensible to local co-op members and employees who had limited numerical and writing skills. The requirement of frequent meetings was seen as a waste of time. So a series of informal procedures grew up allowing substantial abuses of co-op resources.[18]

The domination of cooperatives by government officials may be as

---

[18]The lack of controls was not due to the absence of government regulations (there were plenty of those) but to the lack of community sanctions, which would have been more effective if utilized. Hamer concluded, based on his previous fieldwork in rural Ethiopia (1976), where indigenously based organizations do control corruption, that more decentralized decision making and sanctioning procedures involving members in oversight of cooperatives could have controlled abuses.

damaging to co-ops as corruption.[19] When co-ops are effectively under the control of officials, they should be considered as LA and not as local organizations. On the other hand, administered honestly and efficiently, they may make a contribution to agricultural development even when there is little membership participation in their management. The AMUL dairy cooperative in India comes close to such a situation. Its large scale is such that its base-level societies cannot do more than approve the plans of the managers. This organization is unusual, however, in the extent to which its management has retained high standards of honesty and hard work.

Size presents a dilemma for cooperatives. Control over officers and staff is easier to maintain in small organizations (Doherty and Jodha, 1979; Bennett, 1983:38-40), yet the economies of scale that co-ops can garner for members when purchasing inputs or in processing and selling produce are made possible by larger organizations. Maintaining high standards of conduct within cooperatives generally requires active oversight by members. Unfortunately members' efforts to control abuses are easiest to elicit when a co-op is not being well run. When it is operating successfully, there are few incentives for members to invest time in overseeing management, though an abundance of funds may itself increase temptations. This problem is often dealt with in Latin American co-ops by members' appointing "vigilance" committees that review and report on financial affairs (e.g., Bruce, 1980).

Cooperatives are usually reasonably careful when handling their own members' money. Financial problems arise most often when some substantial amount of money from the government is involved. This was observed in the case of the Comilla farmer's cooperatives in East Pakistan (now Bangladesh). These were one of the most hopeful demonstrations of how small farmers could be enlisted in agricultural improvements (Millikan and Hapgood, 1967; Mosher, 1969; Owens and Shaw, 1972). Members deposited savings on a weekly basis and made loans to themselves as needed with a high rate of repayment. The government later sought to utilize these channels for a large-scale credit program to promote new agricultural technologies. With the large influx of government funds, however, not only record-keeping and management deteriorated but also the incentive to repay declined (Annex Five).

These considerations pose the question of what functions co-ops can best perform in support of agricultural development. Cooperative credit unions and savings and loan associations appear attractive as channels for getting capital into agriculture. Loans and repayments are usually handled more satisfactorily when members' funds are involved as members hesitate

---

[19]The corruption may emanate from officials, as documented in rural Thailand (TKRI, 1980) and northern Nigeria (King, 1975). King presents detailed diagrams showing how both credit and marketing activities of the cooperatives diverged from the way they were supposed to operate under the control of members.

to deprive each other of assets. But there are limits on how much co-ops can expand their loan services with only members' deposits to draw on. Outside resources can be channelled into such co-ops to increase the volume of their loans, but any large infusion of funds is likely to lead to the kind of experience reported from Bangladesh. Whereas people are usually quite concerned to repay private loans, there is an assumption, often created by politicians, that "government" funds do not need to be repaid. Thus, using private or state banking channels, even if some subsidy must be paid to the banks to handle small-scale loans, seems preferable to using cooperative mechanisms for extending large amounts of agricultural credit. The feasibility of this is suggested by experience reported from the Grameen Bank also in Bangladesh (Annex Eight).

If one turns to private or public sector institutions for handling loans to small farmers or landless households, some form of *group lending* may be preferred over giving credit on an individual basis. Group lending reduces administrative costs of processing the loan and increases rates of repayment because the group is collectively liable, as discussed in Chapter Six. This approach underlies the Small Farmer Development Program in Nepal and the Plan Puebla farmer committees in Mexico (Annex Five) as well as various programs for promoting small-scale, nonagricultural enterprises in LDCs (Farbman, 1981; Ashe, 1985). Some effort must go into getting such groups formed and they may not themselves become institutions. But having such groups in operation can become institutionalized as they connect up with banks or government agencies which are institutions.

Cooperative institutions are generally more effective in providing other inputs than credit. However, they must be able to operate in a businesslike manner or they will not survive especially when competing with private enterprises. If input supplies are scarce, as noted already, co-op staff or officers handling them may be tempted to engage in illicit practices. If given a monopoly over inputs, there are similar temptations.[20] On the other hand, if private dealers have a monopoly or monopsony, their performance may be improved and their price manipulations checked by having competition

---

[20]One of the clearest examples of cooperatives producing counter-developmental results occurred in Ghana in 1965-66. Knowing that its popularity was slipping, the government gave the United Ghana Farmers Council, by then a wing of the ruling party, a monopoly over the subsidized distribution of machetes, hoping to boost support for the regime. Machetes, the principal implement for cultivation in southern Ghana, were in short supply because imports had been cut in anticipation of the opening of a new factory to produce them in-country. But co-op officials, having a monopoly and operating more as petty government officials than as cooperative functionaries, held back the machetes supplied, selling them instead on the "black market" for many times the official price. This exacerbated the shortage of farm tools, reduced food supplies and raised food prices in the cities (the price of corn went up to more than three times the world market price). Moreover, it undermined still further the regime's base of support and a military coup shortly thereafter was successful. The UGFC is discussed in Annex Five.

from co-ops. This is yet another example of the value of having combinations of local institutions.

Probably the functions to which cooperatives can make the clearest contribution are *processing and marketing*. These tasks may seem more technically difficult than handling credit or input supplies but they are easier to manage for two reasons: the accounting is quite simple and the problem of collecting payments, which can be such a source of financial losses in supply and credit co-ops, does not exist (Tendler, 1983). Marketing co-ops enable producers to get the best possible return from their output, which gives farmers incentive to increase production and more income to invest in further improvement.

Another reason for marketing co-ops' success appears to be the commonality of interest between large and small producers. In most processing and marketing situations, large producers benefit by having small producers contribute their produce to the cooperative. A larger volume makes processing more efficient, lowers unit costs, and strengthens the market position of the co-op when selling the produce. This is seen, for example, with the Bolivian co-ops and the cotton cooperatives in India reported in Annex Five.

The advantages of cooperative processing and marketing operations are fairly obvious. Sometimes a government, wishing to make such operations more efficient by expanding their scale, and possibly with a view to gaining control over them, has given cooperatives the sole right to buy or process a crop like coffee or cocoa. Organizations nominally established as cooperatives to perform these functions in Ghana and in Jamaica turned out to be man-made calamities (Annex Five). Co-ops as an institutional form are no less vulnerable than state bureaucracies or private firms to the distorting effects of monopoly, and their efficiency and their benefits to producers have usually suffered when given absolute market power. As one among several competing channels, however, co-ops have a lot to offer in agricultural development, but like other channels, they can only contribute to—not by themselves accomplish—local institutional development for agriculture.

5.2.5 Service Organizations

Local service organizations are found more often engaged in activities like education or primary health care than in agricultural development. SOs are often church-related organizations working at the locality level with very poor communities and justifying their efforts as works of charity.

Though few in number, the documented cases we found of SO activity in agriculture were encouraging. One example was a Catholic organization working on small-scale irrigation and ox traction in northern Ghana in the

1940s and 1950s. This effort was quite innovative in its time but was super-seded by less effective government programs (Prosser, 1982). The Catholic-sponsored Kottar Social Service Society in Tamil Nadu, India, though involved mainly with primary health care, helped organize almost 10,000 small farmers (most of them having less than one-quarter of an acre) to install field channels for irrigating their land (see Annex Seven). In Mexi-co a secular organization, FORUSA, established by persons desiring to demonstrate a service orientation of private capital, usefully assisted small farmers on a fee-for-service but not-for-profit basis (Whyte and Boynton, 1983:202-205). Other examples of service organizations, particularly reli-gious organizations, supporting agriculture are cited by Ralston et al. (1983:47-49).

It is difficult to reach judgments about SOs when their number in the literature on agricultural development is so small. When there is sufficient motivation on the part of the providers to sustain a program, whether out of religious, ideological, or personal values, and when adequate resources can be procured, SOs are almost ideal because of the structural flexibility they have, being bound neither by bureaucratic rules nor by profit considera-tions. Institutionalization of SOs, however, depends more on staff and donors than on beneficiaries. The latter are not "members" and have no con-trol over the organization. Accordingly they have no obligations to it and need not support it in a way that would give it broad institutional founda-tions. To be sure, if staff and donors feel a strong enough stake in the organization's continuation, they can make it into an "institution" through their own sustained efforts. Even so, at least some minimum acceptance and valuation within the community is needed for such a service organization to become institutionalized in some substantial way.

The role of service organizations may be more that of a catalytic than an operational agent for agriculture. Three of the four cooperatives that Tendler studied in Bolivia had been started with Catholic Church leader-ship. A case study of cooperative development in the Dominican Republic showed a crucial role played by the local church (Sharpe, 1977). The strong peasant organizations in Honduras, which have helped implement land reform and supported agricultural research activities there, (Whyte and Boynton, 1983:176-190) were launched decades earlier with church sup-port. Thus, service organizations may play an important indirect, if not a direct, role in agricultural development by strengthening other kinds of local institutions.

5.2.6 Private Business

The role of the private sector in agricultural development is rarely ad-dressed in terms of LID. The literature deals mostly with comparative claims of efficiency in resource allocation, while the institutional aspects and contributions of local private enterprises are seldom examined. The literature is also dominated by stereotypes, rendering judgments difficult to make. The image of the money-grubbing village storekeeper who makes usurious loans and pays miserly prices for commodities, clashes with that of the efficient, well-stocked service-oriented store, which gives free agricultural extension advice to all who ask for it. There is little empirical basis for assessing how often either view has validity or for knowing the frequency of positive and negative performances by private entrepreneurs. Complicating these contradictory images are the conflicting interpretations of the role of multi-national corporations in developing countries. Some describe MNCs as serving to modernize production (e.g. Freeman, 1981) while others see them as exploiting farmers and thus leading to economic and social stagnation (Feder, 1978).

A private business, like a cooperative, will seldom be adequate, equitable, or even efficient if it is the only channel in a rural area for handling inputs and outputs. However, private businesses can make very valuable contributions as part of a system of local institutions, mediating between households and individuals on one hand, and district, regional, or higher institutions on the other. The question is where and for what are private businesses especially suited or unsuited.

The first consideration is the potential for profit. Are the operations that support agricultural improvement, such as input supply or grain processing and storage, as attractive as other business opportunities for investment? In certain disadvantaged areas, there is insufficient commercializable activity to make a private enterprise pay. Where yields are poor and uncertain, with incomes accordingly low and variable, businesses are not likely to become involved in input or output services. Changes in the technological level of agricultural production are then more likely to come through government initiative (LA) or possibly from the community itself through collective self-help channels.

On the other hand, private entrepreneurs are generally more attuned to new opportunities than are government institutions. The stimulus of potential profit can induce persons to innovate and persevere where those only "doing their job" would not venture. Thus, private entrepreneurs may be better than official personnel for starting new services in unpromising locations. Any judgment about the comparative advantage of channels would have to compare just how entrepreneurial businessmen are in a specific situation as opposed to bureaucrats. Having some competition between private and public sector channels may itself be worth planning for.

For specific supporting activities, private channels have many advantages in the provision of credit and other inputs. Private enterprises can be attracted to start and sustain businesses wherever profitable opportunities exist. The difficulty is that profitability is not always fully known in advance by producers or by suppliers, and private businesses must be persuaded that there are potential profits before making investments that will permit producers in turn to invest in higher production. To turn all decisions about credit and input supply over to private decision makers can seriously constrain agricultural expansion, which is why most LDC governments have retained at least some role in this area.

The same logic that leads a government to subsidize the use of a new input can justify subsidies for its distribution. What may not appear profitable when used with little experience or on a small scale can indeed produce net benefits once better practices are learned and economies of scale are realized. Whether or not private vendors will be appropriate channels for such inputs depends on whether agreed price levels can be enforced when demand at the subsidized price begins to exceed supply. Private dealers are harder to regulate than government stores or cooperatives though the latter also present problems in practice. Once a technology with the characteristics of a private good[21] has proved profitable for all concerned, the case for handing distribution over to the private sector is strong unless there is a scarcity situation requiring rationing. If there is reason to have competition, possibly distribution can be augmented by cooperative channels. For the functions of processing and marketing, the case for a private sector role is quite strong because one is dealing with commodities that exist rather than trying to elicit ones that have not yet been produced.

State agencies have a rather unsatisfactory record when it comes to buying and handling commodities. The temptation to give short weight and to undergrade produce is notoriously strong for poorly paid government staff.[22] Private buyers and sellers have the same incentive to pay as little as possible but they can be bargained with, and usually sellers can find some alternative buyers. Studies of middlemen in the grain trade in India have shown them to be paying prices that cover real costs of operation and do not produce a profit in excess of other investment opportunities (Lele, 1971).

The basic strength of private businesses is the incentive for efficient and innovative use of resources, which competition can encourage. The option of regulated private monopolies, often used in the area of public utilities, does not seem as feasible in the agricultural area as in infrastructure. Where responsiveness to changing conditions and risk-taking are important, private operations have an advantage over state-owned ones.

One function in which the private sector has a clear advantage over other institutional channels is in the repair of agricultural machinery and generally in its manufacture. There are few cooperative, let alone state, workshops that can compete with private ones. Ruddle and Rondinelli

---

[21]This characterization, which includes divisibility and excludability of benefits, was discussed in Section 3.3.

[22]A government may take over and operate a cooperative as if it were a state enterprise. This happened in Ghana with the United Ghana Farmers Council under Nkrumah (Annex Five).

(1984:80) point out that quite different private enterprises operate at the community, locality, and higher levels in making and repairing machinery. In villages one finds all blacksmith shops where artisans produce simple tools and fix equipment, sometimes even tractors and trucks. More complex manufacture and many repairs are done in enterprises at the locality level with all major production and the most complicated repairs left to companies at regional or national levels.

We began our discussion of private businesses with the observation that no single kind is likely to be sufficient by itself, which applies to the discussion of local institutions in general. Review of LID experience has confirmed our earlier conclusion (Uphoff and Esman, 1974) that promoting a *system of organizations* mediating between the individual or household and higher economic, administrative, and political levels is more promising than establishing any particular single channel.

The complementarities among channels are quite evident in agriculture as each of the kinds of local institutions analyzed has some advantages and disadvantages. For example, if private businesses perform certain agricultural support functions, this costs the government little or nothing compared to what it would pay to accomplish the task through local administration. On the other hand, businesses are set up to advance their own interests not some general public interest, which is the government's responsibility, so they may not be responsive to needs the government has to serve. For some tasks, the least costly method may also be least effective.

This consideration of alternatives has assessed the components of a local institutional network that could inform, encourage, assist, and reward producers as they engage in the activities that raise food and fiber for themselves, their communities, the nation and possibly for export. We need to look also at the *commodities*, the *conditions*, and the *producers* involved to gain a better understanding of how differences in these characteristics affect what will be the most appropriate institutions and combinations for a given situation of agricultural development. But first, we need to consider the general subject of *interdependence and dependence* of producers and its effect on their disposition to cooperate in collective action and with higher level institutions since this interacts with the various characteristics to be analyzed.

5.3 FACTORS OF INTERDEPENDENCE AND DEPENDENCE

Among the most important considerations in LID planning and implementation are the relationships between persons and institutions that physical, economic, and social circumstances can establish or predispose. One needs to look at these relationships both *horizontally* (among persons and institutions at the same level) and *vertically* (between levels). The extent of interdependence or dependence will influence the ease or difficulty of initiating and maintaining collective activity though it does not by itself determine outcomes.

5.3.1 Horizontal Interdependence

Producers may be interdependent in a number of ways thereby creating incentives for cooperation in some kind of local institution—public, private, or volunteer. The following variables can influence interdependence:

(a) **Topography**—hill environments can require cooperation to control water flow so that soil erosion and leaching of nutrients are reduced;

(b) **Location**—in irrigation systems there is interdependence between "upstream" and "downstream" farmers; failure to cooperate leads to crop loss for the latter and to conflict;

(c) **Plant protection**—limiting pests by coordinating planting schedules, by fencing, or by bird scaring (ad hoc bird scaring by individuals has little effect);

(d) **Production activities**—forming joint plowing teams, or planting paddy seedlings by work groups;[23]

(e) **Marketing**—timing harvesting and sales to attain better prices—staggering sales to avoid a glut on the market or coordinating sales to get more favorable terms (through selling in bulk or hiring cheaper transportation);

(f) **Processing**—joint processing to achieve economies of scale and also quality control for better price returns;

(g) **Varietal selection**—coordinated choice of varieties to avoid deterioration of stock, to control pests, to improve robustness, or to spread risks;

(h) **Complementarity**—pastoralists and agriculturalists may benefit by coordinating livestock and crop activities, with livestock grazing on crop residues and providing manure to enhance soil quality for subsequent planting;

(i) **Credit**—moneylending for agricultural inputs or for emergencies;

(j) **Seeds**—some producers can specialize in seed production (e.g., for potatoes or rice) and then exchange seed for consumable or saleable produce;

(k) **Competing uses of resources**—different demands for water, soil, or forest resources can create conflict, but the need to work out some *modus vivendi* to reconcile competing demands can give impetus for cooperation;

---

[23]Most examples of joint labor come from irrigated areas, but dryland agriculturalists can also be dependent on mutual cooperation (Hill, 1982). Getting land prepared for planting and then planting it right after the first rains can make a significant difference in yield. Group action may thus be quite important in rainfed agriculture, as Vincent (1971) shows in a rural community in Uganda.

(l) **Ecological stability**—having to manage natural resources within stable limits to preserve them over time establishes interdependence.

Insofar as these considerations can create interdependence among producers, this does not necessarily mean producers will organize themselves and support institutions to handle the various problems effectively. Program planners should look at the number and kind of factors most likely to dispose agriculturalists to cooperate horizontally as an indication of the probable ease or difficulty with which greater participation in local institutions for agriculture could be promoted.

5.3.2 Vertical Linkages

Given the differences in power commonly entailed by vertical relationships, one should not assume that such relations will automatically establish beneficial interdependence between producers and higher level institutions. Dependence and exploitation may be the result. Whether vertical relations are positive or negative needs to be assessed separately from whether or not producers have reason to interact vertically with local or supra-local institutions. Factors contributing to vertical dependence of producers on institutions outside their community or locality include:

(a) **Inputs**—need for credit, seeds (supply and certification), and other inputs like fertilizer and chemicals:

(b) **Processing**—important especially if the product needs quick and high-quality processing, e.g. milk and tea, as discussed in Section 5.4;

(c) **Marketing**—important especially if the crop is not consumed as food, e.g. tobacco or cotton;

(d) **Transportation and/or storage**—important particularly if the commodity is perishable or especially vulnerable to pests.[24]

Where rural producers depend on assistance from higher-level institutions that are manipulative or extractive, producers are likely to react with antagonism and withdrawal. Such a one-sided situation is not conducive for having and sustaining a dynamic agricultural sector. A relationship of mutual *interdependence* between institutions at local and higher levels will be more productive over the long run than having local institutions that are thoroughly dependent on higher-level institutions in economic, technological, legal, social and other ways.

---

[24]We see from various examples the importance of the nature of the crop, discussed in the next section. Potatoes, for example, present many problems of spoilage and disease during storage and also the problem of shrinkage. Andean peasants store their potatoes separately to reduce risks of loss due to pests or disease, but also because they would find it difficult to determine reduced shares by weight after potatoes have been stored collectively for some time and have shrunk.

Mutually satisfactory terms of exchange should lead to substainable productive activity on both sides, being reinforced by the contributions that each makes to the other's success. This requires local institutions capable of planning and implementing programs of activity on their own and able to "speak back" to a higher-level institution when its proposals are found to be technically unsound or economically disadvantageous.

Local institutions based on horizontal interdependence among members, constituents, or clientele should be better able to contribute to mutually strong and beneficial vertical interdependence over time. By the same token, vertical assistance from higher level to local institutions enabling the latter to function more effectively, should encourage producers to enter into more horizontal cooperation, which strengthens the capability of local institutions. These are general but somewhat abstract principles of LID strategy. They become more concrete by considering the significance of differences in *commodity* characteristics, in the *conditions of production* and in the characteristics of *producers* as these affect LID choices.

5.4 IMPLICATIONS OF DIFFERENCES IN COMMODITIES

Producing different commodities presents agriculturalists not only with varying technical problems but also with varying local institutional requirements. The simplest example is to contrast growing field crops with raising large herds of cattle. In the first instance the area locus of activity is fixed, whereas with the second it must vary unless the animals are stall fed. At the extreme of transhumance, not only animals but whole human communities move hundreds, even thousands of miles a year. The jurisdiction of local governments is territorially demarcated and may become irrelevant to migratory populations. Membership organizations, on the other hand, can be as mobile as the people they serve. Authority relations, for example, being intimately associated with the people who give and receive commands, will be more personal than geographic so conventional LG may need to be restructured for pastoral compared to agricultural production. In order to be effective, local administration will have to "follow the herds" or distribute responsibility among several LA units during each year.

The permutations of crops and cropping patterns are almost infinite so our analysis can only indicate the kinds of LID implications to be looked for in more specific circumstances. The key concepts from organization theory that illuminate these relationships have just been discussed—*dependence* and *interdependence,* viewed both horizontally and vertically.

Two of the most successful organizations-become-institutions currently raising the productivity and well-being of small farmer households are the AMUL dairy cooperative in India (Korten, 1980; Paul, 1982:15-36) and the Kenya Tea Development Authority (Steeves, 1975; Lamb and Mueller, 1982; Paul, 1982:51-62). AMUL is a cooperative in its structure while KTDA is a parastatal body with a network of farmer-grower committees (MOs) attached. These cases exemplify how the nature of the commodity appears to influence the success as well as the form and operation of the institution.

Although these organizations represent different types of local institutions, the structures of KTDA and AMUL are remarkably similar. The KTDA committees operate in much the same manner as the AMUL primary cooperative societies. These base-level units collect the product (raw milk or fresh-picked tea leaves) from farmers twice daily and handle weighing, quality control, and payment. They work with members on behalf of the higher level parent organization to improve the quality and amount of production and also get involved in matters like road improvement because collection must be timely and regular.

The two activities, milk and tea production, have a great deal in common apart from both producing beverages. In both instances production is continuous, not seasonal as with many other crops. Thus, the members are usually in daily contact with the organization through which they deliver and sell their product. It assumes great importance in their lives.

The product itself is dependent on *processing*. True, milk can be consumed unprocessed but it cannot be preserved in its fresh state. It needs to be refrigerated and pasteurized or converted into a dairy product like cheese if it is to last. Tea leaves have no value unless processed and their quality deteriorates fairly quickly thus requiring prompt transportation to facilities for processing soon after gathering. Tea and milk producers are both highly dependent on some organization to ensure rapid transportation since it is inefficient for them to take their produce individually to the factory for processing.[25]

Further, both are commodities for which quality is very important. Spoiled milk becomes worthless and poor tea is undesirable, whereas good milk and fine tea are much sought after and consumers will pay premium prices for good quality products. An organization that can ensure quality generates a good margin of profit and can share this profit with producers who cooperate.[26] Both AMUL and KTDA have devolved responsibility for controlling quality to the base-level groups. If a group's

---

[25] A dairy cooperative in Uruguay found that it could save its members one to five hours a day by taking over the hauling and sale of milk (Annex Five).

[26] There can be problems of adulteration with both milk and tea. Farmers may be tempted to add water or other fluids to milk to increase its volume. (Measuring butterfat content of very small amounts is impractical.) Teapluckers may similarly be tempted to bulk up their pickings by taking also the larger, older, and less tasty leaves instead of just the bud leaves or even to toss in sticks, which add to the weight.

lot is found to be spoiled by careless or deliberate action, all are penalized. If, on the other hand, quality is maintained, all benefit because they get a good return for their labor. KTDA in fact pays a very attractive bonus for quality (Annex Seven).

An additional common feature of milk and tea is that each can be produced by relatively low-resource farmers, who have only one cow or a half-acre of tea bushes, as well as by larger farmers. This relates to the socio-economic characteristics of producers (Section 5.6.3 below). Many other commodities cannot be produced as satisfactorily on a small scale. As long as small producers do not lower the quality of output, their contributing to the quantity of output should be advantageous also to larger producers (as noted on page 133).

The AMUL "model" has been hailed for benefiting small and poor producers by paying a higher price for milk than did the local traders. Its processing facilities for making powdered milk, cheese, and butter (when there was an excess of fresh milk) have enabled it to cope profitably with the seasonal fluctuations of milk output and to share the benefits of this with members. AMUL and KTDA were able to develop strong local organizations that promote efficient production, technological upgrading, and also a broad spread of benefits to small producers in large part because of the structure and incentives the program planners created (see KTDA discussion in Annex Seven). But the nature of milk and tea as commodities should not be underestimated as important factors in the successful operation of these institutions. Not all dairy and tea operations are as efficient as AMUL and KTDA, but few other commodity operations have matched these multi-tiered institutions, which reach down to (and up from) local levels.

Several of the cooperatives that might compare with AMUL or KTDA handle coffee or cocoa, also commodities requiring quality processing and aggregation of produce to receive the best price when selling it. There is not the same continuous contact, however, which creates attachment to the organization, and processing and quality requirements are not as precise though these considerations are important. We have commented already on the Portland-Blue Mountain Coffee Cooperative Society in Jamaica, which has the advantage of producing some of the best coffee in the world and can command a premium export price. Marketing makes grower-members dependent on the organization but they are well rewarded financially for their cooperation.

The AMUL model has been adopted by the National Dairy Development Board in India to promote milk production in other states through cooperative organizations with World Bank funding. Since AMUL has over 200,000 members, it is far beyond the "pilot project" stage. However, it took more than twenty years for the AMUL model of organization to develop and become institutionalized in its environment (Korten, 1980). New problems are likely to be encountered when extrapolating the model into different socio-political environments even with the same commodity, and organizational modifications will be needed.

The Government of India with World Bank funding is now setting up small farmer cooperatives based on this model elsewhere in India for producers of oilseeds. This venture may eventually prove successful like AMUL, but it has already faced certain problems that might have been predicted from an analysis of the contrasting commodity characteristics between milk and oilseeds. The first problem planners encountered was the failure of the oilseed cooperatives to benefit the poor as dramatically as was possible when producing and processing milk. Growers of oilseeds are less often among the very poor because crops cannot be grown without access to land, whereas cows can be raised and grazed by the landless on common property if available. A second problem was that merchants in the oilseed trade (known locally as *telrajah*—"oil kings") are established, powerful figures in the local economy, much more powerful than the village middlemen who buy and sell milk. The vested interests that the AMUL-type oilseed producer cooperatives must confront have more incentive and means to resist the organizational efforts of small producers.[27]

From the farmers' viewpoint, oilseeds do not need to be processed with as much urgency as milk or tea. They can easily be sold unprocessed on the local market thereby reducing producer dependence on an organization. Moreover, compared to milk and tea, oilseed processing can be done by small mills and it offers fewer economies of scale, which in the case of milk and tea create benefits that can be remitted to producers who belong to the organization.[28] In milk and tea production, intense animal husbandry and attention to detail can pay real dividends, whereas such quality considerations are much less important for oilseeds where profit comes mostly from scale of production and the quantity sold. One should not expect the same kind of local institutional strength (or distribution of benefits) emerging from the oilseed cooperatives in India as was possible with dairy cooperatives.

Neither should one expect the KTDA model to work as effectively and beneficially with hybrid maize, for example, a crop which the Kenyan government would very much like to increase. With maize, there is no day-to-day activity that continuously links farmers to the organization. There are long periods during the year when the organization would be irrelevant to producers as was never the case for KTDA and AMUL members. With maize (compared to tea or milk) there is no need for processing, and no

---

[27]This resistance has included violence, as reported in *India Today,* January 15, 1982.

[28]KTDA controls access to the world market for teagrowers to get favorable export prices. AMUL has been able to get into the export business through its marketing strategy. There is some controversy over how beneficial this has been but it certainly has advantages for institutionalization. Being able to export at a premium price is not so important for oilseeds, on the other hand.

comparable need for marketing since much of the maize produced is for home consumption or local sale.

The functions of any supporting institution for maize production would tend to be limited to selling hybrid seed and fertilizer at the beginning of the season, possibly selling insecticides or herbicides during the growing period, and then buying some of the product when harvested. Nothing more would happen until the rains come again the next year. Moreover, the quality considerations, which give AMUL and KTDA "bonuses" of resources to share with producers, would be lacking with maize.

Use of more modern technologies and marketing practices will make producers more dependent on higher-level institutions for specialized inputs and favorable prices. This gives producers an incentive to have their own institutions for horizontal cooperation and to deal vertically with state or private sector organizations. When producing for the market, there is often need to coordinate planting and harvesting schedules, either to sell in greater bulk or to avoid glutting the market and lowering prices. Cooperation in plant or animal protection measures becomes more important as more capital has been invested in the crops, trees, or livestock. To the extent a commodity is commercialized, there is more basis for sustaining local institutions because of the new horizontal and vertical relationships among producers and between producers and higher level organizations. (An exception would be the kind of local institutions established to facilitate barter arrangements in the case of Ayni Ruway in Bolivia, reported in Annex Six.)

The role for local institutions is greater where production is for export because of the stringent requirements for quality control and the timing of harvest and sale. We discussed in Section 5.2.4 the need for cooperative institutions to operate in an efficient manner that serves the interests of producers. This requirement often makes government institutions less viable than cooperative or private channels. The marketing organizations set up by the government in Jamaica, for example, to support and promote the production of bananas as well as other export crops in fact had a disincentive effect that reduced production (Goldsmith, 1982). The fact that bananas are a perishable commodity created requirements for a very responsible institution. Both producers and staff needed to meet high quality standards for export. In an agency purchasing a nonperishable staple like rice or wheat, the bureaucratic approach the marketing organizations displayed would have been undesirable but it would not have been so disastrous as it was with bananas (Annex Five).

Products that involve a greater amount of capital investment and use more modern technologies establish greater dependence on higher level institutions. These products tend to be more exclusive, because of high initial costs, expensive inputs, or delayed production. Some examples are cattle fattening operations, tree plantations, cotton production (which requires a high expenditure on pesticide), or irrigated rice in Latin America where only the wealthy can afford irrigation.

Small farmers who cannot afford such capital investments are usually excluded from local institutions tailored to the needs of these larger producers. In the case of certain Bolivian cooperatives, small cocoa producers could not benefit from the equipment available for mechanization through their co-op, set up originally for its rice-growing members (Tendler, 1983). Cocoa production was feasible in areas that were not suitable for mechanized rice production, but small farmers were excluded from these opportunities. Thus, we see the characteristics of the commodity interacting with certain producer characteristics, discussed in Section 5.6.3.

There is practically no analysis in the literature on institutional requirements or constraints arising from commodity characteristics. We can thus only sketch with examples the need to consider the implications of such characteristics for LID planning and implementation. Once stated, it is obvious that institutional forms are unlikely to be equally effective in support of all kinds of commodities—field crops, tree crops, large animals, small animals. The dependence or interdependence (horizontally and vertically) that producers of different commodities confront should receive more attention to determine the value local institutions will have for producers so as to facilitate cooperation among themselves and linkages outside their group or community.

5.5 IMPLICATIONS OF DIFFERENCES IN CONDITIONS

One should not expect local institutions to be equally effective under all conditions any more than for all commodities. Obviously there are many ways in which the conditions for agricultural development can vary—soil, temperature, topography, etc. The most significant difference for agricultural improvement usually is the availability of water, and we consider this here as an illustration of how *context* can influence LID possibilities. We will examine the implications for local institutional development in rainfed areas compared to irrigated ones. How might LID tasks associated with agricultural development differ when working in less rather than more favored areas?[29]

Areas with limited, excess, or unreliable rainfall will often have a weaker network of local institutions compared to those having irrigation (or

---

[29]Agriculture includes more than crops, though the term as usually used ignores livestock and trees in favor of field crops. Livestock development is likely to become more important where rainfall is too meager or unreliable for good crops. Agro-forestry is similarly related to rainfall, terrain, or other problems that give trees an advantage over other plants. We will be focusing here on issues relating to field crops. To distinguish between irrigated and rainfed agriculture does not mean the former always has abundant water and the latter too little. The distinction is made here for purposes of analysis.

ample, reliable precipitation). Central governments find it difficult to staff and supervise their offices in less-favored areas so LA is usually less effective. Such regions are viewed as "backwaters" by the staff of line ministries. Less qualified or poorly performing staff are likely to be posted there, sometimes as a kind of punishment (Meyers, 1981:56). Local governments have a weaker economic resource base to draw on and commonly display similar limitations of capacity as LA. Because the possibilities for profit are less than in richer, irrigated areas, private enterprises are less numerous and less developed.

Though areas with limited resources face more constraints in LID than other areas, they should not be written off for this reason. Local institutions such as membership organizations, cooperatives, and service organizations may be fewer in number or less capable in less-favored areas. However, traditions of self-help may be more vigorous where the need for them is greater and where the influences of modernization and commercialization have been less pervasive. In our study of local organizations' effectiveness, we did not find that LO performance was higher where natural resource endowments, infrastructre or per capita income were greater. Indeed, the relationship could be the opposite, that LOs perform somewhat better under adverse conditions (Esman and Uphoff, 1984:106-114). Certainly the benefits for producers from horizontal and vertical cooperation may be greater or at least more appreciated.

In a study of agricultural development in the rainfed tribal areas of Zimbabwe, Bratton (1983) found that nearly half of the 500 households randomly selected were members of various agricultural associations, sponsored either by government, private business, or church organizations (Annex Five). To a significant degree, he found that maize farmers who were members of such groups consistently outproduced individual (nonmember) maize farmers. More important, these differences were greater in areas where rainfall and soil conditions were less favorable:

> Whereas group farmers produce nearly twice as much as individuals in Chipuriro, they produce almost three times as much in Gutu (the more disadvantaged area). The implication (which needs further testing) is that farmer organizations make the biggest contribution to production in the more marginal areas. (Bratton, 1983:17)

Oxby (1983:54) has reported higher yields among rainfed group farmers in Kenya compared to nongroup members "who were also assisted by extension workers even though farmers in groups had a lower rate of instructors per farmer." A World Bank project in the rainfed areas of northern Ghana initially failed to set up the farmer groups provided for in the project design. These groups were intended to help operate credit, seed, and fertilizer programs to be run from farmer service centers. The project floundered for some years until such groups were established. (The URADEP project is reviewed in Uphoff, 1985.)

Modern institutions may be less effective in more remote and unfavored areas, which suggests that the strategy for local institutional development should build on any other capacities that exist. Excellent examples of such an approach are the farmers' associations established among the Tiv in Nigeria, which built on traditional rotating credit arrangements, and the development centers set up among campesinos by DESEC in Bolivia, which capitalized on traditional community solidarity. (Both cases are described in Annex Seven.)

Rainfed agriculture, compared with irrigated conditions, is more variable and thus involves more risk. A greater variety of crops will be grown than with irrigation partly to offset the factor of risk. Producers in rainfed cultivation are generally less interdependent and more dispersed than producers with irrigation and this affects the patterns of local institutional development. Without accepting the thesis that irrigation requires regimentation of farmers and necessarily creates power in the hands of a bureacracy (Wittfogel, 1957), it is clear that irrigation reduces agricultural variability and creates more predictability so that agricultural tasks can become more routinized. With more uniform and homogeneous activities, coordination is more beneficial thus establishing a greater role for LA.

Conversely with the greater variety, variability, and risk present in rainfed agriculture, LA is less well suited to be involved in management or even in support of agriculture. Larger responsibilities may be assigned to local government if it can take them on. LG should be better able than LA to respond to local variations and to urgent local needs. More likely it will be private, voluntary, or cooperative institutions, more flexible in their operation and more attuned to risk-taking, that can better exploit what opportunities exist in a less hospitable environment.

One might expect to find households under these fluctuating conditions more inclined to use local institutions to reduce their risks. Cooperative farming would be one such means but it is not common to find such pooling of resources.[30] Families appear to prefer to try to maximize their own production by their own efforts. Labor and other resources such as animal traction are often exchanged but the units of production remain discrete. Mutual assistance is sought and given after the fact in case of crop failure. This means that informal local organizations can be very important and should be respected and preserved. Introducing formal financial guarantees through officially supported local institutions would probably not succeed

---

[30]We found one study of a joint family farm cooperative and an ex-soldiers' collective at village level in Uttar Pradesh, India (Lerner, 1971). Both were able to pool resources to give members better access to water through tubewells for supplemental irrigation of crops. But in both cases, a significant factor which added an element of cohesiveness was having an agrobusiness (an oil press or grain mill) because this created joint assets for members apart from their agricultural production. Both local institutions would have been more successful according to Lerner if more protection could have been given against risk, possibly through linkages to state institutions, since risk was inhibiting investment and re-investment in the co-ops.

because, where risks and variability are so great, their consequences become practically uninsurable. What we see in rainfed areas is usually informal, collective self-insurance with no assured level of protection.

In general there is less interdependence among rainfed producers as compared to irrigated agriculture. Decisions on what to plant and when are made separately more readily under rainfed conditions. Moreover, under rainfed conditions, farmers are usually much less dependent on agricultural inputs from outside the community such as would be supplied through local institutions linked to higher level private, state, or cooperative enterprises. Farmers in rainfed areas are thus likely to have less need for local institutions that handle higher technology inputs and increased saleable outputs. This means there is likely to be less vertical dependence on higher level institutions in rainfed areas. Figure 5.3 contrasts the following situations:

Figure 5.3: ALTERNATIVE CONDITIONS FOR AGRICULTURAL DEVELOPMENT

HORIZONTAL INTERDEPENDENCE AMONG FARMERS	DEPENDENCE ON LOCAL INSTITUTIONS LINKED TO HIGHER LEVEL INSTITUTIONS	
	Low	High
Low	(I) Rainfed Millet Production	(II) Rainfed Hybrid Maize Production
High	(III) Traditional Irrigated Paddy Production	(IV) Irrigated HYV Paddy

In the first situation (I) neither horizontal nor vertical linkages are very important to farmers. Farmers' cooperation, either to produce their own crops or to get inputs or services from outside is by the very nature of the activity not necessary. The opposite situation (IV) with irrigated, technically advanced paddy production, provides many incentives for farmers to work together at field level and with higher levels to acquire an assured water supply and to have the inputs needed for producing high yields.

Agriculture under most rainfed conditions approximates the first situation. Introducing hybrid maize, which requires purchase of seed each year and which gives significantly better yields with use of fertilizer, represents a move toward vertical dependence (toward situation II) without necessarily changing the relations among producers. They may benefit from access to supporting institutions, but there is still no great need for them to cooperate unless local institutions are needed to gain access to inputs and markets.

The experience of Plan Puebla in Mexico is instructive in this regard. CIMMYT, the international center for maize and wheat research, was trying to introduce new maize varieties but with little impact at first. What made a difference was introducing a scheme for group credit. This enabled farmers to get fertilizer and chemicals to increase production from their existing varieties, which were already adapted to the difficult prevailing ecological conditions. This local organizational approach fostered horizontal connections and cooperation among farmers, which in turn supported better vertical linkages with agricultural support agencies. In effect, this moved farmers toward situation IV in Figure 5.3, creating conditions more favorable to local institutional development. Linkages between farmers and agricultural researchers helped the latter to revise their research strategy for maize and this contributed to the development and adoption of better modern varieties (Annex Five).

Agriculture may appear simpler in rainfed areas when the level of "modern" technology is low. Very basic implements are used. Production follows the cycle of the seasons, usually with long slack periods. Yet as more knowledge is gained about the farming systems practiced under such conditions, scientists are gaining more respect for the complexity of these production systems, which utilize a large number of crops and intricate techniques for tasks like moisture retention, weed control, and crop protection. Where the natural resource base cannot be taken for granted, special efforts must be made to coordinate efforts at the farm level and at all levels above it.

One of the few systematic studies of a program operating in a semi-arid environment—in Kenya—highlights the interdependence of strategies for increasing agricultural production, developing water resources, and promoting soil and water conservation (Meyers, 1981). Farmers' receptivity to soil conservation promotion was found to be largely dependent on how well a household succeeds in crop production. Earning some cash income, often off-farm, provides resources for investing in conservation efforts, and conservation efforts in turn become more attractive to a household when it depends on crops as a source of cash income. "Those who seek increased production work harder to insure the continued productivity of their soil and pastures." (Meyers, 1981:87) Off-farm income possibilities were major determinants of a household's ability to absorb the risk involved in agricultural innovation, so nonagricultural activities such as discussed in Chapter Six may contribute to an agricultural development program for a resource-constrained environment.

The operational difficulties of carrying out such a program under adverse natural conditions make it imperative that institutional mechanisms be available to facilitate the day-to-day coordination of various sectoral components. There needs to be mutual reinforcement among activities as well as certain economies of operation such as avoiding duplication and saving trips. Meyers argues that the local level is the best place for achieving such integration because

> from this vantage point, it is easier to grasp and act upon the concrete possibilities for coordination and integration in specific planning and implementation terms. (Meyers, 1981:54)

This does not obviate the need for strong support from central institutions. But particularly in regions where the natural resource base is poor, it is difficult to sustain central capabilities (financial, technological, and managerial) for reasons discussed above. The paradox is that central institutional capabilities are likely to be weakest where they are needed most. This makes all the more significant the findings in Zimbabwe that the agricultural returns to farmer organization may be greater in the less-favored ecological areas (Annex Five).

Strategies for agricultural development in rainfed areas need to be conceived and carried out differently, with more devolution of responsibility, than efforts focused on physically more-favored areas where financial and human resources for a centrally directed effort are more available. Governments in many less-developed countries now wanting to push their agricultural programs into less-favored areas face a growing "fiscal crisis," which limits their possibilities for expenditure. This makes new approaches that rely relatively more on local institutions rather than simply on central institutions all the more appropriate.

5.6 IMPLICATIONS OF DIFFERENCES IN PRODUCERS

Having considered how decisions on the allocation of tasks among local institutions for agriculture could be affected by differences in what is produced and under what conditions, it is appropriate to look at who is doing the producing to see how this may affect LID. To the extent that the agriculturally active population departs from the common image of "farmers" based on Western models—as being educated, male, landowning, and settled—one may expect that standard institutional solutions should be varied.

5.6.1 Literacy

It is widely held that literacy is a requirement for the effective functioning of local institutions. Accordingly it may be thought that where the rural population is largely illiterate, national institutions drawing on an urban-based pool of educated personnel should bear responsibilities for directing development. Yet the basis for this presumption is questionable.

In quantified cross-national analysis of this variable covering experience with 150 rural local organizations, the correlation between their development contributions and community literacy levels was only .08, not at all significant (Esman and Uphoff, 1984:119). Indeed, some of the most outstanding results from local responsibility were achieved where literacy and numeracy were very low.

It is hardly likely that illiteracy and lack of numeracy are advantages for LID and thus to be preferred. But where literacy is low, the local population is likely to include more persons of high intelligence and character who can provide leadership and management talents for the solution of development problems. Where educational opportunities have not been widely diffused, there will have been less social and geographic mobility, and fewer energetic and talented individuals will have moved out of farming or other "low-status" occupations and into towns. Hence, there can be some compensating advantages with low levels of literacy.

If membership organizations can be successful without extensive literacy, so can other local institutions. LA staff can, if necessary, be recruited from areas having more education and can be posted to work where literacy is low. This might not be as desirable as having staff from the area, but it means devolved local administration is possible. Local governments can also recruit from outside to fill certain positions. This was done in Nigeria, where literacy in northern areas was much lower than in the south, to implement the radical decentralization introduced by the federal government after 1967. Even in the wake of civil war, northern LGs recruited personnel from regions with which they had only recently been at war. We certainly know that private businesses can operate with very low levels of literacy as the success of many illiterate business-people in rural communities and market towns throughout the Third World is legendary.

Cooperatives appear particularly fragile under conditions of illiteracy, but this is a consequence often of the paperwork required by higher levels of the bureaucracy which puts an unnecessary burden on the uneducated.[31] The cases cited in Section 5.2.4 show that cooperatives not bound by formalistic requirements can operate at low levels of literacy and numeracy though they may need some assistance from literate and numerate persons.

In practically all communities there are at least some members who can perform roles that require reading, writing, and figuring skills. The chief

---

[31]This has been documented in northern Nigeria where co-ops with mostly illiterate members had to fill out fourteen complex forms and reports regularly even though a few simplified documents would have sufficed (King, 1981). Such imposition of paperwork may also be forced upon local administrative staff, as reported in footnote 23 in Chapter One. To some degree LA may be more sinned against than sinning.

value of literacy appears to be that it gives local representatives more status vis-a-vis higher level officials and greater ability to get those officials to carry out their development responsibilities properly.[32] The crucial factor seems to be the orientation of national government, whether it wants local institutions to succeed despite the impediments that illiteracy can present. Most of the liabilities of illiteracy stem from educated persons taking advantage of their knowledge and status. Governments need to indicate to all personnel that they should be fully supportive of local institutions despite any inconveniences of illiteracy, and that haughty or indifferent behavior toward uneducated members of the public will not be accepted. Bureaucratic reorientation may well need to be undertaken in this regard (discussed in Section 7.5.4).

5.6.2 Gender

Fortunately the assumption of past years that "farmers" are male and rural women are simply "housekeepers" has been shaken by growing documentation and appreciation of the role and contribution of women in agriculture. However, most of the LID literature has been gender-blind.[33] March and Taqqu (1986) have shown that women's associations in rural areas are much more common than previously recognized. These tend to be more informal and less visible than men's associations, however, and to be less powerful because they have control over fewer resources.

Within their limits, women's associations can carry out a great variety of functions. A recent review of the situation in Nigeria concluded:

> In all the States investigated, there is a powerful tradition of voluntary women's groups. These groups are based on many things, age, religion, culture, or they may be traditional savings societies. In all of the States women showed a tremendous ability to organize themselves and get things done. In many areas women organized themselves into cooperative farming groups and pooled their plots. They created and maintained savings societies and other community buildings, often taking care of the organization and staffing of the institution as well. Traditionally women have been involved in cooperative trading and occasionally they handle the marketing of their husbands' farm products or are engaged in the procurement of some farm inputs. (Akande, 1984:132)

Program designers may seek to coopt existing women's organizations into performing project tasks. But the distinction made by March and Taqqu

---

[32]In our analysis of local organization performance, one of the only LO tasks that correlated significantly with community literacy levels was "control of bureaucracy" (Esman and Uphoff, 1984:136).

[33]We were able to find some documentation on women's participation in local institutions for rural infrastructure (primarily for domestic water supply) and for primary health care, but the literature was not very detailed. A state-of-the-art review of irrigation management found documentation on women's role in less than 10 percent of the fifty cases analyzed (Uphoff, 1986a). The number of studies on women in agriculture is fortunately growing, e.g., Nelson (1983) and ILO (1984). A case study of women's agricultural groups in Senegal is included in Annex Five.

(1986) between "active" and "reactive" associations is important to keep in mind. The first category, with formal structure and explicit purposes, may become usefully engaged in contemporary development activities. But the latter, which tend to be tacit and informal responding to particular crises or needs, can be distorted or even destroyed by grafting on new purposes that interfere with their limited but valuable functions for the women who belong to them.

Most of the women's organizations documented in the literature emphasize health, education, or income-earning opportunities outside of agriculture. They may engage in agriculture to support these other activities (e.g. the *mwethya* groups in Kenya, cited in footnote 15), or agricultural improvement may evolve out of cooperation in other areas (e.g. the Mothers' Clubs in South Korea, which were originally organized around family planning—Misch and Margolin, 1975; F. Korten and Young, 1978). It has been suggested that women's church groups in Kenya be brought into agricultural extension programs since they are already important local institutions in rural communities and have ventured into activities like chicken-raising (Moock, 1976:835).

When women's organizations get involved in agriculture, it is most often to support members in their household production activities by channeling technical information, credit, or inputs like fertilizer to them or by helping with marketing rather than by undertaking production directly. While there are some successful cases of women's group production, the record generally is not impressive.[34]

One of the issues debated but unresolved in the literature is whether women should participate as a separate category in local institutions. Women's role in local government has generally been less active than men's, though this does not mean they are without influence.[35] In South Asian countries where there is traditional social discrimination against women's public participation, "reserved" seats have been created in many LG bodies. Reserved seats may enhance women's social status but there is little evidence that they contribute much to increasing women's productivity since local governments have not been engaged very significantly in agricultural

---

[34]Akande (1984) reports successful group production in Nigeria, as does Yoon (1983) in Senegal. On the other hand, women's groups in Burkina Faso had notable failures with group production (Taylor, 1981), and women's production efforts in the *ujamaa* villages of Tanzania have been mostly disappointing (Hyden, 1981). The Umoja women's federation in Kenya, which organized collective work groups that hired out members' labor for agricultural field work, did not engage in pooled production efforts. The group's earnings went into the organization's treasury to fund health, education, and other activities (Staudt, 1980).

[35]In Senegal, for example, of 500 members of Rural Councils, only four were women (Ba et al., 1984:111). In Botswana women were previously excluded from participation in the *kgotla*, the traditional rural LG institution, but now they take part (typically sitting apart from the men, it should be noted). Brown reports: "At the kgotla meetings observed during this research, women generally spoke less frequently than men, though since many women are better educated than men, those women who did speak often carried weight" (1983:22).

development despite their mandate to do so (Westergaard, 1986). Also, the women filling reserved positions are usually chosen by men with the result that strong and independent women's views are not likely to be expressed.

There is some question whether to promote separate membership organizations for women. Especially among poorer strata of the population, solidarity between men and women is crucial in their struggle for survival and improvement suggesting that only integrated organizations be advocated. On the other hand, women without any affiliations outside their families are likely to be more dependent and less ambitious for themselves and their families. Generally it appears desirable to have some separate organizations for women where energy emanating from gender solidarity can be harnessed and given expression.

There will be some social and cultural circumstances in which separate organizations are not viable (though such conditions demonstrate the need for greater autonomy and opportunity for women). In such cases there may be no alternative to "integrated" organizations, in which women's participation is under the control of men. Even the highly idealistic leadership of the Deedar cooperative in Bangladesh was not able to have a strong women's role in that remarkable organization at the start (Annex Six). It took twenty years to get women into full voting and office-bearing roles though this has been accomplished within a very unfavorable environment.

The optimum LID strategy appears to be some combination of women's, men's, and mixed groups to tap the ideas and efforts of different sets of persons working on varied development tasks (ILO, 1985:56). Unless special circumstances require it, women's organizations should not operate in isolation from all contact with men. The case studies of the Senegalese gardening groups (Annex Five) and the Comas Women's Academy in Peru (Annex Seven) show the advantages of cooperation with and even cooptation of men.

There is a question whether the government service should have special cadres for working with women. There is a common bias in agricultural extension toward working with male farmers even when women are more efficient managers of farm resources than men (Moock, 1976; Staudt, 1978). Because women's role in agriculture is so pervasive and because it would be difficult to obtain sufficient resources and status for separate LA units devoted just to women's work it does not seem advisable to press for such units as part of local institutional development for agriculture. Rather increasing the number and proportion of women LA staff, especially in extension services, appears to be the better course.

How difficult it will be for women to play a prominent role in the expansion of local private businesses will vary from country to country. Much of the marketing trade in agricultural products is in the hands of women in some countries particularly in West Africa. In Jamaica female traders known as "higglers" come to the farm gate and in some instances help in the harvesting of commodities (Lewars, 1982:152–153). However, even where historical precedents and cultural values favor women's involvement in private sector expansion, there may still be national policies and practices that limit their participation in support of agricultural development. Rules governing the provision of credit from government programs or banks usually discriminate against women (ILO, 1984:56–57). The imposition of "top-down" forms of organization that are inconsistent with women's existing patterns of interaction can discourage women's participation, whereas working with them in ways that are more socially and culturally sensitive can lead to larger and more viable institutions.[36]

Which women are participating needs to be considered as many of the most visible women's organizations are not suited for work in agriculture.

> Organisations of upper-class women tend to see their function as social. Either they are purely for the social pleasure of the women involved, or they are welfare oriented. Rural women's organisations tend to be oriented more toward self-help (economic) programmes. (Tadesse, 1984:79)

To the extent there are impediments to full participation by women in local institutions that support agricultural development efforts, a significant share of the local talent that could make those institutions more effective will be absent. This can hardly be afforded.

5.6.3 Land Tenure and Economic Status

Agricultural development programs tend to consider only those cultivators who are landowners, regarding those persons who have only labor to contribute as being "inputs" rather than "participants" in the process of development. Local institutional development for agriculture should not neglect the landless and near-landless ("the rural poor") since they are important not only for accepting and using new technologies but also for contributions of resources and ideas. It was the landless and near-landless, as we saw in Chapter Three, who were most concerned that local governments in Nepal and Indonesia invest in increasing productivity rather than in amenities.

There is understandable concern that local institutions' performance will be affected (distorted or diminished) where there is a high degree of socio-economic stratification, usually created by differences in land tenure status. Leonard (1982) has assessed when these differences are likely to create special difficulties at the local level. National institutions may want to

---

[36]This is shown in the case study of Nigerian women's cooperatives by Ladipo (1983). A flexible organizational form for promoting their role in agricultural trade proved successful whereas the authoritarian model, more familiar to the bureaucracy, was a failure. See also Bruce (1980) on experience with market women's cooperatives in Nicaragua.

maintain a greater degree of control over development activities to ensure all cultivators access to resources and opportunities when:

(a) activities are vulnerable to elite manipulation, e.g., distribution of subsidized fertilizer; or
(b) elite interests are divergent from those of the rest of the community, e.g., when introducing a credit program that charges lower interest rates than village money-lenders.

Activities can be delegated to local institutions under conditions of economic and social inequality with fewer adverse effects when, conversely:

(a) the activities are not particularly vulnerable to distortion, e.g., tick-dipping of cattle; or
(b) the interests of the landed and landless do not diverge much, e.g., control of diseases that affect crops, since crop failure will reduce employment and also drive up the price of food.

Relatively few activities fit these latter criteria fully, but decisions about institutional design should take into account how the nature of the activity affects participation in decision making and benefits when dealing with a population where land tenure differences create dynamics for bias.

Where stratification is serious, the choice among local institutional channels may be made differently. "Alternative organizations," discussed more in Section 7.3.3, having membership restricted to the less-advantaged, may become more appropriate to complement LA, LG and private business channels. The cooperative established in Egypt for beneficiaries of land reform were for a while a good example of such organizations, giving political influence as well as economic opportunity and social status to cultivators who had been among the poorest members of society (Harik, 1974). The special land reform co-op helped to break the domination of the large landowning elite over the local government.

Unfortunately in agriculture relations between landless and landed are more likely to be zero-sum and competitive than in other areas of rural development activity. In human resource development education and health benefits for poorer members of the community can be achieved with less likelihood of adversely affecting the interests of richer members. Indeed, richer persons even benefit from better education, health, and nutritional status for poorer neighbors. Though certain public goods like community water supplies or common forests for fuelwood offer advantages to elite and nonelite alike, agricultural programs benefiting the poor often affect labor supply, wages, and competition for land, with a negative impact on the richer community members.

Even private goods like agricultural inputs or marketing services may be provided to the poor in a community through local institutions like cooperatives. Though under the direction of local elite members, nonmembers may also receive private goods as Tendler (1983) found in Bolivia. The reward that elites receive from conferring such benefits can be enhanced social status, which is desired by persons who already have some sufficiency of economic resources. One should not assume that elites will always use local institutions to pursue their own interests to the exclusion of others' advantage. This is an empirical question. Data on the distribution of agricultural inputs, particularly credit, for the Green Revolution in India's Punjab show that even if co-ops there were elite-dominated, they did provide greater access to productive inputs to the poorer sectors.[37]

As a rule, elite interests are more likely to predominate at higher levels than at lower levels. Persons of lower status and income are more likely to play important roles at the group level than at the community level and to have more influence in the community than in the locality.[38] This is true also with respect to the bureaucracy. The poor are more likely to be seen and assisted by sub-district personnel than by district officials. LA staff at the locality level or below are likely to be more responsive because they live in closer proximity.[39] This consideration supports a degree of devolution to local institutions even when stratification confronts decision makers.

When dealing with localities that have a large number or proportion of landless and near-landless, there should be continuing concern over whether local institutions are serving as adequate channels for their participation in agricultural development. Swedish donors assisting the Chilalo Agricultural Development Unit in Ethiopia, operating through local units of the extension service, were appalled to find that their resources for agricultural credit were going almost entirely to large farmers because the LA staff were

---

[37]See Nicholson (1984). Apart from activities in which elite and nonelite members of a community have a common interest, Leonard (1982:18) lists three conditions that make elite-run institutions more likely to be responsive to the needs of the poor: (i) where there is competition for leadership; (ii) where the support of the poor is necessary for elites to achieve and maintain leadership; and (iii) where at least some elite members are willing to appeal directly to the interests of the poor. Nicholson's analysis suggests that reducing the scarcity of desired goods also makes a difference.

[38]This has been documented in Nepal for the panchayat LG system there. The percentage of representatives from low caste or tribal groups declines as one moves from the village panchayat level to the district panchayat, and then to the zonal panchayat. The likelihood that a poor person will be elected chairman also diminishes at higher levels (Gaige 1975:141–165). The Small Farmer Development Program established by FAO in Nepal and other Asian countries recognized this and therefore adopted a group approach for assisting the rural poor. This approach permitted small farmers and the landless to gain some control over LG in their area (Annex Five). The possibility of overcoming this bias toward elite control at higher (locality) levels by focusing programs at lower (group and community) levels is see in the Indonesia case in Annex Seven.

[39]The beneficial effects of having local officials in close proximity to the poor can be seen from an analysis of the outcomes of land reform implementation (Montgomery, 1972). The probability that rural people would get more income, more tenure security, and more political influence in the wake of land reform and distribution of land to the landless was greater to the extent that decision making was carried out at lower levels of government, involving LA, LG, and LOs. See discussion in Section 7.5.3.

making no effort to identify and reach the poor. By working with the staff and redefining eligibility criteria, the pattern of loans was changed markedly within three years' time under a not-particularly-progressive regime.[40]

Working with poorer members of agricultural communities can have substantial payoffs. In the San Martin Jilotepeque cooperative in Guatemala, 60 percent of the members did not own their own land. Yet it was possible to introduce a program that greatly increased agricultural production while reducing soil erosion and promoting nonagricultural activities (Annex Five). Working through a variety of local institutional channels, some specialized and some general, it should be possible to involve and benefit the rural poor, meaning particularly the landless. They are part of the agricultural production process but as tenants or laborers they will have little voice and stake in it unless the pattern of local institutional development gives them opportunities.

5.6.4 Migration

Another popular image of farmers is that they are all settled on the land when in fact agricultural populations increasingly include a substantial number of migrants. Since it is farming communities not just farms or farmers that raise the level of production through technological and institutional innovation, local institutions need to take population mobility into account rather than presume a stable, sedentary population. Friedmann (1982) has put this succinctly in a report on rural development in Haiti:

> Of course peasants do not live in isolation from each other, and more is needed than to work with individual households, though that is necessary too. It is ultimately the peasant community that must be motivated and become the focus for a project.

One needs to distinguish between *seasonal migration*—where individuals or families move regularly during the year to undertake cultivation, tend herds, or earn income where physical or economic conditions are more favorable—and *out-migration*, where adults leave their communities for several years or longer to undertake employment elsewhere. Money is often remitted to their families, and migrants commonly maintain some stake or presence in the community by visits or contributions.

In countries such as Botswana, Nepal, and Yemen, where the Rural Development Committee has worked, it is not uncommon to find

---

[40]Tenants were only 9 percent of loan recipients in 1968 and got only 4 percent of total loans; three years later they were 39 percent of recipients (with 36 percent of loans). Thirty percent of recipients in 1968 were landowners having over twenty hectares (and they got 59 percent of loan funds); by 1971 they were down to 1 percent (with 2 percent of loans) (Cohen and Uphoff, 1977:247–250). We found no data on yield differences by size of holding, but in neighboring Kenya, small farms (under ten acres) had six times more gross output per acre, and almost seven times more net profit per acre, than large farms (averaging 125 acres) (ILO, 1972:167). So the spread of credit opportunities should have contributed to greater total production.

out-migration rates of 30 percent among adult males, and in other countries women may move to cities for short-term or long-term employment. In Central America whole families move to harvest coffee when that is in season so movement may include children though it is adults' participation that is of most concern in LID. Local institutions need to adjust either by moving with the people or by making sure that their activities coincide with people's migration patterns.

In Botswana migration has long been a way of life to accommodate to arid and semi-arid environments. Households spend some of the year in central villages where deep wells give year-round water supply. As soon as the rains start, most households move or send some of their members to "the lands" where arable crops are cultivated while others take cattle still farther away to "cattle posts" where ephemeral sources of pasture and water can be found (Roe and Fortmann, 1982). In the Botswana situation if local government councils and other institutions are based only in the village, they will be made up of year-round residents, mostly older, more prosperous males who stay behind when younger, less well-off persons and particularly women have to leave to exploit available resources. Vesting more authority and economic resources in village-based institutions under such conditions would introduce an undesirable bias into decision making. If local institutions are dealing with agriculture and natural resource management, the persons actually doing the managing need to be well represented.

In Botswana out-migration to South Africa often drains communities of their most vigorous, ambitious, and best-educated potential leaders. The leadership pool, at least for men, will often not be the most capable that the community has to offer. Women, as noted already, do not have equal standing in the public sphere. Ways need to be found to involve migrants while away from the locality by getting financial contributions and suggestions from them and engaging them more actively upon their return to the village. Their experience, their education, and their exposure to new ideas can greatly assist an organization in its development undertakings. Yet it must be kept in mind that returnees may become so distanced from the village that they no longer represent the community (Fortmann, 1982) though this is not always the case. It is interesting to note the case of ex-Gurkha servicemen in Nepal who went as recruits into the British and Indian armies. After returning with pensions they have often become pillars of strength in local institutions (Caplan, 1970).

Perhaps the most dramatic migration effects have been felt in North Yemen, where about 40 percent of males have at one time or another found lucrative employment in the Persian Gulf states. This has led to a decline in agricultural production as women have been left with more work than they can handle, and as maintenance of hillside terraces has not been kept up. Repatriated earnings of migrants have provided a generous capital base for the Local Development Associations in rural areas (Cohen et al., 1981). Unfortunately the LDAs have not systematically channeled such resources into agricultural improvement efforts.[41]

This observation in Yemen is not unusual. A review of literature covering Nigeria, Kenya, Ethiopia, Peru, Bolivia, India, and the Caribbean found that migrants seldom sponsor agricultural extension or other collective investment in agriculture preferring to support buildings and more visible projects (Ralston et al., 1983:38–39). This finding parallels our observation with regard to local government that "collective action" for agriculture seems to be infrequent at the community or higher levels though it is common at the group level especially on an informal basis. It is an important question for LID whether ways will be found to engage the talents and resources of migrants in agricultural development since the phenomenon of migration is likely to increase in the future. The constructive influence of returned migrants in Nepal is of some encouragement though their agricultural contribution has more often been one of setting examples by their own innovative activity than of strengthening LID for agriculture.

5.7 INTEGRATION OF THE AGRICULTURAL COMMUNITY

The implicit model of most agricultural development theories has been one of individuation, from communally oriented and cooperative "peasants" to self-standing and competitive "farmers" (Weitz, 1971). This derives from the increasingly discredited modernization theory, which presumes a unilinear progression from ascribed to achieved status and from particularistic to universalistic norms. In fact, an analysis of the functions of agriculture suggests that change occurs in the forms and not in the extent of cooperation and interdependence. Even in the most traditional modes of agriculture, production is usually by individuals or households, not groups or institutions. There is exchange of inputs and some sharing of outputs in time of need but the balance between individual and collective efforts tends to favor the former.

As the level of technological sophistication increases, individuals require greater access to inputs and to marketing and processing facilities. As individual operations expand and become more differentiated, there is a

---

[41]One problem LDAs face is that women's public roles are culturally restricted, and only men are supposed to participate in public meetings. Swanson (1982) suggests that LDAs' annual meetings be held during the holiday month when many men working in the Gulf return to their communities for family festivals. This would engage more male household heads in LDA decision making and could also mobilize voluntary contributions. Otherwise households where the male head is away send a junior male to represent them in LDA meetings (Swanson and Hebert, 1982). Understandings have been reached in some communities that when important decisions are to be made, the final vote is put off so the issue can be discussed privately in the households with women making their views known. At a subsequent meeting, the male spokesman can then speak and vote on behalf of the household.

concomitant increase in horizontal and vertical interdependence. The balance between private and collective efforts in agriculture may shift somewhat more toward the private side, but it does not tilt from one end of the continuum to the other as modernization theory suggested. Local institutional development becomes more significant as the scale and complexity of agriculture increase as suggested by considering the hierarchy of levels indicated in Figure 5.1.

While the locus of production is usually the individual or household, aggregate levels of production are a consequence of what whole communities are able to accomplish through their networks of institutional support for individual and household producers. In Section 5.6 concern was focused on several large categories of rural residents—migrants, women, illiterates, landless, or land-poor—who together often make up the majority of rural communities (Esman, 1978).

Local institutions that do not bring these people into the planning and implementation of agricultural development will be limiting the scope of agricultural change and the distribution of benefits in the future. Planners and policy makers should be thinking of how to integrate all sections of the agricultural community into productive enterprise. Institutional networks should provide access to resources and services that both increase the output of households and make that production yield more value to its producers and consumers. This access is particularly needed for the majority of agricultural producers who have lacked it in the past. The better-endowed agriculturalists have less need for new efforts at local institutional development because they usually have been able to forge at least some vertical and horizontal linkages of their own—with one another, with government agency personnel at higher levels, with private suppliers, with trade associations representing the interests of larger producers, etc.

What is needed is seldom the strengthening of any single local institutional channel to promote agricultural growth. The good performance of government agencies operating at the local level should help co-ops and private businesses to succeed. The performance of these latter two channels is usually better when there is some competition between them, giving producers alternative choices based on quality of service and cost considerations. Service organizations, because of their different motivation and resource base, can fill gaps that other institutions find difficult or unrewarding to fill. Membership organizations are also important, providing agricultural services of various sorts on a self-help, collective action basis (Oxby, 1983:56). Such groups will be more stable and effective, however, when tied in with other institutions that give them legitimacy at the local level. The significance of this whole range of local institutions is increasingly recognized as a matter of policy (e.g., USAID, 1984). It is up to development professionals to find ways of providing for and supporting LID initiatives in agricultural and related projects.

CHAPTER SIX

Local Institutional Development for Nonagricultural Enterprise

6.1 ACTIVITIES IN NONAGRICULTURAL ENTERPRISE

Nonagricultural enterprise (NAE) can be ignored as an element of rural development only as long as growing populations can be fully and remuneratively employed in agriculture or can be absorbed into jobs in urban, large-scale industry.[1] Since neither agriculture nor industry are providing sufficient employment for everyone, large and growing portions of the population in most developing countries must engage in activities such as artisan manufacturing or petty trading simply to sustain their households. Because these activities are generally not registered, regulated, or recognized, and are usually quite precarious financially, they are often classified as "informal" or "marginal" despite the fact that a majority of the population may be involved in them.[2]

Although NAE may be seen as offering a set of economic opportunities primarily for small holders or the landless, it represents employment and earning possibilities for many rural residents not only for the poorest. Often, in fact, NAE arises out of rural households' search for sources of income that

---

[1]NAE is also referred to as rural-based industry, village industry, off-farm enterprise, agro-industry, cottage industry, decentralized industries, and other terms. The dividing line between agricultural and nonagricultural enterprise is fuzzy with regard to processing of agricultural products (rice milling, oil seed pressing, etc.). As long as such activities are done by the producing unit (usually the farm household), we consider them as an extension of the agricultural process. But once agricultural products are sold for commercial processing and use or when employees are retained an activity will be considered as NAE. Activities of agricultural households that produce goods or services supplemental to their production of food or fiber are regarded here as NAE.

[2]Soares (1983:3) estimates "that the informal sector includes between 40% and 85% of the labor force in developing countries." Approximately one-third of the labor force in rural areas (including rural towns) depends on nonfarm activities as a primary source of employment and earnings. (World Bank, 1978a:7) In addition a large proportion of families depend on nonfarm activities as a source of secondary income.

can be combined with agriculture (Binswanger, 1983:38). Thus, NAE should not be seen only as a full-time alternative to farming.

Governments and international agencies have long been interested in providing jobs for the rural poor if only to slow the rate of rural-to-urban migration. These efforts have failed partly because of the lack of appropriate institutional development strategies. The focus on increasing the number and viability of nonagricultural enterprises has usually overlooked the importance of *institutional networks* that can sustain and expand NAEs through horizontal and vertical linkages. Moreover, "profitability" has too often been regarded as an end in itself rather than as something that contributes to "institutionalization." This is to say that short-term considerations are too seldom directed at also achieving longer-run payoffs.

Conventional programs for supporting the development of nonagricultural enterprises have too often treated them as entities to be serviced directly and separately, for example when providing credit. Unfortunately this approach entails serious costs both in terms of funds and opportunities forgone. Many programs that extend credit to individual NAEs have often worked through staff of national institutions, who have been unable or unwilling to deal effectively with matters such as eligibility and repayment, which require detailed knowledge and attention. Attractive loan funds get siphoned off by the best-off of the target group or even by persons not eligible to borrow them. Funds intended to promote NAEs become dissipated when some borrowers have enough political clout to evade their obligations to repay. Such problems are most visible with regard to credit programs for NAE development, but similar difficulties arise when trying to provide training, technical assistance, etc. without giving adequate attention to, and investment in, the institutionalized bases for NAE development.

The limitations of dealing with NAEs in the same way as with large-scale commercial operations have become increasingly evident. Many NAE programs are beginning to work with and through groupings of enterprises where both the enterprises and the groups are quite small. Loans and technical assistance are provided to the groups which in turn distribute or disseminate the funds and services among members who accept mutual responsibility for their productive use, even repaying loans of fellow members if these become overdue. Regular payments are decided upon and monitored by the group and handled by its representatives. This not only lowers administrative and transaction costs but helps assure repayment so that the funds are truly "revolving," making such programs of NAE assistance both more effective and efficient.[3]

---

[3]An example of such a program in the Dominican Republic is reported in Annex Eight. It channels credit to groups of *tricicleros*, men who pedal heavy cargo tricycles to transport and

The institutional development efforts needed to promote non-agricultural enterprise should focus both on the enterprises themselves, as in the strategy just described for assisting them in groups, and on certain institutions that can strengthen and support such enterprises. In much the same way as for agricultural development (as analyzed in Section 5.1), efforts to enhance local institutional capacity for nonagricultural development need to distinguish between *units of production* at the local level, which may or may not become "institutionalized," and the various possible *local intermediary institutions* considered in Section 6.2. These efforts must then assist both units of production and LIIs in a complementary fashion. Units of production are to be helped to expand, multiply, innovate, and diversify by appropriate local intermediary institutions that make nonagricultural activity more feasible, secure, and profitable.

Much as with other rural development activities, efforts to assist NAE will usually most appropriately be local efforts where familiarity and flexibility permit arrangements that take local conditions into account—particularly as they relate to the ebb and flow of income in rural areas or to matters of time, such as reconciling full versus part-time work schedules or permanent versus temporary or seasonal employment.

Being concerned with approaches to promoting nonagricultural enterprise that draw on and develop local institutional capacities to support NAE, we focus on local intermediary institutions and their connections to local enterprises rather than on techniques for addressing the problems of particular types of NAEs. However, since institutional capacity takes root more readily where suited to the characteristics of the productive task and the operational context, an analysis of LID for nonagricultural development must give some attention to the different kinds of enterprises and services involved, as done in Section 6.3. NAEs can vary in their basis of ownership, their size and technology, and their type of activity. Uniform approaches to working with them are not likely to contribute to dynamic or sustainable NAE performance.

6.2 LOCAL INSTITUTIONAL OPTIONS

In this analysis we are considering nonagricultural enterprises themselves more as units of production than as "institutions" to be developed

---

sell fruit and vegetables or to collect scrap metal, cardboard, etc. in the streets of Santo Domingo. Credit is granted to "solidarity groups" of six to eight members so that they can purchase (rather than rent) their vehicles and then branch out into other enterprises. While each member is individually responsible for some part of the loan, the group's members are also collectively responsible. Asian examples of such a local institutional strategy for handling credit include the Small Farmer Development Programme in Nepal (Annex Five) and the Grameen Bank in Bangladesh (Annex Eight). A similar approach is being introduced in Africa by FAO in its People's Participation Programme (FAO, 1984). Such "solidarity groups" formed the basis for successful savings programs in Cameroon and Zimbabwe (Annex Eight).

though NAEs can become institutions as defined in Section 1.5 if they persist over time, becoming valued structures of activity within the community. The fact of having NAEs can become "institutionalized" to the extent that people attribute enough value to their existence that persons are willing to make contributions to the maintenance of NAEs as a general practice even if not necessarily to the survival of each and every individual enterprise. Here we are interested in the institutional channels through which credit and other services can be provided to NAEs.

Not surprisingly the same six kinds of local institutions as were considered for other sectors offer possibilities for assisting NAEs:

(1) local administration (LA);
(2) local government (LG);
(3) membership organizations of NAE owners or operators;
(4) cooperatives of NAEs themselves;
(5) service organizations, such as might operate a revolving loan fund on a not-for-profit basis; and
(6) private businesses, which provide goods and services for a fee or price.

One can distinguish between *direct* and *indirect contributions* of local institutions to nonagricultural development. The latter include things like local governments building marketplaces and roads that enhance local economic opportunities; private businesses as they expand creating demand for the products of local enterprises; or government schools and clinics at local levels upgrading the human resource base for rural economic activity. Such indirect effects are not dealt with here, however, because they have been covered in the preceding four chapters. We are interested in local institutional activities more directly and explicitly aimed at strengthening nonagricultural enterprise.

We do not often find local institutions presently engaged at their own initiative in systematic efforts to promote NAE. Sometimes church organizations make loans to small businesses to accelerate the growth of the local economy, or local producers may have formed a cooperative to make their marketing or input procurement more efficient. But such institutional activities are the exception and frequently ad hoc. Strengthening them where they exist is a reasonable policy. Usually specific local institutional efforts to support NAE will be at the instigation of some outside agency. A local government body may cooperate with a rural industries program of the national government, represented by regional or district officials distant from the locality. Or a foreign donor, public or private, may provide technical assistance and capital to an association of local producers to upgrade their operations. LID for nonagricultural enterprise should make such programs more extensive and effective.

To refer specifically to local institutions operating in roles that assist and strengthen NAEs we speak of *local intermediary institutions* (LIIs), which make direct contributions to NAE development. These can be local government or local administration units, membership organizations or co-operatives, service organizations or private businesses. Generally speaking different LIIs will have different "comparative advantages" for meeting the needs of local nonagricultural enterprises, whether credit, skills training, information, external representation, or physical inputs.

Figure 6.1: SUPPORT BY INSTITUTION AND TYPE OF ASSISTANCE

TYPE OF INSTITUTIONS	ASSISTANCE PROVIDED	CHANNELS OF ASSISTANCE					
External Institutions (nonlocal)	Support for Local Intermediary Institutions	National Governments International Donor Agencies Private Voluntary Organizations					
	Support for Local Units of Production	*Continuum: Private to Public Sector*					
		PBs	SOs	Co-ops	MOs	LG	LA
	• Credit	(X)*	X	(X)			X
	• Training		X				X
Local Intermediary Institutions (LIIs)	• Information	(X)	(X)	(X)			X
	• Lobbying				X	X	
	• Inputs	X		X	(X)		
	• Services					X	X
Local Units of Production (not necessarily "institutions")	Inputs for Other Local Units of Production	Private Enterprises (of small owner, outside owner, or household)		Producer Cooperatives		Parastatals (rare at the local level)	

*(X) = less important than X

In Figure 6.1 these distinctions are represented, suggesting a division of labor whereby "nonlocal" institutions such as national governments or foreign donors are assisting local intermediary institutions, which in turn support the development of NAE units of production. Some of these local units of production may support others by providing inputs or buying products and services. LIIs are shown ranging along a continuum from private to public sector institutions. Of the local intermediary institutions, LA units (including local bank branches) and SOs have shown the most immediate potential for providing credit and skills training; MOs and LG have some advantage in providing information and lobbying to gain attention to local needs; while private businesses (PBs) and cooperatives are generally best suited to providing physical inputs and certain services to specific enterprises. LG and LA are more appropriate for multi-enterprise services like water and electricity because these qualify as "public goods" as analyzed in Section 4.4.5, with substantial economies of scale in their provision.

Specific LIIs may be able to give certain kinds of support not indicated in Figure 6.1. For instance, a unit of local administration might effectively lobby with higher authorities on behalf of NAEs. The diagram presents no universal claims of comparative advantage but rather illustrates the need to consider where and why such advantage might exist.

One reason for making LID part of any strategy for nonagricultural enterprises is to go beyond simply providing these supports separately. There is need to create inter- and intra-local economic linkages and to have organizational networks that disseminate and share information. In fact, the most fundamental local institution for NAE development is the *local economy*, which can be understood as an "institution" that is not an "organization" (Section 1.5). A local economy is not simply established by the local presence of national economic institutions or by integration of the local community into the national economy. Rather a local economy exhibits some degree of independence from external links and a great deal of mutual interdependence among local producers and households. This not only promotes the generation of value added but retains a large part of it for promoting further NAE development.

The objective of introducing new goods and services to expand the depth and scope of the local economy is to increase the capacity of its components for creating employment and additional income for local households. Some of this income can be invested in other areas such as agriculture, education, or nutrition and health. Furthermore, the overall local institutional framework is strengthened when individual enterprises themselves become established as "institutions" which can buttress the capacity of LG and other local institutions economically and technologically.

This process is evident in the case of group or cooperative enterprises which expand and diversify their activities as did the Mraru Women's Group in Kenya (Annex Six). This group began by raising money to establish transportation service to a nearby town through buying and operating its own bus. Once this activity was established, the group used its profits to build a small retail shop. Eventually, space in the back of the shop was devoted to sewing and family health classes to which the Department of Social Services contributed sewing machines and a teacher's salary. This group moved beyond being simply an enterprise to become a local institution to which women now turn for financial and also social improvement. The *mwethya* women's group in Kenya, discussed in the preceding chapter (footnote 15), showed a similar evolution.

Such changes over time are important to recognize and accept since when supporting nonagricultural enterprise, the accent should definitely be

on the latter word—"enterprise." This means that diversification and modification of activities in response to emerging conditions and new
opportunities are valued as characteristics of institutional capacity.[4] The examples cited from Kenya are quite typical, as entrepreneurs (private or
public) seek to take advantage of whatever lines of activity appear profitable, economically and/or socially. The category in which the "units of
production" are classified may change over time. This is one reason why
local institutional development in support of NAE should not attempt to
work through and strengthen just "one best" intermediary channel. Rather it
will be more effective to have a combination of LIIs cooperating at the various local levels in their support of NAE. As a set they can more readily deal
with the variety of organizational forms NAEs are likely to take and technical tasks they may undertake.

Such variety itself needs to be analyzed and understood. Certain LIIs
will be better suited to working with some kinds of NAEs though no clear
rules on this can be derived from the literature, fragmented as it is on the
subject. Rather assisting LIIs to work with NAEs needs to take into account
the variety to be found among the units of production to be supported. Accordingly some analytical order needs to be brought to this diverse universe
called "nonagricultural enterprises."

6.3 NONAGRICULTURAL ENTERPRISE CHARACTERISTICS

While there may be no general agreement on a definition of
nonagricultural enterprises, distinctions usually focus on *location, type,* or
scale. The distinction between *on-farm* and *off-farm* activities is not very useful because there are various nonagricultural production activities that rural
households can usefully undertake to supplement their agricultural income.
We would include under NAE any productive activities not involving the
producing of food and fiber, and any processing of food and fiber products
off-farm by enterprises that did not produce them. It makes no sense to exclude such employment and income-generating activities as grain milling or
leather tanning if carried out by small, self-standing enterprises since these
have much in common with other small manufacturing and commercial
concerns in rural areas. On the other hand, a household's handling or processing of food or fiber it has produced before selling this commodity does
not constitute a distinct "enterprise" so it is not categorized as NAE.

NAE activities can include *processing* of agricultural products such as
fish canning, hemp retting, or fruit drying; *manufacture* of products such as

---

[4]One of the most striking things about the twenty-five case studies (from almost as many
countries) assembled and analyzed for the ILO/DANIDA project on "identification of successful projects for improving the employment conditions of rural women" (Muntemba, 1985) is
how much the productive activities of these various women's enterprises branched out and
changed over time.

bamboo mats or agricultural implements; *trade and marketing*, including hawking, retailing, or even wholesaling; and *services* such as transport and restaurants—including moving goods by simple means like bicycle or preparing food in roadside stalls. These constitute the main types of NAE activity as discussed below. The characteristics of NAEs that appear most important for adapting LID efforts are ownership arrangements, types of activity, and production requirements. Each characteristic affects the kinds of support enterprises might usefully receive from or through the different local intermediary institutions listed above.

6.3.1 Ownership Arrangements

This aspect of nonagricultural enterprise affects the kind of support that will be appropriate based on the scale of enterprise and the distribution of losses and profits among the producers. It focuses attention on the division of labor within an enterprise, i.e., whether one person performs all tasks, specializes in one of them, or is capable of all but performs them separately. Outside assistance must be tailored to the structure of decision making and operation. It also points to the likely type or level of technology employed as this affects the kinds and amounts of training and capital investment required.

(1) *Private individual or household ownership (micro-enterprise)*. This type of organization operates on a small scale and often with rudimentary technology. If tasks are not divided by gender or age, one individual is likely to perform all of them, either in succession, or separately.

(2) *Private local ownership (small enterprise)*. These enterprises are separate from the household either physically or in terms of financial accounts. They are slightly larger in scale than household enterprises and will often employ some nonfamily members. Depending on the enterprise's size, the owner may either manage or manage and produce simultaneously. Similarly workers will perform one or a variety of tasks.

(3) *Private outside ownership (branch enterprise)*. This type of enterprise, operating on a small or medium scale, will represent an "outpost" of a business from a nearby town or part of a network of enterprises operating within a region. Local employees may perform one task or several depending on the type of organization. Large outside enterprises ("branch plants") generally represent national or international firms locating an enterprise in a locale primarily to take advantage of raw materials or cheap labor. Organization will generally be hierarchical and a clear division of labor will be most common. Technology is likely to be more complex than with purely local enterprises.

(4) *Cooperative ownership (producer co-ops).*[5] This form of enterprise represents cooperative ownership of a business's assets. Profits and losses accrue to members of the enterprise together. Members often know all stages of the production process although specialization may take place in management or as new activities are added. Technology is likely to be simple or only moderately complex.

(5) *Government ownership (parastatal).* Such enterprises are generally large, hierarchically organized, and technologically complex. As publicly sponsored enterprises, they differ from private outside enterprises mainly in having some broader social purpose for locating in a community and in operating with usually less flexibility than purely private sector operations.

Type of ownership does not by itself determine LID needs and opportunities. Rather the extent to which the units of production are purely "local" makes a substantial difference when planning support strategies. Micro and small enterprises and producer cooperatives generally fall in this category and are accordingly more likely to need local supporting institutions than are medium to large private or parastatal enterprises, which can make their own way because of their extra-community commercial connections.

This is not to say that the particularly "local" NAE types (a, b, and d) will respond in the same way to all programs. Rather the analysis suggests, for example, that when it comes to obtaining access to improved technology, units of production that are more "local" are likely to look more readily to local private enterprises, local service organizations, or other local intermediary institutions for assistance because they have fewer linkages to higher level institutions than those with other ownership arrangements (c and e).

NAEs that are more "local" are likely to be based on *already present skills* or *presently perceived opportunities.* If they want to increase employment and income generated through such enterprises, they will need to upgrade skills or introduce new ones (managerial as well as technical) or to increase information about opportunities for local enterprises to make profitable initiatives. In contrast, enterprises with more "extra-local" connections are likely to base their decisions on availability of raw materials or a cheap supply of local labor. Training and information are less likely to figure in their expansion plans. Because of their size and commercial contracts, they are more independent of local intermediary institutions.

While units of production with outside linkages may increase employment or income opportunities in rural communities, they have less stake in the community. They commonly transfer more of their value added outside thereby contributing less to other aspects of local institutional and general economic development. This is not to say that such enterprises should be

---

[5]Buyers' and sellers' co-ops are discussed separately because they represent a distinct form of local institution that can support producer co-ops or other kinds of units of production, by acting as an intermediary for them.

avoided or restricted but rather that a realistic view should be taken of what their "multiplier effects" will be for economic and social development in the area. When deciding how to allocate resources for institutional support of nonagricultural enterprise in rural areas, it is important to take account of the different kinds of enterprises that may be promoted.

6.3.2 Types of Activities

The types of enterprises suitable for a particular location will depend on the availability of inputs, access to targeted markets, and technical and managerial skills to produce the particular good or provide the service. Communities will generally have one or more of the following types of enterprises:

(1) *Agricultural Processing.* Generally the main advantage of enterprises of this type lies in minimizing transport costs from the point of production. This is especially true for high bulk products like sugarcane. For a number of crops, such local enterprises provide efficient opportunities for supporting employment and incomes, especially in the most rural areas. Household, private locally owned, and cooperative enterprises will generally turn to the same local supporting institutions for inputs and assistance while outside private enterprises and state-controlled ones will look very little to local institutions except perhaps to obtain raw materials through small private businesses.

(2) *Manufacturing.* These enterprises may produce either intermediate products (e.g., cloth for a clothing industry located elsewhere or tools to produce other items) or final products (e.g., farm implements to be used locally). The product can be oriented either to a local market or to a regional, national, or foreign one. Local enterprises seem better able to identify and meet local needs for products with their "bottom-up" approach to manufacturing. In contrast, "outside" enterprises concerned primarily with competitive advantages tend to view the local area in a "top-down" way—as a profitable opportunity for producing something for an outside market. In manufacturing, household and private, locally owned enterprises may work cooperatively to purchase raw materials or to gain access to technology although they are less likely to sell cooperatively. Producer co-ops, on the other hand, are more likely to engage in cooperative sales.

(3) *Trade and Marketing.* These enterprises can serve to distribute local goods, bring in goods for local production or consumption, and take out goods produced locally. They represent mechanisms for forging *backward and forward linkages* in the production of goods and the delivery of services. A diversified inventory is generally necessary for marketing so, given the size of the local market, small businesses

seem more likely to grow by setting up additional sales sites in other locations than by expanding their inventory in the first operation (Marris and Somerset, 1972). This may mean either that the entrepreneurs are able to manage several times over the same kind and amount of inventory, personnel, etc., but cannot adjust to the qualitative change in management style that handling one single larger operation represents, or that there is no point in expanding beyond a certain size because the local market would become saturated.

(4) *Services.* These enterprises provide personal services such as tailoring or barbering to local residents or a service required by other enterprises such as transport or storage. In addition, hotels or restaurants may serve outsiders who come regularly (e.g., salesmen who come to weekly markets) or intermittently (e.g., tourists). The services provided represent final products, inputs to other enterprises, or even "export" products. The skill levels required as well as the linkages the enterprise already has will determine the extent to which entrepreneurs will turn to local intermediary institutions for support.

Simple operations like tea stalls or human-powered transport (bicycles) can be assisted by an organization such as the Self-Employed Women's Association in India (Annex Five), which was concerned primarily with providing decent working conditions. Activities like tailoring and mechanical repairs can be sustained through apprenticeship training given informally by small enterprises. With "outside" enterprises such as hotels catering to tourists, the skill level is set externally. The persons they hire must satisfy certain skill requirements to be managers though workers may learn enough through on-the-job supervision for simple tasks.

6.3.3 Production Requirements

Availability of inputs, the conditions for processing, and access to markets affect an enterprise's ability to make its products or deliver its services from beginning to end. Obviously these problems reflect the particular characteristics of each activity.

(1) *Raw Materials.* These are the inputs needed for agricultural processing and manufacture, such as fiber to be spun or parts that go into a manufactured item. Supplier cooperatives and private enterprises (operated by individuals or by households) are the local institutions most likely to be able to provide raw materials. Households and small private enterprises can cooperate by buying together, or a co-op may be formed to sell inputs to producers. Service enterprises like small restaurants need "raw materials" just as much as do manufacturing enterprises.

(2) *Technology.* This includes the implements or machinery needed to

produce an item or knowledge about production techniques. Government personnel if they reach the local level (LA) may be in the best position to provide information about technology, while marketing cooperatives and private businesses are most suited to providing actual physical equipment or inputs to micro, small, and cooperative enterprises.

(3) *Training (for Production and Management)*. The human skills that go with any activity are intrinsically related to the complexity of the technology being used. Skills are often acquired informally through apprenticeship or as a "spillover" from other job experience. Where training becomes more formal, it may well enter from "outside" the locality. With moderately demanding managerial or production tasks, local administration (through extension activities or seminars) and middlemen (a type of private enterprise) seem the most likely channels to turn to. Local service organizations may be best able to work with household enterprises and perhaps with small local enterprises.

(4) *Credit*. Funds for enterprise activity provide opportunity for innovation and expansion of activities over a longer time period. Special lending programs through branches of state banks (LA) are a potential source of credit at least for small private enterprises and formal co-ops. Larger outside and state-controlled enterprises are not likely to obtain their credit from local institutions. The private enterprise channel includes small-scale moneylenders or wholesalers who may make loans in-kind and branches of commercial banks, which lend on a larger scale. Between these two main types of private credit arrangements, all five enterprise types should be able to obtain some amount of credit. Cooperative credit mobilization can be accomplished through rotating savings, credit associations or revolving loan funds. These can be operated by a local service organization or by a producers' cooperative itself, as well as by groups of micro-entrepreneurs.

(5) *Information*. More than market information about a firm's potential clientele is needed. Information is necessary about the availability of inputs, technology, etc. as well as about who might be existing or potential customers. A great deal of information about input, product, and service markets is informally exchanged at the household, small private, and cooperative levels. In addition, market and input information (to be sure, not always unbiased) is provided by middlemen, who represent one form of private enterprise. The possibility also exists of local organizations forming around common information needs. Large private and parastatal enterprises generally bypass local institutions in satisfying their information needs, either by obtaining information elsewhere or by collecting it on their own. Once again, local administration represents a potential source of information for all but the household enterprise.

(6) *Market Control.* This is often an important element in enterprise success. It can be a result of size, or can come from legislation, or even physical force. Local government can play a role in regulating local economic activity; for example, limiting the licenses it grants in order to protect local enterprises from outside or excessive competition. LG and LA are much less likely to regulate or protect large "outside" enterprises, and in fact they may themselves be controlled by these enterprises. Scale is one means of gaining some market protection, or of reducing the uncertainties of fluctuations in supply and demand. It can be achieved through cooperative purchases and/or sales (either through private or cooperative production arrangements). Clearly large private enterprises and parastatals possess a certain advantage in the area of scale.

(7) *Common Infrastructure.* This includes such items as roads, market-places, and electricity. These are generally although not exclusively available through local public sector institutions (LA and LG) as discussed in Chapter Three. Cooperatives may be in a position to lobby for these things or even to provide them if their membership represents an important portion of the population in terms of numbers or status. Large private firms or parastatals may either exert pressure on LA or LG to provide infrastructure services or they may bring this infrastructure in on their own, i.e., through private enterprise.

(8) *Producer Infrastructure.* This includes such things as storage facilities, transport services, and other infrastructure generally available through private sources. Private enterprise and sometimes cooperatives seem the local institutions best equipped to provide such things as warehouses, refrigeration facilities, or trucking, although parastatals can have recourse to local administration where other types of enterprise would not.

There is a great deal of variety in the possible local institution channels for providing a particular input. Each of the six types discussed in Section 6.2 seems to have a particular advantage in some area. Local administration, through extension programs, seems best positioned to provide *information about technology*, though also *training programs* and *subsidized credit*. Together with local government it can provide *market controls* and *common infrastructure*. Besides lobbying, membership organizations seem to have a possible role in providing inputs, but they appear to have the smallest role overall among local institutional channels for NAE development. Cooperatives and private enterprises overlap a great deal in their ability to provide *raw materials, technology, credit* (through banks or revolving funds), and *producer infrastructure*. Local service organizations seem most suited to providing *training* or administering *special credit programs*.

The analysis of production requirements, along with differences in ownership and types of activity, suggests how multifaceted an institutional strategy for promoting nonagricultural enterprise needs to be. While the enterprises involved may be fairly small and even simple, their needs and potentialities are diverse. The array of local intermediary institutions that can assist them is similarly varied. Certainly there are options in most cases as a particular NAE need can be met by more than a single type of local supporting institution though not necessarily equally well by all six kinds of LIIs. NAE planners and promoters need to recognize the range of LID possibilities and to introduce or strengthen those kinds of local intermediary institutions which have some evident "fit" with the units of production to be assisted. While these will vary by ownership type and activity, as discussed above, the production requirements enumerated in this third section will generally apply to all kinds of NAEs.

6.4 INSTITUTIONAL APPROACHES TO NONAGRICULTURAL DEVELOPMENT

A program to promote nonagricultural enterprise development giving due attention to strengthening the local institutional network that supports NAE can have various thrusts:

(a) directly assisting *production units* to help them increase their size and stability thereby contributing to their movement toward status as local institutions;

(b) contributing to the *diffuse institutional environment* at local levels, i.e., to the development of institutions that are not organizations— specifically nurturing the expansion of local markets for goods and services or for supply of inputs (labor, equipment, raw materials, capital, etc.); or

(c) developing *local intermediary institutions* that encourage and bolster NAE units.

We have been focusing on the latter as they should contribute to (a) and (b), improving upon direct efforts to promote these first two strategic aims. Financial resources, training, technical information, etc., can be channeled to NAEs in ways that create mutual regard and interdependence with local intermediary institutions thereby building up the latter for long-run service roles. If LIIs are bypassed, local enterprises will remain dependent on more remote external sources of support. Local intermediary institutions are in a better position to assist nonagricultural enterprises and nurture market and related institutional development as they are rooted in the locality or community. To be sure, the value of these institutions in terms of NAE should always be judged with regard to (a) increasing the size and stability of local production units, and (b) making the diffuse local institutional environment more favorable for enterprise expansion not simply in terms of institutionalizing the LIIs.

The discussion here focuses first on enhancing the services that LIIs are equipped to provide and with encouraging relationships among local intermediary institutions, including cooperation and division of labor among those local institutions which provide NAE support. Services can be provided to enterprises in such a way that a more permanent capacity shared among various local intermediary institutions is established to bolster NAE. One needs to be concerned with how assistance is rendered since this may be as important as what is done for them.

Efforts by "outside" agencies should encourage close linkage of enterprises to any and all supportive elements in their local environment. This includes other enterprises, even competitors, who may derive mutual benefit from some degree of cooperation. Too often an outside agency seeks strong vertical linkages only with itself for purposes of guidance and control.[6] These inhibit horizontal linkages with other NAEs, or even vertical linkages with other sources of support. An enterprise's gaining acceptance from others for operating in what they deem "appropriate" ways substantially enhances its long-run prospects and is the hallmark of "institutionalization."

Recognizing these various needs for linkage directs NAE development strategies to proceed on three operating principles: (a) encouraging cooperation among local intermediary institutions in assisting existing or new enterprises directly, (b) providing assistance in ways that have long-run value, and (c) encouraging local firms to look to one another for goods, services, or information they might require.

6.4.1 Strengthening Local Intermediary Institutions

For government or donor agencies to assist NAEs, which are normally diverse and dispersed, it is usually most effective to work with and through intermediary institutions of various types as described in Section 6.2. Various organizational development services such as staff in-service training can be provided to LIIs, which in turn are assisting NAEs (Looye, 1984). Several examples are given in Annex Six, such as CEDECO in Chile, the local affiliate of Partnership for Productivity in Burkina Faso, and the Micro Industries Development Center (MIDC) in the Philippines. This last institution, a nonprofit, nonstock company, is particularly interesting because it provides assistance to public and private organizations (LIIs) that in turn

---

[6]This subject of linkages, contrasting "assisting" and "controlling" linkages, is treated analytically in Leonard and Marshall (1982:35–38, 220–222 and passim.).

promote small enterprises. It has neither regular offices nor paid staff. Instead, leadership comes from individuals who are "seconded" from the agencies sponsoring and supporting the MIDC. In carrying out its role as "catalyst and facilitator," the MIDC helps

> with the development of skills in project design and implementation, and with the diffusion of information on activities that support enterprise development. It also serves as a vehicle for liaison with government agencies. Liaison activities can include arranging for subcontracting opportunities within the context of the government's development efforts, and consultation with bilateral donors on the resources available for small enterprise promotion. MIDC has also been involved directly in lobbying for the interests of small business. (Hunt, 1984:192)

For example, the MIDC has arranged technical assistance in microenterprise program design and evaluation, business management and planning, socio-economic survey work, and staff training and development for organizations such as the YMCA and the Philippine Agency for Community and Family, which are helping NAEs. In addition, the MIDC brokered a relationship between Appropriate Technology Intl. and Manila Community Services, Inc., an organization directly involved with income-generating activities, so that the latter could raise its credit ceiling for clients with expansion and employment potential (Bear and Tiller, 1982:113). With a fluid organizational structure, an agency like the MIDC can draw upon its broad network of contacts to help LIIs better serve NAEs. These "umbrella" and "brokerage" functions as Hunt calls them, are crucial where LIIs like the YMCA in this Philippine case are isolated or must operate on a severely limited budget.

Enhancing LIIs' capacity to encourage local enterprises directly goes beyond strengthening the capacity of individual LIIs, however. An important aspect of their becoming more stable and productive involves creating some division of labor among LIIs—in effect creating a nonorganizational institution for NAE out of cooperation among the local institutions assisting the process of nonagricultural development.

This principle can be applied with respect to banks and credit provision, for example. In an uncoordinated situation, all LIIs might be giving many different kinds of aid including credit for which some do not have a comparative advantage. Government policy could give incentives for local bank branches to increase their lending for NAE, recognizing that banks (which are not viewed as charities) have higher repayment rates than other kinds of agencies (government or charitable). At the same time, other LIIs could be encouraged to help identify potential borrowers and back them up with technical assistance, training, etc. LIIs should specialize in doing what they do best, e.g., LIIs other than bank branches might concentrate on noncredit forms of NAE support. This of course presumes good working relations among LIIs and that horizontal linkages will be developed between banks and other LIIs so that a network of NAE support activities becomes institutionalized.

6.4.2 Assisting Local Enterprises

Modes and Types of NAE Support. Most NAE support is intended to increase the size or improve the stability of enterprises however small or fluctuating they may be. Size and stability may be thought of as marking a "path" along which an enterprise can travel (or as constituting a continuum along which any enterprise can be located). The most appropriate kinds of assistance, types of program, and mode of intervention will generally correspond to the levels of enterprise development represented by differences in size and stability.

These relationships are sketched in Figure 6.2 with "levels" of NAE development shown on the left as a series of "steps."[7] In the lower left-hand corner, we have individuals who have many social or economic disadvantages and who are practically outside the stream of economic production and income. How one deals with them is quite different from how one deals with formal enterprises represented at the top of the "ladder." Persons below the dotted line in the middle of the figure might be regarded as "pre-entrepreneurs" in the same sense that some governments have set up programs to work with "pre-cooperatives" for some period of time to establish seriousness of purpose and to impart necessary management skills before the enterprise can qualify for registration and assistance as a full-fledged cooperative. The figure emphasizes that agencies working on NAE development should think in terms of a continuum of orientations and capacities with different kinds of support being appropriate at different levels.

As seen from the second column, the kinds of support that are most promising will differ substantially. The most advanced enterprises need capital, management training, and commercial services like insurance, market information, etc.; nothing very different from what large "modern" enterprises require. The most interesting range for assistance is the middle one where the aim is to accelerate activity and strengthen capacity so that enterprises can "move up" the ladder as and when feasible. The least advantaged group needs very basic kinds of education, counseling, and small loans—not even "credit," let alone "capital." With some success in these activities, persons may become economically productive to the extent that they can begin moving along the upward "path" described in Figure 6.2.

---

[7]This scheme derives from the graphic analysis contributed by Cheryl Lassen during the LID workshop held at Cornell in 1984.

Figure 6.2: SUPPORT STRATEGIES FOR DIFFERENT LEVELS OF ENTERPRISE

LEVEL OF ENTERPRISE	KIND OF ASSISTANCE	FOCUS OF PROGRAM*	MODE OF SUPPORT
Urban formal enterprises	Capital loans		
	Advanced management training	Individual	Assistance/ Facilitation
Rural town enterprises (locality level)	Commercial services		
Village enterprises (community level)	Small amounts of capital		
Rural enterprises (group level)	Credit education		
"Micro" enterprise (household level)	Basic management training		
		Group	Promotion/ Facilitation
Self-employed persons (relatively steady cash earnings)	Vocational education		
Seasonal workers (some cash earnings)	Economic organization		
Subsistence producers (not market oriented)	"Entrepreneur" training		
	Marketing assistance		
Individuals significantly disadvantaged socio-economically	Social welfare assistance		
		Community	Promotion
	Basic education		

The paradox of support strategies is that intermediary institutions need to adopt inverted methods of intervention, taking the most collective approach where they need to be working with individuals and working with the individual enterprises where collective capacity has been most strengthened. At

*These are points along a continuum according to Farbman (1981:21).

the lowest levels of enterprise development—where there are no recognizable NAEs and only individuals to work with (and disadvantaged ones at that)—a NAE support program should aim at the whole community, to raise its members' aspirations and competences. When the persons to be assisted are better endowed and somewhat experienced with production processes, a support program can begin dealing more with individuals as members of groups, increasingly focusing on individual differences and capabilities. At the highest levels where NAEs are larger and more established, the strategy can be to deal with enterprises on an individual basis and more as clients than as beneficiaries.

When support for NAE is being provided, the way in which the local community is approached must be considered. Support for local institutional development generally corresponds to one of three modes—*assistance, facilitation,* or *promotion,* as analyzed in Section 7.1.1. In the first, the initiative for getting outside help comes from the local level, whereas in the third, all initiative comes from an outside agency (governmental or nongovernmental). In the second, ideas for institutional strengthening are developed collaboratively between local and outside actors. The first requires some pre-existing local institutional capacity while the third makes no such presumption. With Facilitation, the development of local capacity to set goals and make plans is part of the process.

These three modes are introduced here because they relate clearly to alternative approaches to NAE development. With the least advantaged, the more promising mode of support will usually be Promotion since the individuals involved are too isolated and poorly endowed to be making plans and demands effectively on their own behalf. To the extent they can take some initiative based on their own productive capacity and ambitions, support can be in the Facilitation mode in addition to Promotion. At the higher levels, Assistance can replace Promotion as an intervention strategy with Facilitation continuing to be appropriate.

Local Enterprise Needs. Even though programs that support NAE are usually intended to benefit the communities in which they are located, these programs need to be aware of what makes individual local enterprises successful. Apart from the ability of individuals or groups to manage them, successful nonagricultural enterprises exhibit three basic characteristics.

    (1) They are *demand driven.* In answer to the question "What shall we do?" their first concern is "What is our market?"

    (2) They undertake activities in which they have a *comparative advantage.* This advantage can be at the local, regional, national, or international level, and necessarily takes into consideration the regular availability both of necessary inputs or services along with an assured clientele.

    (3) They operate in a way that maintains the *basic economic viability* of

their enterprise. This need not be to the exclusion of other broader goals, but failure to perform well financially generally precludes attaining other benefits.

This is not to suggest that single-minded business analysis as a basis for NAE support will guarantee the survival of local enterprises or of the institutions that provide such support. Beyond being responsive to these three characteristics, other considerations affect LIIs' utility to NAEs and ultimately their durability. These include attention to local political and economic considerations, cultural practices, and formal versus informal methods of operation.

It is important for program success to consider constraints on the local economy, i.e., how it relates to the extra-local economy and how economic activities may be controlled by elites. Undertaking activities that threaten existing arrangements may well be advisable or even essential but this should be done with full awareness of the risks involved. The Deedar Cooperative Society in Bangladesh offers a good example of working effectively and sequentially within serious politico-economic and socio-cultural constraints. This remarkable case of nonagricultural local development started with regular small group savings and purchase of bicycle rickshaws to get members out of their indebtedness and poverty. As capital was built up, the cooperative diversified into brickmaking, truck transport, and providing marketing facilities, among other activities. At all times, the leadership and membership kept a firm grip on the economics of their operations, which paid off. The co-op has grown from nine members to 1,200, with savings built up from a few annas per member per day to share capital of almost 2 million thaka and cooperative assets of over 6 million thaka. To ensure that control of the co-op and utilization of its assets would not be lost for the poor, a ceiling was set on the number of shares a member could hold, and size of loans was intentionally kept small as part of a "policy of deliberate exclusion of the rich." The board of directors is still made up of landless and smallholder members (Annex Six).

In addition to assessing the economic and political climate, cultural norms must be considered, especially those regarding individual or group undertakings, proper use of profits, the appropriateness of assuming risks and charging interest, and many other things ethnocentrically assumed by Westerners to be a part of "normal" business activity. Programs must carefully examine the points of similarity and difference where local and outside "worlds" come together in business activities. Beyond providing defensible "business advice," LIIs should help enterprises develop operating procedures that bridge both sets of requirements as this will strongly affect their transformation into local institutions.

In Burkina Faso (formerly Upper Volta), Partnership for Productivity/ International has addressed this problem by developing the capacity of an affiliate, PfP/Upper Volta, as an intermediary institution providing locally acceptable credit training, credit administration, and managerial assistance (A. Brown, 1984). Of special interest is their policy of extending credit without requiring material collateral. Instead, creditworthiness is determined on the basis of judgments about character and willingness to cooperate with the lending institution and repay the loan. An equity contribution of 20 percent to cost of the proposed activity is required. Beyond this there is flexibility so that repayments can be rescheduled when clients face difficulties but are making serious efforts to repay their debt. This is how business dealings are conducted "traditionally." At the same time, PfP/UV has a clear and well-publicized policy of resorting to legal proceedings against defaulters when it believes a client no longer intends to pay the debt. Also important, PfP employs only staff from Burkina Faso who may be able to sense what will be accepted locally and what will not (Annex Six). However, character-based screening, which is becoming increasingly accepted as practical, requires a local institutional base with decentralized decision making.[8]

Working in "appropriate" ways, which is essential for institutionalization, is not only a matter of dealing with cultural differences. Frequently when so-called "formal" and "informal" organizations interact, there will be considerable incongruence between the ways they do business. Means that are acceptable to large, formal enterprises may not be understood or appreciated in small ones. This is especially critical where government-supported programs are involved. Costs of registration (in terms of money and time) may preclude "informal" firms from taking advantage of services that require certain paperwork or official certificates for eligibility, for example. Ways of dealing with firms must differ depending on whether there are 500 or 5 employees in the enterprise.

One approach to this problem has been to develop "blindness" to the legal status of firms being assisted. In northeastern Brazil, an intermediary institution (UNO) not only lends to both legal and clandestine firms; it is actually reluctant to encourage small firms to legalize themselves until it is clear that they are developed and stable enough to warrant the expense (Annex Six). Unfortunately such a policy may prevent clandestine firms from eventually availing themselves of formal credit arrangements or from obtaining contracts with business firms or other entities that require documentation. Furthermore, the contradiction of a publicly supported organization encouraging extra-legal operations may ultimately undermine the stability of the LII itself (Tendler, 1983a:124, 137–139).

---

[8]Liedholm (1985:10) observes, based on his review of many schemes for getting credit to small enterprises: "Local institutions are able to have intimate knowledge of their clients that is central to a low-cost appraisal of the entrepreneur. They also reduce the transaction costs of the entrepreneurs desiring loans by reducing travelling as well as waiting time."

6.4.3 Developing Local Economic Networks

The transformation of linkages into networks is particularly important for the development of a local economy. Instead of having just individual connections among enterprises and supporting institutions, whole sets of exchange relations and interactions need to develop so that flows of inputs and outputs become more varied and sustainable, less vulnerable and fluctuating. Several operating principles can guide LIIs in their provision of service to NAEs to maximize their impact in this matter.

Emphasize local economic linkages. Outside agencies should give priority to funding economic activities that establish backward or forward linkages to other economic activities in the community by creating demand for local inputs or outputs. In this way, a network of criss-crossing local economic relationships can begin to emerge. Another approach is to identify products not currently produced locally but for which all inputs and technical expertise are available locally, and then to encourage new or existing NAEs to produce these goods or services. This is something that the PfP program in Burkina Faso has stressed in making loans to small rural enterprises.

Use local expertise in training. One approach to training is to use apprenticeship or training visits as means not only to expose new businesses to established ones, but also to reduce the need for outside agency staff to develop expertise on each area of activity. Staff can then function more as facilitators, by having created a network of people in the local area who function as role models for others. If LII staff have developed a great deal of specific knowledge rather than rely on local sources of expertise, it will be harder for them to "work themselves out of a job" or to want to do so. PfP in Burkina Faso, for example, rather than try to do much technical training itself requires a period of apprenticeship as part of the "feasibility study" a client must do to qualify for a loan. Especially where the proposed economic activity is a new one, PfP believes it is important that the applicant work in an established firm to gain skills and insight into the activity itself as well as to demonstrate sincere and sufficient interest in developing his or her own enterprise.

Form NAE associations. Since many of the relations discussed here can be between cooperatives and private enterprises or other NAEs, it can be useful to create explicit linkages among them. In addition to fostering commercial or collaborative exchanges of goods and services or information, enterprises can be encouraged to meet to discuss credit, management, and other problems as a group. If there is enough common interest among NAEs in economic collaboration, they may form a service cooperative (with pooling of resources) rather than an association (which is like a limited liability company).

Adjust government policies. It is important to consider how national policies affect NAEs. Policies can be adopted that encourage local purchasing of goods and services; for example, government contracts could be permitted with unregistered firms for items such as vehicle maintenance or work uniforms. Another policy modification would be to reduce excessive government regulation, particularly that regarding cooperative enterprises. Frequently regulations for cooperative registration impede institutional development either by dissipating groups' limited resources or by altogether discouraging them from organizing. A case in point is the Chilean precooperative COMARCHI, which had to form a separate marketing agency since it did not have the legal status to market the artisan craftwork it was organized to make (Annex Six).

To summarize, approaches to local institutional development operate at several levels: strengthening local intermediary institutions, assisting local production units in appropriate ways, and encouraging the transformation of linkages among NAEs into a network of interconnecting firms. In addition, there need to be supportive official policies and practices. Efforts along these lines should not represent discrete activities but rather should be parts of an overall program for NAE support that will weave together these LID strategies.

6.5 CHOICES IN PROVIDING SUPPORT

The discussion so far has focused on local institutions and on their operations as they may promote NAE. LID, however, frequently involves outside agencies, whether national government or private voluntary organizations or international donors. Two issues in particular confront agencies: whether to combine financial and nonfinancial aid to NAEs and whether to support individual or group enterprises. A third question is how to evaluate NAE program performance with regard to economic criteria and the broader social goals they embrace since NAE objectives go beyond economic gains for individual enterprises.

6.5.1 Financial vs. Nonfinancial Support

The question of whether to combine credit with other forms of NAE support has different answers depending on the level of development of the enterprises in question. We have indicated in Figure 6.2 the diversity of NAEs, sketching a continuum of initiative and competence.

Where enterprises are at the higher end of the "ladder," they are likely to be able to integrate credit and technical assistance independently. For them, LIIs would be most effective by providing the services for which they respectively have a comparative advantage such as credit or marketing information. This is important particularly for banks, which appear to be best at making and collecting loans rather than providing technical advice and guidance. Bank-sponsored programs are most efficient when providing only credit, not trying to get more deeply engaged in the workings of enterprises (Liedholm, 1985; Stearns, 1985). This minimizes their administrative costs and, perhaps surprisingly, their record in getting repayment of loans is better.[9] This observation applies more to programs directed at advanced NAEs, however, where credit and technical assistance can be separated, and other kinds of intermediary institutions besides banks can cater to other NAE needs.

Nonagricultural enterprises at the other end of the continuum are not so able to manage either credit or technical responsibilities, and LIIs accordingly can be helpful in integrating these. One approach is to use credit as an incentive for other types of assistance, as a kind of "carrot on a stick." In its programs in Burkina Faso, Partnership for Productivity uses the desire for credit as an opening to assist entrepreneurs in developing management skills. For example, applications for loans require applicants to complete a number of small discrete tasks such as doing a market survey or listing all inputs and their sources. Eventually when loans are extended, borrowers have a better knowledge base for dealing with their enterprise's challenges. If a loan is not approved, the applicant should have benefited from the tasks of "management self-training," and this may encourage new and better proposals for credit-supported activities. The entire process is intended to develop NAE capacity at the local level not just to make loans.

6.5.2 Individual vs. Group Enterprises

An important concern in the support of individually owned enterprises is whether it creates or exacerbates differences between the "haves" and "have-nots" within a community. Even if there is some benefit to the community in the form of new products or services becoming available, it seems inappropriate for a development project to knowingly promote inequality. Support for group NAE attempts to address this problem but presents another problem. It is harder to develop capacity with a group than it is with an individual. For example, it may be difficult to get a group to agree to delay withdrawing profits so as to reinvest them in the business since members are not all likely to be equally committed to making the business succeed.

There is a great deal of discussion about the concept of entrepreneurship and whether it is appropriate to attempt to encourage this through group enterprises. Taking business risks does appear to be more feasible for an individual than for a group of persons. Nevertheless, there

---

[9]Liedholm (1985) shows credit-only programs having administrative costs (as a percentage of loans) ranging between 4 and 30 percent, whereas for schemes combining credit and technical assistance, this range is from 19 to 185 percent. On the other hand, arrears in repayment (as a percent of loans outstanding) were only between 6 and 15 percent for credit-only programs while with credit and assistance programs, the range was from 8 to 42 percent.

are enough examples of successful group ventures that no firm rule is established.[10] Perhaps the best policy is to structure NAE support so that whichever avenue small-scale investors themselves want to follow can be accommodated by the program. Staff need to be aware of the pitfalls associated with both individual and group forms of enterprise, just as there are specific problems associated with agricultural processing or service enterprises that staff should know and be able to advise on.

One approach is to mix individual and group activities. In Recife, Brazil, for example, a chain of corner shops called "UNIPOP" (União Popular) was formed by individual store owners who gathered together at first irregularly and then regularly to discuss their problems. They established solidarity and attracted community recognition by adopting a common logo for their stores. Eventually their activities came to include purchasing certain goods (such as telephone tokens) on a group basis in order to obtain wholesale prices. Their uniting did not necessarily spread the risks of business ownership, but it did reduce some risks of operation by diminishing business costs and by spreading information. In addition it offered the individual shop owners a forum for discussion and an opportunity to learn from invited guest speakers.

6.5.3 Ongoing Support and Evaluation

Donor agencies enjoy a distance from day-to-day operations and demands that offers them the opportunity to be concerned with broader social goals, particularly local institutional development. In as much as local institutional development represents a valid goal, donors ought to be willing to evaluate program or project performance in those terms. Right now, projects are usually rated in terms of aggregated numbers of loans granted, repayment rates, and the like. The temptation to do this type of evaluation is obviously great since these things are easily quantifiable. But there is need to develop evaluation frameworks for assigning some explicit value to social and institutional gains as well as to economic payoffs (PfP, 1984:6). Donors should look at outcomes like borrowers' learning from their business failures or connections established among local enterprises rather than just at aggregate measures.[11] The development of appropriate evaluation criteria

---

[10]The risk-taking literature for small farmers suggests that their primary concern is not with maximizing the probability of the greatest single profit but with minimizing the probability of a devastating single loss. This suggests why group activities may remain attractive. The ILO/ DANIDA study referred to above gives many case studies of group enterprise involving rural women (Muntemba, 1985).

[11]Apart from economic benefits to individuals and localities, equity benefits, the empowerment of poor or disadvantaged people through the development of skills, greater self-esteem, and ability to plan and choose among options should be taken into account (PfP, 1984). With regard to the local economy, benefits to be recognized in evaluation include increased variety of consumer goods or lower prices, increased services made available to local producers, and the strengthening of "enabling industries" such as transporters and suppliers.

and techniques for projects that address the development of local institutional capacity will provide better rationale for funding NAE programs in the future and should provide them with more flexibility and incentive to develop new approaches to NAE that incorporate LID as an explicit and attainable goal.

CHAPTER SEVEN

Strategies for Supporting Local Institutional Development

7.1 MODES OF SUPPORT

Establishing local institutional capacity requires not only time and resources but also appropriate strategies and concepts. Demand for LID will not create its own supply any more than supply will necessarily create its own demand. Building local capacities is likely to depend more on how support is given than on how much as this is an area where qualitative considerations commonly loom larger than quantitative ones. Support given in ways that create dependency or that alienate people is likely to be worse than giving none at all. A negative correlation is observed between local organizations' performance and simply the amount of linkage with government. On the other hand, strict "autonomy" is not likely to be most productive for local development as some degree of outside involvement can have positive results so long as it does not become "direction" (Esman and Uphoff, 1984:153–155).

Strategies for support of local institutional development, suggested in Section 1.9, correspond usually to one of three modes: assistance, facilitation, and promotion. These represent different degrees of outside involvement in local institutional affairs but also differ in the kind of relationships established. In working with local institutions in any of these modes, a "learning process" approach is likely to be the most effective strategy for donor and government investments in LID.

7.1.1 Promotion, Facilitation, and Assistance

The most appropriate mode for efforts to strengthen local institutional capacity will depend on (a) what *capabilities* already exist, and (b) where *initiative* for changes in the status quo comes from.

(1) Where there are functioning local institutions such as local govern-
    ments, private enterprises, or cooperatives able to identify needs
    and problems, to develop plans for dealing with these, and to deter-
    mine what outside aid would be helpful, the mode for LID can be
    one of ASSISTANCE.

(2) In some situations local institutions will be less extensive or less ex-
    perienced and thus less able to initiate activities, at least at the
    outset. In such cases a larger role for outside agencies may be appro-
    priate to help create greater local capacity at the same time
    particular needs and problems are addressed. In such a case the LID
    mode can be one of FACILITATION.

(3) In still other circumstances there may be some urgent problem or
    need that an outside agency wishes to deal with, but local institu-
    tions are underdeveloped, at least with regard to that activity area.
    The approach may then be to reorient and strengthen existing insti-
    tutions to further program objectives or to develop entirely new
    local capacities to further these goals. This LID mode is character-
    ized as PROMOTION.

The three modes of support can be characterized schematically as
sketched in Figure 7.1 below, contrasting differences in the strength of existing local institutions capable of dealing with particular development
activities and the source of initiative for addressing certain problems.

Figure 7.1: MODES OF SUPPORT FOR LOCAL INSTITUTIONAL DEVELOPMENT

EXISTING LOCAL
INSTITUTIONAL CAPACITY

SOURCE OF INITIATIVE	Strong	Weak
Local	- - -ASSISTANCE - - - - - - - - - - - - - - - -	
Shared	- - - - - - - - -FACILITATION - - - - - - - - - -	
Outside	- - - - - - - - - - - - - - -PROMOTION - - -	

Which mode is most appropriate depends on the problems that need to
be addressed and on the extent of existing capabilities. Even if one would
prefer that outside agencies respond to initiatives from local institutions,
there will be circumstances where urgent problems are encountered and
local institutions are nonexistent or too weak to identify a problem, to agree
on a solution, or even to seek assistance. When faced with rapid deforestation or a cattle disease epidemic, arguments for a promotion approach are
more compelling than for assistance only.

While it is possible to combat deforestation or disease without concern for local institutional development, achieving even the immediate objective of stemming the loss of trees or cattle will usually require at least some strengthening of the capabilities of a forestry or livestock department (LA) at the local level. This would require some effort in a promotion mode. To go beyond this and to protect reforested areas or to bring about disease control measures, more LID would be needed, such as augmenting local government capacity or starting user groups to obtain and sustain local awareness and cooperation.

A promotion mode is not necessarily dictatorial or unilateral. It is defined by its external source of initiative and its establishment or strengthening of local institutions to achieve a particular programmatic goal rather than to increase local capacity for more general purposes. A facilitation mode is more flexible and accommodating since decisions about goals and methods at the local level are arrived at more collaboratively. A facilitation effort may focus on a specific activity such as irrigation improvement while the outside agency is also helping localities, communities, and groups to develop capacities relevant to other problems they identify for action. In the assistance mode, the outside agency receives requests for technical advice, funds, training, or other kinds of aid specified by a local group or community. However, sufficient local institutional capacity for this mode simply may not exist.[1]

Obviously these three modes constitute a continuum more than a set of mutually exclusive types of action. In what may be formally an assistance mode, the outside agency may be helping local institutions to formulate requests, which represents a degree of facilitation. Or a promotion effort may have spillover effects that strengthen other local institutions so that it involves facilitation. A self-styled facilitation program could operate in such a directive manner that it becomes promotion; or if there is an active community response it could practically become assistance.

Appreciating the differences among these three modes focuses attention on the source of initiative and the existing local capability as important considerations. In the field the analytical distinction can become blurred. The Kottar Social Service Society in India (Annex Seven) made it a practice never to go into a community with its health, agricultural, or employment activities unless it was asked, which suggests assistance. But once working with farmers, mothers, fishermen, potters, or others, it sought to establish cooperatives so that it operated in a facilitation mode as "an organization which organizes" (Field, 1980). The crucial consideration is whose objectives are shaping the effort.

---

[1]A study by the World Bank's Transportation Department of its project experience identified only two cases where it had been able to work in an assistance mode, with municipal (locality) governments in Brazil and with Saemaul Undong community organizations in South Korea

The government of Botswana with foreign assistance embarked on a program to establish communal cattle ranches, offering individuals or groups exclusive rights to use of rangeland. This promotion effort failed because the scheme was presented to people as a package and did not fit their ecologically-based land use practices, discussed in Chapter Two. A more careful examination of what collective action already existed would have revealed a broad range of existing farmer and community groups operating in the traditional land tenure areas, as discussed in Section 5.2.3. These organizations, however, did not involve everyone in the farming community. The extension service was mandated to promote more formal group action particularly through Farmer Committees. Responsibility for decisions and actions was to remain with these groups, making this program in principle more one of facilitation than promotion. In fact, the best results came when the government operated essentially in an assistance mode.[2]

The kind of support given to local institutions by outside agencies can and often should change over time. The capabilities of local institutions in a certain area can increase relative to the problems encountered, justifying an assistance role for outside agencies. If the problems become greater, on the other hand, promotion efforts may be warranted. To the extent that mutual confidence has been fostered, outside efforts are more likely to meet with acceptance and cooperation. The Bangladesh Rural Advancement Committee (BRAC), established after that country's independence, offers a good example of a changing LID support role. Initially BRAC worked in a promotion mode, providing relief services "for" the people. As it gained experience it began working to establish local organizations that encouraged rural people's participation. This eventually transformed BRAC's role to one of supporting local initiatives in an assistance mode (Korten, 1980; Ahmed, 1980).

Assessing modes of support is made more complicated by the fact that they can occur differently at different levels of action. Often local institutional development is furthered by an intermediary organization such as BRAC, which operates supra-locally but seeks to foster local capacity. External agencies may work with an intermediary organization in an assistance or facilitation mode, while that intermediary organization is itself interacting with communities and groups in a promotion mode, to provide and engage people in primary health care, for example. Conversely the intermediary could be the object of promotion efforts from an outside agency while it is

---

(Beenhakker et al., 1984). Of course, there may have been other opportunities to work in this mode that Bank staff and central government officials overlooked.

[2]In a case study of the Mmankgodi Farmers Association, Kloppenburg (1983) shows the potential for good results when a local organization, started at farmer initiative with encouragement from the government, was able to move into the assistance mode by soliciting and obtaining a small grant from the self-help fund of the American Embassy for construction of a cattle dipping tank then moving into other development activities.

assisting or facilitating the local institutional efforts of rural people. Intermediary organizations of this sort are not "local" institutions. Rather they are trying to boost local institutions. It is important to make this distinction when evaluating LID efforts (Olson et al., 1984).[3]

7.1.2 Learning Process Approach

Recent years have seen an evolution in thinking about planning and implementing development projects. The previously dominant conception was essentially a "blueprint" approach. This assumes that all problems and goals can be identified and agreed upon clearly enough for precise interventions to be specified and carried out according to a comprehensive and detailed plan.[4] This approach is sequential with "experts" called upon to design a program and with less qualified or less capable persons then doing the implementation. Usually some technology is recommended to raise productivity, and the project stipulates specific resources—financial, human, and material—needed to apply the technology. If some new or better institutions are thought to be needed, they will also be designed and implemented in a "blueprinted" manner. However, this approach has failed on numerous grounds.

(1) First, it requires a degree of knowledge and consensus on both ends and means that is unattainable. Even if the objective is clear and agreed upon, what needs to be done to reach it can hardly be known in much detail in advance, if only because situations are themselves always changing.[5]

(2) Even if a design is well informed and well conceived, it is not likely to be applicable to the wide variety of circumstances found in the real world. Heterogeneity is usually glossed over in the design process. However, standard organizational models often end up fitting no situation very well. Modification and adaptation are invariably needed.[6]

---

[3]In Chapter Six, we discussed the role of local intermediary institutions (LIIs) in supporting nonagricultural enterprise. These might or might not be entirely "local" in their base and scope of operation, whereas the intermediary organizations referred to here are usually "supralocal." Intermediary organizations are analyzed by Hellinger and associates (1981) in their summary of a research project done for Appropriate Technology International.

[4]Shortcomings of this approach and the "planning" doctrine from which it derives are documented and analyzed in Rondinelli (1982). Earlier critiques of the "blueprint" approach were offered by Morss et al. (1976) and Sweet and Weisel (1979).

[5]Few institutional arrangements have had more deliberate and intelligent advance planning than the Kenya Tea Development Authority, discussed in Section 5.4 and Annex Seven. According to Lamb and Mueller, however, "Despite considerable background work and deliberation, the planners did not know enough in advance to set up a 'perfect' organization immediately, nor could they anticipate all the changes which would affect it over the years. It would have been unrealistic to expect otherwise." (1982:49) Organizational flexibility has been a dominant theme in KTDA's development.

[6]The inapplicability of standardized LID schemes is shown in the case of cooperative credit and marketing societies in northern Nigeria documented by King (1975).

(3) Because improvisation and innovation as well as innumerable other skills are required during the implementation phase, it is a misconception to assume that implementors do not need to be as capable and imaginative as designers, or that there can be a dichotomy between the "thinkers" and the "doers." Implementors of projects probably need to be even more creative than designers for achieving the institutional development that is needed.

What has emerged as an alternative to the "blueprint" approach is what Korten (1980) describes as a "learning process" approach, sometimes referred to simply as a "process" approach.[7] Support for this alternative grew out of practical experience. Lazaro, Taylor, and Wickham, for example, found from their review of irrigation management in Asia, that an inductive experimental approach was more promising than a fixed plan to be implemented on a national scale:

> a strategy tailoring water-user associations to local needs and initiating them on a phased basis, beginning with the situations in which the chances of success are greatest, may be more productive in the long run than the commonly advocated attempts in some countries for widespread and immediate introduction of associations. (1979:7)

The Kottar Social Service Society in India developed a flexible approach to working with communities which Field (1980:161) characterizes as the "art of guiding incremental change." Botswana experience has showed a similar orientation to learning from initial mistakes, formulating a national program that built on these (Kloppenburg, 1983). The San Martin Jilotepeque cooperative in Guatemala (Annex Five) is a good example of how proceeding inductively can produce some remarkable results. Learning process does not refrain from engaging in action because knowledge is less than perfect, but neither does it move farther than necessary in a prejudged direction (Dunn, 1971:156).

Unfortunately the search for "success" in rural development often propels agencies to seek shortcuts, to be overly enthused by any visible gains, and to accelerate or expand activities beyond the knowledge base or the supply of seasoned and committed staff, with unintended results.[8] Developmental change takes time and outcomes may be different from initial appearances. "Successes" can collapse and "failures" may turn out to be successful (Smith et al., 1982). The rush for success, which does not allow time

---

[7]This can also be characterized as "inductive planning" (Esman and Uphoff, 1984:262–265), to emphasize the value of formulating hypotheses about what will probably "work," with continual assessment and revision of strategy. Like Rondinelli (1983), we consider all development initiatives as real-world experiments.

[8]This approach leads usually to failure, where implementors working under time pressure and with mostly outside resources attempt to impose "a new system on a local area rather than go through the time-consuming process of working with local people and their leaders. . . . there is a 'balloon effect': once the external money stops and the foreigners pull out, the system or network made possible by the external funding collapses." (Morss et al., 1976:9).

to experiment, to evaluate, and to develop the human resources needed, can impede achieving objectives or can displace them.

Two examples of large national programs that proceeded in a learning process mode are the self-help water supply program in Malawi and the Saemaul Undong (New Community Movement) in South Korea. The Malawi program started with a pilot project sponsored by the Department of Community Development to show how water could be brought from springs in highland regions to villages needing water on the plains (Annex Three). From the outset community representatives were involved in the planning and design decisions and they in turn mobilized local labor contributions to build the system. Representatives from other communities were brought to observe the pilot scheme and to launch similar efforts elsewhere. At all stages time was taken for consultations and negotiation leading to an understanding of mutual expectations. The communities themselves selected members to be given technical training so that both construction and maintenance could be handled with minimal supervision and input from the Department. Technical and organizational mistakes in the early stages were openly acknowledged and rectified. This gave the program greater strength and momentum, always developing within the limits of its own competence and capabilities.

Neither this program nor Saemaul Undong followed an explicit theory of "learning process" but they demonstrated its elements. Saemaul was much more complex but it also evolved over time (Annex Seven). During its initial phases,

> the national government offered all villages a limited amount of building materials with which to launch small self-help projects. The experience of both successful and less successful communities was analyzed to determine how they organized self-help activities, how they identified and selected leaders, what forms of cooperation they used, and what kinds of government support would be needed to promote self-help projects requiring more extensive cooperation among villagers. (Rondinelli, 1983:92)

The program leadership classified villages into three categories, each receiving material aid on different terms roughly corresponding to the three modes described in the preceeding section.

The Saemaul program actually began more according to a "blueprint," but as experience accumulated, the program's terms were revised accordingly. Acknowledgment of mistakes is never easy, especially in government programs. Korten identifies willingness to "embrace error" as an essential element of a learning process approach. This was one of the most significant features of the small farmer program of the Academy for Rural Development at Comilla in Bangladesh, which has been widely approved as a "success story."[9] The principle of self-criticism stressed by the head of the

---

[9]"The system was developed through a series of trials and errors which involved gathering as much information from the villagers as possible." (Choldin, 1969:485). When the program

Comilla Academy, Akhter Hameed Khan, is valid for any program and is essential for a learning process approach. That trials and errors were documented and shared has helped to encourage a variety of successor programs elsewhere to learn from and avoid some of Comilla's mistakes.

Some governments and donor agencies may think that "learning process" is nothing very new, that they operate according to "rolling plans" and undertake mid-project reviews to make corrections in plan activities. Such plans, however, still presume that some formal document controls actions and that its preparation is the task for skilled professionals (Friedmann, 1976). Learning process does not organize activities into strictly sequential stages, as planning, implementation, and evaluation are regarded as overlapping. Moreover, in a learning process intended beneficiaries are expected to contribute much to the planning, implementation, and evaluation activities along with professionals, which more "formal" planning approaches do not provide for.

Development professionals acknowledge that projects seldom follow the original plans closely. Reasons for alterations range from admitting that certain assumptions did not prove correct, to changes in the political environment that occurred while waiting for final approval of the project. Yet the new or altered documents or the unwritten reformulations that serve as "shadow plans" are more likely to represent administrative expedience than a self-conscious assessment of experience unless an explicit learning process stance is taken. Introducing mid-project evaluations and corrections is better than not having any. But they only convert projects from being like unguided rockets (which once launched cannot have any change in course) to guided missiles which permit some limited reprogramming (or self-destruction) while in flight. Unfortunately government efforts to improve project performance in recent years have resulted in the adoption of "more complex and rigid requirements and procedures for identifying, preparing, appraising and implementing projects" even as the desirability of more flexibility has become increasingly evident (Rondinelli, 1983:47).

Ironically the introduction of more frequent and extensive evaluations of projects contributes to more rigidity when it gives implementors more reason to adhere to initial (and usually inadequate) project designs. Deviations from the design may require not only protracted bureaucratic hassles but may have to be justified later on to evaluators. If one could be certain that a particular modification would produce better results, these would protect one from criticism. But there are more ways for an innovation to go wrong than to succeed, and making adjustments involves personal risk on the part of implementors. Since bureaucratic systems penalize "failure"

---

started receiving major government funding and was expanded into a national program, however, it unfortunately lost much of the discipline and quality that had been built into it by the Comilla Academy as discussed in Section 5.2.4 and Annex Five.

much more readily than they reward "success," most incentives in government and donor agencies work against a learning process approach. Incentives for innovation and adaptation are reduced when evaluation will be undertaken with reference to initial project documentation.

"Learning process" applies to most development activities not just LID, and it can apply to each of the three modes of support analyzed above. There are now quite a number of rich LID experiences to learn from, some of them summarized in the annexes, though the very notion of a learning process implies that each new experience must be treated somewhat differently, remaining open to variations in conditions and objectives as well as means. Such flexibility is important not only for arriving at institutional arrangements suited to and sustainable in the circumstances but also ones that local actors regard as "theirs" and for which they will take responsibility.

7.2 DEVELOPING HUMAN CAPACITIES

Although the term "institutional development" seems to refer to things—to structures, procedures, and abstract performance capabilities—it should always call to mind people, their skills, motivation, and personal efficacy. When one talks of building or strengthening institutions, it is necessary to figure out how the talents and energies in the relevant population can be enlisted, upgraded, and committed on a regular basis to these institutions' operations and improvements. Thus, supporting LID requires particular attention to the human aspects of institutional capacity.

7.2.1 New Approaches To Training

Over the years inordinate expectations have been directed toward training as if the imparting of knowledge and skills through structured programs will necessarily improve people's motivation and ability to carry out organizational tasks. Training centers have been built for many programs, practically as an act of faith, and budget items for "training" have often been substitutes for a thought-out strategy of institutional development. That training has not by itself created strong institutions has led to some disaffection, yet the self-evident need for upgrading human capacities continues to win at least some provision in project designs. The issue is not whether to invest in training but how training efforts might be made more fruitful.

The first suggestion is that training be more dispersed than concentrated. Programs have often recruited one person from a community to attend a conventional training course, expecting him or her to go back and relay the knowledge gained to the rest. This is the way the Training and Visit system works, having a "contact farmer" for each group of "follower farmers" in the program. These groups are often more nominal than real, however, as noted in Section 5.2.1.

A concentrated approach is likely to create both monopolies and vulnerabilities in local institutions. When only one person has information, this can be manipulated to acquire power and advantage, whereas when others share it from the outset the incentives as well as opportunities for diffusion are greater. Moreover, if only one person has the more intensive training and leaves the community (which becomes more likely if training has been concentrated in him or her), the institution receives a setback.[10] Where training has been provided to the whole community, it has more and longer-lasting effects as seen from the carefully conducted experiment by Tandon and Brown (1981). In his comparative analysis of rural development experience in Francophone West Africa and Haiti, Charlick (1984) found a significant correlation between programs' performance and their training of rank-and-file members rather than only leaders.

There are many problems of logistics and resources when undertaking training in rural areas. Some of the more successful local institutional programs have, therefore, tried to make their training simpler and less expensive so as to reach broader numbers directly. As soon as possible, local people should assume responsibility for the training as agents of the local institution rather than of the outside program, as exemplified by the Comas Women's Academy in Peru (Annex Seven).

The BRAC program in Bangladesh is a good example of a program following a highly diversified strategy of training to increase human capacities in many roles—vocational training for women, organizational training for local leaders, specialized training for paramedics, literacy training for almost everyone—to make local institutions stronger (Ahmed, 1980). In her review of health, nutrition, and population programs for the World Bank, Fonaroff (1982) makes the point that there should be training for both health professionals and consumers to participate together in their respective roles. Complementary training of this sort can make both sets of actors more effective. The program in Aceh, Indonesia reported in Annex Seven trained middle-level officials together with villagers to good advantage.

The usual assumption that training is best given to homogeneous groups is quite possibly wrong for rural development since a large part of the behavioral change sought is getting people in different roles, often with different statuses, to work together (RDC, 1974). Training programs that bring such persons together can start new patterns of communication and cooperation whereas segregated training courses reinforce the insularity of different levels that plagues development efforts.

Where not all persons can be trained directly and some members or

---

[10]This is why the Comilla program in Bangladesh had at least two persons from each of its associated cooperative societies participate in the programs at its sub-district training centers.

leaders are to become knowledge brokers, it is very important that the selection of such persons be left to—indeed be required of—local institutions. This was done in Malawi for the technicians who were to guide the self-help water supply program, and because of this, the persons selected were accountable to the community and were more highly motivated both in the training and in the field activities (Glennie, 1982). A problem emerged in the Sarvodaya Shramadana movement in Sri Lanka when the selection of persons to be trained and to operate as community workers was controlled by previous Sarvodaya workers or local leaders. The worker had too little sense of responsibility to the people of the village who had no voice in the selection process (Moore, 1981).

In general the choice of persons for any specialized training is best left to people at the local level. Agencies involved in training should, to be sure, disseminate information locally about what kind of training will be given and for what kind of roles so that local people can attempt to get the best fit between the candidates chosen for training and the course requirements and subsequent responsibilities. If the selection grows out of local discussions about the needs the training will attempt to meet, so much the better. There can be abuses as we saw in a Burkina Faso case where chiefs dominated the selection of women paraprofessionals (Taylor, 1981). But this risk is worth taking in order to encourage closer bonds between those who are receiving the training and those in the community who are to benefit from it. Such responsibility is a stimulus for institutionalization as well as for better results.[11]

Many methods of training need to be revised for working in rural settings. There is some need for various kinds of formal training, but more informal and nonformal methods should be tried. One example is the "evening sittings" used to build a base of understanding and acceptance for the Banki water supply project in India described in Annex Three. Learning is often diffused better in horizontal than in vertical relationships. This means that "trainers" must themselves be willing and able to learn from "trainees." The object of training is to bring about more self-confident, self-directed, self-sustaining efforts within local institutions. The role of trainer becomes more that of facilitator than teacher. Local institutions need to develop problem-solving capabilities, and trainers should be building these up by some combination of sharing knowledge, reinforcing positive attitudes, developing skills, and promoting strategic thinking. Techniques like role-playing and group problem-solving are likely to be more useful than

---

[11]As noted already, one of the weaknesses of the T&V system of agricultural extension is the neglect of such factors in the selection and subsequent accountability of "contact farmers" to "follower farmers." This crucial link in the chain of T&V communication is now getting some consideration (Cernea et al., 1982:150–152). Where it is feared that elites will distort the selection, the community can be asked to nominate several persons, from whom the agency can select "the best qualified" for training.

lectures or recitations. The concept animating the efforts should be one of "developing" people rather than of "training" them (Coombs, 1981:52).

There is also value in promoting what rural people can learn from each other by means of exchanges. Work done among Bolivian peasants is a good example of how training for agricultural development can be facilitated by a program where farmers learn from each other and by getting rural people together to exchange knowledge and experience (Hatch, 1981).[12] Engaging rural residents in programs to help one another learn is a sign of respect for what they know and an encouragement for them to be more self-reliant. Moreover, it can provide more relevant information to those who have responsibility for making local institutions effective. The Malawi water supply program found that visits between communities were a major means of training as well as building support. Strengthening horizontal linkages is discussed below as a separate element of LID strategy, but it should be reinforced by a strategy for training providing for horizontal and not just vertical flows of knowledge. Training can be formulated so as to encourage membership groups of the rural poor to cooperate horizontally and to federate vertically as seen in a new FAO program in Africa (FAO, 1984).

The content of training has to be tailored to the needs of the institution and the persons involved. "Canned" courses or modules are usually less effective than professional trainers like to think. As Early (1984:4) says after surveying training for irrigation management in India, "The major conclusion was that most good training materials are developed for specific purposes and specific programs." Though demand for training materials is often heard from the local level, one of the best ways of developing local capabilities and of encouraging consideration of what the needs and goals of the institution are is to involve local people in planning and designing their own training. Ideas about format and content can be drawn from "examples" developed elsewhere, and outside agencies can make exemplary materials available as a service in support of LID. But participants in the local institution should where possible work out their own training program since this itself is valuable training. A "trainer" from outside can be more effective in a "consultant" or "resource person" role.

In many circumstances part of the effort of human resource development to support LID will involve literacy and numeracy training. Such training is more likely to be effective when tied into the substantive programs of the institution as Hirschman found in a case from Colombia (1984:6-11). Where the operating procedures for an institution are complex enough to require a fairly high order of education, it is worth trying to simplify the operations rather than to train persons up to a particularly high

---

[12]Hatch has taken the process a step further by compiling and publishing in Spanish the local knowledge of agriculture, health, and other practices, thereby making this available to a broader audience than the campesinos involved in the project.

standard.[13] The general level of reading, writing, and arithmetic skills should be raised in most rural areas but not particularly to permit the operation of local institutions. The requirement of literacy is commonly overestimated, as discussed in Section 5.6.1.

Some of the best training will be incorporated in two activities usually regarded as different from training. *Supervision* can provide significant opportunities for training that are seldom seen as such. Studies of the use of paraprofessionals in rural development have found that the field visits of program supervisors to health workers, agricultural assistants, and community organizers often gave the most valuable instruction these persons obtained (Esman et al., 1980; Esman, 1983). Some formal pre-service training is necessary before paraprofessionals undertake their responsibilities, but relevant principles of analysis and action can be more satisfactorily presented and grasped during field visits when personnel are dealing with actual problems at hand. Supervisory visits can be used not just to work with staff or officers of institutions but also to give training to community members if this is planned.

Similarly *evaluation* activities can include a training component, which makes them much more useful for LID. A good example is the Small Farmers' Development Program in Nepal (Annex Five), where group leaders meet periodically with program staff to assess performance. The format developed was to spend the first day reporting on and talking about "problems"—their sources, and how they may be resolved—with discussion of "progress" reserved for the second day. In the course of evaluating problems and progress, much relevant training results from the discussions between farmers and program staff (Joshi, 1983). The sequence followed underscores the positive value attached by the program's leadership to "embracing error" as part of a learning process. It also orients the local institutions to a problem-solving approach, recognizing that often more can be learned from failings than from apparent successes.

7.2.2 Leadership Development

Leadership talents cannot be developed in the abstract. They are the quintessence of skills necessarily embodied in persons, yet they should not be identified just with individuals. Leadership should be viewed as a function that all local institutions need performed not as a matter of personalities and idiosyncratic factors. All institutions need leadership to propose and

---

[13]King (1975) found that cooperatives in northern Nigeria were supposed to maintain fourteen sets of books. When this proved too difficult for local people, the government took over the accounting function. This led to financial abuses by buying agents, which members could not check because they had no control over their own books. King notes that simplified accounting schemes for cooperatives across the border in Niger allowed illiterates to manage their co-ops satisfactorily. The training needed in the Niger case would be different and much easier than in Nigeria because of institutional design factors.

reach agreement on goals, to devise strategies, motivate others, resolve conflicts, oversee implementation, and so forth. These tasks can be carried out successfully by a wide variety of persons. Some societies may have cultural stereotypes that influence effectiveness in leadership roles. Yet many kinds of talent are associated with leadership roles, and effective leaders display many different combinations of qualities and skills.[14] The abilities associated with leadership appear to be distributed fairly widely within populations, almost like mechanical or musical talent. Whether they emerge and develop to others' benefit depends on opportunities to demonstrate them and to gain experience and reputation for leadership.

Attempts to develop leadership as an individual capability miss the fact that leadership depends on the attitudes and actions of "followers" as much as on "leaders." It is a collective phenomenon rather than just an individual characteristic. Leadership amounts to taking or accepting responsibility and then exercising it. This is something in which a number of persons can share.

There are differences between persons in their disposition to take or accept responsibility. Some are reluctant to share responsibility for the understandable reasons that they do not want to be held accountable for what others who are also "responsible" may do. For less commendable reason, some will resist any diffusion of responsibility since credit and other rewards for leadership must then also be shared.

Responsibilities are advantageously shared in many of the *zanjera* schemes in the northern Philippines where two leaders are selected, each having a separate sphere of responsibility. The "external" leader, often a teacher, serves as the link for dealing with government officials or carrying out other tasks requiring formal education. The "internal" leader (*panglakayen*) carries the heaviest load in dealing with the myriad day-to-day managerial tasks (Siy, 1982). This same division of responsibility was found in a Senegalese women's garden group described in Annex Five. The principle of shared leadership has been stressed in the Small Farmer Development Program in Nepal, where even though the groups are small, almost all members will have some committee assignment.

In the preceding section we noted the importance of having trainees selected by the community so that there is a greater bond of accountability. Community members if they understand the objectives of the institution should be in a good position to identify persons who would make best use of training for the advancement of others. Biases can come into local selection processes but it is more likely that persons who have positively impressed

---

[14]It is said that in Latin cultures, for example, the *lider* needs to be very dominant and decisive not consultative or reconciling. Yet even in a situation as freighted with cultural influences and violent conflict as the Mexican revolution, quite divergent leadership styles were successful at different times (Womack, 1968). *Machismo* was less significant for winning and maintaining the public's support than were steadfastness and loyalty to the public's interests, which inspired its confidence.

their friends and neighbors will perform better for the local institution than those who have impressed "outsiders." One of the lessons from the Saemaul Undong movement in South Korea (Annex Seven) was that selection of leaders should be left to the community if the persons given training and responsibility under the program are to exercise influence and accomplish results.[15]

Every locality has some pool of potential leaders, unless it has been affected by substantial out-migration (Section 5.6.4). Even this may deplete only the male leadership ranks or certain age groups, in which case LID should encourage leadership talent in nonmigrant categories. Usually relatively fewer leaders come from the poorer strata of rural society because of various biases and burdens (Ralston et al., 1983:22–24). Yet examples of good leadership being mobilized from poorer sections by outside catalysts are reported in the Mae Klong integrated rural development project in Thailand (Annex Five), Ayni Ruway in Bolivia (Annex Six), and the Aceh community-based program in Indonesia (Annex Seven).

Still, rather than emphasize the social origins of local leaders, we would focus on the mechanisms for maintaining *accountability* of leaders to their constituencies. There is no guarantee that persons from a humble background will work for or persist in advancing the interests of the disadvantaged, and one can find numerous examples of persons who grew up in privileged circumstances who are willing and able to promote the interests of the poor. The key issue is how fully and freely the persons who speak and act on behalf of rural local institutions are accepted in those roles by their constituencies. This depends in large part on how the institutions are designed and operated and for what purpose.

Provisions can and should be made for *replacement* of leaders who no longer enjoy the confidence of a majority within the local council, co-op, or association. The more explicit these procedures the more of a deterrent they are to misconduct and the more easily they can be utilized when needed. Like all techniques they can be abused, but the alternative is less desirable—having no rules or having ones that are not clearly understood or widely known. While it is often desirable to have informal rather than formal

---

[15]"Anybody over 20 years old, regardless of education, income, or social status, who was chosen by his neighbors, could become a Saemaul leader," reports Rondinelli (1984:101). "The success of Korea's Saemaul Undong can be attributed largely to the dedication of Saemaul leaders, who were chosen by villagers and who served without pay. They organized and prodded villagers to cooperate in self-help projects and mobilized resources within the community. Their effectiveness was due not only to their own leadership traits, but also to their selection by villagers, the training provided by the Saemaul Leaders Training Institute, and the competitive approach used by the government to stimulate village development." The "competitive approach" referred to implicitly pitted elected Saemaul leaders against traditional village headmen (see Goldsmith, 1981). This has now been dropped with Saemaul leaders taking over the functions of headmen (Yoon, 1985:157). Except for the competitive approach, practically the same things can be said of the program to improve irrigation management through water user associations in the Gal Oya scheme, Sri Lanka (Uphoff, 1986).

procedures and practices, this is one domain where strong arguments can be made for formal or at least very explicit provisions.

Another measure for promoting accountability is to provide for *rotation* of officers or staff in their positions, so no personal monopolies of authority or access to information and contacts can be maintained. This has the added advantage of spreading experience more widely within the community and of reducing the dependence of institutions on a very few persons. If rotation is applied rigidly, however, it can be disruptive of programmatic efforts and can reduce people's sense of responsibility for their institutions by taking control out of their hands. This suggests a LID strategy of recommending rotation as a possible rule, leaving acceptance and implementation to local decisions. There may be provision made for exceptions if the persons involved determine this is in the best interests of promoting local institutional effectiveness and building capacity.

When trying to attract leaders, the question of *rewards* must be addressed. Leaders who serve without pay can gain a certain legitimacy based on their motivation of public service, and this can enhance their claim on others for cooperation. However, not all local institutions can be developed entirely on a volunteer basis. Certainly local administration must operate on a paid, professional basis, and businesses need to pay their managers and employees and return a profit. Many voluntary organizations also find that they need to provide some salary or emoluments. Some indigenous water user associations give group leaders use of a small piece of land or exemption from certain responsibilities to compensate for the time devoted to organizational tasks (Uphoff, 1986a). Even the Yachiho village health organization in Japan, which receives a huge amount of contributed time from volunteers, gives its health instructors and health officers some stipend.[16]

The possibilities of accomplishing considerable improvements through mobilization of local leadership have been seen in an irrigation rehabilitation project in Sri Lanka, where water user associations have been introduced (Uphoff, 1985 and 1986). Two simple methodologies appear to have helped in getting committed and energetic leaders. First, farmer-representatives are selected (a) after extended discussion of what qualities members of the field channel group want to have (or avoid) in their representative, and (b) after the group has already carried out some work on an informal basis showing who among them can make group action most effective. Second, the choice of a representative is made by *consensus* rather than by vote. The discussion preceding selection narrows the field of candidates

---

[16]This remarkable case is reported in Annex Seven. The Saemaul program in South Korea, it should be noted, provides a number of benefits that substitute in part for cash payment—transportation, discounts, scholarship opportunities for leaders' children, and social recognition. Leaders are kept in check by the expectation that successors will be chosen within five years. The possibility that a community will extend the term of a leader who is unusually effective creates an additional status reward for good leaders.

by tacitly and tactfully screening out undesirable candidates. Whoever is finally agreed upon knows explicitly what members expect of their representative. Further, all members, by having assented to the representative's being chosen to act on their behalf, are publicly committed to cooperate. If several persons are qualified and supported, responsibility can be shared or rotated among them by mutual agreement. These representatives are not paid and appear to get considerable satisfaction from their roles of responsibility in a popular program. Similar mobilization of local talent is seen in other cases described in the Annexes.

We need to consider also "structural" features of LID, but these "behavioral" aspects are basic to successful programs. One of the most commonly cited constraints on rural development is "lack of management capacity" for carrying out programs. In fact there is substantial capability already present at local levels for managing a wide variety of development undertakings, as reported from rural Thailand and Northern Yemen in Annex Eight, for example. Efforts to upgrade rural people's skills and to encourage local leadership to take more responsibility could help accomplish much more in all areas of development.

7.3 STRENGTHENING INSTITUTIONAL CAPACITIES

The structures of local institutions differ enough that there is little point in trying to propose general strategies for making certain structural improvements in institutions. When it comes to modifying sanctions and incentives, for example, one cannot equate the relationships between businesses and *customers*, service organizations and *clients*, cooperatives and *members*, local governments and *constituents*, or administrative agencies and *citizens*. Each kind of institution needs to operate somewhat differently even when it is the same rural persons who are functioning in these various roles. Having made sector-specific suggestions in preceding chapters, we will consider here some generalizable elements of strategy with regard to local institutional development.

7.3.1 Working With Existing Institutions

When one hears complaints about local institutions "not working," the reference is most often to introduced institutions.[17] Pre-existing institutions for all their faults—and one can identify many—have the advantage of being familiar and of having accumulated some legitimacy, support and

---

[17]Because of the ambiguities and controversies surrounding the terms "modern" and "traditional," we try to avoid them. The distinction between "tradition" and "modernity" has little theoretical power for prediction or explanation, having at most some descriptive value (Bendix, 1967; Portes, 1972). A distinction between existing (or pre-existing) and introduced institutions is the most serviceable.

commitment over time. There are sometimes objections that existing institutions embody certain socio-economic or anti-modernization biases. Where serious biases exist, LID strategy should steer toward alternative institutional channels. But any efforts to institute new channels must reckon with the fact that existing institutions will be competing for people's resources, time, and loyalties and usually begin with a head start in any competition, as illustrated in the Jamaica case discussed in Section 2.5.5.

The alternatives are: (a) to oppose and to try to undermine existing institutions, (b) to ignore and work around them, (c) to try to use and work through them, or (d) to try to work with and build on them. The last two options are generally more promising though there is more difference between them than may be evident on the face of it.

The third alternative corresponds to a promotion mode where persons in traditional institutions or roles are coopted to work on activities essentially defined and determined from outside. A community health program in Ghana which recruited indigenous healers proceeded in this mode with considerable tact and sensitivity and had some progress to show for the effort (Annex Four). The healers as well as their patients apparently were willing to accept certain aspects of Western medicine as complementary to traditional practices when no choice between them was forced.

Many primary health care programs have trained traditional birth attendants in simple modern practices. Some programs like that in Burma described in Chapter Four have produced positive results by encouraging newly trained midwives to work supportively with their traditional counterparts, while others like the Sine Saloum project in Senegal have encountered difficulties in involving traditional midwives.[18] Outside the health area, we found some impressive examples of what might be considered "cooptation" of traditional leaders. The Malawi self-help water scheme (Annex Three) is a good case where chiefs became engaged in the decision-making process. An evaluation of the Lilongwe integrated rural development project also in Malawi, funded by the world Bank, indicated that

> the primary factor contributing to (its) progress . . . was its ability to involve both tribal units and their chiefs in the project's operations, encouraging the chiefs to serve as members of the land board overseeing implementation of one of the project's vital activities. (Ruddle and Rondinelli, 1983:82)

Hence there are examples of where a promotion approach coopting existing institutions can be successful provided that the activities are clearly desirable and the pace and manner of implementation are not forced. Such

---

[18]The method of cash payment introduced was at variance with traditional practice and led to a reduction in the use of the midwives' services (Hall, 1981). Since then the project has been reorganized. In particular, village health committees have been given clear responsibility for the "health huts" and more flexible arrangements for payment have been introduced (Bloom, 1984a).

cooptation has been less successful in range management efforts in Botswana as reported by Roe and Fortmann (1982).

Some of the most impressive cases of LID involve not cooptation so much as cooperation with persons in traditional roles. Rather than try to convert existing institutions to new activities and purposes, new ones are established that build on the patterns of organization already familiar and accepted. Some of the best examples are found in Africa where so-called traditional institutions and leadership remain stronger. In Cameroon informal rotating credit associations were used as a basis for developing a network of formal credit unions. Within twelve years this included more than 180 credit unions with 26,000 members and capital assets of 400 million CFA francs (Annex Eight). In Nigeria traditional savings societies among the Tiv ethnic group provided a base for establishing a regional system of farmers associations that contributed to a 72 percent increase in income in ten years (Annex Seven). The Pikine health care project in Senegal, described in Annex Four, patterned its health committees after the elders' committees which already existed, and the Sine Saloum health project also in Senegal regained lost ground by adopting a similar approach (Bloom, 1984).

These are encouraging cases, but all that can be said is that they establish a presumption one should try to work with or build on existing institutions and roles. Evaluation of their capacity and appropriateness obviously is needed on a case-by-case basis. Sometimes there are no pre-existing institutions with which to work as for example in the Gal Oya irrigation resettlement scheme in Sri Lanka (Uphoff, 1985). Where they exist, some initial experimentation may indicate they are not suitable channels for promoting collective action for a particular activity as discovered in the Orangi Pilot Project in Pakistan.[19] In the rural development project in Aceh, Indonesia, traditional leaders at first dominated the newly established committees at the locality level. However, their influence gradually diminished as community and group-level activities took root and brought forth new leadership. The older leaders were gently moved into advisory rather than authoritative roles because the "action" was occurring at a lower level (Annex Seven).

There is always a question whether existing institutions and leaders can be involved in development projects without losing the legitimacy that made them effective in the first place. Much depends on whether they are seen as maintaining some independence of action. The cooperation and compliance traditional institutions and leaders can elicit derives in large part

---

[19]This is directed by Akhter Hameed Khan, the founder of the Comilla experiment in Bangladesh. Khan worked with the elected councillors of the existing local governments and with Islamic religious leaders in the mosques, but these prominent figures failed to provide the expected leadership on behalf of Orangi residents. Fortunately the neighborhood groups set up under the project did accomplish a great deal (Annex Three).

from their working within common understandings of what is or is not legitimate and from familiar mechanisms for maintaining accountability, often by quite subtle means. If these understandings and mechanisms are undermined by their annexation to government programs, their value will be greatly reduced (Coward, 1979).

Hunter (1980) suggests that traditional institutions in any event make important social and psychological contributions and thus deserve acceptance as a necessary and helpful part of village society's network of local institutions even if they appear irrelevant to development activities. This is stating the weakest case for working with existing institutions, but his comment is worth noting since Hunter previously took a more negative view of such institutions (Hunter and Jiggins, 1977). Stated positively agencies should think through and experiment with cooperative approaches toward existing institutions (Cernea, 1982).

7.3.2 Catalytic Approaches

Where local institutional capacities already exist and need only to be strengthened, LID tasks are easier, though not necessarily assured of success. Prompting or promoting such capacities where they are negligible presents outside agencies, whether governmental or nongovernmental, with special challenges. There is growing support in the literature for recruitment, training and deployment of "catalysts"—persons who specialize in community organization and are given responsibilities for getting institutional processes started. Even where the assistance mode is being followed, there could be a role for such persons—to work with and strengthen local governments, cooperatives, or private businesses, to help them make better use of outside resources and their own. Where the mode of support is facilitation or promotion, the role for such specialists is more evident.

The designations for such persons are various, some of them paralleling our typology of LID support modes. The terms "promoter," "facilitator" and "community development assistant" can be found in different situations. "Change agent" has been used as a designation for persons seeking to achieve behavioral change and sometimes institutional development (Tilakaratna, 1984). "Promoter" can be used as a generic designation (Esman and Uphoff, 1984:253–258), but the term "catalyst" is probably more neutral and more descriptive, implying that the person initiates a change process but is not absorbed by it (Lassen, 1980).[20]

---

[20]Hirschman (1984:78–79) objects to the terms "broker" and "intermediary" as having somewhat derogatory or condescending connotations and he dislikes the term "facilitator" on esthetic grounds. "Promoter" he also considers to have derogatory connotations, so he concludes in favor of the term "social activist." In the French tradition of *animation rurale*, one can speak of *animateurs* (Charlick, 1984), while in Spanish, the term *promotores* is often used

A number of the most successful LID experiences in South and South-east Asia have used catalysts.[21] Hirschman (1984) in his survey of "grassroots" programs in Latin America finds many good examples of such catalytic efforts. The Plan Puebla in Mexico (Annex Five) is an example from that part of the world. In Africa a seven-country program supported by FAO is similarly using group promoters to establish small working groups in rural areas (FAO, 1984).

One can ask whether catalytic (promotional or facilitational) efforts require setting up a special cadre with its own recruitment, doctrine, supervision, career paths, etc. The establishment of the Saemaul Undong program in South Korea, for example, proceeded through government channels, though the program did develop its own staff. The same is true for the Kenya Tea Development Authority. A profoundly innovative rural health program based on village health committees and federations was introduced in Panama by Ministry of Health personnel between 1969 and 1973. This was accomplished without catalysts but under unusual circumstances as ministry personnel were put under extreme pressure by their minister and the president to serve the health committees (LaForgia, 1985). An innovative rural development program in Thailand (Annex Seven) managed to utilize regular government staff after a process of bureaucratic reorientation and training.

More typical of government programs may be the commendable but vulnerable progress of *promotores* from the Ministry of Agriculture assisting cooperatives in the Dominican Republic (Sharpe, 1977). Unless government agencies have gone through a process of bureaucratic reorientation, it is unlikely that official staff will be able and willing to act effectively as "catalysts" given a lack of appropriate attitudes and skills. The situation is often aggravated by a legacy of distrust, resentment, or fear on the part of the rural people whose participation in these new or refurbished institutions is desired. Quantitative analysis of performance of rural local organizations has found that those initiated by personnel working in a "catalyst" mode were markedly more successful than organizations set up by government staff in the usual top-down manner (Esman and Uphoff, 1984: 163–165).

There are a number of variables in formulating a "catalyst" role.

(1) Should the person be someone from "outside" the community or locality, or an "insider" recruited locally and given special training and

---

(Sharpe, 1977).

[21] A partial listing includes the "social organizers" in the Orangi Pilot Project in Pakistan (Khan, 1983), the "group organizers" of the Small Farmer Development Programme in Nepal (Ghai and Rahman, 1979), the "institutional organizers" for the Gal Oya irrigation rehabilitation project in Sri Lanka (Uphoff, 1985), the "community organizers" of the National Irrigation Administration in the Philippines (F. Korten, 1982), the local organizers of the Bangladesh Rural Advancement Committee (Ahmed, 1980) and the Thai Khadi Research Institute in Thailand (Rabibhadana, 1983), the health workers of the Kottar Social Service Society (Field, 1980) and the cooperative organizers for the NDDB dairy scheme also in India (Paul, 1982).

status? Opinions differ on this, e.g. with Flavier (1970) and Hunter (1980) strongly favoring the former.[22]

(2) Should the person be a paid professional or a volunteer? As with local leaders, unpaid catalysts have some special credibility and legitimacy. The latter alternative may be attractive also for its budgetary implications. However, there is less control over the persons, and turnover is likely to be higher. Also, there is something to be said for "professionalism," so long as "burnout" (a real danger in this kind of work) can be avoided.

(3) Should the person begin by working on a particular, often technical, task around which people can be mobilized, or should the organizer emphasize building up more generalized local institutional capabilities first? There are proponents of the more technical approach who emphasize tangible benefits as an incentive for organization, and others who stress the need for developing group and individual skills first.

(4) Should the approach be one of compromise and reconciliation or confrontation and conflict? There are advocates of a methodology that seeks to build commitment to group effort stimulated by the latter (Freire, 1970). Yet, in many circumstances it may be untenable or counter-productive.

There are many other questions such as what kind of training and supervision are best, how should catalysts be deployed, whether women can work effectively in such roles, where should catalysts live, should they attempt to support institutions directly or by training local people to do this? This is a subject area where systematic observation and evaluation are lacking so a "learning process" approach is clearly necessary.

The catalyst approach is gaining support in many quarters as the limitations of working through conventional bureaucratic or technocratic channels become more apparent. Since NGOs and PVOs often operate in a manner quite similar to government, they too may need to think in terms of establishing specialized cadres with the task of working with local people to strengthen whatever local institutions are identified for assistance, facilitation or promotion.

7.3.3 Alternative Organizations

Most development programs of governments and donor agencies have

---

[22]An instructive compromise is the National Community Development Service's recruitment in Bolivia of local leaders who have demonstrated CD skills and assigning them to other communities within their locality or to other localities within their region so they are only partially "outsiders" (Savino, 1984). Savino reports the problem, noted also by Colburn (1981) with health committee organizers in Guatemala, that "locals" may be regarded as "prophets without honor in their own country." Still, there are arguments for having locals—quicker orientation, less cost, likely to remain longer in the community. Experimentation is needed to determine which approach will be most satisfactory in a particular context.

as one of their objectives to improve the productivity and well-being of the disadvantaged and the less well endowed. There has been much concern in the literature that promoting development through local institutions, where rural elites can exercise greater influence than the rural poor, will be to the advantage of the former and disadvantage of the latter, as noted in Section 5.6.3. In particular there is apprehension that cooperatives operate in this manner (Münkner, 1976; ICA, 1978; Lele, 1981), but local administration and local government, not to mention local merchants, are also widely seen as contributing to inegalitarian outcomes. There are contrary examples, however, some cited already which show benefits reaching the poor in rural communities through cooperatives and other local institutional channels.[23]

The question is whether to emphasize special or separate institutional channels for the poorer sectors—"alternative" institutions, which exclude the more advantaged sectors (Leonard, 1982)—or try to make the regular, more inclusive institutions better serve the poor (possibly through special programs). A strategy focusing on "alternative" LID would include the following:

(a) special agencies or offices of local administration that deal exclusively with poor clienteles;

(b) "exclusive" membership organizations including only the poor in cooperatives, tenant unions, women's associations, etc.;

(c) service organizations assisting only the poor; and

(d) special enterprise promotion, aimed at establishing or strengthening petty manufacturing and commerce (often referred to as "the informal sector") which generates employment, income and capital for the poor (Chapter Six).

Local government is usually by definition "inclusive" since its jurisdiction is defined territorially. One step in the direction of "alternative" institutions tried in several South Asian countries has been to reserve some number of seats on local government councils for representatives of poorer castes and tribes. This is not generally regarded as having done much for the

---

[23]In one of the few quantified evaluations comparing the outcomes of working more through central or through local institutions, Montgomery (1972) studying land reform implementation found more benefits reaching the rural population when local governments and membership organizations were involved, contrary to the expectations of many critics of local institutions. If a centralized approach worked exactly as intended under the leadership of a strong and egalitarian central government, it might be more beneficial to the poor. But a top-down approach is, if anything, more liable to manipulation and subversion by educated and influential rural elites. They find higher-level institutions more physically and socially accessible than do the poor, who can have relatively more influence on local institutions.

poor. More important is the influence such groups are gaining, however slowly, through the regular electoral processes for local government.[24]

"Alternative" membership organizations may make a real contribution to the advancement of the poor. There are several impressive cases from the Philippines, for example, where the power of rural elites, often in league with local administration, was curtailed by mobilizing the less advantaged (Hollnsteiner et al., 1979; Paul and Dias, 1980). The Small Farmer Development Program in Nepal excludes from membership in its groups, and therefore from credit and technical assistance, any person with landholdings over a certain extent, in a way that targets benefits to the poor (Ghai and Rahman, 1981; Rahman, 1984). There is no special agency working with small farmers, but the Agricultural Development Bank of Nepal has special staff assigned to work with SFDP groups in a Facilitation mode. Loans are applied for and given through the regular banking institutions, backed by program guarantees. Although beneficiaries are almost all from among the rural poor, they are as in most programs still not often the very poorest of the poor (IFAD, 1984).

Service organizations (SOs) have traditionally "targeted" the poor, a good example being the Kottar Social Service Society in India (Annex Seven). There is little that a government or donor agency can do to create SOs, however. It can encourage them through tax laws or can give them subsidies and contracts, but they must come mostly from private initiative. There is considerable evidence that such organizations can work more effectively with the poor (e.g., Hyden, 1983; Hirschman, 1984). Nonetheless, any major role via government instigation can change the nature and effectiveness of SOs, if only because larger scale affects performance capabilities. Another approach, promoting small-scale private enterprises for the poor, is getting more attention now with some promising results when even quite small amounts of capital and technical assistance are made available (Farbman, 1981; Soares, 1983).

While there is often reason to promote "alternative" institutions, these should not be seen as the sole or sufficient solution. Institutions with weak client groups tend themselves to be weak (Tendler, 1982). The tradeoff with regard to local administration is between the poor having strong claims on weak agencies, or weaker claims on stronger ones. If there is clear political support from above for advancing the poor, the latter is a promising approach. Where there are well-functioning cooperatives, membership, and service organizations that speak for the interests of the poor, and they have representation in local government, the chances of local administration

---

[24]"There are indications that newer and younger faces have been recruited to sit in panchayats in all states where elections have recently been held, and there is also evidence that some groups and castes have increased their representation. Such changes, however, must still be described as slow-paced and incremental . . . [It will be] a minimum of another two or three decades before power could pass to the most disadvantaged rural groups." (Franda, 1979:146).

being responsive to the needs of the poor will be considerably enhanced. This is another example of how local institutional networks are more important than the structure and program of any individual institutional channel, as discussed in the next section.

A combination of "alternative" channels and "regular" ones is likely to be optimal, recognizing that regular institutions are prone to discriminatory or disadvantaging performance vis-a-vis the poor. There can be bureaucracies that defend the interests of the poor in their performance of duties. The Kenya Tea Development Authority is an example where the staff have upheld reasonably well the ceiling on tea plantings to minimize unequal benefits from tea-growing, when richer members wanted to evade or change the limit.[25] Efficient private local enterprises operating with good infrastructure and sufficient competition can also benefit the poor. One should not assume that only "alternative" institutions can help them.

Another option is "alternative programs," activities and investments that are of most value to the poor because richer persons cannot or do not want to benefit from them. Such programs can be carried out through regular institutional channels with less fear of monopolization or diversion.[26] Practically speaking, there will always be some bias in the spread of benefits. In general this will be less in the case of services compared to goods (Hunter, 1981), though the bias in provision of extension services in favor of larger and more advantaged farmers was noted already in Section 5.2.1.

Where providing goods or services intended for both the rich and for poorly endowed persons in rural areas, it is important that the executing agency be oriented to reaching and benefiting the poor, otherwise they are unlikely to get much benefit. Agencies that have not had this orientation will need to go through a process of bureaucratic reorientation (Section 7.5.4). With this must go substantial effort directed toward training and leadership development that enhances the human resources of the poor as discussed in Sections 7.2.1 and 7.2.2. The poor are most in need of networks of institutional structures at local levels. The worst situation for the poor is an institutional vacuum with neither horizontal nor vertical linkages, for

---

[25]This was found by Steeves (1984), whose thesis on KTDA (1975) is the most detailed analysis available and who did follow-up fieldwork in Kenya in 1979. Richer farmers engage in some subterfuge to circumvent the ceiling, but it has been preserved better than Steeves expected given that country's general policies (Annex Seven).

[26]Benefits will be less vulnerable to being diverted away from the poor for whom they are intended if: (i) they are indivisible, rather than being separately available to individuals or families, e.g. public sanitation compared to bank loans; (ii) getting the benefits is linked to use of a resource the poor have in abundance such as labor-intensive public works; (iii) they relate to problems or opportunities more relevant to the poor such as improving cassava production; (iv) their quality cannot be upgraded at the expense of quantity; (v) they are provided actively rather than passively (only upon demand); (vi) supply exceeds demand or is provided in units that exceed the demand of local elites such as a primary school; (vii) the goods or services cannot be accumulated and sold for profit such as vaccinations or primary education (Leonard, 1982).

then they lack both the personal resources and institutionalized opportunities for influence beyond the community.

7.4 INSTITUTIONAL NETWORKS AND SUPPORT BASES

The value of horizontal linkages among institutions and of their being vertically linked to higher and lower levels of organization has been seen previously. While isolated instances of local institutional development can be impressive, their cumulative effect is negligible.

> What count are *systems or networks* of organization, both vertically and horizontally, that make local development more than an enclave phenomenon. (Uphoff and Esman, 1974:xi)

This conclusion has been accepted as applying across activity areas. In natural resource management, for example, Ruddle and Rondinelli point to the need for "appropriate institutions (that are) vertically linked into an organizational network, both to provide a 'hierarchy' of services and to increase the quality and reliability of service delivery" (1984:79–80). Because primary health care involves so many activities (curative medicine, agriculture, water supply, etc.), Hollnsteiner (1982) says that a number of strong local institutions may be required before results can be shown—a strong local institutional network with horizontal linkages is needed to address the underlying problems affecting people's health.[27]

Although the importance of strengthening linkages is increasingly recognized, various impediments need to be pointed out. Project design and implementation are usually conceived and carried out in compartmentalized sectoral terms, even though it is clear that this may be counterproductive. It is difficult to work at strengthening whole systems or networks of institutions when agencies focus on those tasks that are most clearly "theirs" within some fixed division of bureaucratic labor. It is not easy to have influence and to use resources across bureaucratic lines or at different political-administrative levels. Yet this is what is required if links of communication and cooperation are to be forged both horizontally and vertically.

This applies no matter which mode of LID support the outside agency is working in. Responsibility for fostering linkages is greater with promotion

---

[27]A recent USAID policy paper on local organizations endorses this concern with institutional linkages:

> A.I.D. has determined to give explicit consideration to the strengths, weaknesses, and linkages among local organizations, as well as those between local and national organizations, before embarking on programs of development that explicitly or implicitly depend on local organizations for successful implementation . . . . the development literature is rife with examples of development projects that failed to achieve stated objectives because important linkages to essential organizations or institutions were never made. (1984:4).

because the agency has taken the lead role, but one of the most important contributions in an assistance mode can be support (even instigation) of linkages with other institutions.

One means for dealing with the linkage problem in the Philippines, where the National Irrigation Administration (NIA) undertook to establish a network of water user associations, was to create a formally recognized Communal Irrigation Committee. This had representation from the top ranks of NIA, the Ford Foundation (which was providing technical assistance to the program), and several knowledge-building institutions that were helping with the training, monitoring, documentation, and evaluation (D. Korten, 1980 and 1982; F. Korten, 1982). This committee had both the knowledge of the program's development needs and the status to take initiatives to foster horizontal or vertical linkages where deemed useful.

Such a formal structure may not always be feasible if consensus on LID itself is still being fashioned. Informal "support groups" at various levels can be established by a sponsoring agency or even a donor agency through an investment of time to get appropriate persons interacting and creating a common stake in the program's success. The role of knowledge-building institutions like the Asian Institute of Management or the Institute of Philippine Culture (of the Ateneo de Manila), which backstopped the NIA experiment, can be invaluable because they can be more independent in their judgments and initiatives. In addition they are not burdened with implementation responsibilities and have less stake in tussles over bureaucratic turf. The Cornell Rural Development Committee played an informal "linkage-supporting" role in the Gal Oya project in Sri Lanka in conjunction with the Agrarian Research and Training Institute (ARTI), a Sri Lankan government institution assigned to manage the project's socio-economic activities (Uphoff, 1985).

The Philippine and Sri Lanka experiences, though both aimed at improving water management, have some instructive differences. The first program has been closely linked at all levels to the irrigation agency involved; the latter program was only passively accepted by the Irrigation Department at the outset. On the other hand, the farmer groups in the Philippines have not developed as much horizontal or vertical linkage among themselves as in Sri Lanka. In the Sri Lankan case, farmer representatives themselves took initiative to join their field channel groups up to the locality level, with three assemblies of seventy-five to one-hundred of them engaging in regular meetings with officials. The top administrative officer for the district invited these area meetings to send representatives to his monthly meetings with district heads of government departments in order to avail himself of some authentic farmer input into planning and decision making. Farmer groups have also cooperated with one another at the level of the distributary canal so that horizontal and vertical linkages evolved rather extensively, supported by the organizers (catalysts) in the field and by ARTI.

One of the early lessons from the Sri Lanka experience was that one could not expect to build up effective water user associations without linkages with the field staff of the Irrigation Department as well as other departments. An isolated LID effort just with the farmers to form water user groups was doomed to failure. Even when taking a "sectoral" approach to something as specific as improving irrigation, linkage to other institutions having complementary functions is very important. Such linkages could be at the same level, as when the extension service works with farmers' associations and other local institutions, or at different levels, as when local government works with specialized project committees and a district planning authority. Two examples show such linkages in action.

In Costa Rica, a program of agricultural research carried out in a "farming systems" mode was effective when the extension service followed a local linkage strategy. To introduce stall feeding of cattle and reduce environmental degradation, extension agents had been asked to carry out field trials with cut fodder for cattle with the technical backing of the Inter-American Center for Tropical Agriculture (CATIE). In one locality they worked closely with the local school, the local dairy plant, and the cooperative, and gave moral support to a newly formed farmers' association.[28] The school and the co-op at different points in time, were responsible for certain aspects of the project. Local people (particularly high school students) were hired to help. When the CATIE project ended, the co-op took responsibility for promoting the extension program to disseminate the results of the research. As a consequence of such a collaborative strategy, nearly all the farmers in the locality were switching to growing and using king grass as fodder for their cattle.

Another good example is the bridge building committees in Baglung district of Nepal, which made remarkable contributions to rural infrastructure under adverse conditions (Annex Three). These could not have functioned effectively without significant horizontal and vertical linkages. They were legitimated and assisted by the sponsorship of the village panchayat at the local level. Links up to the district panchayat and beyond that to the Local Development Department of the national government helped establish a five-year plan and gave them access to needed resources.[29]

Vertical linkages can be of two kinds: (a) to higher level bodies of the same organizational structure, e.g., connections within a federation of cooperatives, between retail and wholesale enterprises, or between different

---

[28]These represent four different types of local institutions: local administration, private business, cooperative, and membership organization. This case was observed by Jorge de Alva and reported to a member of our LID working group, Katy van Dusen who was doing field work in that region during 1982.

[29]The committees unfortunately did not continue in existence after the planning and construction phases were completed and thus did not become "institutions." Responsibility for maintenance of the bridges rests with the panchayats, which are institutions. This indicates the importance of having multiple channels to carry out activities at the local level.

levels of the bureaucracy; or (b) across kinds of channels, as when a local government gets grants and technical assistance from a national-level private voluntary organization, or a farmers' association has ties to the Ministry of Agriculture and to state banking institutions. Both kinds of linkage are obviously important, but any analysis of vertical linkages should distinguish between those that are "intra-channel" and "inter-channel."

One of the least examined areas of local institutional development concerns the formation and strengthening of *federations* of membership organizations or cooperatives. An evaluation of health committees in Panama has found that one of the main reasons such committees (and the primary health care program they support) remained effective in certain parts of that country is the establishment and functioning of active federations of health committees (LaForgia, 1985). The health committees set up under the Pikine project in Senegal were similarly strengthened by joining together in an Association for Health Promotion (Jancloes et al., 1981). Examples of such organization for agriculture would be the DESEC centers in Bolivia, which numbered 200 at the base, grouped in eight regional bodies and one national body, and the Tiv farmers associations in Nigeria, which grew into a four-tiered structure with village, district, and divisional bodies and a regional council at the apex (Annex Seven).

Multiple-level institutions have various functional or technical contributions to make, but they can also provide the political support base needed to sustain development programs. This is documented in the Panama primary health care case noted above. A similar experience is reported from the Philippines where a national community-oriented nutrition program might have disappeared but for political support mobilized through a National Coordinating Committee on Food and Nutrition established in 1960. It brought together representatives of a wide variety of organizations in what Montgomery (1977) characterizes as a "semi-government operation working through community leadership, and embodying private as well as public leadership and funding." Village and provincial support for the nutrition programs that the Committee sponsored made it a wise political move for national leaders to continue funding them.

National leaders may welcome these multiple-level institutions or may be averse to them. Their acceptance of local institutional capacities may well be a consequence of how much economic and political resource mobilization these channels can manage consistent with national regime objectives. To the extent that local institutions produce satisfaction with the pace, scope, and direction of development efforts, there is political profit for any regime that promotes, facilitates, or assists them. Further, where local institutions permit greater mobilization of financial or material resources and more efficient use thereof, there are economic incentives to tolerate and even support such linkage. Better economic performance is likely in turn to contribute to political satisfaction and support. The subject of mobilizing and managing economic resources is taken up in Chapter Eight. We turn here to a consideration of how national institutions can become more effective in support of local institutional development.

7.5 RESTRUCTURING AND REORIENTING NATIONAL-LEVEL INSTITUTIONS

Our discussion of how local-level institutions can be assisted and strengthened has presumed that some national institutions, public or private, are willing and able to support such local institutional development. International-level institutions are considered in the concluding section (Section 8.5). We start with the question of "willingness" on the part of national institutions to support LID (Section 7.5.1) and then address how they can improve their "ability" to do so (Sections 7.5.2, 7.5.3 and 7.5.4).

7.5.1 National-Level Orientation

To the extent that the national leadership of a country is opposed to or unsupportive of LID, the prospects for developing local capacities on any widespread basis are diminished. There may be pockets of initiative and self-reliance, sometimes given impetus by the neglect or the negative orientation of the center but their sustainability and expansion will be in doubt. On the other hand, the presumption that strong and consistent central support is needed as a precondition for LID is not correct. There needs to be at least tolerance of local capacity building, but support should be optimal not maximal, as the quality of support is generally more important than the quantity and support can be built up over time based on good performance.

Some national governments may feel threatened by an increase in local institutional capacity (Ralston et al., 1983:52–53) and thus may undermine, or at least not promote, LID efforts. On the other hand, there are certain incentives for national governments, even relatively conservative ones, to accept and even promote local capacity (Esman and Uphoff, 1984:34–40). While the political orientation of the government will affect the climate for LID, it is not necessarily a determining factor because central governments are seldom monolithic. Within a government, various agencies and leaders may have significantly differing attitudes and motivations. We would discount the possibilities for LID only in extremely unfavorable situations, such as in parts of Central America currently.[30] One of the most impressive coun-

---

[30]Even in Guatemala and in pre-1979 Nicaragua we found governments accepting efforts to develop village health committees, though the degree of institutionalization is not clear. See Colburn (1981) on such LID efforts in Guatemala. Dr. James Sarn, for a time USAID Agency Director for Health and Population in the Bureau of Science and Technology, has reported in a personal communication that VHCs started during the Somoza years in Nicaragua are still continuing, though with a different designation.

tries for local institutional development has been Taiwan, which has had a relatively authoritarian regime. There Farmers Associations and Irrigation Associations carry out wide-ranging responsibilities including hiring and supervising their own technical staff and mobilizing and managing substantial amounts of resources (Stavis, 1983).

The central consideration is whether the objectives of the national government are at variance with those of the majority of rural people. "Power" is not necessarily a zero-sum phenomenon. It represents the ability to achieve goals despite resistance, regardless of the basis on which that ability rests (to paraphrase Max Weber's formulation). When goals are in conflict, assessments of power turn on which party prevails. *To the extent that national institutions desire for rural people what they want for themselves, however, building up local capacity helps both the center and the periphery to advance their respective objectives.*

One needs to look at the compatibility of local and national goals in order to evaluate the acceptability of LID to national institutions. If the center is trying to extract resources from agriculture to pay for industrial investment or for urban consumption, LID is likely to produce political conflict as communities and localities become better able to represent their interests at higher levels. LID can proceed, however, even where the government is not fully supportive of economic and social gains for the peripheral population if it concludes that there is more to gain from promoting a self-reliant path than from continuing rural dependency, especially where it faces mounting budgetary constraints. The scope for LID will be narrower in this context but there will be some basis for central support.

Support might be measured in terms of the financial resources provided to underwrite local institutional activities, but as we have noted already, quality is more crucial for LID than quantity. "Commitment to LID" should not be assessed just in terms of the amount of funds channeled to and through local institutions. The decentralization of authority, of personnel control and organizational structures is especially important and deserves consideration as a special topic (Section 7.5.3), as is the reorientation of government staff toward working more constructively with local institutions (Section 7.5.4).

Apart from providing economic resources and authority to local institutions through budgetary and legal provisions (Section 7.5.2), LID will be helped by national leadership showing respect for what various local institutions can and do accomplish, endorsing their legitimacy either directly or indirectly to encourage others' acceptance of them as institutions. Status and legitimacy are important resources for local institutions to enjoy, though for institutionalization to occur they are needed from local populations more than from national leaders. Leaders' conveying status and legitimacy to local institutions should encourage other persons to do the same. Actually even a neutral stance by national leaders toward local institutions that are meeting people's needs may be enough to allow these institutions to take root and expand. But more active signs of support are usually helpful.

The literature is full of analyses identifying "political will" as crucial for local institutions to develop. But the amount of support does not appear to be that significant.[31] Rather it is the way in which support is given—how reliably, how tactfully, how flexibly—that makes a difference. Because we are talking about local institutions, there is no substitute for commitment of local resources and sense of responsibility, which outside efforts may displace as readily as they encourage. This conclusion departs from the predominant opinion in the literature, which emphasizes "political will" at the center as a requisite for LID. While national opposition can stifle or sabotage LID, national support is at most a necessary, but not a sufficient, condition.

National leadership may not be entirely convinced about LID in advance. Even where they might welcome LID in principle, there have been enough misconceived and failed experiences with local institutional development that a considerable amount of skepticism on the part of national decision makers is understandable. The question is whether enough scope and support will be given for LID experimentation and "learning" (Section 7.1.2) to proceed. Governments are usually quite differentiated internally. If some ministries or departments are willing and able to take LID initiatives, possibly with donor assistance, it is up to them to show results that can win greater support from national leaders.

The argument can even be made that it is not particularly advantageous to begin an LID effort with full backing from on high, where everything has been formally agreed on in advance. Some skepticism on the part of top leaders may well be a spur to more energetic and innovative performance by government or PVO personnel. Equally important, the personnel will be less tempted to try to impose certain structures or formulas on local people. They will have to seriously solicit local cooperation and to be open to local ideas and criticisms in the process of developing new or better local capabilities.

Indeed, strong national support may encourage a "blueprint" approach in practice even if it has been foresworn in principle. With such support there is usually strong pressure for quick results, which is inimical to LID success as seen during the "villagization" period of *ujamaa* in Tanzania (Fortmann, 1982a). Local institutional development involves not just local

---

[31]In our analysis of the performance of local organizations, we found essentially no correlation (−0.02) between extent of "political support" and LOs' performance (Esman and Uphoff, 1984:122–123). This could be explained by the frequency with which a great deal of government support smothered local initiative or was aimed at establishing organizational capabilities that members had no particular interest in.

people learning new patterns of expectation and performance but also some learning on the part of national leaders and personnel. The support sought for LID should not be for a specific program so much as for a learning process, which takes place at all of the levels depicted in Figure 1.3. With each gain in local institutional development, there should be some changes in the way in which work is planned and carried out at virtually all levels, from the individual up to international institutions.

7.5.2 Legal Framework

One of the elements of support that needs to be considered is the legal framework for LID, which can only be provided from the national center. The desirability of having appropriate laws is commented on in reports on activities as diverse as forest management and women's small-scale enterprises (GAO, 1982; Jules-Rosette, 1982).

Care needs to be taken when formulating new legislation to take account of any existing beneficial but uncodified practices, for example in the area of land tenure (Noronha and Lethem, 1983). There is also a need to understand that even mandatory legislation is more effective when authorizing than when establishing. Even if new institutions or practices are required by law, they are not likely to become social facts without a great deal of investment by authorities in communication, education, and enforcement. There needs to be political support that goes beyond the enactment of a law and helps agencies and communities redefine their relationships and roles, as shown by Nellis' analysis (1981) of decentralization experience in North Africa.

One debate in the literature is the extent to which legal initiatives should precede LID efforts, setting forth new relationships and giving them sanction in law, or should follow some experimentation, consolidating in law the relationships that have evolved. Sometimes the very legalistic context in which governments operate makes it difficult to take the latter approach, in which case there may be no choice. But where possible the latter approach seems preferable, in keeping with a "learning process" strategy of LID.[32]

---

[32]In Chapter One, we suggested an analogy between LID and the task of laying out sidewalks to go with new construction. Architects can try to anticipate and plan all pedestrian movement, laying out all walkways in advance. But some inconvenient or unnecessary sidewalks are bound to be put in if there is no test of use based on actual practice, and some potentially useful ones are bound to have been overlooked by planners. Alternatively planners can put in only the most obvious or necessary sidewalks and let subsequent foot traffic indicate what additional ones are needed. Only where "shortcuts" are damaging might traffic be constrained physically. We suspect that many laws are put in like sidewalks not because of functional reasons but because of planners' preconceptions about how people "ought" to behave or how something "ought" to look.

In Thailand it is reported that the government undertook to "modernize" existing irrigation systems by upgrading the physical structures and imposing a uniform system of local irrigators' associations, with standard bylaws, centrally sanctioned personnel, etc. However, farmers already had developed and operated existing irrigation systems for generations through their own local associations which were not uniform.

> Each has it own approach to selection of leaders, organization of maintenance tasks, regulation of water use, punishment of cheaters, flood protection, etc. If notions of bureaucratic "efficiency" dictate that all such associations be reorganized to fit some externally designed template, there is grave danger that local skills will be blunted and irrigation water used less efficiently.... Any decision that imposes *ex post* local uniformity (e.g. by threatening to cut off resources) should be supported by evidence that local efficiency and production will be enhanced, and not by unspoken, aesthetic judgments regarding bureaucratic order. (Calavan, 1984:221–22)

There is a common disposition when formulating legislation to establish uniformity that is neither efficient nor necessary but primarily serves bureaucratic convenience and desires for control. While legal frameworks are important, they are at most enabling; and if rigidly or complexly formulated, they can be disabling. As with other aspects of outside support for LID, how legal frameworks are provided is more significant than whether they are established or how elaborate and extensive they are. In facilitating irrigation water users associations in Sri Lanka, we found good reason to defer enacting legislation until some experience had been gained with what kind of structures farmers could and would make operational (Uphoff, 1982).

7.5.3 Decentralization Strategies

Local institutional development is itself a strategy of decentralization, to create capacities at several local levels for handling authority and responsibility. But for LID to proceed very far, it requires a degree of decentralization within the government structure itself so that official decision making is brought closer to local levels.[33] Decentralization is not a homogeneous category. The two major kinds of decentralization discussed in the literature are *deconcentration* and *devolution*. But devolution in turn needs disaggregation as can be done with our LID analysis. The initial distinctions to be considered are:

(a) whether the decision makers in question are located centrally or "de-centrally"—whether political authorities and administrators are physically in the capital or in provincial, regional, district, or other centers;

---

[33]We are using "decentralization" as Leonard (1982:4) defines it, as the process through which government agencies or local organizations obtain the resources and authority for timely adaptation to locally-specific conditions in the field. This is a broad but suitable definition.

(b) whether the decision makers in question are accountable to authorities at the center or to publics in the provinces, regions, districts, localities, etc.

These two variables together produce four combinations of circumstances as suggested in Figure 7.2.

Figure 7.2: CENTRALIZATION AND DECENTRALIZATION ALTERNATIVES

Decision Makers Located:

Decision Makers Accountable:	CENTRALLY	DE-CENTRALLY
CENTRALLY	(I) Centralization	(II) Deconcentration
DE-CENTRALLY	(IV) Democratization	(III) Devolution

As suggested by this matrix, we are usually dealing with departures from the "norm" of *centralization* (I), where decisions are made centrally by persons who are accountable to central authorities. To the extent that decision makers are physically re-located in dispersed offices closer to the activities and person for which they are responsible—or to the extent that authority for making decisions is transferred from persons who are located at the center to other persons within the bureaucratic structure who are located in dispersed centers—there is deconcentration (II), a kind of decentralization.

To the extent that authority is handed over to persons or institutions at regional, district, or lower levels who are accountable to the publics in these locations, one has devolution (III). This is a more profound form of decentralization, though deconcentration should not be dismissed because it can represent a great improvement for LID. If devolution goes down to one or more of the "local" levels we identified in Section 1.6, this represents a form of LID. But even where devolution of authority reaches the provincial or district level, the institutions at those levels are in a better position (and more likely) to facilitate the performance of what we are regarding as local institutions.[34]

When the highly centralized Egyptian government concluded that there were great inefficiencies in maintaining so much decision-making authority within the central ministries in Cairo and delegated a good deal of

---

[34]The fourth possibility, that decision makers located centrally become more accountable to local populations, is best characterized as *democratization*. This is not conventionally classified as a mode of decentralization though within this analytical framework, its common ground with the two major forms of decentralization becomes clear. All three represent different kinds of departures from "centralization" of government such as originated in monarchial, military, or colonial rule.

authority to executives and administrative personnel at the governorate level, this represented a major step toward deconcentration. In the process, village (locality) councils, which had been rather moribund, found it easier to take initiatives and get certain problems acted upon (Mayfield, 1975). The decision makers whose approval had been needed for so many things were not physically more accessible than before, no longer shielded by geographic and social distance as they had been when hidden away in the massive agency headquarters in Cairo. This process has been taken further with the Basic Village Services project, discussed in Annex Three, which has both devolution and deconcentration elements that strengthen the capacity of village councils for economic and infrastructural activity.

With deconcentration to the local level, there is an increase in the potential capacity of local administration (LA) to undertake development activities because the number, quality, and authority of the local administrative cadre will be boosted. This cadre includes technical personnel such as veterinary officers and public health inspectors as well as administrative staff like sub-district officers or more empowered village headmen. They remain accountable to central authorities but they have more resources to work with and more authority to exercise in the name of the center.

Devolution offers a number of possibilities. The standard mode of devolution is to delegate authority to a local government (LG) body accountable to the public under its jurisdiction, exercising powers prescribed by law with the backing of the state behind its actions. However, other kinds of devolution deserve consideration, because they involve other local institutions apart from LA (deconcentration) and LG (classic devolution).

Intermediation involves a larger institutionalized role in development activities for membership organizations like cooperatives, farmers organizations, health committees, etc. such as described in Esman and Uphoff (1984). These local organizations may even be given some limited authority in certain areas (such as health committees being authorized to make inspections of the sanitary conditions in homes), or some economic resources (subsidies for operating grain storage warehouses). Under such circumstances organizations act on behalf of members, providing services that might otherwise be undertaken by government agencies or local government bodies. However, they may also lobby with the authorities for favorable policies or act as watchdogs vis-a-vis the bureaucracy to obtain better performance from it. Some of this kind of devolution may be tacit, resulting from policies (stated or unstated) favorable toward a larger role for local organizations in development activities rather than through formal legislation.

Philanthropization occurs where the state allows private voluntary organizations (PVOs) to channel resources to the local level and work with local institutions directly, particularly service organizations, which are the counterparts of PVOs based at higher levels (up to and including the international level). *Marketization* is a form of devolution where services to the local level are provided through private enterprises responding directly to local demand. Enlarging private sector alternatives to public sector activities is not usually seen as "devolution," but this is what it amounts to since decision makers are then purely local and are more locally accountable.[35]

The four modes of devolution can be distinguished analytically by considering two variables:

(a) the extent to which the activities are collective or private; and

(b) the extent to which the activities are done for and to other persons, possibly in a paternalistic manner, or are more in the tradition of self-help.

Compared along these two dimensions, we see the devolution alternatives arrayed in Figure 7.3, with the respective types of local institution shown in parentheses. LA is associated with deconcentration, as shown in Figure 7.2. The analysis here shows what the different modes of devolution at the local level have in common with each other and in what ways they are different.

There is an additional kind of deconcentration that could be mentioned, which Leonard called *delegation* where the government hands over responsibility (authority and finances) to a government corporation or parastatal enterprise operating outside the formal structure and control of government. Examples would be the commodity corporation CFDT, which promotes cotton production in Francophone West Africa, or the Kenya Tea Development Authority (Annex 7). Such institutions are seldom local, but they can work with farmer groups, which are local and may promote LID, as KTDA has done rather effectively (Lamb and Mueller, 1982).

Figure 7.3: ALTERNATIVE FORMS OF DEVOLUTION

Purpose of Organization	Mode of Action	
	COLLECTIVE	PRIVATE
FOR OTHERS	(I) Classic Devolution (LG)	(III) Philanthropization (PVOs and SOs)
SELF-HELP	(II) Intermediation (MOs and Coops)	(IV) Marketization (Private Businesses)

Donor agencies are often more enthusiastic about decentralization efforts than are national governments (Ralston et al., 1983:12–13). However,

---

[35]These distinctions are an application of the analysis proposed by Leonard (1982) and which he suggested in our 1984 LID workshop.

governments are going to find it ever more difficult to pursue their preference for centralized control as fiscal constraints become increasingly severe. Moreover, their effort to receive all the credit for government actions makes them liable to be blamed for all the failures.[36] The extent to which a government "loses" power by decentralization measures depends, as pointed out above, on how congruent its objectives are with those of the public. A process of decentralization does not mean the elimination or even necessarily a substantial weakening of the central government since as Leonard says with regard to Kenya:

> In a decentralized administrative structure, the center needs to be every bit as strong as in a centralized one, but the reorientation required is one of [providing] technical services rather than of hierarchical control. (1977:213)

Decentralization is essentially a matter of degree as well as kind, involving several kinds of reallocations of authority, finances, information, and other resources. The experience with devolution of authority to state and local governments in Nigeria (discussed in Section 8.4) shows how a far-reaching decentralization could touch most sectors of rural economy and administration. The Malawi self-help water program (Annex Three) represents a narrower decentralization, focused on planning, constructing, and operating village water systems. For this, authority was decentralized to regional engineers and to user committees in a combination of deconcentration and devolution.

Many nominal decentralization measures lack substance as powers over the issues and resources of most concern to rural people may be withheld. Effective decentralization requires some combination of authority, finances, information, personnel, expertise, equipment, and facilities. The lack of any of these can make the others ineffective, e.g., if there is no approval from the Civil Service Commission to hire technical staff even if LG has funds for this in its budget to do so, or having staff to work with rural communities but no vehicles and fuel to give them mobility.

The Tanzanian experience with decentralization is sadly instructive in this regard. A new system of party-bureaucratic units was set up at regional, district, and village levels, replacing the local government bodies established during the colonial period, and ujamaa collective production was promoted instead of the cooperatives that were in place. The new system gave at most the appearance of participatory, decentralized governance (Fortmann, 1982a). President Nyerere, the architect of this new scheme, has now called his abolishing local governments and cooperatives the biggest mistake of his twenty-five-year rule (Nyerere, 1984:228–229).

One possible difficulty with decentralization efforts in support of LID is

---

[36]Ralston and associates (1983:216) cite Mawhood's argument with regard to Africa that "the ruling elites ought in their own interests to be abandoning the attempt to monopolize all available resources."

that the intermediate-level institutions to which authority and control over resources might be delegated are often not disposed to pass these on to local-level institutions. In Latin America, for example, regional development organizations and second-tier local governments tend to be dominated by urban-based elites and middle sectors (Gall, Corbett, and Padilla, 1975), while agencies at the block and district levels in India are so tied to bureaucratic structures at the state and national levels that decision making does not pass down to lower levels (Nicholson, 1973; Reddy, 1982).

Something similar is reported in Kenya with a program for natural resource management and agricultural development (Annex Two). Even when a degree of decentralization to the district level was achieved, decisions were still not made flexibly and quickly enough to achieve the results intended on the ground (Meyers, 1971). The Kenyan government has now embarked on a "district focus" strategy for rural development that has more merit than the previous approach. But unfortunately it has made little provision for LID. It concentrates attention entirely on strengthening institutions and processes at the district level—despite the fact that according to its own plan, the identification and initial approval of projects is to come from the locality or community levels.[37]

With decentralization there is the common problem of getting coordination of activities at various levels. Formal committees are generally without authority to control the work of participating agencies. If binding decisions are to be made, agency heads commonly send subordinates to meetings to be able to avoid making firm commitments. We cited in Chapter Four the plaintive observation of an official Indonesian report on primary health care experience in that country that coordination has been mostly ineffective as each agency finds ways to resist others' having any influence on its program. Commenting on experience with health programs in the Philippines and elsewhere, Hollnsteiner (1982) notes that linkages between agencies and between the national health service and local organizations cannot be fostered without some alteration in the "turf protection" orientation of technical and administrative personnel.

It is likely that if any avenues of coordination are effective, they will be informal ones. These are more likely to develop where:

(a) the offices of various LA units are geographically close, e.g. in the

---

[37]"The identification of projects is a continuous process; it goes on all year around. The initial idea for a project should come from the area that will benefit from its implementation (village, sub-location or location). After being discussed and agreed upon locally, the project suggestion is forwarded to the Divisional Development Committee (which discusses and ranks all such suggestions from localities and then forwards them to the District Development Committee)." (Republic of Kenya, 1983:8) The District Development Committee includes chairmen and clerks of local authorities (LG) as well as chairmen of the sub-district Divisional Development Councils. But no provisions are made for strengthening any sub-district institutions in this document which establishes "district focus." Indeed, there is no other mention of local authorities or of Divisional Development Councils in the document.

same market town, and even in the same building or compound, as done in Bangladesh as part of the Comilla program;

(b) local administrators have extensive informal contacts, e.g. if there are social clubs where people can interact outside of work, these will facilitate cooperation;

(c) local administrators have sufficient discretion to be able to accommodate one another and their clienteles; and

(d) local organizations can press for coordination from below by demanding integration of services.

This last consideration is crucial in our view. If there are lapses in coordination and conscientiousness on the part of intermediate-level institutions, it will be local persons who know this best. If higher level institutions can be made in some way accountable to localities and communities through local institutions, the prospects for improved performance should be improved. We recognize that this presents a troublesome circularity. While some degree of decentralization is useful for supporting effective LID, at the same time some amount of LID contributes to making decentralization work better.

This points to the fact that LID is not something that can be promoted in neat, sequential fashion. Capacity to support LID through decentralization and other measures should be strengthened at the same time direct efforts are being made to create local capacities with work at different levels becoming mutually reinforcing.[38] Increased capacity of intermediate-level institutions is to be welcomed so long as they do not stifle local institutions below them. The objectives of development are best served by having a full range of institutional capacities from the group level up to the national level. The limitations and lack of linkage observed for most local institutions in developing countries prompted this analysis of LID since it has a very insubstantial foundation in most LDCs if local institutions represent the "base" of a national institutional "pyramid." This contrasts with the institutional structures found in economically more advanced countries, which are much better grounded at lower levels.

7.5.4 Bureaucratic Reorientation

Too prominent or too paternalistic a government role can defeat the expansion of local responsibility, even in the private sector. We have stressed the quality rather than the quantity of official interaction with local institutions. Too often the kind of relationship government personnel presently

---

[38]This may appear to suggest a LID equivalent of the "balanced growth" strategy proposed for economic development in the 1950s. But in concept and spirit it is closer to Hirschman's proposal for "unbalanced growth." One is best advised to proceed incrementally, doing those things that give the process the biggest boost through forward and backward linkages rather than try to plan and put in place all parts of the process at the same time.

have with local institutions is more of a deterrent than encouragement for LID. This makes necessary what can be called "bureaucratic reorientation" (BRO), which encompasses some combination of changes in the structure of organization, the procedures of operation, and the doctrine of a bureaucracy, as well as in the career paths, the criteria of promotion and reward, and in the attitudes and values acted upon by personnel. BRO is a complex social process, having structural and behavioral, objective and normative aspects (Korten and Uphoff, 1981; Bryant and White, 1984:50–58; Blair, 1985).

Application of this rather broad concept must be tailored in each situation. Even within a single country, somewhat different approaches would be necessary for the agricultural sector compared to public works, for example. Engineers' competence and performance are much more ascertainable in the design and construction of a bridge than can be determined for agriculturalists who are developing and promoting an improved crop variety for adoption by farmers. Many more extraneous factors beyond the professional's control will affect the latter outcome than the former. Peer judgments and pressures would be a more useful influence for engineers than for agriculturalists and thus the avenues for improving performance would be different. One would expect "user" input and influence to be more beneficial for getting better performance from agriculturalists than from engineers, quite apart from how much local knowledge is relevant to the technical tasks of extending a new crop compared to designing a bridge.

For many years, the emphasis in development administration has been on planning rather than on implementation. It was assumed that a proper design could and would be implemented satisfactorily. Some would say that the real objective of design efforts has been to justify and capture funds for the bureaucracy, but this underestimates the faith placed in "design" and the derogation of "implementation" as something almost anybody could do if the plan was followed. The realization that blueprint approaches are inappropriate has helped to refocus attention on implementation, going along with increasing acceptance of "learning process" approaches as discussed in Section 7.1.2.

Getting administrative and technical staff to work more respectfully and cooperatively with local public and private institutions involves a number of changes. The conventional prescription of training and indoctrination to change attitudes and values is not very promising unless coupled with various structural and career-related changes. A simple but interesting example of a BRO measure that cost very little but which elicited improved performance from rural schoolteachers and principals in Kenya (and which narrowed differentials between more and less advantaged areas) was the innovation of publicly posting the average examination results for each district and also for each school. This gave parents and pupils a better idea of how well the latter were performing on a comparative basis and consequently how well the teachers and schools were doing their job. This ran the

risk of heightening exam-centered pedagogy, but teaching was already oriented to passing the exams; only too often the instruction was careless or
neglected. At both the district and community level, low ranking in exam results was a spur to parents and teachers as well as to principals and
supervisors to "catch up." Teachers who had been neglecting their work in
favor of private activities were brought around to refocus on their duties.
Without hiring more school inspectors or introducing heavy penalties for
absenteeism from the classroom, teacher and pupil performance was upgraded as community efforts were enlisted in the improvement of education
simply by giving out information.[39]

Building up local capacities is bound to be seen by many staff as threatening to their prestige and power if not their material interests. There need
to be some concrete rewards for working in a new mode with local institutions, since such work is likely to be in the most difficult areas. Cleaves
writes that

> national leaders and policy makers must change their frame of reference as to the defi-
> nition of personal and policy success and (must) reward policy implementors
> accordingly . . . . While appeals to altruism are legitimate ways to build motivation
> they cannot completely substitute for direct compensation especially when
> implementors sense that they are bearing the brunt of responsibility for national de-
> velopment. (1980:296)

Along with individual incentives, there needs to be some structural reorganization creating collective incentives for the bureaucracy in question to
reorient its efforts to serving the needs of local institutions. One of the clearest examples of such a shift is reported from Mexico. As part of a major rural
development project, a special unit was set up within the public works ministry, a Directorate for Labor-Intensive Works (DCMO), which had little
access to heavy machinery. To accomplish its assigned goal of rural road
building, the agency had to work closely and cooperatively with local communities, which would provide the labor needed to build roads only if
satisfied with the proposed feeder road, its design, and the schedule of
work. When satisfied, progress could be quite rapid as community road
committees took full responsibility for the mobilization and management of
labor. The road network in the project area went from 25,000 to 100,000 kilometers in six years' time by this method (Annex Three).

A significant change resulting from setting up a separate program rather than a special division has been documented in the Philippines. The
National Irrigation Administration started a new program for improving
small-scale communal schemes in which farmers who were to benefit from
the proposed permanent irrigation structures were expected to repay the

---

[39]This discussion draws on a 1981 paper for the World Bank prepared by Tony Somerset, Institute of Development Studies, Sussex.

capital cost. To negotiate from the farmers' side about improvements, to mobilize labor and materials to defray the costs of construction, and to be responsible for repayment, Irrigators Service Associations were set up with the facilitation of organizers sent out by NIA (catalysts as discussed in Section 7.3.2). Engineers who were assigned to work on communal schemes had to be responsive to farmer suggestions and interests because farmers' through their membership organization could refuse to accept improvements that they were expected to pay for. Engineers who did not work in harmony with the farmers' groups would have nothing to show for their efforts because new schemes would not be approved or built. This bureaucratic incentive helped to change the way technical personnel related to rural people (D. Korten, 1980; F. Korten, 1982).

The basic requirement for BRO is that the bureaucracy become more client-oriented, reflecting many of the operating features that Peters and Waterman (1982) have identified as central to the success of the best American corporations.[40] One of the recurring themes in their analysis is the importance of "commitment." Training can compensate for lack of skills but not so readily for deficient motivation. BRO needs to increase both skills and motivation for working with local institutions. But enhanced commitment, whether achieved through persuasion or incentives, is the more essential task in bureaucratic reorientation.[41] It is difficult to promote value change but the theory of "cognitive dissonance" gives some encouragement (Hirschman, 1965). To the extent that reward structures encourage bureaucratic performance in support of LID, officials' attitudes and values are likely to accommodate and become more favorable toward local institutions.

Positive results from local institutional performance can in turn reinforce such an orientation. This was observed in LID for water management improvement in Sri Lanka. At first it appeared that water users would not change their attitudes and behavior unless and until the engineers changed their attitudes and behavior because farmer performance was in large part a consequence of the way the irrigation system was managed (poorly). Indeed, the concept of BRO was formulated in response to the task of setting up farmer organizations in Sri Lanka where the bureaucracy that worked with them was initially unsympathetic.

---

[40]Included in their listing were: a bias for action; staying close to and learning from the people they serve; encouraging autonomy and entrepreneurship on the part of staff; recognizing that productivity comes through people and their ideas; having a strong, broadly shared normative orientation that gives the organization direction and cohesion (despite the autonomy noted above). Structurally there is considerable decentralization matched by active "hands-on, value-driven" central leadership.

[41]Interestingly a study of the development of cooperatives in the U.S. has concluded that staff who are "technically incompetent but dedicated" are more effective than those with reverse qualities, competent but not supportive on normative grounds (Leonard, 1982a:204).

There was no opportunity to defer organizing work with farmers, however, because the project design required their participation right away so that they could make some input into plans for rehabilitation. In fact, farmers' progress in improving water management very quickly helped to change the orientation of the technical staff to be more favorable toward farmers, and this in turn encouraged further LID. As engineers found themselves interacting in new ways with farmers, they became more supportive of this change especially as it produced some good results and in this way raised their self-esteem (Uphoff, 1985).

The actual LID work was carried on by organizers who cooperated with the engineers but who operated outside the Irrigation Department in a "catalyst" mode. Whether working from inside or outside the bureaucracy, there is need to consolidate support for LID within the relevant agency. The Saemaul Undong experience in Korea is an example of reorientation within a bureaucracy noted for excessive centralization and unresponsiveness to local needs. Within a few years, there were recognizable changes in the way its staff related to communities (Annex Seven). On a less grand scale but within a large irrigation scheme in India, engineers began spending more time with farmers and working more responsively once irrigation committees had been set up—so long as the top administrative leadership set an example of paying attention to farmer ideas and needs (Singh, 1984). Similar experience is reported by an engineer, now head of the Mahaweli Engineering and Construction Authority in Sri Lanka, when he introduced farmer organization in the Minipe irrigation scheme (de Silva, 1981). The experience in Panama in introducing village health committees as part of a primary health care program showed how rapidly BRO could be accomplished with firm ministerial leadership (LaForgia, 1985). So although reorientation of bureaucracies for supporting LID is a difficult undertaking, there are examples that show it can be accomplished.

CHAPTER EIGHT

Mobilizing and Managing Economic Resources for Local Institutional Development

8.1 RESOURCE DYNAMICS

The effectiveness of local institutions in mobilizing and managing resources is crucial to their ability to provide valued goods and services for their constituencies and to establish and sustain themselves over time. The resources involved in institutional development and performance are not restricted to the economic ones usually classified as *goods* or *services*. There are various other kinds of resources that institutions need to mobilize and manage. *Information* is an obvious one. It is acquired, accumulated, generated, and dispensed by institutions though it is difficult to denominate. *Status* and *legitimacy*, likewise hard to measure, are resources of real importance to institutions' effectiveness as suggested in Chapter One. Indeed, the extent to which an organization is accorded legitimacy from its relevant publics is an indication of its having the status of an institution.

The resources that are most tangible and most amenable to generalizable strategies are ones denominated in *economic* terms: cash and credit, in-kind payments (material goods), and labor (services). In this chapter we focus on how these resources can be mobilized and managed at the local level, and how outside resources can be provided in a way that enhances rather than compromises local institutional capacity, concluding with some general observations on donor agency contributions to LID.

There are several reasons why local capacity for economic resource mobilization and management should be of concern:

(a) it can *expand the resource base* for dealing with development needs by increasing the amount of resources available or the efficiency of their use;

(b) it can *encourage local commitment* to sustaining an activity and maintaining an institution over time; and

(c) it can *improve the application of scarce resources to priority needs* in ways preferred by the public with enhanced local control over the course of development.

From a local perspective, it can also strengthen institutions' claims for getting more resources and assistance from outside the locality though government and donor agencies will not regard this as important except as it reflects better local institutional performance according to the other three justifications. The third rationale (c) reflects important "qualitative" concerns. It is often overlooked in favor of "quantitative" measures (a) and "sustainability" (b). If local people have more control over program activities, they should be more willing to accord an institution the status and legitimacy it needs for effective performance over time and for its local standing as an institution.

When people collectively mobilize economic resources, this can produce some social and political resources for them. In the Pikine primary health care project in Senegal (Annex Four), one reason for having community residents pay a fee for drugs and services was to make government staff more accountable to the community for the timely supply of drugs and more respectful in their treatment of patients. In the Gal Oya irrigation project in Sri Lanka, discussed in the preceding chapter, the fact that farmers were expected to contribute their labor for rehabilitation of field channels gave them some bargaining power vis-a-vis engineers. Engineers designing structures and scheduling work had to consult farmers more seriously and respectfully than farmers had experienced before. This unanticipated gain in influence and status for farmers gave a boost to the establishment of water user associations (Uphoff, 1985).

With the growing "fiscal crisis" in developing countries, there is reason for governments to look toward local institutions to help with resource mobilization (Howell, 1985). Yet, even without consideration of fiscal constraints this is important in terms of the effectiveness of development efforts themselves. Morss and associates (1976) found that small farmer development projects were more likely to be successful if the intended beneficiaries contributed some of their own resources to the effort. Charlick (1984) found this same effect in *animation rurale* projects in Francophone countries. When local organizations made some initial contribution of resources, subsequent growth in financial capacity and in managerial capacity at the local level was greater. Also, the higher the initial level of contributions the greater the ensuing levels of local participation and the more ability to get external support in terms of resources, programs, and personnel (1984:108).[1]

---

[1] Charlick studied agricultural and rural development projects in Cameroon, Haiti, Niger, Senegal, and Burkina Faso (Upper Volta). Projects where there was no resource contribution

Of the three different modes for giving support to local institutional development reviewed in Section 7.1, the assistance mode presumes that there is already some local capacity for resource mobilization and management. Where this mode is feasible, the amount of outside resources needed relative to local resources should be less and the efficiency of their use increased. A good example is the Mmankgodi Farmers' Association in Botswana, whose members had already organized themselves to carry out rotational grazing and to spray their cattle to reduce insect-borne diseases. To have better disease control, however, they wanted to construct a tank for dipping their animals. A small grant (less than $1,000) was sought and obtained from the self-help fund of the American Embassy to pay for cement and other materials. Members contributed their labor to build the tank and a storehouse for the dipping supplies. To cover costs of maintenance and operation (mostly chemicals), the organization charged a small fee for each animal brought for dipping, and it was collected before the animal could enter the tank. The Association's activities were successful enough that it moved into developing an irrigated fruit orchard so the outside assistance had a multiplier effect (Kloppenburg, 1983). In facilitation and promotion modes, external agencies take a more active role in strengthening institutional capacities for resource mobilization and management with a view to ensuring their financial viability over time.

There can be situations where local institutions do not need or want any outside assistance for mobilizing or managing resources. This may be because they have limited objectives and are able to support these adequately already or because they do not want to compromise their independence for carrying out their own program of activity. Rather than try to inject external resources into such a situation, it is preferable for government or donor agencies to carry out programs with other institutions in the locality or nearby localities. Where these programs are successful, local institutions that previously rejected links may decide to expand their objectives or change their mode of operation so as to enter into collaborative relations with outside agencies.

To use their limited resources to best advantage in working with local institutions, agencies need to make their contributions additive rather than substitutive or possibly subtractive. We first look at ways in which institutions can be helpful with mobilizing local resources (Section 8.2) and then in managing them better (Section 8.3). This leads to consideration of how outside resources might be used more assuredly to augment rather than reduce local resource mobilization, as sometimes happens (Section 8.4).

To use the language of game theory, we need to ask: How can external

---

(no resource mobilization) had an average success rating of 13 percent whereas those with some contribution, even if low, had a rating of 43 percent. Those with moderate to high contributions were rated 51 percent successful. These were projects in some of the least favored areas of the Third World.

agencies contribute resources to have a positive-sum effect, instead of producing zero-sum or even negative-sum results? The metaphor of "pump-priming" is also appropriate, where by expending some amount of resources a greater and steady flow can be induced. We see this dramatically, and perhaps coincidentally, with some of the water supply projects documented in the literature; for example, the Malawi and Indian cases in Annex Three. Given the growing consciousness among governments and donor agencies of intensifying financial constraints, their interest in improving local resource mobilization and management is increasing.

8.2 METHODS OF LOCAL RESOURCE MOBILIZATION

While there are numerous ways in which resources can be mobilized at the local level, not all are equally suited for all purposes or institutions. Taxes, for example, involve an exercise of authority that only government-linked institutions possess, whereas mobilizing people's funds in the form of investments requires the probability of some profit. User charges cannot readily be applied to "public" goods and services, as discussed below, though any kind of institution can levy them. Lotteries can be used by private, public, or membership institutions to raise money and so can savings schemes if an adequate rate of interest can be paid to depositors as an incentive.

Some of the most efficient schemes can be extremely simple such as the arrangement in certain Indian villages where teachers' salaries are supplemented in-kind by having each child bring to school a stick of wood that can be used as fuel for cooking (Douglas Pickett, personal communication). Local institutions may benefit from ideas about schemes that external agencies know have been successful in other localities. However, one important principle is that agencies should *avoid standardization* of local methods of resource mobilization. The success of a particular technique often depends on its "fit" with the local environment such as whether children can readily find fuelwood on their way to school, to refer to the example just cited. There will be much variation in acceptable and productive resource mobilizing methods. Taking advantage of whatever methods are most feasible in the particular locality will best add to the total flow of resources.

The other general principle is to *encourage a multiplicity* of locally operable methods, not relying too much on any one of them as seen in the Japanese case in Annex Seven. This should spread burdens more broadly (and more fairly) as well as make resource flows less vulnerable and less fluctuating. In Table 8.1, we list different types of resource mobilization at the local level and also types of supra-local mobilization, discussed in Section 8.4. We suggest for which local institutions each type is most relevant using the classification and abbreviations for local institutions introduced in Chapter One, and the kinds of goods or services it would apply to, discussed next.

Table 8.1: Types of Resource Mobilization for Local Institutions

Type of Resource Mobilization	Type of Goods or Services for which Appropriate	Local Institutions for which Appropriate
LOCAL		
Taxes (general revenue or specific purpose)	Public/mixed	LA and LG (MOs may have levies with similar effect
User charges	Private/mixed	All
Savings and credit	Private	All
Revenue from productive schemes	Private/mixed	All, especially MOs, co-ops and PBs
Collection schemes including lotteries and competitions	Mixed/private	All, but less for PB
In-kind contributions —land, supplies, equipment, food, etc.	Public/private/mixed	All
Labor contributions	Public/private/mixed	All but PB
SUPRA-LOCAL		
Local shares of taxes (remitted after being levied and collected supra-locally)*	Public/mixed	LA, LG, possibly MOs, co-ops, SOs
Block grants	Public/mixed	LA, LG
Matching grants	Public/mixed	LA, LG, MO, SO
In-kind contributions	Public/mixed	All but PB
Subsidies	Private	MOs, co-ops, SOs and especially PBs.

*This category can include a share of supra-local taxes collected locally and kept by LA, LG, or maybe MO or SO as a commission. The Taiwan Farmers' Association example is discussed in Section 8.4.1.

8.2.1 Public, Private, and Mixed Goods

Public goods cannot be produced or utilized without cooperation among persons because of indivisibility of benefits, nonexcludability from benefits, scale of investment required, or interdependence of users, as analyzed already in Section 3.3. It is usually accepted that such goods and services should be paid for by general revenues.

Private goods on the other hand are divisible, excludable, and have no significant externalities. User charges are feasible and usually desirable unless some subsidies are deemed appropriate through public decisions, e.g. for purposes of familiarizing users with a new good or service or making it available to low-income users.

Mixed goods are ones such as agricultural research, water supply, irrigation, extension advice, and education, which produce benefits for society as well as for individuals, as discussed in Section 4.4.5. These may justifiably be funded partly from general revenues and partly from resources raised in other ways. The proportions should reflect the balance of public and private benefits.

One may be concerned about the desirability depending on local contributions of resources because of possible undesirable effects on distribution. If local resources are the main source of program support, relatively more developed areas may be better able to benefit and to advance more quickly (Golladay, 1980). However, more advantaged areas are likely to fare relatively better under almost any system—the more so if the central government matches the resources mobilized locally as Thomas (1980) found with the *harambee* self-help movement in Kenya. In practice, poorer areas generally have less political influence and are less likely to get government assistance other things being equal. So in absolute terms, a self-help approach may be more likely to produce local improvements for poorer areas than waiting for official largesse.

One way of reducing the bias that existing inequalities in resource endowment can create is to establish different formulas for central matching of local resource contributions as done with the Saemaul Undong movement in South Korea. To create incentives for self-help, the largest government contributions went to the middle range of villages, which were making the greatest development efforts, while wealthier communities got relatively less funding (Annex Seven). Some adaptation of this approach appears appropriate for many local institutional development situations.

8.2.2 Taxes

Local governments in developing countries usually have less authority for levying taxes than in more developed nations and often what authority they have is not fully utilized. Further, because a higher proportion of total tax revenue comes from indirect forms of taxation like import and export duties, local administration is less involved in the tasks of tax collection. Scholars and consultants have often recommended an increase in resource mobilization through locally levied and collected taxes, but there are various reasons why the current situation prevails.

In rural localities the absolute amount of resources available for development efforts appears relatively less and the difficulty of collection is relatively greater than in urban areas in part because rural economies are less fully monetized. Local bodies are often reluctant to raise tax revenue even when empowered to do so and reluctant to take action against those who do not pay. This is particularly true when it comes to conventional taxes on income, sales, and property.

National governments may be satisfied with this state of affairs because often they do not want local governments to have an autonomous financial base. It has been part of the prevailing ideology of "national planning" that investment decisions should be made under central coordination or direction. Local decisions might contradict national ones or at least compete for resources. There may also be the political fear that more self-sufficient local governments, not dependent on financial handouts from the center, might become an independent base of opposition, a fear made more real when ethnic or other distinctions create centrifugal tendencies within the state.

These considerations would not explain why authorized local taxing powers are not fully used, however. First, in areas where much of people's real income is in kind rather than cash or where few commodity exchanges take place through the market, it is difficult to assess accurately the amount of taxes owed. Second, there may not be agreement on the economic unit on which to base taxes, e.g. when land is held communally or when "families" are very ambiguous. Third, the financial and administrative resources available may not be adequate for collection of the conventional taxes, which can have very high costs of collection.[2] Finally, the persons who have the most resources to tax are usually in control of local governments and may be averse to taxing themselves very substantially, or to contributing as much as other community members consider proper.

Local bodies often tap a number of "minor" sources for funds. Village panchayats in India, for example, collect a variety of house taxes, profession taxes, labor taxes, pilgrim taxes, drainage taxes, water and lighting taxes, taxes on fairs, festivals, and entertainment, on ferries and fisheries, animal taxes, vehicle taxes, taxes on agricultural land and on commercial crops, etc. (Vyas et al., 1983:61). In North Yemen, the Local Development Associations (Annex Eight) collect a *zaqat* tax, which is like a tithe on production, and are

---

[2]In the Indian state of Uttar Pradesh, the cost of collecting property tax amounted to 50 percent of the revenue (Vyas et al., 1983:70).

considering a tax on the income of migrants returning from jobs in the Gulf states (Cohen et al., 1981).

Strategies for improving resource mobilization through taxes would include:

(a) *combining a wide variety of less conventional taxes* (like those just listed from India) *with taxes from conventional sources like income, sales, and real estate,* whenever possible tying them to specific purposes to allay suspicions that the funds may be misused;

(b) *finding simpler and more inclusive ways to assess conventional taxes,* such as the Graduated Personal Tax in East Africa and the tax on "trades and professions" used in some Indian states to reduce assessment problems by taxing potential income;[3]

(c) *using very simple fiscal cadasters instead of more expensive, legally precise land cadasters for property taxation* (Kent, 1980);

(d) *developing more fair, flexible, and effective ways to collect taxes,* where possible applying quicker and cheaper social rather than legal sanctions.[4]

One hesitates to recommend "raising taxes," since it can be reasonably argued that most rural areas are more underserved than undertaxed. But it is not possible to develop strong local institutions without a firm financial base. If sufficient taxes are not levied and collected, other resource mobilization methods need to be introduced.

8.2.3 User Charges

Although user charges tend to be underused as a strategy for funding certain activities at the local level, they are only appropriate for private or mixed goods, which yield a clear benefit to specific persons. Some of the direct taxes listed above, such as water or vehicle taxes, practically amount to charges. Road or bridge tolls, payments for using a public well, fees for

---

[3]The GPT is based on the family unit and was devised in lieu of property taxation when land was held mostly by the tribe. Like the Indian tax, it uses an estimate of the average income for given occupations. Successful assessment is achieved in part by consulting local committees that know how much wealth or income people have. In event of a disaster, reductions can be made for areas or individuals. The tax provides an incentive for greater production since any income earned over the average for one's category is tax-free. The tax appears to be regarded as fair and to be accepted because taxpayers realize that the revenue will be applied to locally desired improvements. The Indian tax on trades and professions is like a poll tax based on the average earnings of the taxpayer's occupational category (Hicks, 1976:33).

[4]In a Bolivian case when male heads of households declined to pay their assessment for community development work, the women in the community confiscated their portable radios and other moveable property until the assessment was paid (Savino, 1984). In Peru one rural community has an annual round-up of cattle, and anyone whose local taxes are in arrears has the choice of paying them up or having one of his cattle sold at an auction. Any proceeds from the sale in excess of taxes due are contributed to the community's fiesta, so anybody getting "caught" is not particularly angered (Whyte and Boynton, 1983).

health care services, and levies for electricity provision are examples of user charges. Irrigation water issues, schooling for children, and curative health services are things that people seem particularly willing and able to pay for.

The main issue when levying user charges comes with mixed goods, where there is some public interest in having many people share in the benefit. If the requirement of fee payment excludes poorer members of the community, from primary education for example, there is reason to consider some subsidy from general revenues or to adjust charges to match ability to pay. Some sort of "progressive" fee structure can often be established. [5]

Prices are in effect "user charges" for goods and services provided by private businesses. Upon occasion private providers may adjust their prices to suit customers' or clients' financial circumstances. This may be done through some credit mechanism rather than through differential prices; that is, by not charging interest or by forgiving or reducing the debt at some future time.

8.2.4 Savings and Revolving Credit

One of the most widespread methods for mobilizing savings for private purposes, informally institutionalized in many countries, has been "rotating credit" schemes (Ralston, et al., 1983:108-100; March and Taqqu, 1986:54-66). The credit union movement in Cameroon, where such a mechanism has been developed into a national system of savings associations (Annex Eight) is particularly impressive. Traditional local savings institutions also served as a basis for farmer associations in Nigeria (Annex Seven). Rotating credit schemes are often not institutionalized, however, because members do not feel a need to continue the group effort because the scheme was mismanaged or because members lack the financial means to keep participating.

Institutionalized credit schemes involving some savings component are of more interest for development purposes. These programs create funds that can be borrowed and replenished by repayments. Their size increases if interest payments more than make up for any defaults, and their real size increases if this growth exceeds the rate of inflation. Jayaraman (1980) recommends revolving credit as a means of financing soil conservation investments in watershed management.

Such schemes have been more successful where all or most of the funds were contributed as savings by members and where there is peer pressure for repayment. Unfortunately the pool of resources available is less likely to be maintained or increased when most of the funds are from the government. As discussed in Chapter Five, the repayment of loans from Bangladesh cooperatives was quite respectable when mostly members'

---

[5]Examples can be found in the Tunisian water supply case in Annex Three and the Mexican primary health care case in Annex Three.

money was at stake, but the revolving funds stopped revolving after there was a huge infusion of outside credit (Blair, 1982). The Grameen Bank in Bangladesh (Annex Eight) has done well so far with revolving credit using outside funds, having an almost perfect rate of repayment. The rural savings movement in Zimbabwe (also described in Annex Eight) is an excellent example of mobilizing savings for use as productive credit without any infusion of government funds.[6]

Those who participate in member-operated funds are in the best position to judge ability and willingness to repay. Persons' "reputation" has been found to be an adequate and cost-effective form of security for loans if assessed by local residents (Ashe, 1985). Such credit mechanisms can deal with very small loans and savings deposits, obviating the heavy overhead costs of a more formal institution. However, they cannot compensate for the poverty of members where this is extreme. When this became a serious problem for poverty-oriented programs in India and Haiti, the solution was to establish more formal "banks" that mobilized also the savings of the less poor to help absorb and buffer costs of operation.[7] More resource mobilization and management can be done through such mechanisms but only if the skills and judgment of members are fully engaged in their operation.

8.2.5 Revenues From Productive Schemes

Income-generating mechanisms should be built into LID strategies whenever possible so long as it does not detract too much from institutional objectives. A graphic example is the decision by the YMCA in Kitwe, Zambia, when planning to construct a new building, to raise more money than needed to build its facilities so that it could construct a row of shops on the ground floor. These could be rented out to earn revenue to pay some of the organization's operating expenses (Leonard, 1982a:203). Another good example is the practice of a water users' association in Tamil Nadu, India

---

[6]This savings movement has provided one of the organizational bases for the network of agricultural associations (groups) in the rainfed commercial areas of Zimbabwe, described in Annex Five. These associations in turn have contributed to the dramatic increase in agricultural production in Zimbabwe during 1984 despite the devastating drought that affected it and other African countries. As Bratton (1986) showed, maize production in "member" households was almost double that of "nonmember" households though their landholdings were equivalent. Moreover, the amount of maize marketed by "member" households was seven times greater without reducing household consumption. In 1984 these smallholders produced for sale about 400,000 tons of maize, more than two and one-half times as much as the government had expected from them. (*New York Times*, December 2, 1984.)

[7]The Working Women's Forum in Madras, India found that many women seeking to establish small enterprises could only gather enough means to begin repayment after they had gotten three small loans. (The ceiling for loans was relatively low.) To absorb the costs of being flexible with these women, the Forum opened its own bank (Chen, 1983). FICOP in Haiti evolved as a bank-like institution owned and managed by a cooperative in an attempt to improve its ability to lend to the poor (personal communication, Tony Barclay, Development Alternatives, Inc.).

which auctions off the right to catch the fish remaining in the bottom of the irrigation tank at the end of the dry season. The money from this goes into the association's treasury and helps pay for waterguards who oversee the distribution of irrigation water (Annex Eight). Such fund-raising means are reported from some other "active" communities in India (Wade, 1984; Sharma, 1985).

In these cases the revenue generated does not detract from institutional objectives. The "price" paid by YMCA members for their income to cover recurrent program costs is having to walk upstairs (something that might not be acceptable to an institution with elderly members). Auctioning off fishing rights does not interfere with the functioning of the water users' association and even generates some social excitement.

There is always the danger that a commercial operation can divert some of an institution's talent and energy from other tasks since once begun it cannot be allowed to fail. This does not seem to have happened with the Taiwan Farmers Associations, discussed in Chapter Five. They finance a considerable range of extension and other services including scholarships from the proceeds of their savings and loan operations and from their sale of fertilizer and other inputs (Stavis, 1983).

8.2.6 Collection Schemes

A variety of often ingenious means for collecting money are found in practically every society. Examples would be the large lotteries run in some Latin American countries by the *sociedades de beneficiencia,* service organizations that raise funds to defray operating expenses of local hospitals, or the fiesta queen contests that generate money for local governments in the Philippines. These may be ad hoc or done on a regular basis.

A case from Burma reported in Annex Four indicates the wide variety of collection schemes that can evolve when local institutions are given responsibility and latitude for mobilizing and managing resources for a program the people value. To support the primary health care program put under their charge, the Village People's Councils (local governments) have developed the following contribution systems with the kinds of taxes and user charges already discussed:

(1) fixed or variable payment for services;
(2) voluntary donations for services;
(3) fixed payments for drugs;
(4) fixed or variable household levies;
(5) special donations by wealthy villagers;
(6) periodic donation campaigns; and
(7) cultural programs with admission charges dedicated to support the primary health care program (Chauls, 1983).

Not all of these arrangements are institutionalized. If accepted by the public, however, they become part of the resource-raising repertoire of local institutions, available as needed and thus useful adjuncts to other methods for mobilizing resources. Governments or private agencies can encourage these arrangements by providing recognition or rewards through publicity or prizes for localities that excel in such resource mobilizing efforts. They may consider not only the amount raised but also the originality that was demonstrated.

8.2.7 In-Kind and Labor Contributions

Given that providing substantial quantities of cash is often difficult for rural residents, local institutions may find it easier to arrange for contributions of materials, equipment, land, or labor. Schemes like the Malawi self-help water supply program and the Baglung bridge-building program in Nepal have mobilized substantial resources of this sort.[8] Where pilot projects can be undertaken first there is an advantage to the extent one can show some tangible and impressive results to enthuse potential contributors. Subsequently, once a larger program is started, it needs to be carried forward quickly and steadily so that momentum is maintained.

The potential for in-kind and labor contributions is limited to certain types of activities since many tasks will require large amounts of cash. The Malawi and Nepal cases cited here, to be sure, produced substantial cost savings over what it would have cost the government to provide the infrastructure. Another significant case of in-kind resource mobilization is the Chattis Mauja irrigation scheme in Nepal. This 7,500 acre scheme, built by local people about 150 years ago, takes water from the Tinau river through a diversion structure and main canal to serve fifty-four villages. The farmer-members contribute about 60,000 man-days of labor each year for maintenance of the main system (the river coming out of the mountains carries a large quantity of silt) and also perform maintenance work on distributary and field canals. Cash and in-kind contributions (rice) are made in addition to cover the salaries paid to the organization's officers and the technical staff it employs to oversee operations and maintenance. As seen in Annex Eight, such massive resource mobilization requires a well-institutionalized organization, in the Chattis Mauja case having three tiers with the highest one corresponding to the sub-district level.

Procuring such contributions will, to varying degrees, be influenced by

---

[8]Both Glennie (1982) and Pradhan (1980) report that unskilled labor was given free, but skilled laborers from the community were paid. In the Nepal case most of the unpaid volunteers who helped carry the steel cable from the road to the village and rocks to the bridgehead sites were from higher castes, while it was lower-caste blacksmiths and masons who got paid for their work. In Botswana, however, members of the Mmankgodi Farmers Association who were masons were not paid, even though they had special responsibilities during construction (Jack Kloppenburg, personal communication).

cultural predispositions. The tradition in Nepal and other South Asian countries of giving labor for community purposes (*shramadana*) facilitates the mobilization of labor for irrigation maintenance and other collective action tasks. Another example of resource mobilization for irrigation comes from a different cultural area in the Northern Philippines. In one recent year, nine zanjera groups are reported to have contributed nearly 16,000 person-days of effort and over 22,000 pieces of local materials (Siy, 1982). Chauls (1983) suggests that the primary health care program in Burma is able to attract volunteer health workers partly because of the "merit" which Buddhist beliefs associate with community service. In fact, there is value attached to participation in community activities in many if not most rural areas, no less in the Andean highlands of South America (Isbell, 1978) than in the Hindu or Buddhist localities of Asia.

In-kind resource mobilization may be preferred in some local institutions because it reduces the likelihood of mismanagement, a problem discussed in the next section. Cash in hand can create suspicion of malpractices if not malpractices themselves. In one of the Local Development Associations studied in North Yemen, the prevailing attitude among many LDA members was that the officers were "thieves" even though our researchers found no evidence to support this view (Swanson and Hebert, 1982). One of the reasons the Baglung bridge-building efforts in Nepal succeeded quite well was because of the small amount of cash involved since conflicts over money have so often undermined trust in the local panchayat system (Pradhan, 1980). With only small amounts of cash given to cover the payment of skilled labor, there was little scope for suspicion (the rest of the inputs were contributed in-kind by community members or the government). The requirement in Botswana that small dam groups (Annex Two) collect a fixed watering charge per animal was ignored by the groups partly because the amount set by the government was higher than needed to cover operation and maintenance costs but also because having cash in hand was a source of difficulty. Groups preferred to mobilize labor from members to do maintenance work whenever it was needed and to take up ad hoc collections for any unavoidable cash expenses like replacing pump parts or buying diesel fuel for the motor (Roe and Fortmann, 1982).

Knowing about such problems and appreciating local adaptations throws a different light on the conventional concern with "resource mobilization." In our review of LID experience, we were struck by the frequency with which rural people could devise effective means of financing efforts and investments they understood and valued by some combination of cash, labor, and in-kind contributions. Resource mobilization requires matching proposed activities to recognized local needs. Institutionalizing resource flows is a valid concern to outside agencies, especially as they become ever more acutely aware of the problems of financing recurrent costs of local programs. The two rules of thumb, which we proposed at the beginning of this section for taxes, apply to all resource mobilization efforts at the local level—*flexibility* to suit local conditions and *diversification* of sources. Additionally we have been impressed by the extent to which resource mobilization depends on good resource management at the local level so that locally recognized needs are dealt with effectively by the activities undertaken. This points to a separate but certainly related consideration of resource management capacity.

8.3 METHODS OF LOCAL RESOURCE MANAGEMENT

The activities of resource management and mobilization are more closely linked for local institutions than for institutions at higher levels where specialized personnel and coercive means of enforcement are provided to ensure that resources are collected. At local levels even payment of taxes is often as voluntary an act as the contribution of labor. Resource mobilization is generally contingent on how well the resources are used and whether they are used for things that local people value. Any inefficiency or corruption in resource management is a direct and obvious impediment to resource mobilization, and conversely effective application of resources to meeting local problems is a definite stimulus for mobilization.[9]

8.3.1 Financial Accounting

Technical assistance to local institutions from government or private agencies in the techniques of bookkeeping, inventory management, cost-accounting, and investment decision making may be some of the most important aid outside agencies can give. Poor record keeping is one of the most frequent causes of misuse of funds and breakdown of trust, which leads in turn to institutional decay, according to Fortmann (1982) writing on rural local institutions in Botswana. One of the kinds of training that the Bangladesh Rural Advancement Committee (BRAC) found most important for the local groups formed under its auspices was in accounting (Ahmed, 1980). Both the Mmankgodi and Pikine cases referred to already report establishment of very strict financial management procedures intended to give members confidence in the program.

We discussed in Section 5.6.1 the potential difficulties for LID presented by illiteracy and lack of numeracy. Probably the key element in improving financial management in local institutions is simplification of the record-keeping and reporting requirements to deal with only the essential information, which can then be more easily understood by everyone

---

[9]An evaluation of the Pikine primary health care project in Senegal noted that improvement in the quality of services was a more important incentive for getting community members to make contributions than were financial savings they might have from the scheme (Annex Four).

concerned. As discussed next, this also helps deal with problems of financial mismanagement (Esman and Uphoff, 1984:227-233).

8.3.2 Controlling Dishonesty

There are two main approaches to addressing dishonesty, external or internal. Some institutions like BRAC have found it important for an outside agency to conduct audits of local institutional finances to ensure proper use of funds (Korten, 1980). In the Puebla project in Mexico, when some members were flouting the group credit scheme by not repaying loans, the intervention of the authorities to arrest these *banditos* was a boost to the local organizations (CIMMYT, 1974). Outside agencies may be especially helpful in the recovery of loans where "insiders" are reluctant to apply pressure to friends and neighbors (Tendler, 1981). On the other hand, one can rely more on internal mechanisms. A "goldfish bowl" technique of reporting and conducting financial business in the public eye can be more of a check on misconduct than paper transactions with outsiders. Very successful indigenous local institutions in Indonesia, the *subaks*, have established the practice of assessing all fees in public meetings so that all members know how much should have been collected, from whom, and for what (Birkelbach, 1973).

Financial matters arouse suspicions easily in any society. Openness and accessibility are likely to provide more protection than auditing procedures, which may be circumvented by fraud or connivance however complicated they may be. One of the most interesting LID examples of this was reported from Aceh, Indonesia, where villagers involved with a community development program turned out dishonest leaders who were defrauding the organization once finances became a matter for the whole membership to review (Annex Seven).

8.3.3 MAINTENANCE OF EQUIPMENT AND FACILITIES

There are various reasons why maintenance is so unevenly and poorly performed, as discussed in Section 3.4.4 with regard to rural infrastructure, where the issue most often arises. A study of local organizations' potential for promoting rural development concluded, as we would, that maintenance presents a special problem because:

> Many rural organizations are mobilized on an irregular basis for a particular purpose or event. Continuous, intensive organization is not sustained. Examples of successful, locally organized self-help usually exhibit periodicity and a purpose-specific character. Maintenance requires a new structure of incentives, rewards for leadership, a building of new capacity into organizations. (Ralston et al., 1983:117)

The problem referred to is that of institutionalization, of going from uncertain to predictable performance by "a building of new capacity into organizations." Ability to carry out maintenance on a regular basis could well be one of the tests of institutionalization.[10]

Maintenance activities are difficult to institutionalize at the local level unless there is some evident need for them. We found in studying the role of local organizations for managing catchment dams in Botswana that maintenance was periodic, done only during the months of the year when the dams were most needed (Annex Two). Outsiders had the impression that there was no maintenance being done because it was not evident at times when they visited the rural areas. But a field study showed something akin to "optimal" maintenance—just enough to protect the dam bund and control cattle access. The dam groups preferred to keep maintenance below a level that would require their assessing and handling regular cash contributions, for reasons discussed above. Instead, they relied on contributed labor and materials and on occasional emergency collections of cash (Fortmann, 1985).

The fairly common reluctance of organizations in rural areas to mobilize cash because of the potential for misuse and distrust presents a problem for local institutions needing to carry out maintenance functions. One element of strategy can be to make certain procedures for nonmonetary resource mobilization or ad hoc cash collection routine.

One way in which local institutions can be encouraged to take on more regular maintenance responsibilities is by providing them *technical supervision* as seen from experience with water supply projects in Peru (Haratani et al., 1981). One of the inhibitions holding back local initiative on maintenance there was a lack of confidence that sufficient technical expertise was available locally. After obtaining technical training and backstopping, local governments were more willing to carry out maintenance work on water systems as needed. Giving technical assistance for maintenance tasks and routines is one of the more straightforward kinds of LID support that can be provided by outside agencies.

Local institutional problems with maintenance arise most often when jurisdictions are unclear or when the facility or service is not well understood or needed by the community. In Chapter Three we considered circumstances under which good maintenance is more likely—where the need for maintenance is obvious, where responsibility for repairs can be clearly fixed, or where the users are particularly concerned and influential. Gradual deterioration of a road is less likely to be taken care of than a landslide blocking it, just as the breakdown of a diesel electricity generator is more likely to be attended to than a leak in a water supply pipeline. Where need, responsibility, and demand for maintenance are clear, local

---

[10]Ralston and her associates (1983) observe the same distinction between "organizations" and "institutions" that we spell out in Chapter One.

institutions seem to be able to find the means, including technical know-how, to do the job.

This observation applies more generally to resource management by local institutions. While need for management does not always create its own supply of management skills or of resources to make the skills effective, local management capabilities can be substantial where the objectives of local institutions are understood and supported. Some examples of this from rural Thailand have been noted in Annex 8. For such management capacity to be tapped, however, there must be what Calavan (1984) calls "appropriate administration," the managerial equivalent of appropriate technology. Calavan suggests some ways in which outside agencies can create "space" for local initiative and responsibility to become linked to development activities being introduced. This is a useful perspective to bring to issues of resource management for LID.

8.4 LINKING SUPRA-LOCAL RESOURCES WITH LOCAL RESOURCE MOBILIZATION

If there are appropriate local institutions backed by conducive policies, national and international resources can be used to elicit greater local resource contributions for the sake of a wide variety of development efforts. The objective as suggested in Section 8.1 is to create a "positive-sum" dynamic so that outside resources do not replace local contributions but rather increase them. For external resources to "prime the pump" of local effort, *the framework of institutions and policies is more important than the amount of resources expended by government or donors.*

The return of such resources can be phenomenal if institutions and policies are supportive; for example, the ten-fold or more expansion of investment that Atteh (1980) reports in one of the poorer states in Nigeria. In 1967 the government decentralized its structure creating nineteen states where before there had been only four regional governments; subsequently it established district and local government bodies. As discussed in Annex Eight, communities in Kwara State in ten years' time carried out twenty million naira worth of projects, including roads and bridges, court-houses, classrooms, dispensary-maternity centers, postal agencies, market stalls, libraries, hospitals, dams for water supply, and electrification of larger settlements.

All these projects were initiated by local people and their children living in urban centres. Villagers determine priorities, plan, finance, and execute development projects on their own. The people therefore have provided themselves with more amenities than the government did. Most of these projects are financed from the sale of crops produced by 'traditional' agriculture which is deemed primitive. Yet government appreciates and coordinates these efforts, lending a hand through grants, technical supervision of projects, etc. (Atteh, 1980:421-422; statistics are given in Annex Eight).

What makes this mobilization of resources more remarkable is that it occurred during a period when the central government of Nigeria was well endowed with petro-dollars and one might have expected local people to sit back and wait for official largesse. There were many justifiable complaints about corruption, foolish investments, and technical errors in the years right after this immense redistribution of authority in Nigeria, but the scope of work undertaken made some problems unavoidable. Against these complaints one should set the scale of accomplishments attained.

Too often the way outside resources have been provided has not had such a positive-sum effect. Instead the result has been zero-sum with external resources simply substituting for local resources. Indeed, sometimes negative-sum consequences have resulted when external inputs reduced the level of local contributions by more than the amount provided from outside, as with certain food-for-work programs discussed in Section 8.4.3.

Contrasting approaches can be illustrated with examples from Ecuador and North Yemen. In the first case, a local institution handling electrification began raising its own funds before the end of the project to install new facilities, so the donor agency cut its allocation by the amount of funds mobilized. This created a disincentive for institutions to begin raising funds until the project was terminated, when they would have to start without experience or precedent (Tendler, 1979). In contrast, the Ministry of Health in North Yemen made grants to Local Development Associations for part of the costs of construction of primary health care units, expecting the community to come up with the balance of funds needed. If an Association raised more funds than needed for its health unit, the grant would not be reduced and the LDA could use the extra funds for other purposes. This gave incentive to put real effort into the fund raising (Cohen et al., 1981).

8.4.1 Local Shares of Taxes

Collecting taxes levied by government is always difficult and costly. One practice, which has advantages both for national and local governments, is to delegate collection of certain taxes to the latter, giving them a fixed share of revenue as a commission for their work. In Taiwan this has been extended to membership organizations where the Farmers Associations (FAs) get a percentage of the land tax, which they collect in kind (as rice) for the government (Stavis, 1983:218). This provides a stable source of income to the associations, reducing their need for subsidies to cover the cost of certain services (mixed goods) that the Associations provide.

In countries where the revenue structure is convoluted with a variety of earmarked taxes, local jurisdictions may receive revenue (certain shares) from specific taxes on exports or on commodities originating in their region. Such special taxes are common in countries like Argentina and Peru and cover much of the cost of public works in the Philippines (Caiden and

Wildavsky, 1974:, 271-273, 285-287). An alternative source of funds is the remission of some share of general revenues to local governments according to certain formulas. Such systems have the advantage of giving some fiscal stability to local institutions, but there may then be little incentive to generate additional revenue locally. Earmarked funds are not easily adjusted or eliminated, though formulas can be set that reward special resource mobilizing efforts (Bahl, 1982). Such systems present the same problem as tax collection commissions, namely that the flow of resources to different institutions is likely to be unequal, reflecting existing patterns of development. Here too, formulas for revenue distribution can be adjusted so that they compensate for economic disadvantage. To deal with this problem, however, it may make more sense to transfer some funds as grants.

8.4.2 Grants

Grants can be designed to further a wide range of objectives and can be directed to the whole range of local institutions with a view to increasing the overall volume of resources devoted to development. Two issues of special concern are the use of grants to ameliorate inter-regional or inter-locality inequality, and the choice between categorical and general purpose grants.

Grants promoting equalization may provide a needed stimulus to poorer areas, but they can also create disincentives for local resource mobilization, discouraging richer areas that may feel discriminated against while encouraging poorer ones to accept gifts in lieu of self-help. We have referred already to the way the Saemaul Undong program in South Korea handled this. At first it gave all communities the same grants in kind (a standard amount of cement and steel for construction). But this was inefficient and had no incentive effect so villages were classified as "basic," "self-reliant" and "independent." The middle category got the most aid as a reward for their own effort with the first getting more than the last. The apparent disincentive to "graduate" into the third category was compensated for in part by the status given such villages as good examples for the others. As reported in Annex Seven, much "graduation" occurred.

Having three categories like this is simple administratively but it creates sharp differences in assistance which might be avoided with more incremental changes. An alternative is a progressive grant structure in which communities receive decreasing increments of aid as their ability to mobilize their own resources increases. Kenya established such a system during the late 1950s to assist the newly established District Councils (Hicks, 1961:422-424).

Determining some common denominator on which to base an "equalization" criterion is difficult. Should it reflect current income levels if these can possibly be known? The number or proportion of households demonstrably "poor"? The potential for rapid improvement? Systems of fiscal equalization presume that there is a relatively uniform system of local taxation, yet standardization can undermine creative local resource mobilization. In the name of establishing equalizing grants, one would not want to reduce local initiative.

With regard to types of grants, block grants and matching grants have different characteristics. Comparing the grant systems in countries having a British colonial past, Hicks remarks:

> Block grants as a type get good marks both from the point of view of leaving Local Authorities to plan their own priorities unfettered, and from the consideration that an equalizing element can relatively easily be included. Their main drawbacks are firstly, absence of direct stimulus to activity, and secondly, that unless specific conditions (for instance concerning general standards of performance) are written in, they give no incentive for careful management . . . .
>
> In contrast to block grants, the main advantages of specific grants are stimulus and control, and these are very valuable factors. At the same time there is a danger that they may upset the balance of local budgeting. (Hicks, 1961:309-310)

Obviously there are arguments to be made for and against each kind of grant from an LID perspective. To the extent that either block grants or specific grants are given on a "matching" basis to reward local resource mobilization, they can make a positive-sum contribution. Whether they aid the process of institutionalization is not so clear. The village subsidy program in Indonesia (Annex Three) provided block grants with some restrictions on what the funds could be used for and it mobilized some "match" in the form of local labor and management (Prabowo, 1973). Workers were paid a wage but not necessarily at market level so the difference amounted to a kind of local contribution which augmented central resources. It appears, however, that the village governments were not uniformly strengthened by this program, especially where the projects undertaken were chosen by local elites and not particularly popular with the people. There was no systematic effort to build up local capacities for planning and implementation, and maintenance has reportedly been a problem. A similar program in Thailand (Annex Eight) has been making more progress in this direction, partly because the local government units handling the funds are more freely elected and more readily held accountable by the community for results.

A major advantage of giving block grants in the assistance or facilitation mode is that they provide some *core funding* for local institutions. It has been observed in the rural infrastructure area that the stability and predictability of funding levels is often more important for LID than the amount of funds provided (Garzon, 1981). Core funding is essential for institutions to have incentive to focus on future-oriented activities like planning. The quality of requests for assistance and the kind of things asked for will be affected by whether institutions are thinking in terms of "windfall" benefits or of things that need to be (and can be) developed and maintained over time.

There are hazards in having too much as well as too little funding from outside. Generous and unconditional block grants can undermine local institutional capacity as surely as can scarcity of resources. This happened with a rural works program in Bangladesh (then East Pakistan) that was reasonably disciplined and productive in its early period. Both characteristics declined once large amounts of money began flowing to the union councils (Thomas, 1971). The matching grant requirements were relaxed in order to "move money" faster, and more of the implementation was carried out by private contractors who often did not give value for money. Such poor performance detracted from the legitimacy and support that the Union Councils (locality-level LGs) enjoyed. We find that grants, especially if given on a matching basis, can be useful financial mechanisms for supporting LID capacity, but the Bangladesh experience confirms the adage that there can be "too much of a good thing." Large amounts of funds flowing into a local institution are no solution for inadequate capacity and indeed can become a problem.

8.4.3 In-Kind Contributions

There are a number of documented cases where external gifts or grants of materials elicited matching local inputs of labor. The example of the Local Development Department in Nepal assisting the work of local bridge-building committees in Baglung district by providing steel cable has been cited previously. The value of communities' contributions of labor and material inputs was many times greater than that of the cable. Similarly the Community Development Department in Malawi gave pipe as well as training and technical assistance to committees that managed the installation of extensive gravity-flow water supply systems. The women's garden groups in Senegal, described in Annex Five, were greatly aided by a donor giving them improved wells for irrigation and trucks to transport produce to market.

The material contributions not only spur local effort, but their being given in-kind reduces possibilities for corruption and institution-corroding suspicion that would have existed with grants of money (Pradhan, 1980). This was one of the reasons why the government in South Korea gave its initial Saemaul Undong aid to villages in the form of cement and steel reinforcing rods. However, the inefficiencies resulting from providing the same materials to all villages shows why grants should be tailored to local priorities and needs.

One objection to such a strategy can be that the provision of materials with the expectation that communities or localities will provide matching labor for construction can be a regressive form of resource mobilization. Particularly in communities that are highly stratified, poorer members are likely to have to provide proportionally more labor even if they derive relatively less benefit.[11] How unfair the impact of in-kind contributions from government, PVO or donor agencies may be depends on the task at hand, the prevailing stratification, and the policies followed in apportioning contributions.

A more serious problem with outside in-kind contributions can be the disincentive effect that commodity aid (often given as "food for work") may have. We have seen in Botswana and Sri Lanka how community customs of voluntary work—for road maintenance and cleaning irrigation channels—can be undermined by introducing payment in kind, so that people subsequently refuse to continue doing maintenance work they previously undertook unless given free food. An evaluation of a rural water supply project in Peru concluded that:

> The interjection of 'food for work' in development projects where a tradition of voluntary community involvement exists can produce more harm than help. (Haratani et al., 1981)

The result of such outside resources will be negative-sum—resource demobilization—as the total amount of resources mobilized for development tasks over time is diminished due to a withdrawal of local resources previously contributed on a regular basis.

We would not take a firm position against this form of outside assistance, however. The Kottar Social Service Society in India has made good use of such aid to cite a contrary example (Annex Seven). There are situations where emergency relief needs to be given, and rather than provide free rations, food may be provided as part of a program to build up community assets with the labor that would otherwise produce nothing. Food-for-work can provide some dignity to individuals in circumstances that are otherwise demeaning. It could also be argued that one should not require rural people to provide services like roads or water supply for themselves at their own expense when urban dwellers seldom have to make similar investments. In any case, if one accepts the practical and ethical justifications for food aid, its

---

[11]The roads built under the rural works program in Bangladesh, for example, were chiefly of value to larger farmers who produced a surplus to market, though the poor who derived relatively fewer benefits had to provide most of the labor (Garzon, 1981:18). It is often thought to be beneath the status of richer members to contribute labor, though they may be expected to contribute money to the effort in lieu of work. Whether this happens depends on local norms and leadership orientation. In a water project in Ethiopia, not only did the rural poor contribute most of the labor to dig the trenches and lay pipes for the system, but once it was finished they had to pay for water when they had previously gotten it free (Uphoff, Cohen and Goldsmith, 1979:274). In neighboring Kenya, Thomas (1980) found less regressiveness in self-help projects because outside grants were matched more often by money than labor (and the money was used to pay for labor). Richer members of the community, partly to gain prestige, gave a larger share of resources, though poorer members might be expected to contribute some labor in lieu of cash.

implications for the strengthening of local institutions should be carefully weighed before embarking on such a program.[12]

8.4.4 Divisions of Responsibility

One of the ways in which outside resources can be provided with less likelihood of reducing local resource mobilization is to work out formulas for sharing financial responsibility that are understood and accepted at the local level. In the primary health care area, one common formula has been for the community to construct part or all of a facility, such as the health hut in the Sine Saloum project in Senegal, with the understanding that the project will provide training and salaries for the personnel who staff it. The cost of drugs is also fairly readily assigned to the local level, since user-charges can be levied for such "private" goods.

A systematic study of financing primary health care programs found that costs for supervision of staff, logistical support for the program, and referral services usually had to be assumed by the sponsoring agency, and that sustainable local contributions were most likely to take the form of voluntary labor and possibly some payments for services or sometimes paraprofessional salaries (APHA, 1982b:41). The Sine Saloum project referred to above found it difficult to mobilize cash resources at the outset. But after a more socially sensitive approach was taken, it was able to make a new division of financial responsibility work (Bloom, 1984a). In the Pikine primary health project, also in Senegal, the division of labor was arranged so that the government pays staff salaries and the community pays for services and drugs.[13]

There can be various difficulties with sharing of responsibility. Rural people may have difficulty in coming up with cash (often depending on the time of year) and it is therefore sometimes suggested that their contributions

---

[12]In research on local institutions in sixteen villages in Sri Lanka, Uphoff (1979) found one case where controversy over apparent corruption in distributing food-for-work aid had undermined an active Rural Development Society (RDS). Some other communities experienced no debilitating effects. The ability of a community to continue voluntary labor alongside "paid" labor was said by local leaders interviewed to depend on the pre-existing strength of the Rural Development Society. This suggests that food aid is not a promising means for strengthening local institutions if they do not already have some cohesiveness and integrity as institutions.

Negative experience with food aid in Botswana is discussed in this regard in Brown (1983:70-73). A more positive view is offered by Gooch and MacDonald (1981:58-59) who suggest that "the nature of self-help is changing with cash becoming the main contribution, "so disincentive effects are less important even if free labor contributions are discouraged by payment. Indeed, they argue, food-for-work schemes have sometimes had a "positive effect in that they have mobilized communities and enabled people to keep their resources intact."

[13]Both projects are reported in Annex Four. This division of labor can be debated. Often it appears that local people can best provide materials while the government covers salaries. The opposite view is that salaries paid locally may cost less than if paid by government and can be paid more flexibly, reflecting seasonal variations of work load, for example. Also, this would make the personnel more accountable to the community. There are pros and cons for either division of responsibility. The India and Nepal irrigation examples reported in Annex Eight suggest advantages of having salaries paid by the local organization.

should be only in kind. This caution is worth noting because it restricts the scope for local resource mobilization and the kind of development activities that can be undertaken locally if all financial resources must be provided from outside. The primary health program in Burma suggests that cash can be mobilized even in poor communities if the services being offered are highly valued (Annex Four). From an LID point of view, this underscores the importance of undertaking activities that meet local expectations.

There may be misunderstanding about the terms on which the respective local and outside resource contributions are to be made. In the Philippines, the National Irrigation Administration (NIA) must work out a formal written agreement with the water users' association that NIA organizers (catalysts) have helped to establish before rehabilitation work is started.[14] If the Association's members are not willing to accept the design prepared by the engineers in consultation with farmers, the capital improvement will not be undertaken. If the agreement is signed, members agree to repay the capital costs, which are reduced by whatever amount of labor and materials they contribute to the construction (Bagadion and F. Korten, 1985).

In North Yemen, where literacy levels are lower, a very simple physical formula has been worked out for building schools. If the Local Development Association builds a school up to the level of the windows, the national Confederation of Yemeni Development Associations gives a grant to fund the rest of the construction, and when that is done, the Ministry of Education provides a permanent roof for the building as its contribution (Cohen et al., 1981). This example is offered not as a formula to be replicated but rather as an indication of the kind of innovativeness and clarity to be sought in working out divisions of financial responsibility to promote postive-sum results in resource mobilization.

8.4.5 Procedures

Requirements accompanying outside provision of resources can have an adverse effect on local resource mobilization. Local institutions may be discouraged from seeking matching funds or grants by complicated budgeting procedures and long approval and disbursement cycles. It often happens that the government's bookkeeping requirements for handling and later auditing its funds are forbidding, and if foreign assistance is involved, two or more different accounting systems may be required. Even if such complexities do not deter local institutions from seeking outside support, they may absorb enough effort that the net contribution of the external aid is diminished.

---

[14]These catalysts start in a promotion mode, but switch to facilitation and eventually assistance, according to the distinctions made in Section 7.1.1.

One unfortunate circumstance for local institutions is the lack of fit between external and local budget cycles. Getting expenditure of funds approved in advance of activities is often difficult for rural institutions. Local administration, being already part of the government's fiscal system, may fare better than other local institutions, but even it will have problems of fitting into the national budgeting system. Even when an expenditure has been approved in the budget, obtaining authorization to actually spend the money is a hurdle frequently difficult to deal with from a distance. Opportune times for construction and slack times in the agricultural cycle may come and go without receipt of promised outside resources. Rather than encourage more local effort, funds so unreliable or inaccessible will dampen it, as seen in the Indonesian case in Annex Three.

Compounding the deterrent effect is the general rule that within any budget year, authorized but unexpended funds must revert to their source. Matching resources are difficult to mobilize locally on a rushed basis. The consequence of annual budget restrictions can be activities that are done haphazardly or are only marginally useful. One of the major improvements that could bolster local institutions and make external resources more productive would be to relax restrictions on retention of unexpended funds. Authorization to carry funds over to the next year without losing them would be one of the least costly impetuses to expanded and more sensible local self-help activity.

The feasibility of allowing local institutions to carry forward some reasonable surpluses for future use depends in part on the availability of financial services from banks, credit unions, and accountants. National and donor agencies may be reluctant to give up tight control over "their" resources. But then it should not be surprising if local actors are not so conscientious or self-exerting in their use of resources which, by external definition, do not "belong" to the local institution. It would also be useful if, instead of the penalties so commonly threatened for misuse of outside resources, there were rewards given local institutions for careful and innovative application of external inputs, especially when these were multiplied or extended by local resources.

8.4.6 External Inputs

Having considered how outside contributions, including resources in kind, can augment local efforts, it should be said that having to use external materials can itself constitute a barrier to local resource mobilization. An evaluation of a domestic water supply project in Peru concludes:

> Imported materials tend to become the limiting element in development projects and produce rigidities in project design and construction. (Haratani et al., 1981)

Yet external inputs can also be valuable contributions. The success of bridge construction in the hills of Nepal was dependent on both the provision of steel cable from outside and the use of locally available materials and local technologies—indigenous rockworking techniques instead of cement, connecting rods forged by traditional blacksmiths. This meant that people had more confidence in their ability to build and maintain the bridges themselves, which was an incentive to contribute their own labor and funds. Self-help water supply projects often combine external inputs such as PVC piping with local resources and skills.

The challenge is to identify which outside inputs can have the most resource-mobilizing effect at the local level. Strong cables and durable faucets, for example, can in certain circumstances be important attractions to villagers who are expected to contribute their own labor and money to a bridge-building or water supply project.

Yet reliance on resources from outside the community can present problems. The Burmese primary health care program discussed previously found that the enthusiasm of village volunteer workers sometimes flagged when the supply of drugs from the capital city was interrupted due to problems of logistics or weather. The supply of drugs had been an inducement for local participation in the program. Where outside resources figure centrally in a project's strategy for local institutional development, the project design and budget should ensure the reliability and adequacy of supply.

More serious effects of outside aid can come from sheer magnitude, which dwarfs the share of local resources and distorts local people's sense of responsibility for maintaining their flow. As the proportion of outside resources increases, invariably so will external controls. Even a development organization as committed to the principle of self-reliance as the Sarvodaya Movement in Sri Lanka found that an influx of overseas funds led to a centralization of activity in the national headquarters (Moore, 1981). Local initiative and planning activities had to give way to central assumption of responsibility to satisfy all the approval, reporting, and accounting requirements that came with external aid, even aid intended to buttress a self-reliant approach.

8.5 DONOR AGENCY CONTRIBUTIONS

Outside assistance, whether national or international, should not have to compromise local institutional integrity and capacity. Donors should understand that their objective is not to accomplish certain "targets" through the expenditure of their funds, so much as to strengthen local capacities to meet those and other targets on a sustained basis, relying as much as possible on local resources. Outside assistance can be given in ways that offer inducements to local effort if the amounts are manageable, the procedures supportive, the kinds appropriate, the pace of expansion flexible, the approach experimental, and the expectations reasonable.

Most of the cases reported in Annex Eight as well as many in other annexes give examples of imaginative and intelligent uses of external resources—funds and materials as well as technical assistance and administrative support. In particular it is important for donor agencies to appreciate that there is considerable management capacity in local communities even if levels of education and literacy are not high. These talents can be mobilized if forms of "appropriate administration" as described by Calavan (1984) are utilized.

It is widely appreciated that avoiding "dependency" is essential for development, and this is more true for LID than for any other aspect of development. At the same time, it is clear that outside assistance is needed for most widespread advances of local institutional capacity. This suggests a strategy of "assisted self-reliance" (Esman and Uphoff, 1984:258-261). While this concept may seem contradictory, it is not. It is only paradoxical, and much of the development enterprise is pervaded with paradox. The development process at once moves toward greater independence of individuals by creating new productive capacities, and more interdependencies as mutual resource flows and accountability are established.

There are many ways in which donor agencies can support processes of local institutional development in specific situations. As a rule, they will not work directly with local institutions, instead cooperating through national or regional agencies—public or private sector intermediaries that operate in an assistance, facilitation or promotion mode vis-a-vis local institutions. As we have seen, the donor support itself can be in an assistance, facilitation or promotion mode with the intermediary institution that seeks to strengthen local capacities. Sometimes donor aid may be even more indirect by channeling funds through an international organization or a private voluntary agency operating as an intermediary with national or regional institutions.

The learning process approach discussed in Section 7.1.2 is something most national or intermediary institutions understand and accept by now but only in principle. In practice, most still operate according to blueprint ideas and procedures. A donor agency that recognizes the value of a more inductive approach to LID can encourage those institutions directly involved in planning and implementation efforts with local institutions to revise their approach by providing them with training and financial support to bolster new kinds of development work. Arranging and funding visits by agency personnel to countries and programs that have made the learning process effective may be one of the most valuable forms of donor assistance, and one fairly easily approved by funding agencies.

As suggested in Section 7.5.4, donor agencies need to engage in their own version of "bureaucratic reorientation." Donors' prevailing methods of operation and the usual reward structure for their staff commonly work against a realistic approach to LID. Until such constraints can be changed, donor efforts to promote LID with and through national and intermediary institutions will ring hollow.

Chief among the biases that work against LID is the preoccupation with (one could call it a pathology of) "moving money." This comes from assuming that *the amount of money spent equals the amount of development achieved* (Korten and Uphoff, 1981). It takes very little reflection to recognize that this equation of expenditure with results is fallacious. Yet it dominates so much of the thinking and activity of donors and national governments that "moving money" becomes a source of distortion and sabotage for LID efforts.[15]

Actually the notion that investment in and through local institutions must always be slower than other kinds of development expenditure is mistaken. The Basic Village Services project in Egypt, to which USAID has contributed over $230 million, has shown that small-scale investments made in and through Village Councils can proceed more expeditiously than other kinds of projects as this huge project has managed to keep ahead of schedule in its disbursements (see Annex Three; also Mayfield, 1985). Another most impressive case of an "accelerated" development project, in one of the most depressed environments, is reported from rural Haiti. There, an agroforestry project working through PVOs with existing local peasant organizations (*groupmans*, small farmer groups of seven to twelve members) managed to reach not 6,000 peasants planting 3 million trees as originally planned but 75,000 peasants who planted some 20 million trees in four years (Murray, 1986). The Grameen Bank experience in Bangladesh (Annex Eight) has given similar encouragement that large amounts of funds can be beneficially used in very small amounts through an appropriate channel linked to local organizations.

LID-oriented projects can utilize money reasonably rapidly and productively, but a rigid pace of expenditure will not produce good or optimal results. For LID even more than for other activities, the amount of

---

[15]Writing on efforts to strengthen municipal government capacity in Latin America, Gall et al. observe: "In those instances where funding has been provided for municipal development, many observers find that decentralization has been hampered by the pressure to produce a given number of subprojects. Donor loans have been made for short-time periods (three to five years) and thus pressure exists to place subloans as quickly as possible to meet pre-established disbursement projections. This then produces a situation in which the following things happen: (a) Rapid start-up of lending activity is necessary, so pre-planning of priority areas of lending either does not occur or is ignored; and (b) The institution-building and technical assistance activity (which is by its nature slow and gradual) takes second place. This overtakes the need to reform municipal personnel and tax laws, to define a clear role for local government in the overall scheme of development, to build linkages with regional plans, and to upgrade the quality of local development plans and service delivery. In short, the capacity building that would make decentralization effective is bulldozed aside by the pressure to disburse funds for works." (1975:11).

development achieved is not necessarily proportional to the funds expended. Donors need to be devising new and better indicators of development, including LID, so that they can get away from the mistaken and misleading equation of expenditure with development, as suggested at the end of Chapter Six.

A second way donors can prepare themselves to be more effective in supporting LID is to take a longer time perspective. Institutionalization as a process almost by definition requires time. Valuations of an organization and its performance need to become widely shared and strongly held and this seldom happens quickly. A three or four year life-of-project is unlikely to suffice for advancing changes in the bedrock acceptance of an institution. Fortunately donors appear to be lengthening their time horizons on projects though they still are often fixated on quick finite results.[16]

The concern with precise planning targets itself contributes to a displacement of LID effort, focusing attention more often on superficial or spurious "outputs" than on sustainable processes and capacities. Rondinelli correctly observes that:

> The insistence of funding organizations—whether they be international aid agencies or central government ministries—on precise and detailed statements of objectives at the outset in order to facilitate systematic planning, management and control often leads to game-playing, phony precision and inaccurate reporting that create severe administrative problems later on. (1983:81-82)[17]

More emphasis should be placed on signs of progress toward institutionalization. These would include performance measures attributable to the institutions in question, as well as indicators of acceptance and support from the persons on which they depend for sustained activity. The number of farmers who have "joined" water user associations is less significant from a developmental viewpoint than declines in the number of water disputes reported or increased farmer and official satisfaction with water delivery.

We have noted frequently the importance of having a network of local

---

[16]In work on water management improvement in Sri Lanka, the government and USAID agreed on an unusual but reasonable twenty-year time horizon, including establishing a system of farmer organization. The Gal Oya project was to be the first in a series of projects and was initially planned for eight years. Bureaucratic considerations, however, caused this to be reduced to four, which among other things meant that the master planning envisioned had to be done concurrently with the rehabilitation work.

The project itself "quantified" farmer organization goals in an unrealistic way, specifying that all 19,000 farmers in the project area would be "organized" by the end of year four. (The actual number of farmers in the area turned out to be almost twice as many.) In the haste to promise results, little thought was given to how organizations so rapidly established would become permanent, sustainable institutions (Uphoff, 1982). In water management particularly, one does not want organizations that subsequently lose their effectiveness. In fact, the process of institutional development went faster than those responsible had "planned" (Uphoff, 1985).

[17]The way target setting can lead to absurd performance reporting was documented in a district of Tamil Nadu, India when Cambridge University researchers found that the area actually planted with high-yielding varieties of rice in 1975-76 was only one-third the area officially reported to and by the Ministry of Agriculture (Farmer et al., 1977:96).

institutions that mutually strengthen one another. Donors usually want to focus simply on assisting a single channel, such as cooperatives or local governments or private businesses. But this is probably not even the best way to build up the particular favored channel. This is not to suggest that donors must undertake the LID equivalent of "integrated rural development," investing in all kinds of local institutions simultaneously. Rather a broadened focus should be adopted so that linkages extending beyond the institution receiving aid are recognized and supported by the donor. To make an institution independent of all others may be unwise, because this can disengage it from relationships with complementary and collaborative institutions.[18] If there is no such network, its prospects for effectiveness as well as institutionalization are accordingly diminished.

The fact that assistance to local institutions can weaken them is reflected in the distinction made between *enfeebling assistance* and *supportive assistance* by Peterson, (1982:118-119). The former makes the organization dependent on outside sources of support, smothering its independence and initiative, perhaps unintentionally. Supportive assistance, on the other hand, is characterized by stimulating local commitment and initiative, through the kind of cost-sharing practices considered in Section 8.4. Peterson cites the government policy in Taiwan of contributing no more than 50 percent of construction costs for Farmers' Associations facilities to ensure a substantial local contribution, in part so that people regard the facility as "theirs."

Donors should determine what they can do internally to begin reorienting their efforts toward more effective support of LID. One relatively low-cost reform would be to change the sequential and dichotomized approach to projects where certain persons do the planning and then others do the implementation. A learning process is hampered by discontinuities of personnel. The Ministry of Public Works in Venezuela has come to realize how costly such segregation of roles can be. It now requires design engineers, early in their careers, to manage for at least two years one of the irrigation schemes they have laid out on paper (Gil Levine, personal communication). Getting away from having the design and the management of projects handled by completely different teams is a good first step. A second step would be to have longer tours of duty for staff in the field so that "donor memory" can be improved. LID suffers greatly when those responsible for overseeing it change frequently as is too often the case now.

To supplement donor inputs and to increase institutional memory as well as expertise in the management of social change, there is good reason

---

[18]USAID's policy paper on local organizations takes note of the value of horizontal linkages and advises: "Providing support for new organizations outside the existing network of institutional linkages may thus be ineffective. Furthermore, offering outside assistance that enables or encourages existing local organizations to withdraw from this supporting network may over the long term be counterproductive." (1984:4).

for donors to enlist and contribute the services of knowledge-building institutions. Examples of this type of contribution are the previously mentioned
Asian Institute of Management and the Institute of Philippine Culture,
which bolstered the efforts of the National Irrigation Administration to introduce water user associations (D. Korten, 1980; F. Korten, 1982), or the
Planning Research and Action Institute of Lucknow, which spearheaded
the UNICEF-backed water supply project in Banki, India (Misra, 1975).
Where there is institutionally perceptive leadership within a government
agency such as with the Kenya Tea Development Authority or the Malawi
self-help water scheme, LID can proceed without such assistance. But even
with aware leadership, broader or quicker progress may occur if a
knowledge-building institution is involved as a partner in implementation
and adaptation if only because agency personnel are usually so overloaded
with administrative tasks.

An additional change that some donor agencies have already implemented is to move away from evaluation as an end-of-project activity and to
undertake evaluation and redesign on a more frequent, periodic basis, so as
to incorporate ongoing learning into the project cycle. Since project designs
are intended to get resources allocated and flowing to a certain activity, they
should be regarded more as a license than as a contract. Reassessments and
reformulations are part of any complex management task. These activities,
to be sure, should not be allowed to become all-consuming. The first rule in
Peters and Waterman's excellent book (1982) is to be action-oriented. But
action should be undertaken thoughtfully and self-critically, informed by
feedback from one's clientele. The fact that circumstances always change
and analyses are always fallible or incomplete should make the revision of
plans, based on experience, an act of wisdom not an indication of incompe-
tence. If donor agencies can convey this perspective to national
governments and implementing agencies, a real service will be done for LID
and for development generally.

Development itself is the most demanding learning process there is. Individual learning is difficult enough, but the learning required for
development is all the more complex and ambiguous because it must be collective learning. It must be incorporated in the experience and actions of
hundreds, thousands, and even millions of people who day in, day out,
struggle to gain a better understanding of how they can make their lives
more productive, satisfying and secure. The limits of individual action are
reached fairly quickly and this realization leads to collective action at group,
community, and locality levels, as discussed by Hirschman (1984). These
learning processes are unwieldy and diffuse, often not conclusive and certainly not identical.

The task of planners and implementors within higher level institutions,
from the international level of donor agencies down through national, regional, district, and sub-district levels, is to launch and sustain their own

complementary learning processes in support of what people at local levels are doing. This is a vision of what donor agencies can and should do. Their role has previously been defined principally in terms of providing capital and expertise, as "giving" productive capacity and "giving" answers. The function of outside resources should rather be to help in identifying problems and finding solutions across a broad range of human needs. This includes strengthening the development of local institutions, which are crucial for improving both productive and problem-solving capacities.

In so many cases, as seen in the annexes, we find that lack of local institutional development was a constraining factor, or conversely, LID was the key to making impressive, often rapid and inexpensive improvements in many sectors. Introducing appropriate local institutions led directly to the spread of new agricultural technologies, improvements in health, construction of water supplies and bridges, protection of forests, more reliable and equitable distribution of irrigation water, etc. With such a realization by donor agencies, LID should assume greater salience in their planning and investments. For donors to be effective promoters, facilitators, or assistors of LID, however, they will need to change some of their own ways of working, in directions that have been pointed out in this concluding section. Acceleration of progress toward local institutional development may, paradoxically, have to begin at the international level.

ANNEXES

Rural Local Institutions in Kenya

The following two diagrams were prepared by Mary Tiffen of the Agricultural Administration Unit of the Overseas Development Institute (ODI) of London on the basis of data gathered while evaluating the Machakos Integrated Development Project in Kenya. She has kindly given permission to reproduce them here as examples of the kind of institutional levels, channels, and networks our analysis is concerned with.

The first figure (A1.1) shows how the institutions "reaching down" to the local level appear from above. Note how from this top-down perspective, both the specificity and differentiation of local institutions diminish at lower levels.

The second figure (A1.2) is a view "from below." It reflects the quite differentiated organization of people that exists at the local level and gives details on the various committees, government agencies, and nongovernmental organizations (NGOs) to which local roles and local bodies relate.

The structures established "from above" and "from below" may not meet. Four years after the project had started, Tiffen found herself introducing the MIDP project manager to the head of the County Council for the first time. The lack of connection between these key central and local decision makers who were operating essentially at the same level prompted her to prepare these diagrams in such detail (Tiffen, 1983).

Figure A1.1: GOVERNMENTAL STRUCTURE

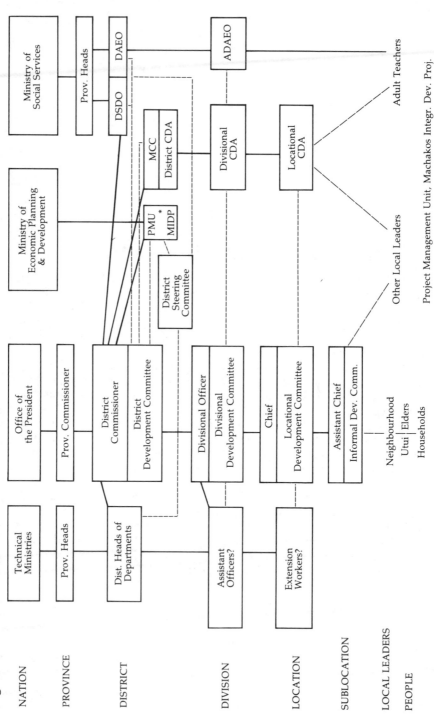

*Source: Tiffen (1983)

Figure A1.2: COMMUNITY STRUCTURE (SIMPLIFIED)

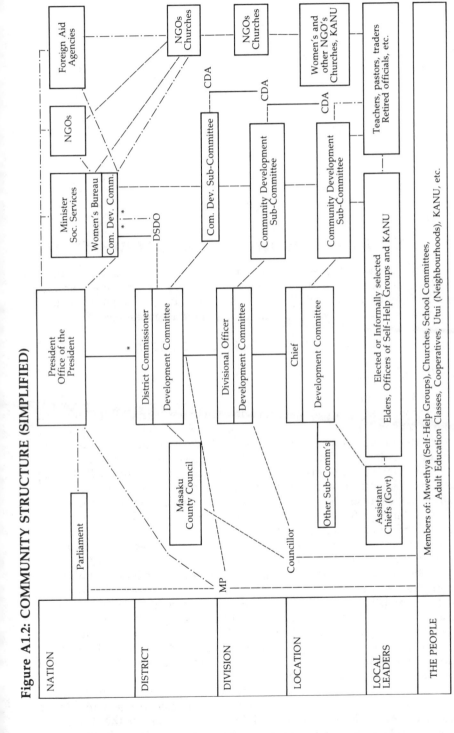

Source: Tiffen (1983)

Key: —— Responsibility lines – – – ex officio ——— sends up elected member –·– pressure group route

* Chairman in this line always an official. ** Chairman in this line always elected.

Members of: Mwethya (Self-Help Groups), Churches, School Committees, Adult Education Classes, Cooperatives, Utui (Neighbourhoods), KANU, etc.

Natural Resource Management

To share with readers some of the most instructive LID experiences, positive and negative, that we have found in our review of the literature, we are presenting capsule descriptions of some of these experiences. Readers are referred to the referenced sources for fuller accounts.

IRRIGATION WATER MANAGEMENT

CHILE: San Pedro de Atacama Irrigation

Irrigated agriculture goes back at least to 500 A.D. on the high desert plain where San Pedro de Atacama is located in northern Chile (10,000 feet above sea level, less than 100 mm. of rainfall annually). We know that by 1000 A.D., a society based on a complex system of irrigation existed, and in Incan times the population was 20,000, greater than it is today.

After mining enterprises were developed upstream from San Pedro and began to take off substantial amounts of water that were uncontrollable by farmers, their investment in agriculture lagged, and the area reverted largely to subsistence cultivation. Locally elected associations manage the distribution of irrigation water at canal level and at the area level, but they have come under the control of officials of the national irrigation bureaucracy since it lined some of the canals in San Pedro in the mid-1960s.

The agricultural system is languishing because the national administration is not very responsive or flexible. Some delegation of authority to the local administration would help to resolve uncertainty about conflicting uses of water and encourage farmers to undertake more investment and active water management. Farmers cannot reach the productive potential of even their current technology, let alone what could be done with construction of storage tanks, because of the rigid pattern of operation that has been imposed from outside (Lynch, 1978).

LESSONS: To be effective, local institutions need to encompass the interests of all the relevant actors and to be able to reach authoritative decisions. Being "local" may be a liability if persons outside the area or at a higher level can negate local decisions. This applies to local administration as much as to local government or local organizations. Irrigation will not approach optimum productivity unless it has appropriate local institutional support.

PAKISTAN: Daudzai Irrigation in Northwest Frontier Province

The system of water management at Daudzai has been developed by local residents over centuries. Water rights, responsibilities, and rules for distributing water were codified first in the early 16th century and revised several times in the last two centuries. A complex system of rotational irrigation with schedules specified in units of time per *tarib* (half acre) is managed by farmers, who also clean and operate all channels.

All members of the village participate in discussions, but the village elders who function as the local government make all decisions. *Chowkidars* are appointed from and paid by the community to supervise water deliveries on its behalf. The government irrigation department provides assistance in managing conflicts when these cannot be handled by the elders and in constructing and operating some control structures that the community has difficulty handling (Bhatty, 1979).

LESSONS: Local communities have considerable capacity to deal with the technical and organizational tasks of water management, though their performance can be usefully augmented by local technical staff of the government. Where the whole community relies on irrigation, its management can be undertaken by local government. When traditional institutions are functioning well, it is advisable to work with them, making accommodations in government procedures as necessary for a good cooperative relationship.

MEXICO: Indigenous Irrigation in Oaxaca State

Water management committees in Oaxaca, where the practice of canal irrigation goes back more than a thousand years, have been operating as part of the village government (LG) there. The great diversity of ways in which different villages manage their irrigation water, as documented by Lees (1973), is quite impressive as is their effectiveness in this task.

In her study of twenty-three communities, Lees found no simple or direct relationship between the irrigation technology used and the social organization utilizing it. Rather "the form of water use management emerges from the social structure of the society where it is found." Unfortunately where these old irrigation systems have been upgraded by the government, the role of local government in water management has been abridged as it was given no legal sanction by the national government.

LESSONS: Again, local technical and organizational capacity is significant. There are many different ways of organizing decision making, resource mobilization, communication, and conflict management at the local level. National government would do well to accept and work with such diversity, including granting the necessary legal recognition for such local organizations, if it wants to capitalize on indigenous social infrastructure.

PHILIPPINES: Zanjera Irrigation Organizations

Among the most sophisticated indigenous irrigation organizations in Southeast Asia are the zanjera schemes in the province of Ilocos Norte. Although each base organization is separate, there are numerous federations which jointly operate diversion dams and common main canals. Members contribute labor and materials to the construction and maintenance of the systems in proportion to the amount of land they cultivate under it.

Land shares, called *atars*, are often divided into several separate parcels to ensure that locational advantages and disadvantages are shared equally. At the tail of each system, a section of land is set aside for the organization's elected leader, which gives him some compensation for his duties and also gives him an incentive to ensure that water gets all the way down to the lower reaches.

One indication of the resource mobilizing capacity of the zanjeras is the report that one zanjera federation made up of nine organizations mobilized nearly 16,000 person-days of labor from members for maintenance and other work without monetary compensation (Siy, 1982).

In 1980 the Japanese aid agency in conjunction with the National Irrigation Administration undertook to install a 10,000 hectare irrigation project in Ilocos Norte. The agency completely ignored the existence of the zanjeras and proposed cutting new canals across nearly all existing channels. The organizational integrity of the zanjeras could have been destroyed by such intervention, but fortunately this approach to design and construction which ignored what was already in place, was revised (Visayas, 1982).

LESSONS: The zanjeras represent an elaborate form of "social infrastructure" to make irrigation more efficient and beneficial. To ignore them represented a form of "disinvestment" by the Philippine government and the donor agency. Water users have an interest in achieving both productivity and equity. Donor agencies should assess existing local institutional capacity before introducing new development programs to determine how best to relate to local organizations and LG where they are operating effectively for irrigation water management.

SOCIAL FORESTRY

SENEGAL: AFRICARE Reforestation Project

The Senegal Forest Service works with Rural Community Councils on this project, providing implements, tractors, seedlings, transportation, etc., while the community through its local government Council contributes labor to plant the trees. The division of responsibility is such that the Forest Service continues to oversee the plantation once established, but the Council can decide independently what to do with the wood. Income generated from the sale of wood goes into the Council's fund for rural development, to be used according to its own priorities.

Maintenance of the planted area is the responsibility of the Council. Nonetheless, the Council was not "abandoned" since at one point, when the villagers could not keep up with the weeds, the Forest Service moved in with tractors and disks to help out. Due to the efficient cooperation and co-management between the Forest Service and Council, almost double the targeted area was planted without additional funds. However, a local nursery could not be planted due to a shortage of water and Forest Service field agents (Weber, 1981).

LESSONS: Such locally managed reforestation programs are less costly, higher yielding, and more successful than the large-scale, government-sponsored industrial plantations in Senegal, according to the evaluation by Weber (1981). This collaboration is possible if technical assistance, material, equipment, and funds are provided by the administration, and if the local government, in return for contributing labor, enjoys the economic benefits of the project.

NEPAL: Panchayat Forest Management

Deforestation is a serious problem in many areas of the Nepal hills. Previously communities were responsible for local forests through their traditional local government (panchayats). In 1957 the government vested ownership and control of all forest areas in its Forestry Department because it regarded local management as inadequate. (Later the rule was relaxed to permit private or community development of small planted forestry areas.) This approach to forest conservation proved largely ineffective.

The Divisional Forest Officer (LA) at Chautara decided to reinstitute community responsibility on an experimental basis. Working with the assistance of the Nepal-Australian Forestry Project and involving local panchayat leaders in the planning, the officer got the government to declare the area a fuelwood deficit area so that export of fuelwood to other places could be banned.

The cooperating panchayats (LG) were authorized to make use of the forests in their areas. These actions made the local people believe that the forest was now their property and their responsibility, to be used for their own benefit. They began protecting the existing forest and planting and caring for new trees (without the expense of putting up costly wire fencing). People kept their livestock out of the planted areas and the forest quickly regenerated. This program became the basis for a new national effort at community-based reforestation beginning in 1977, when the government restored communities' right to own and manage forests (Dani and Campbell, 1986).

* * * * *

In 1957 forests in the Nuwakot District, as elsewhere, came under more direct government control when they were made the responsibility of LA. During subsequent years the cutting of trees by villagers, in the words of a former Joint Secretary in the Ministry of Local Development, turned entire hillsides "into an unsightly ochre-red spectacle, but also causing the villagers themselves a great deal of hardship in finding fuel and fodder supply" (Shrestha, 1980:89).

The small farmer groups in Nuwakot District, established under the Small Farmer Development Program sponsored by FAO (described in Annex Five) have in some places branched out into forestry. In one location the groups in nine contiguous wards (subdivisions of the panchayat) undertook to reforest their area. They employed six local persons as watchmen to prevent trespassing while the area was allowed to regenerate. The watchmen were paid 120 rupees a month from funds collected by the panchayat from residents in the nine wards. When it was discovered that the money collected in this way did not always reach the watchmen, responsibility was decentralized to the ward representatives who supervised the collection of contributions from local households and paid the watchmen directly.

Shrestha says: "The forest continues to be protected and it is growing luxuriantly. The watchmen continue to be interested because they think that it is their own forest. In addition, their efforts are massively supplemented by those of the individual households themselves who, because of their emotional and material involvement in the maintenance of the forest, do not stand for anybody trespassing on it.

In one of its meetings last year [1979], the village assembly reaffirmed its continued interest in protection of the forest, decided to increase the number of watchmen where necessary, and resolved to request the government to desist from putting a barbed wire fence around the forest, suspecting that such an act on the part of the government might alienate them from their right over it."

Shrestha's conclusions apply also to the Chautara case. "This example of forest development not only demonstrates that the villagers, given the opportunity, have the capability to plan and implement their own development programs, mobilize their own resources, and manage the project on a continuing basis, but also that the areas of development intervention by the government have to be judiciously identified so that they do not bring about any negative effects on local initiative" (Shrestha, 1980:90).

* * * *

The Madan Pokhara village panchayat has been cited as another successful example of community-based forest management in the hills of Nepal after national policy gave local people more responsibility for the forest resources in their environment. Village leaders enforce rules for forest protection but also help meet local needs for wood by designating several days each year when villagers can enter the forests to remove dead trees. By not allowing free access, the felling of living trees can be controlled. In addition, the panchayat supports planting of large numbers of private fodder trees and successfully lobbied for a rural electrification project to reduce the need for wood to provide interior lighting. Moreover, households have stopped using open pit fires for cooking in favor of more efficient mud ovens.

Despite all of the positive achievements, a study of this panchayat by

Acharya (1984) showed that the resource management practices were partly achieved at the expense of less well organized neighboring communities. Since all the forests around Madan Pokhara are so well protected, its villagers frequently take wood from the forest of a village panchayat about one half hour's walk away. This is not protected because the leadership of Bandi Pokhara panchayat is weak. Also, more openly, Madan Pokhara villagers have reduced their grazing demands on their forest area by arranging to graze approximately half their livestock in other communities where grazing regulations are relatively lax.

LESSONS: Although local government can be an effective institution for forest management, NRM activities by units of local administration may be necessary to prevent well-organized villages from taking advantage of villages with weaker LID. Coppee (1980) reports a similar case in Bihar state of India where villagers' protection of their forests is facilitated by their collection of fuelwood from the forests of other villages, where the people are not organized. This suggests the need to deal with forest management at the locality or sub-district level, not just at village level.

INDIA: Chipko Forest Protection Movement

The hilly area in the state of Uttar Pradesh where Chipko got its start is inhabited mostly by a so-called tribal population. The initial organization was a labor cooperative, formed with the help of an outside organizer, to get income for males by taking road-building contracts. Earnings were invested in setting up a wood products cooperative. But members found their supply of trees threatened by timber merchants who received permits to cut the forest by distributing gratuities or who simply moved in without a permit.

When members protested and threatened to block the saws and bulldozers, government officials used a ruse to trick them out of the forest. Even so, the saw crews that came surreptitiously to cut the trees were thwarted by the village women, who had figured out the trick and fastened themselves to the trees. ("Chipko" is a local word meaning "clinging.") The struggle widened as the initial leadership got other communities to join in the resistance, and the government had to support them publicly.

There are now Village Forest Councils covering a large area and undertaking significant planting activities in twenty-seven villages. When the Councils first discussed this, the men spoke for fruit trees and the women for fuel and fodder sources. The compromise was to plant both kinds of trees. The involvement of villagers in reforestation has given them legitimacy in the eyes of the wider community and they have set an example for local-level social forestry elsewhere. Unfortunately these membership organizations have sometimes come in conflict with local government bodies. (Bhatt, 1980; Agrawal and Anand, 1982; Fortmann and Rocheleau, 1985:261-264; Sharma et al., 1985).

LESSONS: Both the form and objectives of local institutions can change and evolve over time and with experience. The contribution of an outside catalyst was important, though it was crucial that leadership of the organization pass into local hands. The legitimacy gained by Chipko from reforestation activities has helped to "institutionalize" it by gaining national recognition and support.

SOUTH KOREA: Village Forestry Associations

The tradition of community-supervised common forests goes back a long time in Korean history. Private ownership of forested land was first recognized only in 1910, though village forests were not recognized until 1951. In 1961 a system of four levels of forest was established (national, provincial, district or county, and village forests). Village Forestry Associations responsible for the lowest level were managing more than 2 million acres by 1978.

The law required all land with more than a certain slope to be planted with trees. If any private forest owner did not comply or did not manage his land acceptably, the VFA could plant it or take it over (with the owner getting 10 percent of any subsequent sales of wood from his land). That the government saw this program as both important and sensitive is indicated by the fact that the VFAs were set up by the Home Ministry, and the army was mobilized at the time in case there was any opposition from disgruntled local owners. VFAs manage both planting and caretaking, usually having two teams, one for patrolling the forest and the other serving as a fire brigade. (Ahn, 1978; Eckholm, 1979; FAO, 1982).

LESSONS: The Village Forestry Associations might be considered an arm of local administration, except that their heads are elected by a meeting of all household heads in the village, and the forest management is undertaken within government guidelines for community benefit. In their form and operation they thus combine features of local administration and local membership organization. They build on local traditions of community management of natural resources rather than impose a wholly new set of norms and practices. They reinforce a sense of village ownership and responsibility for forest resources. Moreover, they mobilize a great deal of local leadership in conjunction with the Saemaul Undong movement (described in Annex Seven).

RANGE MANAGEMENT

KENYA: Turkana Indigenous Range Management Organization

The Turkana pastoralists in Kenya have a very loose tribal organization. Livestock movements are decided by the *awi*, which is a collection of families and their livestock. This is the basic unit of organization and management, operating quite independently to take advantage of available resources. There are loose informal organizations known as *adekars*, which are groups of awis, but these are transient and cohere only on a seasonal basis. The adekar might look attractive as an indigenous institution to work with and through, because it operates on a larger scale than does the awi, but it could not function in any decision-making or coordinating role. The overarching tribal organization, which serves to resolve disputes not handled at lower levels, is not a decision-making institution either. It does not have sufficient knowledge or standing to manage rangeland resources (D. Sandford, 1981).

LESSONS: The basic unit of range management is the family or group, which is small and only loosely knit with others because of the need for mobility and flexibility. Some higher level institutional links can be useful but more in a negotiating or advisory role than an authoritative one.

BOTSWANA: Range and Livestock Management Project

This project was to develop socially acceptable and economically viable groups of small stockholders that would utilize improved range and livestock techniques. The approach was to fence in large areas to be managed by the groups along classic rotating three-paddock lines—"Texas ranches for groups," as they were informally referred to. Although the project was designed to be an experimental one to do research and establish what would work, it changed course to concentrate on implementing a dozen such ranches. This target was subsequently reduced to three, and the project was finally "phased out after having managed to get only one ranch, with fifteen members, off to a very shaky and problematic start" (Odell and Odell, 1980).

LESSONS: Importing organizational models from the West into pastoral environments is not likely to be successful. Group ranches in Kenya and Tanzania have encountered similar difficulties (Hoben, 1976). Even when a project is designed for experimentation (recognizing that the knowledge base for action is limited), there are great pressures to convert it into one for implementation, seeking to "run" before government managers really know how to "walk."

Small Dam Groups

The Ministry of Agriculture at first built small catchment dams for herders' use without regard to how they would be managed or by whom. This was unsatisfactory so the government decided it would construct no more without first identifying a group of local residents who would accept this responsibility. Officials had to get a group to sign an agreement in return for which it would be given a dam to manage according to rules set by government.

The traditional water use norms were such that the groups found it very difficult to exclude anybody who wanted to use the water, especially since the group had not invested any of its own resources in creating the water source, a criterion traditionally recognized as creating rights over water use.

The government thought these groups were ineffective because they did not meet regularly, did not collect the prescribed watering fee per animal, and did not regulate use of the dams year-round. Closer examination established, however, that the groups did function as actively as necessary during those months of the year when the dams were needed as water sources. At other times, people and animals were elsewhere, exploiting ephemeral water sources or were back in the main villages during the dry season where deep wells gave them assured water. The small dams could not and should not have been expected to give year-round water supply.

Moreover, the fee prescribed by the Ministry was greater than needed to maintain the dams, and collecting it would have created a fund that would itself have to be managed and would be open to disputes. It was simpler and sufficient if members gave labor or special contributions whenever these were needed to repair or upgrade the water facility (Roe and Fortmann, 1982).

LESSONS: Government investments cannot override established norms and conventions at the local level, especially in an area as sensitive as water or grazing rights. It is not reasonable to expect that people will accept and sustain prescribed patterns of behavior that are inconsistent with technical and ecological relationships. Nor should financial arrangements be prescribed without a proper investigation of the economics of the activity. Creating cash funds is frequently a source of mistrust and conflict and should be avoided where other methods of resource mobilization are feasible. The capacity of rural people in Botswana to organize and manage local resources very informally and successfully is documented by Willett (1981).

BURKINA FASO: West Volta Livestock Project

Intended to establish group ranches, this project was hardly more successful than the one reported above in Botswana. After two years, not one group ranch of the six envisioned had been created. The Fulani pastoralists did not trust the government's purpose since it was seen as representing the interests of sedentary agriculturalists. One problem was that the project ignored the existing Cattle Owner's Union, made up of Fulani herders. This is one of the few formal membership organizations we have found reported among pastoralists. It was bypassed in project planning with predictable and unfortunate results (Gooch, 1979).

LESSONS: Again, where local organizations of users exist, they should be consulted and involved in project management. When there are conflicting interests, as between herders and agriculturalists, these need to be sorted out. Organizational mechanisms should be established to enable project staff to work with pastoralists directly. A current USAID Range and Livestock Project in Niger is seeking to work more closely and collaboratively with pastoralists (Wall, 1983).

BOLIVIA: Highland Community Range Management

There is much erosion visible in the highlands of Bolivia, in part due to the soil types, the topography, and the rainfall, but also due to extensive livestock grazing. Though there are strong local traditions of community problem solving, it appears that indigenous institutions are failing in their resource management responsibilities.

On closer examination, it becomes clear that the erosion is not a threat to people's basic subsistence food system, and the animals grazed are the major insurance for families during years of crop failure. During dry years, there is reason to keep animals on the ranges or pastures for a longer time, increasing the extent of overgrazing. However, it is not established that degradation is due to overgrazing. Most of the fields where animals graze longest are those which are fallow and due to be cultivated the next year. Grazing all the stubble off does no harm if the fields are to be planted to crops in a short while, and the additional manure from longer grazing improves soil fertility (LeBaron et al., 1979).

LESSONS: The specific physical, social and economic conditions of an environment need to be examined carefully before making a judgment about resource management or mismanagement. The existing strategy of resource use is heavily influenced by the prevailing factors of risk. Without understanding risk, and the methods local institutions have devised to cope with it, there is little chance that NRM practices or institutions will be changed by outside intervention.

WATERSHED MANAGEMENT AND SOIL CONSERVATION

INDIA: Mahi-Sukhsar Watershed Management Project

In principle the watershed management projects set up in the state of Gujerat are quite participatory, aimed at achieving contour bunding, terracing, and gully plugging in catchment areas. An initial economic survey by project personnel brought them in contact with farmers, and it was envisioned that the project's extension staff would work under the elected district panchayat.

However, in practice the panchayats were not involved in the appraisal or approval stages of the project. The implementation team, which was to have included two progressive farmers, was never formed, and execution work was entrusted solely to a soil conservation officer. Administrative blockages constrained the officer's interactions with (and support from) the government system, and his lack of linkages at the local level meant there was limited communication and cooperation in support of the program. One cannot know how capable the panchayats would have been of taking more responsibility for planning and implementation because they were never given a definite role (Jayaraman, 1980).

LESSONS: Fine-sounding provisions for working with and through local institutions put into project documents in the planning stage frequently get left out in the rush for implementation. While it may be thought that consultation and participation will slow down progress, in fact impediments within the bureaucracy are at least as great, and inputs from local institutions may be one of the best ways of overcoming such barriers.

JAMAICA: Two Meetings-Pindars River Project

This integrated rural development project serving small farmers in two highly erodable watersheds was intended to introduce soil conservation measures along with improved agricultural production. The project design called for farmer participation through Development Committees but these were set up only after implementation had begun. Applications for, and approvals of, the highly subsidized soil conservation treatments on steep farmed hillsides were handled directly through the extension service (LA) with no role for the committees (MO).

When farmers put in bench terraces as advised, the runoff from their fields created even more of an erosion problem for their downhill neighbors, who then had to do something or suffer the consequences. This was hardly conducive to farmer cooperation. Piecemeal efforts at soil conservation understandably produced little improvement.

The program was made even more ineffective by trying to "buy" cooperation. Farmers who put in terraces only because of the subsidies offered were not willing to maintain them without further payment because there was no individual or collective commitment to the program. Persons were mostly trying to get as much immediate income as they could from the project.

No significant role was provided for local governments in the area because the project was planned for farms in the two watersheds, and LG boundaries did not correspond to these hydrological lines. Neighbors used to working together might find themselves separated by the project boundary, with one eligible for subsidies and the other not. This sundering of social and political connections among rural people came from a narrowly technical view of watershed management and soil conservation (Blustain, 1982).

LESSONS: It is not reasonable to expect membership organizations to take root when they have no particular function. The Development Committees were not involved in planning the project, and they did not approve activities (though they could propose things like improving roads or capping a spring). The technology being introduced was "individualistic" in that it did not require "collective adoption" (West, 1983). It would have made sense for all the farmers on a hillside to plan soil conservation measures jointly through the committee. This would have given the LOs a real role, but the project did not take this approach.

KENYA: Machakos Integrated Development Project

This project with eleven components covered an area of 14,000 square kilometers of semi-arid area. Soil conservation measures focusing on subcatchment areas averaging seven square kilometers were a major part of the project. Plans were formulated by project staff and presented to farmers who were asked to contribute to implementation through improved practices on their individual farms and through collective action in their local area. Activities included terracing, digging cut-offs, afforestation and pasture rehabilitation.

It was found that farmers' receptivity to soil conservation measures was closely related to how well households succeeded in crop production. Hence, soil conservation efforts should have been closely coordinated with attempts to increase production. Although project documents called for decentralized decision making (decentralized to the district level), numerous implementation problems arose due to delays in taking action in the district offices. Delays in payment to laborers, in procurement of handtools, and the lack of promised counterpart personnel contributed to reduced effectiveness in the soil conservation program. Moreover, most farmers did not see themselves as being involved in a collaborative effort (Meyers 1981).

LESSONS: Decentralization efforts that moved the center of decision making from Nairobi to the district level did not accomplish day-to-day coordination of soil conservation and crop production activities. This represented a necessary step toward deconcentration (7.5.3) but there was still no devolution to local institutions. To achieve effective coordination, effective institutions at the locality, community, and group levels were needed since as Meyers says, at these levels "it is much easier to grasp and act upon concrete possibilities."

ANNEX THREE

Rural Infrastructure

ROADS AND BRIDGES

COLOMBIA: Pick and Shovel Road Project

The Small Farmer Market Access Project, more commonly known as *Pico y Pala* (Pick and Shovel) signifying its labor-intensive construction methods, began in 1970. It undertook to build more than fifty all-weather unpaved mountain roads averaging five miles in length. Most of the work was done by small farmers and landless rural laborers under the direction of a Colombian government agency, *Caminos Vecinales* (CV), a semi-autonomous agency under the Ministry of Public Works.

An evaluation in 1979 found that there were already tangible economic improvements as transportation costs had been dramatically reduced resulting in better prices for agricultural produce, more varied products, and improved farming practices. There were also improvements in access to health services. Unfortunately the agricultural extension system (LA) had not been strengthened at the time of evaluation to support and accelerate these changes.

Applications for roads were received from informal village organizations, *Juntas de Acción Communal,* which also organized the construction work. However, maintenance was lagging behind because the resources allocated to it in the state's highway department maintenance budget were meager. The evaluation report states:

> We were told by CV personnel that the communities that participated in the building of the *Pico y Pala* roads will maintain them to the best of their abilities. The team did, in fact, observe several instances of *campesinos* working without pay (at the request of their leaders) to clear landslides, and we accept the fact that *campesinos* can and will clear their roads whenever possible. The system breaks down, however, when the nature and extent of the damage exceeds the *campesinos'* physical resources.

> In practice, communities have in such cases sought and obtained help wherever they could get it—from CV, the state and national highway departments, and from the Federation of Coffee Growers. Such assistance is, however, *ad hoc;* no reliable mechanism

exists through which major maintenance can be undertaken. The problem of preventive maintenance also persists. On only one of the roads visited had farmers kept the drainage ditches clear of growth and debris. [Elsewhere] it is only a matter of time before the water rediscovers that the shortest way downhill is across the road surface (van Raalte et al., 1979:12).

LESSONS: The potential for activating such local organization is substantial in this kind of project where there is a great need and demand for transportation facilities. The project itself has serious limitations for lack of local institutional development provision, however. Responsibility for major maintenance was not established; the national government had not allocated adequate funds; and no mechanisms for communities to raise funds had been established. No institutionalized linkages had been developed between communities and the Ministry of Public Works to get assistance to deal with major landslides.

The project was scheduled to end in 1981 in spite of impressive accomplishments, because CV had failed to build support for its work among higher Colombian officials. Since the program was very popular in the communities it served, various local organizations could have provided a better base of support for the program's continuation if more local institutional development had occurred since such institutions can mobilize and direct political support as well as manage construction and maintenance activities.

NEPAL: Baglung District Bridge Program

In the mountainous Baglung district of Nepal, where most paths between villages are made difficult by steep ravines and by rivers that become dangerous during the rainy season, one of the leaders in the district panchayat got the idea for a self-help bridge program. All villages were invited to submit requests through their local panchayat for assistance to build needed bridges. Whether their request would receive priority depended on its justification in terms of travel time saved, increased safety, and promises of local labor and materials to carry out the project.

The district panchayat sponsored the program and gave some modest funding. The central government's Local Development Department contributed steel cables, which would make the bridges stronger and more permanent and which are difficult to obtain in the remote communities in the hills. Villages had to mobilize labor to carry the cables many miles from the nearest road to the building site. The project relied on local technology and materials. Masons were enlisted to build the bridgeheads with traditional rockwork instead of using cement, which is costly and difficult to transport. Blacksmiths made connecting rods in their own forges, and villagers provided unpaid labor for gathering rock, cutting boards, and putting up the bridge.

All work was done under the direction of bridge construction committees set up under the aegis of their respective Village Panchayats (LG). Within four years, sixty-two bridges had been built, some as long as 300 feet in length. They were put up in much less time than it would have taken the government to build them, and their cost was as little as one-quarter what it would have cost the government (Pradhan, 1980).

LESSONS: The combination observed here of a membership organization working in conjunction with the local government has been effective in a number of other successful programs also. Reliance on local technology and materials was crucial for the communities' being able to take responsibility for planning and construction. The amount of outside assistance was limited, but was of critical importance because the strength of the cable was an incentive for local efforts to put up a permanent bridge. Because the amount of actual cash handled was small, there were fewer opportunities for corruption and disaffection with the program on that basis.

MEXICO: PIDER Rural Roads Program

Mexico's huge Integrated Rural Development Program known as PIDER found in its first evaluation that its most successful component was the building of rural roads with community organization and participation. This increased the road network in the project area from 25,000 to 100,000 kilometers in six years.

A special office within the Ministry of Works, a Directorate of Labor-Intensive Roads (*Dirección de Caminos de Mano de Obra, DCMO*), was assigned responsibility for construction. Since it had little heavy road-building equipment to work with, meeting construction targets was dependent on labor contributions from communities. These were represented by Road Committees, which would not agree to provide labor unless they were satisfied that the proposed road would be worth their effort.

According to a World Bank report, "The success of the local level committees for the labor-intensive rural road construction program suggests that an organizational structure at the local level can be established and can facilitate the execution and operation of the program" (Cernea, 1979:70). During a five-year period, the 64,000 kilometers of road built amounted to 35 percent of the total length of the road network in Mexico and served a population of 6 million (Edmonds, 1980:129).

LESSONS: The fact that the government agency was dependent on rural communities for achieving its bureaucratic goals meant that it had to work in a cooperative, nonauthoritarian manner. The communities responded positively through their local organizations to support the program of rural road building when given a voice in determining what would be built, where, when, and how. Linkage between the local unit of administration (LA) and membership organizations proved mutually beneficial.

RURAL ELECTRIFICATION

INDIA: Rajasthan Decentralization Experiment

Given existing budget constraints, only about 2 percent of Rajasthan's villages could be hooked up in any one year to the state electricity board's grid. Prior to 1969 all decisions about which villages would be connected were made by board personnel. The criteria were to be (a) potential for increased production indicated by the presence of groundwater that could be pumped for irrigating agriculture, and (b) investment efficiency, estimated by a village's proximity to the grid, so that the cost of connecting a village would be minimized.

Hadden (1974) found that when village and district panchayats were involved in determining which communities best met these criteria, the productivity and efficiency standards were met more often than when decisions were made bureaucratically by the board. Administrative decision processes had been less open to public scrutiny and thus were more vulnerable to unwarranted political intervention. When all applicants for connections were listed publicly and assessed in public LG discussions, there was better adherence to objective criteria.

LESSONS: Contrary to common thinking, political interference and corruption may be less when responsibility is devolved to lower levels of decision making. Resources can be used more productively and efficiently in a decentralized system when people with knowledge of the real conditions on the ground are able to contribute this to decision processes, to which they have access in a decentralized mode. Such decentralization need not occur "without strings." Because of policy concerns, the government can set criteria to be followed, in this case for awarding connections. The locality should often be able to apply them better than higher level bureaucrats.

BOLIVA: Rural Electrification

Under a $29.5 million project initiated in 1973 and financed primarily by USAID, seven rural electrical systems were constructed in six of Bolivia's nine departments (states). The national parastatal corporation was to generate electricity, which would be distributed through separate grids operated in each department. Five of the new rural systems were connected up to existing municipal systems in departmental capitals; the other two were laid out to be exclusively rural.

Providing light to poor households was the primary objective of the program. Project designers also hoped that provision of electricity on a twenty-four-hour basis would stimulate small rural nonagricultural producers to expand. This hope generally was not realized because use of electric power for productive activities seldom proved to be profitable. Moreover, where such opportunities did exist, the project did nothing to foster forward or backward linkages. Construction of smaller, dispersed generating plants under local control was precluded by the designers' assumption that twenty-four-hour service was to be provided.

The designs of the central systems themselves were sub-optimal because this phase was handled by foreign consultants who had a construction orientation and were little concerned with how the system would be operated. The municipal organizations to be responsible for distribution had no input into the design. Many potential hookups were overlooked in the design as the planners worked with outdated information. Overdesign of the system using U.S. design standards and faulty assumptions about use by producers, the extent of nucleation in settlement patterns, and the level of household consumption led to overcapacity, high per unit costs, and subsequent difficulty in operating the system.

LESSONS: An evaluation by Tendler (1980) concluded that the institutional arrangement (perhaps intentionally) had some redistributive effects. By serving both urban and rural consumers and charging both the same rates (even though the unit cost of supplying electricity to the latter was three to four times greater than in market towns), the systems made power more accessible to poorer areas. For both technical and financial reasons, utility companies generally attempt to connect as many households as possible within reach of their distribution lines. If poor and better-off households are interspersed, as in the case of Bolivian villages, economic and distributional objectives coincide.

Project designers, however, by and large failed to take advantage of this redistributive potential because they were insensitive to institutional considerations. Failure to link design and construction to operation and maintenance undermined the viability of the utility companies. Since project design was determined by design engineers, rather than by those responsible for operation and financial performance, technical specifications were established without regard to their impact on operating costs after construction.

The design consultants also overlooked possibilities for fostering forward linkages by working with or promoting organizations that could contribute to the secondary but important objective of increasing economic activity through electrification. Small farmer groups in the Cochabamba area, as Tendler notes, "had been quite capable of forming informal organizations for obtaining and managing pump-irrigation systems, and of contributing financially to the undertaking" (1980:26-27). If such organizations had been formed (which Tendler says are "compatible with traditions of intercommunity cooperation among Bolivian peasants"), the objective of promoting productive use of electricity could have been furthered.

ECUADOR: Rural Electrification

Between 1964 and 1976 two cooperatives and six private companies operating on a regional basis were assisted under three USAID loans totaling $5.6 million. Although USAID initially emphasized the cooperative model of organization, it gave responsibility for establishing cooperatives to the National Electricity Institute (INECEL), an agency opposed to cooperativization.

One of the cooperatives was dissolved after its distribution system was connected to that of a major city, Guayaquil. The remaining co-op survived because it was in a frontier area and had been formed by local businessmen and agricultural colonists during the early 1960s when INECEL was a fledgling organization. It retained the support of local commercial, industrial, and agricultural interests though only a small minority of members attend annual cooperative meetings.

In contrast to the Bolivian systems discussed above, which emphasized rural electrification as such, the programs in Ecuador were designed to serve primarily the market towns. Electrification made major contributions to the development of agro-centers. Although the projects were not aimed at benefiting the poor, increased access to employment, income, agro-processing facilities, and some social services produced definite benefits. Furthermore, rate structures and surcharges on industrial users provided modest income transfers from urban to rural areas (Kessler et al., 1981).[1]

LESSONS: Under favorable conditions, private enterprises can take root and provide a spread of benefits as seen from the growth of productive activity in the market towns once electricity was available. The institutional channel for distributing electricity could be either private or cooperative, as there was no evidence that either was more effective than the other.

When it comes to promoting cooperative forms of local institutional development through a national agency, its orientation is understandably crucial. It can discourage, and lead to the demise of, co-ops by its actions or indifference— though we also see in this case that where a cooperative has a strong local base of support, it may be able to resist even bureaucratic opposition. Several of the private companies had been conceived as cooperatives but were implemented as private enterprises to avoid problems with INECEL.

DOMESTIC WATER SUPPLY

MALAWI: *Community Self-Help Water Program*

This impressive rural infrastructure program is one which has in ten years' time laid 900 miles of piping to serve 2,000 village taps and over 500,000 persons in rural areas at a cost of about $4 per person. The program was evolved in a "learning process" mode (Korten, 1980) under the auspices of the Department of Community Development and is now being further expanded with donor assistance.

Malawi has springs and streams in the hills which can feed gravity-flow water systems in the plains. The Department devised a method of approaching communities through their traditional chiefs and elders to propose cooperation. The message conveyed is essentially as follows:

> "This is to be your project, not the government's. If you want to have better water, the government is prepared to work with you to get it. But the responsibility is yours, to manage as well as to build." (Liebenow, 1982)

The government offers to supply pipes, materials and training if the people will provide labor to dig trenches and lay the pipe. They should also select someone from their community to be trained as a para-technician, to

---

[1]It should be stated that the extent of benefits depended heavily on a huge subsidization by the government (approximately two-thirds) of the price of diesel used to generate electricity. This was possible because the government was itself producing and exporting petroleum. The resources forgone through this policy might have been used more productively. Arguments to justify the subsidy in the name of helping the poor are weakened by the fact that the poor were not the principal beneficiaries of the subsidy.

supervise the work and to oversee maintenance of standpipes and water lines afterwards.

A Main Committee is formed for each service area (usually a locality), supported by Section Committees established in each village within the area, to organize the self-help labor, to arrange work schedules and allocate work among the villages. Branch line systems operate from each storage tank along the main line, with each branch line committee responsible for maintenance of its own branch. This complex structure works quite well in a decentralized manner under the supervision of what is now the Ministry of Community Development. (Robertson, 1978; Glennie, 1979; Liebenow, 1982)

"The pivot of the Malawian program is the District Development Committee. This is an administrative and political body chaired by the district commissioner and includes the district's members of parliament, the chairpersons of the ruling Malawi Congress Party, League of Malawi Women and League of Malawi Youth, the district medical officer and other technical personnel" (Chauhan, 1983). All requests for a piped water scheme proceed through this committee.

LESSONS: This program is similar in many respects to the Baglung bridge program in Nepal though it is instigated by the government rather than from the locality. Its committees have become institutionalized as was not achieved in Baglung. The philosophy of self-help in both is similar and the reliance on local managerial talents has produced impressive results.

The recruitment, training, and use of paraprofessional technicians is one of the most important parts of this scheme, as these roles give the community an opportunity for management, not just participation. Williamson (1983) makes this distinction with regard to community water supply efforts in Nepal very similar to these in Malawi. Another important element appears to be that following construction work each day, the water is allowed to run through the recently installed sections of pipe so that some immediate benefits are visible.

Working through traditional leaders is fairly unusual but clearly effective. Chiefs and elders in other countries may be less respected and thus less able to provide leadership or at least legitimation than in Malawi. In any case, the potential for such a constructive role should be explored.

The "reticulated" structure of local organizations, paralleling the structure of the water distribution system, provides a matrix for decentralizing responsibility downward and for aggregating labor and other resource inputs upward. If sections fail to mobilize the resources necessary for construction or maintenance, they are the ones who suffer the consequences.

TUNISIA: Rural Water Supply Project

A water supply project supported by USAID introduced motorized pumps that required fuel, which the government was not prepared to provide on a permanent basis. The project had provided for "guardians," local persons hired to look after the wells, but they had not been authorized to collect user fees.

At three of the five project sites, users took collective action to establish fees assessed on a household basis, ranging from $1.25 per month to nothing for those households too poor to pay. In one community a local organization grew out of its quarterly clan meetings and provided basic types of assessment, collection, and accounting of water use fees. In Kairouan, the driest area, users were the most ready to assure that their critical water supply continued to function by levying a fee on themselves to cover costs of fuel supply and maintenance.

At two sites, guardians were resented because they imposed a fee system without community agreement. In one instance, the community forced the guardian's removal. Whether these two communities, having gotten off to a bad start due to the matter of fee imposition, would follow the good example of the other three was not known at the time of evaluation (Bigelow and Chiles, 1980).

LESSONS: The prospects for community members to organize themselves for achieving important objectives like water supply are not hindered by low material well-being or little formal education. Relying on the communities' own methods of organization and decision making is important, however, as imposition from outside can deflect community energies from constructive efforts.

INDIA: Banki Water Supply Program

One of the best documented cases of LID for water supply with resulting improvements in health conditions is from Uttar Pradesh state in India. The Planning, Research and Action Institute of Lucknow began in 1962 to work with the heads of seven village panchayats (LG) in Banki locality to develop a piped water supply, which the people would own and manage to improve health conditions.

There was initial resistance to changing water habits but this was overcome through house-to-house visits to identify health problems that could be resolved by having cleaner water, and through "evening sittings" where misconceptions about costs and water quality as well as health benefits could be discussed and dealt with in small public gatherings.

A Waterworks Executive Committee was set up in consultation with the panchayats, consisting of one member from each village. This committee evolved into a body recognized by the government, appointed by the people, with full responsibility for the operation of the system.

By 1973, 40 percent of the 836 families had piped water and the rest obtained water from forty-two public standpipes. Dramatic health improvements were documented, with diarrheal diseases greatly reduced and cholera eliminated in the population. Through user fees, the system became self-sufficient and the outside actors withdrew (Misra, 1975).

LESSONS: As noted above, the combination of LG and LO seems quite advantageous for such undertakings. The program proceeded through persuasion rather than trying to impose new activities through state government or local government authority. The principle of self-financing of the scheme's operation was made clear from the start though some initial capital funding was secured from UNICEF and WHO. Outside resources were provided in a way that did not create a "dependency" complex.

COMMUNITY SERVICES

EGYPT: Basic Village Services Project

This massive project has funded more than $200 million worth of construction of roads, water supply, sewerage, and other facilities through *local councils.* At the project's outset there was great diversity in the capability of local councils with which the project was to work. Nonetheless, both the government and USAID were anxious to expedite the work so that villages would receive the anticipated effects on income and employment as soon as possible. The project has contradicted the conventional view that undertaking such expenditures in a highly decentralized way must slow progress in construction.

The rate of work and disbursement of funds through local councils has been more than satisfactory. Local councils have generally been able to select, plan, and carry out rural infrastructure activities in a timely manner once loans were available and the government adopted procedures that reduced the immensely complicated bureaucratic requirements previously inhibiting local councils (Mayfield, 1985). A recent evaluation that examined a substantial number of the 869 participating localities found that with few exceptions, local personnel are sufficiently competent to design and construct the types of sub-projects funded under the project (Chetwynd and Samaan, 1984).

LESSONS: A system of support for local institutions can add up to a very large program if the volume of small activities is great, as in this project. The project has made a major investment of training to upgrade the management capability of local councils, directly training 5,000 Egyptian project managers and 20,000 persons indirectly. This has contributed to project performance (Odell, 1982, and personal communication). The project has been supported by a relatively small but active nation institution, the Organization for Reconstruction of Egyptian Villages (ORDEV), with only 260 employees. It operates in a manner more supportive of local councils than would be found with most other national agencies. This has also been an important factor.

PAKISTAN: Orangi Pilot Project

Orangi is a squatter town outside Karachi with a population approaching one million. While not exactly "rural," the LID implications of this pilot project deserve consideration. The project is directed by Akhter Hameed

Khan who pioneered LID work while director of the Academy for Rural Development at Comilla in Bangladesh (then East Pakistan). Khan first visited Orangi in 1980, and after a month of observation and discussion launched the pilot project in collaboration with the All-Orangi United Federation (OUF), a collection of more than thirty membership organizations in this slum area with nearly a decade of experience.

The Orangi Pilot Project (OPP) hired three "social organizers" to work full time with community groups and shared an office with the OUF to strengthen collaboration. Efforts made to support OUF over the first half year included assistance with gaining legal recognition, starting a newsletter, and organizing various social events. During this time OUF lobbying efforts with government agencies to improve physical conditions gradually turned toward more direct action.

At first the neighborhood *(mohalla)* was the unit of organization but this was replaced by the lane *(tanzeem)*, which grouped twenty to thirty households into a more solid social unit. These groups, brought together by the organizers, were asked to cooperate with OPP engineers in devising appropriate waste disposal systems, which had earlier been found to be of great interest to residents.

After considerable experimentation and a number of technical failures, appropriate designs and materials were agreed upon that allowed installation of sewerage systems at a low enough cost for the slum residents to finance the improvements themselves by providing labor and about $25 per household. Experiments to provide drinking water proved less amenable to technical-organizational breakthroughs. A wide variety of other activities, outside the infrastructure area, were also undertaken with different degrees of success.

LESSONS: The experimental approach taken by the OPP under Dr. Khan's leadership produced some very promising socio-technical methodologies for providing low-cost, maintainable sanitation infrastructure. His quarterly reports show a continually self-critical inductive approach to developing local institutional capacity which is essential for achieving this goal and which is regarded as ultimately more important even than improved sanitation per se (Khan, 1983).

The use of "social organizers" for forming local organizations was an important part of the strategy for local institutional development. Such use of "catalyst' is being increasingly recognized as a valuable component of LID strategy in other kinds of rural development work as discussed in Section 7.3.2.

INDONESIA: Village Subsidy Program

This broad national program was instituted in 1969 to create rural infrastructure through block grants to local governments. Beginning with subsidies of $250 for each project, the amount was raised to $750 by 1975. Funds have been used to purchase construction materials for irrigation facilities, roads, markets, etc. As might be expected with a program of this magnitude, there have been many shortcomings in the program's administration but it provided considerable infrastructure at relatively low cost (Patten, Dapice, and Falcon, 1973; de Wit, 1973).

One detailed case study of developing irrigation infrastructure through this program (Hafid and Hayami, 1976) found it to be quite cost-effective where there was good local leadership. In some of the cases analyzed, activities were organized by the *lurah* (village headman), whereas in others, responsibilities were devolved to unofficial community organizations, operating much like the bridge committees in the Nepal case above.

Although the program intended to mobilize village labor during periods of reduced agricultural demand, government budget allocations did not always reach the villages in a timely manner thereby slowing or halting construction plans. For instance, funding for work scheduled in the first quarter of the year when much village labor is otherwise unemployed often did not arrive until the second, third, or fourth quarter, and in some cases not until the following year (Prabowo, 1973).

LESSONS: The program did not have a strategy or even an objective of strengthening local institutional capacities to handle the subsidies most efficiently. Quality of output depends very much on the talent and commitment of the lurah and on the leadership of the *bupati* (head of the district administration), as documented by Hafid and Hayami (1976).

The selection of activities has not always been democratic, so the more advantaged minority tends to get its preferred projects such as roads built more often than does the poorer majority, which usually favors improving irrigation and drainage to provide more production and employment. (This is similar to the results of a survey in rural Nepal reported in footnote 18 of Chapter Three.) The program seems to engender more enthusiastic participation from villagers when sub-projects that generate employment are undertaken (personal communication from Don Emmerson, based on field observations).

The funds expended would have had a more lasting effect if there had been an explicit LID strategy, including training (as in the Egyptian BVS project described above) and if there had been a more concerted effort to strengthen networks of local institutions that can complement the existing local government (the lurah and other local officials).

OMAN: Community Development Centers

Until 1970 the Sultanate of Oman was almost completely outside the realm of deliberate development activities. One of the first major development programs begun in 1976 with UN assistance was to establish community centers for the isolated and often nomadic population. At the district (*wilayat* or governorate) level, Local Community Development Committees (LCDCs) have been set up with the *wali* (governor) as head and with representatives of several ministries participating. Having village sheikhs and *rashieds* (headmen) as members at this level does not provide much participation, but there is some linkage.

More important are the Village Community Development Committees

(VCDCs), made up of rashieds and other community leaders. These are responsible for activities at the community or locality level, depending on the size and dispersion of population. As of 1985 the program reached 142 villages and fifty-four settlements, with a population of about 42,000 persons. The VCDCs discuss possible projects with government staff (LA) and when agreement is reached, responsibility is given to small committees of interested villagers (similar to the institutional arrangements for bridge construction in Nepal, reported previously). The facilities constructed include repair and maintenance of canals, digging and deepening of wells, construction of village meeting halls, Koranic schools, village and feeder roads, public baths and latrines, and women's centers.

The 261 projects completed so far have had a monetary cost of over $12 million, almost half of which has been contributed by the rural communities. In addition they have provided labor and local materials. In some cases funds are raised to buy special items like rugs or air conditioners for community centers as a mark of local pride. Monitoring Committees of local leaders are maintained to follow up community proposals and requests. Though Oman has considerable oil revenue, this approach is approved by the government because the arrangement strikes a balance between community resource contributions and those from outside agencies and the government.

LESSONS: According to a report on the program prepared for a U.N. Inter-Regional Workshop on Community-Based Approaches to Rural Development in Geneva, December 1985, it has been found that "projects implemented by self-help efforts with the assistance of the government cost less, save time, and avoid complicated bureaucratic procedures, besides its benefits in building community will, skills, and self-confidence in undertaking developmental activities. Moreover, it increases service utilization and support. It is quite evident in the villages where the community helped construct latrines, public baths, water systems, garbage disposal areas, and repair of irrigation canals that they have adopted the improvements into their daily life." This contribution of LID for rural infrastructure to greater utilization and adoption is often overlooked in agencies' preoccupation with magnitudes of construction—which are impressive in this Oman case but more significant because of the subsequent impact on people's lives.

Primary Health Care

BRAZIL: Project Esperança

This primary health care program evolved from a curative program supported by a missionary organization with limited participation by beneficiaries into a regional program stressing community-based health. The transition occurred with assistance from private foundation funding. The participating areas have a population of over 30,000, served by seventeen rural health posts and a training center-clinic complex with administrative offices in the city of Santarem. The complex has forty employees who provide technical services and support to seventeen licensed rural health aides and fifty-six rural health promoters.

Experience with full-time health aides suggests that older, functionally literate women seem to do better with maternal and child health and community organization work. In contrast, the more numerous volunteer health promoters, who work fewer hours, include farmers, fishermen, *curanderos* (indigenous healers) and traditional birth attendants. Incentives include a painted signpost in front of the promoter's house and free transportation, room and board for training. In addition to training aides and promoters, the clinic complex in Santarem reinforces their position by treating any patients referred by them before treating nonemergency cases that have bypassed the rural health posts. Two U.S. surgical teams still visit annually but only perform types of surgery not available in Santarem.

Esperança provides unusual support to the community health committees with special training in management and organizational tasks. Some committees are composed of representatives of existing local institutions, though this is not always the case. Federal and state government health agencies provide vaccines and medicines for the rural health posts, while local governments pay the salaries of eleven health aides (Favin, 1982).

LESSONS: Primary health care programs need a vital network of local institutions collaborating on several fronts. Strong vertical and horizontal linkages have enabled the rural health aides and promoters to increase their level of activity over time. This has been facilitated by having strong community health committees, not just health workers. Furthermore, by enlisting a substantial number of volunteer health promoters, Esperança has increased its base of support and access among project beneficiaries.

BURMA: *Community Health Care Program*

This program relies on volunteers who serve as community health workers (CHWs) and auxiliary midwives (AMWs). Nationally, health services are available from division and state hospitals, township hospitals at district level, rural health centers at sub-district level, and sub-centers at locality level, in ascending administrative order. There is about one sub-center for every twelve villages. At the community level, the CHWs and AMWs operate under the local government body, the Village People's Council, which serves as their institutional base. There were nearly 30,000 volunteer workers by the program's fourth year of service.

Villagers have contributed their labor to help build the health centers and sub-centers. However, most sub-district health centers are fully staffed only three days per week, with staff devoting Thursday through Saturday to field travel to supervise CHWs and AMWs at the sub-centers while concurrently conducting mobile clinics. Locality sub-centers are visited by health center staff at least two or three times per month. Standard protocol for each visit entails meeting with a member of the local government.

Community health workers are chosen by LG and the fact that they are not paid tends to militate against selection of health workers as a "political prize." Tasks include distribution of drugs, encouraging people to construct latrines, taking malaria blood slides and assisting school health programs. CHWs work approximately two hours per day with no precise routine; however, the curative role clearly occupies the bulk of their time. Auxiliary midwives deliver two to three babies per month, often in conjunction with traditional birth attendants. Since the AMW does not interfere with the traditional birth attendants' income, friction is generally avoided.

Although CHWs receive a kit containing eleven types of drugs following their training, this supply is not replenished by the national government. Instead, each local government must devise its own system of raising funds for this. There is a considerable variety of systems that have emerged including fixed or variable payment for services, voluntary donation for services, fixed or variable household levy, donation by wealthy people only, periodic donation campaigns, etc. These efforts seem to be quite successful. Unfortunately shortages at the national level have at times caused delays even when local funds are available for purchasing drugs (Chauls, 1983).

LESSONS: Though it is not possible to list all of the reasons for the high level of activity generated, one important reason appears to be that villagers consider CHWs to be part of "their" local government rather than an arm of the government health system (LA). As seen from the frequency of supervisory visits each month, LA does play an active and critical role, however. While there are cultural, political, and religious bases for volunteerism in

Burma, the devolution of responsibility for health beyond the Health Department to the communities, especially in regard to financing, appears to have contributed to the program's vibrancy.

CAMEROON: Village Health Committees

In 1972 the University of Pittsburgh medical school began a demonstration project in the Department of Mefou to promote self-reliant health care practices with a special emphasis on preventive measures. To achieve this, auxiliary nurses already in government employment were selected by the Department physician for training as visiting health workers to assist village health committees that were set up in four pilot villages. The committee membership consisted of acknowledged local leaders. The VHCs functioned in a formal manner, probably not consistent with community practices. ·

Two years after the project ended in 1976, a survey found little or no change in health status, despite construction of a number of latrines, protected springs, and garbage pits by the communities. At best, one-third of the health committees continued functioning, and the impact of the VHWs was accordingly limited (Isely, 1979).

LESSONS: One conclusion reached was that the VHWs had taken a very mechanistic approach to the formation of the committees. They were satisfied with the formal existence of VHCs as having met their "targets." Also, the committees were probably less effective because they were composed of existing leaders, without establishing who had the most interest in improving community health and who had the most support of villagers.

One VHC had remained active. It had previous experience with community projects affiliated with a church group, suggesting that it had a reservoir of collective action capacity to draw on. More thought should have been given in project design to the process of setting up and sustaining a membership organization relying on volunteerism. Four years is probably too short a time to expect a high degree of institutionalization and represents too little investment to have a significant impact on health status.

GHANA: Association of Ghanaian Psychic and Traditional Healers

Indigenous health practitioners have organized themselves into a national organization, which has formal membership requirements and fees. To become members, practitioners have to be licensed by the District Council (local government) where they practice.

A project to improve village health in Techiman District initially trained and relied on newly recruited village health workers and traditional birth attendants. This proved rather unsuccessful because of lack of community support. (Communities were expected to pay VHWs' salaries but did not always do so.)

Then in 1979 it was decided to involve herbalists and other traditional healers. A training program was provided for them by staff from a private rural hospital. The Ministry of Health, which had had extensive informal consultation with healers through their organization before the course started, helped by encouraging attendance.

Pre-training interviews with the forty-five prospective participants guaranteed that information about existing techniques and beliefs was taken into account in the course. Classes were held in the homes of healers with each participant paying a small fee to cover the costs of material received. Feedback from the trainees was actively sought from them in their homes on a weekly basis. All discussions and printed materials were in the vernacular language.

The main focus of training and subsequent activity included environmental health, preventive and promotive health, family planning, and home remedies. Established remuneration practices were preserved and sufficient (Warren et al., 1981).

LESSONS: The success of this program indicates the potential of working with and through indigenous health practitioners although such programs might not work everywhere. Ghana had been experiencing severe shortages of professional medical personnel and an irregular supply of factory-produced drugs. Thus, such an approach made a low-cost contribution to rural health by upgrading existing local roles (nonorganizational institutions).

GUATEMALA: *Rural Health Paraprofessionals*

Beginning in 1971 the Ministry of Public Health and Social Assistance initiated efforts to improve curative and preventive services in rural areas. With support from USAID and UNICEF, two new roles were incorporated into the health system. Sub-professional Rural Health Technicians were given a two-year training course in preparation for a four-year contract under which they would in turn train and supervise paraprofessional volunteer Health Promoters on a full-time basis. The training of paraprofessionals stressed preventive measures, although each promoter was given a kit containing simple medicinal supplies for which villagers paid a small sum to replenish or enlarge the stock.

Though the program did not take root everywhere, a 1981 study found promoters working in a number of villages, usually devoting about one hour per evening to their activities with some promoters actively working on preventive projects such as water supply construction. Promoters tended to be more active where they had worked in conjunction with the Rural Health Technicians to create elected village health improvement committees.

Interestingly these committees rarely contained a village authority figure but in many cases they had to be "reorganized" several times until they secured enough energetic and effective committee members. One paradox faced by the program was that although paraprofessionals from the community in which they lived were more easily accepted than outsiders, this tended to lower expectations about what these persons could accomplish.

The key to raising expectations appears to have been frequent visits by the Rural Health Technicians. These person's information and friendship were highly valued by the promoters, and they enhanced the status of the promoters in villagers' eyes. The promoters maintained a sense of comradeship and collective endeavor via semi-annual training sessions and a self-run newsletter that shared experience and "tips" (Colburn, 1981).

LESSONS: Effective support and supervision of community health workers need not come from highly trained professionals, especially in programs attempting to reach the most remote and inaccessible areas. Sub-professionals are frequently able to give more support and supervision to community health workers and village health committees than higher salaried professionals. Having health workers volunteering on a part-time basis to serve a smaller population may be a viable alternative to full-time paid workers. An active local committee adds greatly to the paraprofessionals' effectiveness.

INDONESIA: Dana Sehat Health Cooperative

In 1972 staff from a church-affiliated health center in Central Java's Purworejo-Klampok subdistrict undertook efforts to reach relatively distant and poorer communities by devoting more time to preventive measures and opening three new health posts. Though these activities kept the staff quite busy, the center's director and his associates could see that the program had "no firm roots in the community."

Following extensive discussions with community members, it was decided to recruit and train volunteer health cadres to work on a part-time basis, one cadre for every fifteen households. At the same time, local government officials and health center personnel worked to organize a cooperative health insurance program. This was implemented through the existing village administrative structure of neighborhood organizations. Each city or community had been divided into districts and then into hamlets, which were subdivided into "blocks" (or neighborhoods), of fifty to one hundred families—the group level in our analytical framework.

Each household pays a contribution of fifty rupiah (U.S.$ 0.12) per month for curative services and medicines. This covers the cost of total family care by cadre, which includes nutrition, health education, and public health services. The fee is collected by the block headman. If the funds collected are insufficient, the cooperative can get credit for one or two months' expenses from the health center. When there is a positive balance of funds, the community decides how to use them for health-related activities such as building community latrines or improving the sewage system.

Some communities have used a balance to start a village credit cooperative. Funds generated from this activity provide a "reserve" to cover any shortfalls in the health program. The community meetings established as part of this program provide an excellent opportunity for practical health education by the cadres as well as for undertaking broader problem-solving for the community (Hendrata, 1976).

LESSONS: By establishing village-based health cadres backed by community cooperatives, access to preventive and curative services was increased. Fee collection was facilitated by handling this through local government officials, to achieve self-sustaining financial status and low costs for beneficiaries. Where excess funds were accumulated, the development of semi-autonomous credit cooperatives provided further benefits and greater economic security. As predicted by Isely and Martin (1977), such village health committees can provide impetus and channels for more broad-based rural development.

MEXICO: Project Piaxtla

This pioneering health project was begun in the mid-1960s in the village of Ajoya. Over almost two decades of activity, a program that initially centered on curative problems evolved to address preventive and social issues. The most interesting aspect of the experience was the way health professionals from outside were used to support a local health program without creating social hierarchies or dependency.

Project guidelines provided for outside professionals to come only by invitation of the community health team, and only for short visits, to make clear that the team itself was self-managed and not dependent on the continued presence of outsiders. Visiting professionals had to speak the local language and were asked not to dress in white. Doctors were to teach, not practice their skills, assisting the village's own primary health workers. Since doctors also came to learn, relations with VHWs were on a peer basis. To reinforce this, visiting professionals were expected to participate in agricultural work too.

When persons required care beyond the village's capacity, they were referred to the nearest city, four hours away by bus. Several doctors in the city agreed to charge for their surgery on a sliding scale, giving substantially lower rates to the poor. The determination of financial status was left to the VHWs, who would send a note with each person indicating the family's ability to pay. The urban physicians provided important services to the rural community while at the same time strengthening the status and legitimacy of the paraprofessional VHWs. The VHWs reciprocated in a small way by referring also their more financially prosperous patients, who paid normal fees and thus increased the size of the cooperating physicians' practices (Werner and Bower, 1982).

LESSONS: The capacity for communities to operate quite autonomous PHC programs is considerable if outsiders approach them in a respectful and supportive way. Some back-up with higher level technical services is needed for even the most idealistic PHC efforts.

PANAMA: Community Health Program

In 1969 the Ministry of Health launched an ambitious national program in which over 500 health committees were established in rural areas during a five-year period. Community participation through the legally recognized health committees was considered the principal mechanism for the planning, implementation, and distribution of program services. Activities included construction of water supply and waste disposal facilities, establishment of community gardens, small animal projects, health education seminars, vaccination campaigns, and health status surveys.

In those areas of Panama where the Community Health Program remains active, federations of village health committees at the district or provincial level are very important. Federations provide a valuable intermediary service linking the communities and the health system. They serve as a mechanism by which individual health committees can approach and pressure the health system for more and better quality services. For example, during federation meetings (usually held twice a year), health committee representatives publicly present their problems and requests for assistance to a group of senior health officials, politicians, and military officers from the region the communities represent. These items are openly addressed and discussed by the health officials, and a tentative solution is agreed upon.

During the week after the meeting, a delegation of federation officers (who are elected by the health committees) formally present a written summary of the requests and proposed solutions to the regional director of the health system. Informal meetings between federation officers and health officials continue until "all requests have been checked off the list." In some cases the officers visit the communities to confirm that problems have been satisfactorily resolved. In one list of twenty "problems" noted by La Forgia (1985) at one biannual meeting, sixteen had been resolved within two months. Similar problems were not addressed in the districts and regions lacking a federation.

After a number of years of educational activity, a 1976 study by the Ministry of Health found 68 percent of the community members contacted requested sanitation and potable water and only 4.5 percent were interested in health centers for strictly curative medicine. Local health staff and VHCs pointed to diarrhea, gastro-intestinal disorders and malnutrition as the principle causes of ill health. Later research suggested that higher level officials believed curative services were in greatest demand by the communities. This apparent difference in perception suggests that in contrast to the 1970s, health officials do not now visit communities or attend health committee meetings as frequently as before (La Forgia, 1985).

LESSONS: Strong support for PHC from the national level clearly assisted local-level efforts for the first five years of the program. Thereafter without such support the program still continued to be effective where local institutions remained strong. One of the key elements was the formation of VHC federations, which were in a position to discuss and negotiate issues with MOH personnel. While this level of support from the top levels of Panama's MOH have subsequently receded, continued interest by some medical directors of district health centers as well as by rural communities themselves where they maintain health federations has resulted in strong, ongoing PHC activity in several regions.

SENEGAL: *Pikine Primary Health Services*

This project was begun in an area near Dakar in 1975 to provide health care to dispersed rural hamlets. The plan was to have many small health units rather than a few large health centers. The project was started in a two-room private house with staff provided by the Ministry of Health.

The community's contribution, apart from paying fees for treatment, was to co-manage the health services by electing a health committee, to control the internal financial procedures, and to provide a link between the primary care practitioners and member families. At regular intervals, new health committees were formed and new health units opened.

All the health committees were unified into an Association for Health Promotion, officially recognized by the government in May 1980. The role of the government in backing up its staff is to monitor the effectiveness of coverage, plan programs and logistics, stimulate community capacity to solve problems, provide efficient technical guidance, support the accounting system, and take care of seriously ill referred patients (Jancloes et al., 1981).

LESSONS: A well-conceived government effort can elicit an effective community response. Few PHC programs have had such a federation of health committees providing vertical linkage to strengthen the program. It may put some uncomfortable pressure on the government agencies to perform their tasks better, but it also creates a constituency for health care that can support the Ministry when political clout is needed.

Sine Saloum Rural Health Project

The Sine Saloum project, begun in 1977, was sponsored by the government of Senegal and USAID to create a new and more extensive layer of health services for the Sine Saloum region's rural population. Instead of relying on a single health worker, the program trained teams of three paraprofessionals for each rural health post—a dresser (first-aid worker), a midwife, and a hygienist. Midwives were chosen from among existing traditional birth attendants. Management committees were formed within each community to oversee financial affairs including payments to health workers who were to receive a percentage of the funds collected. The committees did not have any promotional or mobilizational role.

Unfortunately the program encountered some serious difficulties. Information about the program was channeled through village chiefs, with the result that few women understood the program or considered it as "theirs." The high academic standards required for dressers meant that many were not from the community they were to serve or were frequently not available. (Given their educational level, they also left for more desirable jobs whenever possible.)

The participating midwives were required to charge a relatively high fixed fee and were therefore rarely called upon. Neither their traditional status nor their more modern training were attractive enough to overcome the barrier of a cash charge. The fact that only one person in the management committee had control over cash receipts also made the treasurer susceptible to requests for loans from his relatives, which undermined the program's financial viability. Finally since USAID paid most of the cost of construction, too many villages located near one another went ahead and built health posts. As a result, the first-aid workers found they had an insufficient number of patients to earn even a minimum salary (Hall, 1981).

As these problems became apparent, AID and the government of Senegal undertook actions to save the project. Agency staff moved their office from Dakar to the Sine Saloum region. Efforts were made to improve supervision. The Ministry of Public Health issued a directive endorsing VHC's responsibility for overseeing all the activities of the health huts including financing. Significantly all members of the VHC now receive training in health-hut operation and financial management so that they are in a good position to support the health workers. Formation of a women's committee for each hut, in keeping with traditional village organization, gives women a greater voice and broadens the network of supporting institutions (Bloom 1984).

LESSONS: When educational standards for health workers are set too high, local residents may be ineligible to serve or may leave for better opportunities after a short period of service. Treating villages all as separate local entities rather than planning programs (with people's participation) at the locality level led to a waste of capital and human resources.

The use of traditional health practitioners is likely to be less effective when long-established forms of remuneration are substantially altered. This project like so many others would have done better if it had adopted a "learning process" approach from the outset instead of following a predetermined "blueprint." Also, involvement of a wider group of beneficiaries in the initial planning and management, getting beyond the village chief and his associates, would likely have avoided major pitfalls.

SIERRA LEONE: Serabu Village-Based Public Health Program

A missionary hospital at Serabu had sought to meet rural health needs by sending a mobile clinic around to villages on a regular basis, but after ten years it was apparent this approach was having little impact. In an effort to increase their effectiveness, the hospital changed its approach to one of having nurses make periodic visits (usually for two days) to the villages on foot, not even carrying medicines with them.

Committees including the village chief, persons with indigenous knowledge of "medicines" and traditional midwives were organized and would meet for informal discussions similar to traditional village meetings. Although the meetings were not regularly scheduled, they were frequent, usually once or twice a month and open to any interested member of the community.

Within three years the committees were instrumental in building a number of wells, rubbish pits, and latrines. They did not see a need for having individual health workers appointed and trained because disease prevention activities were always undertaken on a group basis after discussion involving the whole village. For the first several years, curative care continued to be provided by indigenous practitioners with certain serious cases referred to the hospital (Ross, 1979).

LESSONS: Villagers can be interested in public health programs if approached in a sustained and sensitive way. Although one normally finds a distinction between village health workers and the village health committee, this case suggests there need not be. If VHC members are active enough, they can become de facto health workers. It is instructive to contrast this experience with that reported previously for Cameroon and also with a case study from Liberia documented by Sheppard (1981).

THAILAND: The Population and Community Development Association

This private, nonprofit service delivery organization has had great success in getting contraceptives to the rural population by supplying them at low cost to village storekeepers who sell them for a modest profit. The shops also provide information about family planning methods.

The considerations were that for birth control to be practiced, devices had to be available near the population and in a setting that was familiar and congenial. They had also to be available continuously with no interruptions of supply as was common in government offices.

The Association has trained family planning program participants in more than 16,000 villages, a third of all those in the country. However, efforts aimed at expanding activities to include control of parasitic diseases and pig production have not, unfortunately, been as successful. The program is credited with having made a substantial contribution to Thailand's decreasing population growth rate, falling from over 3 to almost 2 percent within a decade (Korten, 1980).

Now that the acceptability of contraceptives has greatly increased because they are so readily available, rural people are increasingly taking advantage of the free birth control pills distributed through the government's sub-district clinics, according to Bruns (1981). This presents a LID dilemma—whether the two channels can and should co-exist.

LESSONS: There are some kinds of distribution tasks for which the private sector is uniquely well suited, though paradoxically the success of the private distribution channels in this case has now bolstered the government's distribution system. The role of a dynamic leader, PCDA's founder, Dr. Mechai, has been pointed to in many evaluations, yet his "genius" was most concretely expressed in his choice and development of local institutional channels.

Agricultural Development

LATIN AMERICA

BOLIVIA: Agricultural Cooperatives

A recent evaluation of four peasant cooperative associations assisted by the Inter-American Foundation provides a number of insights that contradict the conventional wisdom about cooperatives (Tendler, 1983). The co-ops, which have been in operation for almost ten years and continue to receive donor assistance, have familiar administrative and management inadequacies. Their membership, for example, is small and appears to have levelled off after reaching only 25 percent of the families in the communities. The prices charged to cover the co-ops' merchandise and services are sometimes too low to cover costs, and collection of loans is casual. The organizations exhibit many of the "pathologies" frequently found in cooperatives in Latin America as well as in other parts of the world.

Yet upon closer examination, Tendler found some very positive aspects of their performance. The average donor investment per member family ($1,000) might be judged higher than "reasonable." But when the benefits to nonmembers are considered along with those for members, the cost per beneficiary goes down markedly, and the ratio of benefits to costs is substantial. Aside from serving as a voice with the government for all farmers on issues that concerned them, two of the co-op organizations undertook public infrastructure projects—potable water and road construction— which benefited most of the community. The cooperatives also worked to control contagious crop and livestock diseases, an effort that required (and received) the support of nonmembers as well as members, benefiting them all.

One instance of what appeared at first to be "loose management" turned out to exhibit a good (if intuitive) understanding of the difference between average and marginal costs. Nonmembers were allowed to ship their produce in the cooperative truck for a small charge if there was space available. This looked as though nonmembers were not contributing their "share." But the co-op was increasing its income to cover more of its operating costs for the truck. This was economically advantageous for members even if the nonmembers did not pay an equal proportion of total costs.

Management inadequacies were not randomly distributed but were greater or less depending on the nature of the task. Agro-processing was consistently the best-performed activity, and cooperative stores and credit the worst. Agro-processing worked well because the commodities in question "belonged" to the members and their return from their produce depended on good processing (and storage and marketing). Also, the members regarded the processing facility very much as "theirs" because they had contributed the labor and materials to build it. This created social pressure from among farmers for efficient and honest operation. Furthermore, improving the management of agro-processing called for technical decisions that did not involve politically or socially difficult problems.

The store and credit operations, on the other hand, did not generally perform well. Prices were set too low, and there was no systematic effort to get loans repaid on time. The social norms associated with "cooperatives" apparently made it difficult to charge prices or to follow procedures that might resemble those of "exploitative" middlemen. In contrast when one of the co-ops rented out a bulldozer to members who needed its services for clearing land, there seemed to be no difficulty in charging a rate that covered all costs. There were no private competitors whose presence would "obligate" the co-op to keep charges lower than private operators.

The leadership of these co-ops came from some of the more prosperous members of the community who rarely relinquished office. However, since they were also farmers the leaders shared with members the same economic interests, e.g. the desire for better crop prices and lower transport costs. Activities such as marketing, processing, and stores benefited many nonmembers thereby spreading benefits beyond the self-interested control of the entrenched leaders.

LESSONS: Evaluating cooperatives, like other local institutional development efforts, calls for closer and more multifaceted scrutiny than standard accounting procedures normally provide. The fact that co-ops had several activities underway simultaneously allowed one activity to subsidize another and to give the institutions some stability and attractiveness difficult to achieve in single-function organization. (Note: This conclusion by Tendler differs from that of her 1976 study of farmer organizations in Ecuador and Honduras.)

Co-ops may be more useful institutions at an early stage of LID, diminishing in utility as some of their functions can be taken over by state or private institutions. This is not proven by the Bolivian case studies but rather inferred from the fact that these co-ops filled functional niches often filled by the government or by businesses in other settings. The fact that more advantaged persons joined and led cooperatives did not mean that these organizations' benefits accrued only to such persons. If the activities of co-ops produce positive-sum (rather than zero-sum) benefits, members and leaders should be willing to have the benefits of co-ops go also to nonmembers.

GUATEMALA: San Martin Jilotepeque Cooperative

World Neighbors, the agency which in 1971 helped initiate project activities, already had a well-established reputation in the region from work begun in the 1960s. Planned originally as an "integrated" project, the undertaking started with one agency staff member and six part-time extension workers concentrating on a small geographic area attempting to learn from the residents through interviews and data collection involving almost 600 families. Activities narrowed fairly quickly to focus on agricultural development.

A review of the data found that corn yields were among the lowest in Guatemala due in part to soil erosion problems. With funding from Oxfam and World Neighbors, a weekly training program on agricultural practices to combat erosion and raise production was organized for two groups of farmers. Each course followed an outline suited to their abilities and learning methods. Members of the training staff visited the farmers in their communities to help put classroom ideas into practice. After nine months, twenty-seven of the forty original participants agreed to work as unpaid rural promoters and themselves to adopt the "technological package" which, because of its cost, required that each promoter be loaned $15 for one season.

Subsequent efforts involved the organization of a credit cooperative and a small input supply store. The cooperative, called Kato-ki (self-help), had 732 members and over $38,000 in share capital by 1978. Loans are made for agricultural inputs, livestock, land purchases (60 percent of the members are landless), commerce or small industry, housing, and consumption. The cooperative established a banking service for members' savings. The input supply store was established to meet the emerging demand for agricultural inputs. Prices and quality remain attractive enough to draw customers even though four nearby competitors have gone into business selling supplies in recent years, and members of the co-op are free to choose any store they like. Sales in 1977 totaled over $23,000 (over $300 per member).

New members must attend classes where attention is given to the uses and management of credit. Loans are reviewed by a credit committee and if a request is reduced or denied, the reasons are fully explained to the member. Important decisions are made by the cooperative's general assembly with more routine matters handled by elected leaders who, after two years, must relinquish their position.

The project has demonstrated some impressive results. Farmers' average net income using the improved technological package on one hectare of corn and one of beans has increased over 160 percent within five years. With cooperative-sponsored training and credit services, average yields increased 110 percent for corn and 60 percent for beans. By 1978 sixty-three members had been able to leave the "landless" category by acquiring land.

The default rate on loans has been only 8.5 percent. Many members report they no longer have to engage in seasonal migration or seek work on nearby haciendas (Gow et al., 1979:153-170).

LESSONS: By becoming well acquainted with residents, maintaining continuity of field staff, and showing flexibility, the project was able to focus on the priorities of the residents and not those of the planners who initially advocated an "integrated" approach. This is a good example of "learning process." When organizing the training program, the outside agency closely consulted with existing religious institutions to identify potential local leaders. Since activities began in a small, staff-intensive manner, important individual and group learning could emerge before undertakings were expanded.

The fact that all new members of the co-op complete the same program means that the entire membership has relatively equal information about organizational procedures and methods of operation. Limited terms of office and reduced external funding when there was evidence of appropriate local capacities to continue the institutionalization process helped preclude a dependence relationship.

JAMAICA: Agricultural Marketing Boards

When the government waited to increase production of food crops and particularly to promote export crops like citrus, bananas, and coffee, it established an Agricultural Marketing Corporation (AMC) to give marketing services and guaranteed prices for commodities. To boost export crops, various commodity associations were set up, officially as membership organizations, but practically as state enterprises. Private buyers and handlers were thought to be too exploitative and thus to be a deterrent to farmers' expanding production (Lewars, 1982).

The prices offered by the AMC were usually too low for farmers to get what they considered sufficient return for their effort. Moreover, the buying system was chaotic, with drivers not always coming when scheduled to pick up produce or demanding bribes before they would buy perishable foods. Farmers with foodstuffs soon learned to bypass the AMC and returned to dealing with private buyers. They did not have this option for export crops like coffee and bananas, however.

Banana exports, for example, require effective organization to collect sufficient quantities of assured quality produce that can maintain the satisfaction of foreign consumers. A banana growers' association was set up by the government and all sales for export were required to go through it. Farmers being compelled to "join" took no interest in the association. They often did not even know they were "members" because their dues were automatically deducted from the proceeds of their sales.

The alienation of farmers from "their" association was increased by the high-handed way the staff treated them and their produce. Rejection of hands of bananas discolored by tropical snails was not explained, for example, and this caused much resentment because members saw the fruit as edible, not knowing that foreign consumers would shun it. Farmers had no control over the price paid. (It was kept low for the sake of government prof-it.) Eventually substantial interest in banana production was lost (Goldsmith, 1980 and 1982).

LESSONS: Although set up to promote production, the govern-ment agency and the commodity associations (pale versions of membership organization), ended up reducing it. Both farmers and gov-ernment were the losers from this. When organizations like the commodity associations and the AMC (whose buying centers operated as LA) develop no awareness, commitments, or support within the pub-lic and particularly among those persons whom they are supposed to serve, they cannot become "institutions."

MEXICO: Plan Puebla Farmer Committees

This project was started in 1967 by CIMMYT, the international wheat and maize research center in Mexico, to improve the production and in-comes of rainfed farmers in the State of Puebla. The National Agricultural University at Chapingo supported the effort. By 1973 it covered thirty-two municipalities (counties) and involved some 43,000 small farmers (CIMMYT, 1974).

Initially the project emphasized the adoption of new, high-yielding maize varieties, but it soon became apparent that under the prevailing agro-nomic conditions of Puebla, the traditional varieties did practically as well since farmers needed to maximize combined maize and bean production on their small fields and not just the output of maize. However, maize produc-tion could be increased by adding fertilizer and trace minerals that were deficient in the soil (Whyte and Boynton, 1983:37-41).

For farmers to buy new inputs they needed credit. Upon arrival in the field of a second generation of field staff, an extensive system of credit groups was organized. This was based on the notion that groups would be better able to apply pressure on members to honor the repay-ment obligations than an administrative arrangement that extended credit to individuals.

In a site visit to the project area, Swanberg (1982) found the system was still functioning well after several years. The use of "community organizers" in forming the farmers groups was apparently quite successful. To increase their capacity to negotiate for better prices among other things, farmers got the government to construct a warehouse. Perhaps even more important was their increased level of knowledge about plant fertilization.

LESSONS: Building a program based on small groups of ten to fifteen farmers proved very successful here, similar to the spread of irrigation water management groups in Sri Lanka analyzed in Uphoff (1985) and more gen-erally shown by Oxby (1983). Farmers welcomed the "group discipline" that upheld the integrity of a program that provided real benefits to them. An-other important element in the Puebla experience involved the sensitivity of project staff to farmers' limitations, constraints, and needs (Swanberg, 1982). Specifically time was invested in observing the performance and ra-tionale of the existing agricultural system instead of stubbornly insisting that farmers adopt the new technology, which it turned out was not as superior as the technicians assumed. Upgrading the existing technology in conjunction with local institutional development opened the door to subsequent introduction of more appropriate new technologies.

URUGUAY: Durazno Dairy Cooperative

This cooperative, organized around the provincial capital of Durazno, has not had time to become institutionalized. Yet it has gotten off to a very promising start because of the profitable combination of technology and organization put together with help from the Inter-American Foundation. A dairy plant run by the cooperative is seeking to encourage small and medium-size milk producers to raise output by guaranteeing stable demand. With pasteurization and packaging of milk in attractive containers, consumers are willing to pay more for the milk they get. In addition the plant produces butter and is in the process of expanding production of cheese with the expectation of export sales.

The dairy producers previously marketed their own milk individually, which required making one or two trips daily by horsecart to distribute milk along an extended route that sometimes resulted in spoilage problems. The cooperative employs a truck to collect the milk at members' homes, thereby saving them from one to five hours of transportation labor a day. This has freed up time for farmers to increase crop yields or improve pastures and herds. The advantages of group transportation, processing, and marketing give members a tangible stake in making the co-op a success (Hirschman, 1984:18-21).

LESSONS: Though the dairy cooperative with its modern plant and transportation system has clearly increased the economic welfare of producer-members, the status and prestige they have gained also provide a strong inducement for supporting the co-op. "Now they are associates of a much admired, technologically progressive undertaking, whereas previously their daily milk-peddling treks caused them to be viewed as quite lowly members of the rural society" (Hirschman, 1984:21).

The differences in commodities should be noted, illustrating issues raised in Section 5.4. For some producers, such as wool growers, yearly deliveries or sales can be an exciting variation on their daily routine, giving desired opportunities for social contact. For dairy producers on the other hand, since marketing is a daily activity it is mostly boring and little valued. When developing local institutions one needs to take into account the nature of the goods produced and the less tangible social aspects of agricultural life.

AFRICA

BOTSWANA: Drift Fence Groups

Drift fences are wire fences built to separate crop land from grazing land. They are usually put up to protect against crop damage though they can also ease herd management problems or serve as the basis for grazing management schemes. A few bush fences had been built in the 1920s and 1930s, but the first wire drift fence in Botswana was completed in Southern District in 1975. After this there was a phenomenal growth in drift fencing. By August 1980, 109 fences were either completed or underway with a total length of 1040 km (Willett, 1981,II:9).

The configuration of each fence is broadly determined by ecological considerations (the location of crop and grazing lands), though the exact line takes into account such things as access to water points and the need for future expansion of crop land. Most fences are locally initiated; indeed all ten in the area studied by an Institutions Research Project of the Ministry of Local Government and Lands were locally initiated. Often the idea for a fence comes from the example of a neighboring community that has built a fence. In some areas adjacent fences are linked up to form one long line. In the Iswapong Hills area one fence made up of ten to fifteen km. segments, each built by a single community, now stretches almost 200 km.

Government assistance to the fence groups is part of its overall support program for farmers' groups. The group is expected to provide voluntary labor to cut poles, clear the fence line, and build the fence. It must also contribute cash equivalent to 10 percent of the capital costs. In return the government provides fencing material (wire and gates), equipment (for tightening the wire and digging holes), and extension advice. Maintenance of the fence, once completed, is the responsibility of the group (Chris Brown, 1983, and personal communication).

LESSONS: Where a local organizational form provides manifest benefits it can spread rapidly if easily manageable by members. The support given by the government has been limited but very effective in spreading these groups and fences. It is a good example of "assisted self-reliance" (Esman and Uphoff, 1984:258-264). The maintenance of fences has been reasonably good partly because any need for repair is quite evident and failure to make repairs will result in obvious damage (this was one condition mentioned in Chapter Three for local institutions handling maintenance effectively). Also the "ownership" of the fence is clearly with the group not the government—an important condition.

GHANA: United Ghana Farmers Council

The cocoa industry in Ghana, presently in a shambles, was once the economic mainstay of a prospering economy. Cocoa farmers developed their production beginning in the 1890s essentially on their own with little help from the government. Indeed, the colonial government at times discouraged the nascent industry. Farmer entrepreneurs made this small country the world's leading producer by the 1950s (Hill, 1963).

The UGFC grew out of cocoa producers' cooperatives, which were started in the 1920s in response to the low price paid by private (European) buyers. At that time several groups of small producers (most illiterate) tried to sell directly to the London market but were swindled by their agents. Thereafter co-ops stuck to purchasing cocoa beans from members and selling them to European companies in-country to try to get the best price.

During 1937 when it became apparent that the European companies were in collusion to hold down the price paid to growers, Ghanaian farmers boycotted them holding back the entire crop, almost 300,000 tons, for six months until the colonial administration intervened to raise the price. After World War II, growers became one of the main organized "pillars" of the independence movement as the UGFC was formed and allied with the Convention People's Party of Kwame Nkrumah.

One of the first problems confronting Nkrumah after his party took over the government in 1951 was to combat a serious epidemic of the black pod cocoa disease. UGFC branches (MOs) cooperated with government staff (LA) in explaining to farmers the need to cut and burn infected trees on a mass scale. The campaign could hardly have gone as quickly and successfully without the UGFC's assistance. Partly as a "reward" to the UGFC for its role in helping to win independence but mostly to get control over the crop so as to divert revenue to the government, Nkrumah gave the UGFC a monopoly on cocoa purchasing.

The result was to destroy it as a cooperative form of organization. Clerks, previously accountable to farmers, now cheated on weight and grading, giving "chits" instead of cash and demanding bribes to convert the chits later into money. Both farmers' incentive to invest in planting new trees and the regime's popularity suffered as a result. (The UGFC's disastrous monopoly over distribution of machetes is discussed in Section 5.2.4, footnote 20). When Nkrumah was overthrown in 1966, one of the military government's most popular acts was ending the UGFC monopoly (Beckman, 1976).

LESSONS: Farmer's indigenous organizational capabilities can be substantial as demonstrated in Ghana by their action to start cooperatives without outside assistance and to hold up an entire cocoa crop in 1937. Cooperatives, if given monopoly and state backing, may act irresponsibly once accountability to members is severed. The political and economic consequences of this can be quite unfortunate as seen also in the Jamaica case cited above.

NIGERIA: Gombe Local Authority

The policy of indirect rule by the British colonial regime left considerable authority in the hands of traditional leaders in northern Nigeria who headed what were called the Native Authorities governing each sub-district area. (Native Authorities were renamed Local Authorities in 1968.) A case study of the Gombe Native Authority by Tiffen (1980:25) concludes that this region's comparative success in agricultural development has been due in large part to the performance of its local authority (LG).

All NAs had taxing authority for making local investments but some mismanaged this authority creating a disincentive to individual farmers to improve their production. The Gombe NA, however, carefully invested the taxes it collected in education, health, veterinary, and agricultural services. The Gombe traditional leaders were generally progressive in encouraging agricultural modernization and setting a good example in their own fields.

The traditional district and village heads, in turn, "propagandized innovations such as the use of fertilizer, worked their own farms actively, and keenly cooperated in the distribution of cotton seed, the organization of cotton markets, etc." (Tiffen, 1980:29).

After 1945 the government started "democratizing" the system of local government by establishing offices for elected representatives. In Gombe where the Native Authority heads were progressive, they were elected to the new Councils. The government, however, was reluctant to give much independent taxing and spending authority to local councils, thinking village people too illiterate to be allowed any control of funds. In Gombe this mattered less because there were many active interest groups that put pressure on higher authorities to invest in agricultural improvements the local government could not undertake.

In communities with strong local leadership, despite the lack of formal taxing powers, "Village Heads who were good organizers could get rough roads constructed or classrooms built by voluntary labor, and they might be able to influence the central NA to allocate the necessary funds for staffing and maintenance" (Tiffen, 1980:32).

> The Village Head is the main channel for Government advice and orders to his people. The Agricultural Officer expects him to enforce the cotton close season (to curb diseases), to provide cotton seed dumps, to organize seed distribution and to disseminate information. The Veterinary Officer expects him to maintain cattle tracks and to inform cattle owners about innoculation facilities. The Forestry Officer expects him to protect Forest Reserves. He has to recruit labor for local public works. The Education Officer expects him to keep this village school full despite prejudice against Western education. The District Officer expects him not only to collect taxes but to maintain law and order, and all for a salary which in 1967 ranged from £42 to £345 per annum.

The government and donor-assisted development projects in the area that have not succeeded have been those that bypassed the Local Authorities, whereas those that had worked with and through the local government have had considerable success, Tiffen reports. One water scheme pushed through by high officials without local review and support was a waste of £245,000.

LESSONS: As Gombe has benefited with so little expenditure of centrally directed funds, we can take it as an example of the success of the policy of strengthening the rural institutional base of the Nigerian economy. The special political and administrative factors which favored its development are to be found locally, in the power structure that favors majority rural interests; in the effective leadership given by locally rooted families at District and Village levels; and in the comparative absence of extortion, which has meant that local farmers are not afraid to work for, and display, wealth (Tiffen, 1980:35).

SENEGAL: Women's Garden Groups

The establishment of women's garden groups built on traditional cooperation among Senegalese women in agricultural tasks, especially rice production. In the mid-1970s the government initiated an agricultural development project during a period of drought when there were serious food shortages. Though a similar garden promotion scheme had failed a decade earlier for lack of demand, recent growth in tourism had created an increase in demand for tomatoes, potatoes, etc. and villagers' need for income had greatly increased. Hence, the prospects of successful collective action were more favorable.

Since land could not be purchased outright, the groups began by securing use-rights from village authorities. Land was cleared and fenced by relying on the traditional division of labor; men cleared and prepared the land and also provided the labor for well digging. Because the wells frequently became saline, limited but essential technical assistance was given to the groups by UNICEF and by units of local administration. Of particular value was the provision of cement and hand tools to line the wells. As no pressure was applied by outside agencies on the groups to take on a particular organizational design, each of the more than fifty groups has adapted its form to meet local needs and norms. A discussion of two groups indicates their diversity.

The women's garden group in Boucotte Ouoloff has 160 members, each of whom paid a membership fee of 1000 francs to join. Two presidents serve concurrently, the younger being in charge of "external affairs" (since she is bilingual) and the senior woman handling "internal affairs" (within the village). With assistance from village men, three hectares were cleared and fenced, and a 12-meter well dug. Each member has individual rows to oversee on the plot. However, following the sale of their produce, members must individually contribute 2500 francs to a common fund. Monies have been used for such items as construction of a health/maternity center and construction of a road to the garden so it would be easier for the UNICEF-donated truck to transport commodities to city markets and hotels. Five hectares of trees have also been planted by the group to help alleviate fuelwood scarcity.

In the drier area of Dianky, another gardening group has 260 members of whom forty-eight are men. Leadership remains exclusively with the women, however. This group works two hectares on a more collective basis than Boucotte Ouoloff. According to the group's president, the organization has "matured" rather quickly due to a previous experience with women's banking and a tradition of cooperative agricultural labor for growing rice and peanuts. Discipline within the group is strict. If a cultivator does not tend her rows, an empty basket is placed next to them. If the basket cannot be filled with produce from that person's row in the group plot, produce from her or his own individual plot must be contributed. With outside assistance three improved wells have been built. The group has agreed to take on several experimental projects using new varieties of seeds, provided that they plan and decide what the projects will be. As with Boucotte Ouoloff, provision of a UNICEF truck has facilitated shipment of produce to Dakar, thereby increasing the quantity sold and the profits each member received (Yoon, 1983).

LESSONS: The dynamism in women's garden groups comes from their building on indigenous patterns of cooperation and because outside agencies were able to support the organizations without trying to determine how the tasks would be organized and what kinds of sanctions were appropriate. External aid for water source improvements complemented the labor and skills already available. Provision of the truck allowed for new marketing linkages, which brought groups together in ways that would not have occurred otherwise. An example of innovation in organizational structure when groups are left to determine this themselves is the selection of a president for external affairs, i.e., someone who is wise in the ways of Dakar and can speak French.

ZIMBABWE: Farmers' Associations

A systematic study was done by Bratton (1983) to determine the extent, functions and effectiveness of farmers associations in the rainfed communal (African-operated) areas of Zimbabwe. Interviews with a random sample of 494 households in four districts revealed that 44 percent of cultivators belonged to some form of voluntary agricultural association. The groups themselves covered a wide range of activities and had connections to a variety of public, private, parastatal, and nongovernmental agencies—the Ministry of Agriculture, the Windmill Fertilizer Company, the Agricultural Finance Company, the Cooperative Marketing Union, the Adult Literacy Organization of Zimbabwe, the Savings Development Movement (Annex Eight), and the Catholic Church.

A classification of associations according to their sponsorship is understandable from the perspective of the capital city, but Bratton says:

> For several reasons it is seriously misleading when viewed from the village. (a) Farmers and not field staff are the prime movers in creating and sustaining the farmers' organizations. Farmers justifiably resist being defined as appendages of large, distant agencies. Example: a farmer in Wedza sternly corrected me when I asked if his was an "extension worker group"—"Does he [the extension worker] come here to join our group when there are fields to be planted or weeded?" (b) Farmers in groups feel free to enter transactions with several different agencies and are rarely bound by loyalty to only one. Example: a group leader in Mtilikwe explained that "we can't just speak with one government worker to get all the things we need." (c) Most important, farmer groups with nominally different "labels" perform essentially similar functions (Bratton, 1983:5).

In terms of the activities undertaken, 60 percent of the groups identified in the study engaged in *exchange of information* so as to diffuse technical "know-how" in agriculture. In part, groups form to overcome the shortage of extension agents in the field and in part to consolidate and dispense existing indigenous knowledge." Just over half the groups engaged in mutual *work exchange* through work parties for planting, weeding and harvesting, sometimes sharing scarce capital resources like farm implements or draft oxen. Almost half of the organizations (47 percent) made *bulk purchases of inputs,* particularly fertilizer, and about one third (36 percent) did *joint marketing* to attain transport savings and better prices. About one-quarter of the groups were *multi-purpose,* usually with supply and marketing functions having been added to production (labor exchange) groups.

> The survey results confirm that, within each agro-ecological setting, maize farmers in groups *consistently outproduce* individual maize farmers. The effects of group organization on maize output appear to become *more marked* as rainfall and soil conditions become *less propitious.* Whereas group members produce nearly twice as much as individuals in Chipuiriro, they produce almost three times as much in Gutu. The implication, which needs further testing, is that farmer organizations make their biggest contribution to production in the more marginal areas. (Bratton, 1983:17).

LESSONS: We had already formulated our framework for agricultural LID analysis before receiving this empirical study, which supports our analysis very directly. Actual production is likely to remain an individual or household responsibility, even if there is some collective action during the production process. The main "institutional" functions are to provide inputs and to dispose of outputs on advantageous terms. Even when there is exchange of labor or implements, each participant gets (only) the produce from his or her own field, so there is not cooperative production with a sharing of risks.

The extent of farmer organizations in support of agriculture is itself quite impressive. The mix of governmental, private, and NGO initiatives to promote farmer agricultural associations has been fruitful. Yet these connections have not been overwhelming. As a rule, the farmer groups have been able to maintain their own identity and capacity. Groups' significant contribution to greater productivity is demonstrable from comparative data on yields. (See footnote 6 in Chapter Eight.)

ASIA

BANGLADESH: Comilla Small Farmer Cooperatives

The farmer cooperatives sponsored by the Academy for Rural Development at Comilla started out with considerable promise. The groups met regularly and each member made a deposit into his savings account, becoming eligible for loans administered by the group. Farmer representatives from each group went regularly to the sub-district (thana) training center run by the Academy to gain new agricultural knowledge which was brought back to the group, with demonstrable gains in productivity. The Comilla "model" became one of the most hopeful examples of how small farmers could be enlisted in agricultural improvement (Millikan and Hapgood, 1967; Mosher, 1969; Raper, 1970; Owens and Shaw, 1972).

When the government and donors became enthused about the Comilla cooperatives, they wanted to expand them to the whole of East Pakistan (now Bangladesh). The leadership of the Academy knew that the success depended in large part on the thoroughness of the training and supervision that brought out the best in the groups' membership and leadership. But they had no control over the larger program (Blair, 1978).

The main undoing of the program was the infusion of huge amounts of credit from the government to be passed on to co-op members. The discipline that had characterized repayment of loans when the funds were mostly the members' own savings dissipated and arrears began piling up. In 1967-68, 1,000 co-op societies with 25,000 members paid in 1.6 million thaka as shares and borrowed 5 million thaka in loans—with only 2.2 percent overdues. Five years later, the "movement" was expanded to offer 5,000 societies with 125,000 members, over 10 million thaka in shares, almost 60 million thaka in loans, and 25 percent overdue (Blair, 1982:438). Before long the program was as insolvent as other government-run credit schemes.

LESSONS: Over-rapid expansion of even a good program can kill it because training, communication, discipline, supervision, and other crucial elements get diluted or destroyed in the process. The philosophy of "self-help" with which the organizations began was washed out by the flood of resources that the government poured into the program. In an attempt to have a larger impact, the government lost most of the effectiveness the institutional model possessed.

INDIA: Gujerat Cotton Cooperatives

Many people know about the AMUL dairy cooperatives, which started in the Indian State of Gujerat, but few people realize that they were preceded by similarly successful cooperatives of cotton producers. At the turn of the century, new technology, new markets, and better transport made cotton a more profitable crop in Gujerat. However, the benefits of increased production tended to go to the merchants who bought the crop from producers.

A cooperative sales society established in 1919 grew in the next decade into a cooperative doing ginning and pressing, financed and managed by growers. Efforts by private gin owners to suppress it failed. Between half and two-thirds of the cotton grown in Gujerat was eventually marketed through cooperative channels. Growers were paid 80 percent of market value upon delivery (minus the value of any loan they had taken out in advance of the season) with the balance paid at the end of the season when the crop had been sold. The societies were able to get a better price for the crop because of their economies of scale and their quality control.

This structure of cooperatives has supported considerable technological advances in cotton production. A steady flow of new varieties with features of disease resistance, higher yield, and better fiber quality have been introduced in the last two decades (Nicholson, 1975).

LESSONS: Cooperatives can expand in scale and can become both technologically and commercially sophisticated in competition with private buyers. A similar example is seen with the Sukuma cotton cooperative in Tanzania, which grew into a regional federation with its own cotton ginneries and which contributed to a doubling of production (Lang et al., 1969).

A cooperative form of organization for processing and marketing can provide greater returns to farmer-members. These benefits can provide a stimulus for adoption of new technology and raising output as seen also in the Bolivian cooperatives reported previously.

NEPAL: Small Farmer Development Program Groups

The SFDP was set up in 1975 by the Agricultural Development Bank of Nepal (ADB/N) with support from the FAO. This was an unusual donor-assisted project in that only $30,000 was provided at the outset and the design of the program emerged from intensive field visits involving consultations with small farmers and landless laborers about their problems (FAO, 1978-79).

The program recruited, trained, and sent Group Organizers (catalysts as analyzed in Section 7.2.2) into communities to set up groups of ten to fifteen small farmers, including landless laborers, to whom credit would be made available on a group basis without collateral to improve incomes. The initial focus was on rice production, small animals, poultry, buffalo raising, vegetables, etc. Women's groups were also started up with activities on nutrition, literacy, and cottage industry production. The groups often supported building or upgrading schools, improving roads, water supply or irrigation, and establishing first aid centers and meeting halls. The savings program included a fund for emergency loans so that members could stay out of the thrall of moneylenders. Food banks were also introduced to help members out in time of need. Member households would make a "deposit" of grain in the bank, withdrawing it and more if necessary, replacing the amount as soon as possible.

Groups often branched out into other activities making, for example, agreements to limit expenditure on weddings (thereby reducing a major cause of indebtedness) or to curtail drunkenness, gambling, and theft. Incomes have increased by 20 to 30 percent, according to a mid-project evaluation by the International Fund for Agricultural Development, though it also finds that the improvements have been somewhat greater for the better-off within the large category of "rural poor" in the Nepal hills (IFAD, 1984). There has also been some reduction in ethnic and caste discrimination and improvement in the status of women, through groups often mixed by social background but with separate groups for women (an issue for LID discussed in Section 7.2.3).

One important consequence has been to increase small farmers' political influence in their communities. In Tupche where the program was started, the rich family that previously dominated the panchayat was ousted from control, and about forty-five small farmers were elected to panchayats in the area through the group solidarity introduced by these membership organizations (Shrestha, 1980; Ghai and Rahman, 1979 and 1981). Small farmers have also gained a larger role and voice in the government-sponsored cooperatives (IFAD, 1984:36).

The Group Organizers work with remarkable freedom and initiative according to the IFAD evaluation. None had been withdrawn from communities by 1984, though this had been envisioned within three to five years. But their role had changed to perform a variety of functions: "motivator, mobiliser, credit and investment officer, extension agent, spokesman with government departments, conciliator and arbiter of conflicts, data and information gatherer, evaluator, thinker, philosopher and friend." (1984:33) They now look after a much larger area with membership ranging from 500 to 1300, up to almost 100 groups. There may have been some decline in the overall performance of the project with this expansion. Still, what impressed an evaluation team most was the effectiveness of the project's decentralized, flexible mode of operation.

The IFAD evaluation described one group in Khopasi, which it found to be among the most active, indicating the potential of this kind of local organization.

Formed 2½ years ago, the group has 19 members, including 4 landless. The maximum holding is 0.5 hectares. The group meets once a month and participation in the meeting is compulsory. There are four sub-committees dealing with group savings, group farming, purchase and sale of paddy, and loans utilization and repayment. The sub-committees meet as and when necessary. So far the group has not had any loan repayment problems. Nor has it experienced any serious conflict within the group.

Its group savings based on a contribution of Rs. 15 per month amount to Rs. 29,000. The group has instituted group grain storage to be used in emergencies. It has a number of group activities such as potato cultivation; seed multiplication; and vegetable gardening. The members participated in road construction in the panchayat, donating a total of eight days' labour each last year. Fourteen members have undergone vasectomy; the other five have not done so because they have only one child each.

The group leader estimated that their incomes have been rising at the rate of 10 to 12 percent per annum and that differentiation among members has been reduced. Early this year the group made a loan of Rs. 1000 to another group to set up a pharmacy in the village. This will also benefit their members with supplies of medicine. The group keeps complete and up-to-date records and has drawn up an impressive five-year investment and development plan comprising 13 items. (IFAD, 1984:35).

LESSONS: Starting with small, cohesive groups is important for building a structure of local institutional capacity. Leadership responsibilities within the groups have been passed around, revealing a considerable breadth of talent among this largely illiterate population. The gaining of political influence has been an important aspect of the institutional development process as the panchayat local government now supports the expansion of the program such as into social forestry (as described in Annex Two).

Small farm households may best begin their institutional development by concentrating on agricultural and other directly productive activities. But as organizational capacity is developed, there are other needs such as literacy, hygiene, and family planning that can be promoted through these same organizational channels if members have confidence in them.

The role of catalyst, discussed in Chapter Seven, was crucial here, as the group organizers initiated new social processes that members could and would then continue and elaborate.

The program's style of operation has been important as the IFAD evaluation particularly noted. This supports the general rule in organization theory that organizations will tend to replicate in their environment the kind of values and relations they exhibit internally. The ADB/N has set an example of innovativeness, flexibility, and sense of responsibility that has carried over into the way the Group Organizers work. This in turn has elicited such qualities in many small farmer groups.

TAIWAN: Farmers' Associations

The Farmers' Associations (FA) (and parallel Irrigation Associations) in Taiwan are credited with making a significant contribution to agricultural development there, attaining some of the highest yields anywhere through a system of very intensive production practices (Mosher, 1969:37-40). The FAs provide extension advice and physical inputs (seeds, fertilizer, chemicals, etc.) as well as credit. They also handle purchasing, processing, and marketing for their membership, which includes most farmers in the country though membership is at least nominally voluntary.

Taiwan was ruled by Japanese authorities from 1895 until 1945, with the object of producing food for the colonizing country. During this period investments were made in irrigation, fertilizer factories, and agricultural research to improve rice varieties. After World War II when the Chinese Nationalist government moved to Taiwan, great attention was given to rural areas including an extensive land reform program and investment in health, education, and law and order.

While farmers in Taiwan have had various forms of local agricultural institutions since 1913, the present form of Farmers' Associations including credit cooperatives has been in operation since 1953. The FA established in each township (locality) is financially self-supporting by having several sources of income. First, the government stipulates that all farmers pay their land taxes (in rice) through the FAs, which receive a portion of the tax as commission to cover expenses. Second, all fertilizer sales are channeled through the FAs, which make some profit on these though the price paid by farmers is fixed and subsidized by the central government. Corrupt practices are relatively uncommon because the supply of fertilizer has been kept plentiful and the government keeps a vigilant watch against corruption (through Nationalist Party cadres). Third, the FAs each have a credit department, which functions like a bank. Profits on savings and loans are kept by the Association and used to fund extension services, scholarships, etc.

In certain respects the FAs operate, and are even perceived by some farmers, as arms of government. Indeed, the government has 480 pages of general laws for FAs. On the other hand, selection of the salaried FA staff is made by elected FA boards of directors, subject to some minimal specification of qualifications by the government. Decisions on who will get allocations to grow highly profitable market crops such as asparagus and mushrooms are left to the FAs. This is an attractive resource which FAs control. Moreover, each Association has autonomy when it comes to spending the profits of its various input and output operations (See Stavis, 1983 on both FAs and IAs).

LESSONS: Even though the FAs have operated under much supervision and control from the center, they have created a degree of farmer involvement in managing agricultural improvement that has contributed to making Taiwanese farmers among the most productive in the world. In particular, many local staff (equivalent of LA) are employed, supervised, and controlled by the FAs rather than by the central government ministry, creating an accountability of officials to farmers that is rare in agricultural development.

A number of financial mechanisms are helpful such as using FAs to collect land taxes and giving them a commission for this service. This permits the government to accept payment in kind, freeing farmers from the need to convert rice to cash at harvest time when prices are low. It also gives the local institutions a stable financial base, while helping the central government with its finances. The FAs handle rural banking quite efficiently and finance useful services and benefits for the whole community from these operations, which would otherwise benefit only a few private moneylenders.

Because of their evident success in Taiwan, Farmers' Associations have appeared attractive as an organizational model to other developing countries. Indeed, the FA model was imported to Malaysia in the later 1960s with great disappointment. One cannot transfer an organizational design from one socio-political-economic environment to another any more than a biological specimen can be expected to survive where temperature, soil, and other conditions are quite different. Some of the organizational principles such as accountability referred to above, however, can be extrapolated to new environments. Subsequent adaptations of the model in Malaysia that enhanced members' loyalty to their organizations through greater devolution of authority and more active measures to alter existing rural social relations resulted in a greater degree of success (Mohamed, 1981:38).

THAILAND: Mae Klong Integrated Rural Development Groups

The Mae Klong Integrated Rural Development Project was initiated in January 1974 with the collaboration of three Thai universities each of which intended to address broad development objectives in the region. Project activities began in villages in the sub-district of Yokkrabat, some fifteen to twenty kilometers inland from the sea. Approximately half the villagers relied on production of palm sugar as their primary source of income, while the other half were rice farmers with a lower average income and standard of living.

During the first year projects were implemented through the formal village leaders and included attempts to improve an earthen flood dike to provide more irrigation as well as adult education, dressmaking classes and village health worker training. These efforts were not well accepted and were not continued in the second year. However, the university researchers persevered with their efforts to increase rice yields which were low because of high levels of soil salinity and rodent problems. Suggestions for transforming the rice areas into palm production did not appear promising since this would require a large investment and a long gestation period until the first crop. This meant the innovation could not benefit the really poor.

In mid-1975 a newly arrived university staff member, in the course of visiting rice-growing households, found that many people supplemented their incomes after the harvest season by selling fish trapped in mud dams they had constructed. Based on this information, researchers began to work toward developing socially cohesive groups of households organized around the prospects for larger-scale fish production.

The organizing activities involved: (a) facilitating small, informal evening conversations among farmers to discuss their knowledge of different varieties of fish and the feasibility of raising fingerlings (this social methodology resembles that of the Banki water supply project reported in Annex Three); (b) sending a number of farmers selected by the groups to observe fish raising at the National Institute of Fresh Water Fishery; (c) starting an experimental fish pond on land owned by one of the informal leaders; and (d) overcoming resistance by the local rice mill owners who were initially able to prevent the group from obtaining loans from the agricultural bank.

By 1976, over 100 households had significantly increased their income through involvement with fish culture. The villagers also began raising fingerlings for replenishment of the ponds. Although the groups remain loosely structured, each household's fish harvest is timed to allow for work groups to do the harvesting collectively and to prevent oversupply of the market. These loosely structured groups have developed roles, practices and procedures to promote a collectively valued purpose and are thus on the road to "institutionalizing" their organizations (Thai Khadi Research Institute, 1980; Rabibhadana, 1983).

LESSONS: The outsiders had to learn to observe and listen before their expertise could become useful to the rural people and before institutional development, based on valued new opportunities, could begin. The evolution here of a production-centered program out of an "integrated" project is similar to that reported above from Guatemala. The fact that the new technological opportunity was very productive was certainly an important factor favoring the groups' "institutionalization."

When the organizers worked through the established village leadership, they got conventional advice which did not lead to a fruitful agricultural-cum-institutional development approach. By going door-to-door to meet informally with households, the organizers were able to identify new leadership within the community, coming from the poorer strata, who had ideas and talent previously overlooked or excluded. These persons' experience, and the confidence they could generate from others, gave the effort a new impetus.

The program was able to proceed without much formalization of the organizations, which would have given vested interests more opportunity to oppose or thwart the program. Such informal groups are vulnerable but also flexible. If the commitment of members is strong enough, even outside obstruction may not succeed.

Nonagricultural Enterprise

BANGLADESH: Deedar Cooperative Society

This cooperative was founded in Deedar village in 1960 by nine members, all but one of them rickshaw pullers, among the poorest of the poor. They agreed among themselves to make daily thrift deposits in a co-op savings account (the savings from drinking one less cup of tea a day). The group's first major investment was to buy two rickshaws through hire-purchase arrangements to be used by members to save the onerous charges imposed by rich persons from whom they rented the vehicles. Within a year of its founding, the society had grown to fifty-five members and owned eleven rickshaws—all acquired without obtaining any outside loans.

From the beginning the society emphasized "collective self-discipline." Members who defaulted repeatedly on weekly savings were threatened with fines or confiscation of their savings or eventually with expulsion. At the same time interest-free loans (limited to one-fourth of the amount of a member's savings) could be taken out for productive as well as for "nonproductive" purposes (for marriages or religious festivals, for example). Participation was sustained by a "fine blend of strictness and leniency, disincentives and incentives" (Ray, 1983:12).

The Deedar Cooperative expanded in two ways. First, women and youth were included in savings and training from early on. Then in 1978 and 1979 separate weekly general meetings were organized for women and youth respectively. Women now participate with men on the board of directors. Membership has grown to virtually the whole community, 1200 persons—400 adult males, 300 adult women, 200 youth and 300 juniors from all the households in the village.

The second type of expansion was in economic activities. With a goal of generating employment and dividends for members, a truck was purchased in 1963. In 1964 a loan was taken out to establish a brickfield. Further activities were undertaken: purchase and installation of deep tubewells to increase the rice production area by double and triple cropping (augmenting employment opportunities as well as income for the landless), a paddy husking mill, a consumer store, and a cooperative marketing center. Share capital has grown to 2 million thaka, and the cooperative's assets exceed 6 million thaka. Scholarships and free books are given to children of members to encourage educational advancement. The cooperative has sponsored a "model" secondary school in the village. There is also a health insurance scheme (Yeasin, 1984).

Ray concludes from looking at Deedar's annual reports that "Deedar does not look upon profit as the principal aim when it launches commercial ventures or many other activities. Profit may be just one of the aims. But a cooperative society must aim at providing employment to members and also some tangible services, e.g. in matters of education and medical treatment. Only in this way can a cooperative society win the hearts of the poor people and ensure its survival despite losses in commercial ventures, which may sometimes be unavoidable." (1983:42).

LESSONS: Deedar is a good example of a comprehensive community development institution that has grown out of self-help savings and income-earning activities. It shows the importance of careful selection of economic activities with a guiding concern for self-reliance. The order in which activities were adopted was based on an awareness of the existing power structure. Furthermore, they were selected not only for profitability but also for "community contribution" and employment generation. Last, and certainly not least, activities were selected in which there was at least some prospect of breaking even.

BOLIVIA: Ayni Ruway Exchange Networks

This program, focused in the Department of Cochabamba, was formally started in 1974 among Quechua-speaking people in the Bolivian Andes. It sought to gain more benefits for rural households than they could get by selling their produce in excess of family needs and buying the goods they could not produce themselves in the monetized commercial sector. The commodities traded through the emergent network of local organizations are both agricultural and nonagricultural but the institutional structure can be classified under the rubric of "nonagricultural enterprise" since the agricultural goods are leaving the household enterprise where they were produced.

Ayni Ruway (which means "collective work" in Quechua) sought to link communities together through an institutionalized network of productive exchanges using the traditional barter mechanism. In practice this involves linking communities in diverse ecological zones through a chain of carefully located storage-exchange centers. These are called *pirwas* or *ayni wasis* (houses for everyone) and are managed by local leaders called *kamachis*. Each community offers a specific product such as wheat or wool that can be traded for other locally produced items such as soap, candles, or noodles. The latter items are produced by recently organized cottage industries. In this way villagers can acquire things they need without having to engage in monetized exchange through traders and shopkeepers who have been found to be very exploitative. Ayni Ruway has also organized handicraft producers to sell their wares to nearby urban consumers and now to enter the export market in Western Europe.

The network covers more than eighty highland communities, and administrative responsibility for overall coordination rests with an "external team" comprised of five rural schoolteachers, a psychologist, and an economist. They are the persons who launched the program to improve the standard of living—and the status—of the Indian population with which they identified. They wanted to break the grip that merchants and other *mestizo* outsiders had on these communities. Once the effort was begun, assistance came from the Inter-American Foundation. The most tangible form of aid has been some pick-up trucks acquired to transport appropriate quantities of goods to the various locations.

The operations are managed by twelve *jatun kamachis* (locality leaders) and sixty kamachis. The majority of these are women in their teens and twenties who are not formally elected but who demonstrate the most talent and commitment to this kind of self-help effort and who are agreed upon by consensus. The external team spends about three-fourths of its time working with these leaders and their communities with the rest spent in Cochabamba handling financial and administrative details. Although decision making is generally informal, it occurs only after a great deal of consultation among the staff and with people in the communities. No central executive makes unilateral decisions.

The day-to-day tasks carried out by the kamachis include: administration of the storage-exchange centers, bookkeeping, establishing exchange values between and among commodities, communication with other communities, and recruitment and orientation of new members. These rather substantial responsibilities provide opportunities for the kamachis to take on other women as "apprentices" for on-the-job training in administration and other more technical tasks (Healy, 1980).

As part of the founders' and members' concern with the integrity and preservation of Indian culture, Ayni Ruway sponsors over fifteen theater groups, organized by the kamachi, which perform dramas in Quechua on a regular basis. These serve both to increase awareness of the project and to revitalize Quechua culture. The Ministry of Education has signed an agreement with Ayni Ruway to work through the theater groups to provide nonformal education to the communities (Breslin, 1982).

Over six years the network expanded its base of support in the highlands and gradually began selling some of its members' produce outside the network to acquire cash for them. The external team with its multidisciplinary skills has provided some guidance and protection in these endeavors. Both barter and theater contributed to supportive exchange relationships that enhanced productivity and cultural pride. Ayni Ruway also appears to have been able to foster cooperation with the local administration.

LESSONS: This project successfully built on indigenous traditions and values, recognizing that barter was a long-standing and accepted "nonorganizational" institution in the Andes. The potential of barter for meeting local needs was severely limited however by the lack of accompanying organization to make it more versatile and productive. The feeling within Indian communities that they got "cheated" whenever they engaged in monetized exchange with others was an inhibition to their expanding production of food and other goods.

Rather than attempt to introduce "cooperatives," a conventional organizational form previously tried and discredited in the area, a new organization with traditional form was created. It has minimal formalization. There are no formal officers and no full-time management staff at the center. Yet it has become "institutionalized" according to our definition, to the extent its roles and practices have acquired intrinsic value in the eyes of community members. The economic value the incipient institution provides to members is greatly added to by the social and cultural values it promotes on behalf of the population, giving them satisfaction in their own identity. The handicrafts it promotes are not simply a means to earn income but also an expression of Quechua creativity and tradition.

BRAZIL: Northeast Union of Assistance to Small Businesses (UNO)

UNO (União Nordestina de Ajuda as Pequenas Organizações) was set up in Recife in 1972 by a U.S. private voluntary organization, ACCION International/AITEC. UNO received additional support from the business community in Recife, from other foreign donors, and from the Brazilian public sector. After six years of providing credit, UNO began to receive funding from the World Bank and from the Brazilian public sector to expand the number of loans it granted in Recife and to set up programs in the "interior" (Hunt, 1984; Tendler, 1983a).

AITEC had two objectives in setting up this program for providing credit to small businesses not having access to banks. First, by encouraging labor-intensive technologies, AITEC hoped to increase employment, production, and income among the poor. Second, AITEC hoped to establish a Brazilian PVO that would be able to stand on its own.

From the start UNO concentrated on bringing its microenterprise clients to existing banks for credit. The UNO methodology, which evolved over the early years of its operation in Recife, involves first screening and training clients (mainly in bank procedures) and then forwarding their loan applications to participating banks. In turn, the banks "double-check creditworthiness, process the proposal, and issue a loan agreement" (Jackelen, 1982).

When UNO expanded into the "interior" after 1979, as a part of its participation in the World Bank-Government of Brazil integrated rural development project (POLONORDESTE), its program adjusted to the needs of "monoproducers." The original Recife methodology was modified to include cooperative or association formation, appropriate technology, and training—with credit remaining as the backbone of the program.

UNO's institutional development, including autonomy from local elites, was furthered by its informal alliance with a broad mix of local, national, and international supporters. Initially UNO was backed by the local federation of industry and commerce, a well-established and influential institution at district and regional levels. In addition UNO gained the support of nationally important persons. Together these eased the way for obtaining backing from three local banks. Although UNO had extensive local support from the private sector in its first four years (banks, primarily), private financial support never exceeded 30 percent. Public sector funding represented 30 percent of the UNO budget during this period, while foreign donations started at 60 percent in the first year and varied from 40 to 47 percent in the next three years.

Eventually the private sector lost interest in UNO — in part because private backers felt their responsibility was fulfilled once public or international funding had been obtained. In addition UNO cut loose from AITEC three years after its founding, finding that being tied to a U.S. PVO was becoming a liability for operating as a local organization. However, UNO was able to continue operating as a result of its participation in the POLONORDESTE project in 1979. In fact, this insulated it from the federal small-and-medium-business administration (CEBRAE) and assured UNO's autonomy in pursuing and adapting its microenterprise assistance methodology.

LESSONS: Although UNO is weak as a "model program" in terms of its unit lending costs and staff productivity, the program's survival through a period of national economic austerity, and its stubborn ability to continue lending small amounts to worse-off firms is no small accomplishment, especially given the natural tendency of the better-off small firms to exert pressure for obtaining the highly subsidized loans.

UNO's development of institutional ability appears to be attributable in part to the "premature" withdrawal of AITEC funding and technical assistance; its being limited to one task rather than many; slow expansion in terms of budget and types of activities; and an institutional network that protected it from political interference.

This case shows the importance of establishing links with institutions that can provide the technical, financial, and especially political support necessary when a new organization is being set up. What is remarkable is that this arrangement allowed for survival in spite of operating costs and procedures considered by observers as less than "exemplary." With its program known and supported by Recife's elites as well as UNO's former staff and clients, UNO's solid institutional position offered it the opportunity to expand its lending and to modify its credit techniques later.

BURKINA FASO: Partnership for Productivity

Partnership for Productivity (PfP) began working in two locations in the Eastern Region of Burkina Faso (previously Upper Volta) in 1977. With a grant from USAID, it planned to promote rural enterprises generating employment and income—particularly those with potential for becoming self-sustaining, perennial enterprises. Credit, technical assistance, lectures and seminars were to be the core of the project (Goldmark et al., 1982).

Initially, PfP employed fairly traditional techniques for providing credit-cum-management training, with courses being offered in elementary bookkeeping, inventory control, and completion of monthly balance sheets and profit-and-loss statements. Although special management and accounting techniques were developed for illiterate managers (including pictographs and colored boxes), use of these techniques by credit recipients was discovered to be directed more at satisfying PfP staff than at practical management. Some of this became clear because PfP was working with and through an affiliate, PfP/Upper Volta, which had only Voltaic staff.

The procedures recommended by PfP evolved as the initial techniques' limitations became evident. The program's newer approach was to replace the courses with general business planning and working capital management. The first was approached on a task assignment basis. Prospective clients were asked to develop a budget, survey a market, or identify a source of supply as a requirement for obtaining a loan. Their performance allowed PfP staff to gauge both the commitment and competence of potential borrowers. Qualifications are assessed on an individual basis, with enterprise managers physically separating working capital from profits.

Credit is extended only in small amounts, with timing and repayment suited to the individual enterprise. Subsequent loans are contingent upon repayment and successful performance. By providing credit in a manner tailored to local economic and cultural circumstances, PfP is making credit available in a region that has virtually no banking infrastructure. At the same time it has modified its techniques, PfP has established regional branches in two new locations and has plans for opening other branches (A. Brown, 1984).

In addition to delivering credit and training to individuals, PfP's program reflects concern with the community as a whole. For the local economy, this "systems approach to human and economic development" means assisting "the entire range of productive activity necessary for an economy to grow . . . . Clients are encouraged to analyze the needs and opportunities in the local economy and to propose enterprises that will fill them" (Lassen et al., 1985:9-10).

The fundamental guideline is to concentrate support on enterprises that provide new goods and services or reduce the prices of ones already present. The growth of a supported enterprise is to be to the benefit of— not at the expense of—the local community. One relevant technique that focuses on developing business networks is to urge new enterprise managers to visit former ones as part of a feasibility study, a process that encourages the development of mutual technical assistance. Project "graduates" have been quite willing to help new enterprises get started.

LESSONS: This program is an example of culturally sensitive credit and business training in a setting that is only now becoming monetized. Some initial mistakes were made in formulating the program because outsiders did not understand that "borrowing" was regarded with disapproval in this culture (as previously in England—remember Shakespeare's advice, "neither a borrower nor a lender be"). Also, failure in business was seen as reflecting one's fate rather than one's management decisions and skills. The program had to learn and take such cultural conceptions into account.

The program offers a good example of learning process by modifying its practices such as developing a system of "character-based" collateral and a system of credit approval that was itself educational for the applicant. By making access to advice easier for clients and adopting flexible repayment practices, the program was able to fit into the existing socio-cultural matrix. Establishing local branch offices also brought the program physically closer to intended beneficiaries.

Finally PfP's focus on creating local economic linkages and of filling gaps in the local economy has been important for nonorganizational LID. Unfortunately some of these approaches have come into conflict with conventional concepts of project evaluation, which has prompted PfP along with other PVOs to reconsider what are appropriate norms for NAE evaluation by donor agencies. Unless the criteria used are attuned to reinforcing LID concerns, innovative programs (specifically, donor funding for them) will be diminished.

CHILE: Women Artisans in Santiago

The Centro de Desarrollo Comunitario (CEDECO), a private nonprofit foundation, was originally founded in 1968 to provide educational and technical assistance to then-flourishing local community development groups, largely encouraged and legitimized by the Frei government of the 1960s. Until 1975 CEDECO offered leadership training as well as courses in manual arts in local mothers' centers (Centros de Madres, or CEMAs). However, when the Pinochet government no longer permitted CEDECO to give instruction in the CEMAs, this deprived CEDECO of access to its previous constituency as well as to an important means for earning income even though CEDECO was allowed to continue providing training in its own building.

In 1976 the Inter-American Foundation (IAF) reached a grant agreement with CEDECO "to train community leaders and provide technical assistance to the remnants of community organizations formed in the sixties" (Dulansey, 1980). The income-generation portion of the multipurpose project included organizing women in small groups to produce hand-knitted wool garments. The goal was to train community leaders while setting up self-sufficient and self-managed artisan production.

COMARCHI (Cooperativa Multiactiva de Mujeres Artesanas de Chile, Ltda.), a pre-cooperative, was founded as a result. It brought together forty production groups (talleres) of eight to twelve members who are usually neighbors. Communication between COMARCHI and the talleres is achieved both formally and informally. Formally group representatives meet at the headquarters twice a month for courses on such things as participation, organization, or principles of cooperativism, and they then communicate with talleres members at meetings held at least monthly. Informally skill training and quality control take place both in the talleres and at the COMARCHI center when finished garments are turned in.

The income-generating aspect of the multipurpose project was for awhile blocked by the legal status of the two groups. Because CEDECO was nonprofit, and COMARCHI was still a pre-cooperative (not yet a legal enti-ty), neither could engage in marketing. So a marketing agency, SOARTEL, had to be co-founded as a *sociedad colectiva* by representatives from both or-ganizations. Marketing was further inhibited by the legal requirement that women's husbands join any sociedad colectiva as founding members. Ac-cordingly SOARTEL was established with twenty women and their husbands (forty in total) and five representatives from CEDECO.

An integral part of the strategy was to create and co-manage this com-mercial agency so that ultimate "control and management of the garment industry would be vested in a cooperative, self-managed enterprise estab-lished by the women." Initially SOARTEL was not located in the same building as CEDECO. This made transferring the management of finances, marketing, and personnel to COMARCHI (located in a separate building) more difficult. Fortunately the situation improved when COMARCHI and SOARTEL were moved under the same roof (Dulansey, 1980).

LESSONS: The case shows the importance of forging formal and infor-mal linkages among funding agencies (IAF), local intermediary institutions (CEDECO), and NAEs (COMARCHI and its talleres). Each had its speciali-ty: (1) IAF in providing assistance when needed and in reinforcing a "collegial and collaborative" posture; (2) CEDECO in conceiving the idea, developing the proposal, securing the funding, organizing the women, pro-viding training, technical assistance, and administrative support, and gradually handing over management responsibility to the artisans; and (3) not least, COMARCHI in providing a structure that sustained communica-tion and allowed women the flexibility to earn money while accomplishing other tasks.

The case also shows how local groups can employ apprenticeship and informal communication as a training and information strategy. Furthermore, it shows how in spite of bureaucratic barriers there are ways to support income-generating activities locally by improvising new forms of organization.

INDIA: *Self-Employed Women's Association*

In 1972 the Self-Employed Women's Association (SEWA) was legally registered as a trade union of self-employed women with the support of the nationally recognized Textile Labor Association of Ahmedabad (TLA), which was originally organized with the help of Mahatma Gandhi. Falling into three primary groups—small-scale sellers, home-based producers, and laborers—the "invisible" women who were brought into SEWA found themselves "outside the reach of labor laws and (lacking) protection in terms of wages, health insurance, retirement, pensions, and numerous social secu-rity benefits. . . . [in contrast to] workers in the organized sector who, through unions, had pressured the government to provide protection in these areas" (Sebstad, 1982).

Early organizing involved hundreds of meetings in working class neighborhoods throughout Ahmedabad in order to establish "trade groups" whose leaders provided the link between SEWA and the workers throughout the city. Initial organizing centered around three major problems the workers faced: lack of capital, harassment by police and municipal authorities, and poverty-induced family problems.

Using strategies that (1) increased the women's visibility as workers, (2) raised women's incomes, and (3) increased women's control over income and property, SEWA has developed from an organization into a widely recognized local intermediary institution. It is credited with lobbying for the self-employed women, bringing groups of women together and linking them to outside organizations, organizing cooperatives, establishing a women's cooperative bank, and other accomplishments. Most unusual, however, is the mix of two types of joint action: labor unions and cooperatives. SEWA first forms trade unions among traditionally unorganized women workers and subsequently helps them set up cooperatives. For example:

> Women *chindi* (waste cloth used to make patchwork quilts) sewers who previously worked on a piece-rate basis for merchants have formed a cooperative production unit. Supplies of raw materials, credit for sewing machines, and markets are provided through the cooperative. Vegetable sellers have organized a marketing cooperative and take orders for vegetables from government-run hospitals, jails, and hostels. The cooperative members previously worked as street vendors (Sebstad, 1982:61).

Similar organizations have been formed with carpenters, junksmiths, wastepickers, bamboo workers, and handblock printers.

SEWA itself is made up of several branches: the Union, the SEWA Bank, the Economic Wing, and the Rural Wing. The union is patterned after trade unions where members are grouped by trade or occupation. Leaders who "emerge" (rather than being elected) from these groupings are supposed to participate in decision making through a system of committees. In reality a fairly "top down" style was inherited from the TLA and decision making usually rests with the president and the general secretary. Each trade group in the union has a low-paid organizer assigned to it. These organizers function as the link between members, the different branches of SEWA, and "outsiders." Through joint action SEWA leaders, organizers, and members have struggled for and obtained such things as fixed wages and secure vending space from employers or local police.

In contrast to the struggles of the union, activities in the other SEWA operations are development-oriented. The first of these was a credit program, which began with SEWA serving as an intermediary for nationalized banks. Initial difficulties led to the establishment of the SEWA Bank, which in the beginning mobilized savings while continuing to function as an intermediary for the nationalized banks for two years. Later, and until 1976, SEWA disbursed money that the banks deposited in a savings account of the SEWA Bank. After 1976 SEWA began to lend out its own funds, partly because of difficulties with repayments to the banks and partly because it now had sufficient resources to do so.

The Economic Wing was established in 1978 and works on technical skill training, forming production units, obtaining raw materials, and improving marketing skills. The Rural Wing's activities began in 1975 and center around organizing agricultural laborers, although they also include nonfarm employment activities for off-season months. In 1981 SEWA was ousted from the Women's Wing of the TLA. The reasons are complicated, but it appeared (at the time of Sebstad's evaluation) that SEWA would continue to function effectively on behalf of the women with whom it works.

LESSONS: The SEWA case is remarkable because it explicitly addresses the economic and social needs of a very marginal group: self-employed poor women. Initially concentrating on organizing its members to struggle against injustices of the "institutional environment" in which they operate, the group expanded later to "development activities."

In spite of the wide range of SEWA's undertakings, the organization's survival after a split from its sponsoring organization speaks well of its status as a local institution. SEWA seems to belie recommendations for specialization in areas of comparative advantage, although closer inspection indicates that expansion has depended on capacity to recognize problems and adjust as new activities are taken on. Specialization occurs within special sections of SEWA.

It is also worth noting that SEWA has a large latent membership. Formal membership fluctuates as economic conditions change. This indicates that it serves a function in women's economic lives, but that active participation is not always necessary or possible. As long as SEWA can survive in this manner, it is clearly more an "institution" than an "organization."

KENYA: Mraru Women's Group

The Mraru Women's Group began in 1970 like most of the groups affiliated with *Maendeleo ya Wanawake* (the national women's organization). Initial discussions in the meetings called to set it up centered on crafts and homemaking. Eventually however, because reaching the market center twelve kilometers away from Mraru was difficult, the fifty group members decided to save money to purchase a bus. Their decision reflected the particular problems with transportation in their locality: (1) the existing bus was often full when it got to Mraru, and (2) men rode instead of women if space was limited (Kneerim, 1980).

The women formed a savings society in August 1971. They met once a month and each member contributed what she could—in cash or in kind. By 1973 they had saved enough to place an order for a bus. At this point enthusiasm grew and the pace of saving increased. *Harambees* (public fund raisings) were held, a local government social service worker helped the group obtain a loan, and a special last-minute fund-raising event amassed the money needed for a complete down payment. The bus was delivered in 1975 and bus service was initiated immediately.

After one and one-half years, the group declared half of its savings (from earnings on the bus service) as a dividend and decided to invest the remaining money in a new enterprise—a *duka* (retail shop). This was chosen because the land and building would be a solid asset, unlike the bus, whose value deteriorated with time. Within six months the duka was constructed with space for the shop plus three small rooms. A loan helped the group acquire stock and open its small enterprise, which does a steady, though not necessarily large, business. The group plans "to expand the building to include quarters for employees of the bus service and the shop, an office, a meeting room that could double as a classroom, a kitchen, an indoor toilet, and five bedrooms that would serve as a small hotel" (Kneerim, 1980).

Subsequent activities of the Mraru Women's Group have included goat raising and personal improvement (including classes in sewing and family health). The goat raising is a riskier investment than earlier ones but it is a traditional activity for women in the area. The sewing classes are possible because the government donated two sewing machines and sewing materials. Many of the class members' products are sold in the duka next door.

LESSONS: The Mraru Women's Group represents the process of transforming a group enterprise into a local institution. By focusing on local demand, the bus service opened possibilities for expanding the range of goods and services available locally. The initial focus on profitable activities allowed the scope of the women's activities to reach beyond financial to social undertakings.

PHILIPPINES: Micro-Industries Development Center

The Micro-Industries Development Center (MIDC) was formed as an umbrella organization in 1980 by a number of public and private associations providing support to microenterprises in the slum areas of Manila. The different participating organizations recognized they each had different resources and experiences to offer small firms as they grew and required different kinds of support over time. MIDC hoped to achieve greater efficiency and impact in the microenterprise sector by coordinating previously scattered resources and experiences.

Operating as a nonprofit, nonstock company, MIDC has no paid staff. One member of its board of trustees (made up of seven individuals from the public and private sectors) serves voluntarily as managing director while office space and administrative support are contributed by the participating agencies. MIDC views itself not as an implementing agency but as a broker or facilitator with two broad tasks: (1) to assure "that people and programs interact to maximize their learning and the quality of their project design and implementation," and (2) "broker" suitable matches between funders and programs, e.g., between international donors and public and private agencies in the Philippines, between the Philippine business and social service communities, between formal sector financial institutions and microentrepreneurs, or between small or medium-sized businesses and microenterprises (Bear and Tiller, 1982:113).

As of 1982 the MIDC had held a workshop for program staff and microenterpreneurs "to explore the constraints to microenterprise development," supported a training course "to prepare community leaders to become business management extension agents," arranged a credit line between two participating organizations so that one of them could charge commercial rates of interest, and brokered funds from Appropriate Technology International to assist one organization "in raising its credit ceiling for clients with expansion and employment potential."

LESSONS: While its short period of existence precludes any conclusion about the success of its "brokerage" approach or its "institutionalization," MIDC's structure for channeling cooperation among organizations (sharing areas of comparative advantage) provides a working model for how a local intermediary institution might operate without necessarily becoming a local funding agency. MIDC's priorities (leadership development, design and testing of program expansion mechanisms, technical assistance, and influencing government policies) represent areas to which few local institutions have sufficient staff resources to devote much of their energies. The umbrella format provides economies of scale that make these long-range priorities a possibility (Hunt, 1984).

Experiences in Local Institutional Development

BOLIVIA: Center for Social and Economic Development (DESEC)

The Center for Social and Economic Development (DESEC) began on a regional basis in 1963. Its founder has been a driving force behind this private service organization. Initially DESEC worked closely with Catholic parish churches and associated groups. But the emphasis given to economic activities and insistence on remaining clear of partisan politics led to a break with the church. For two years after this, DESEC continued its efforts holding meetings in rural schoolhouses and peasants' homes to encourage neighbors to consider forming a local association.

Two types of organizations were formed: community groups termed "centers," and functional activity groups called "committees." A center is a membership organization composed of peasants who live in the same village or community. They work to resolve common problems collectively and elect representatives who participate in a regional federation, which in turn has a representative in the national-level federation, Acción Rural Agrícola de Desarrollo Organizado (ARADO).

Members who are interested in a particular activity such as milk, potato, or rice production join specialized committees that focus on improving production, marketing and so forth. These committees are organized into centers, cooperatives, and producers' associations. They have also established a chain of local stores and an outlet in Cochabamba for the sale of items produced by ten artisan committees. An indication of the linkages within this network of organizations is the fact that fifty-two committees participate in DESEC's adult literacy program.

Under the DESEC umbrella are four service organizations (Asociaciones de Servicios Artesanals Rurales) which have professionally trained staff (many of whom are from the region) to provide technical assistance to the peasant-based committees and center organizations. These organizations work with DESEC-sponsored activities but also have the autonomy to work with other programs involving housing, health, education, and agriculture.

It is the intention of each service organization (ASAR) to become self-supporting. In the meantime support from the German-based foundation MISEREOR has been crucial. In addition DESEC has worked to find funding from other international agencies for specific projects and its members have themselves taken on consulting work to help maintain their financial viability (Morss et al., 1975:G2–G13).

LESSONS: DESEC has involved many thousands of people in efforts to work collectively in improving their own lives. Its understanding of the need for a network of local institutions operating at several levels has helped to increase the incomes and confidence of rural households. Often beginning in the Promotion mode, DESEC has shown itself capable of recognizing when and how to "pull back" as a local organization's capacities emerge. In practice DESEC is engaged in an amalgam of assistance, facilitation and promotion modes (Section 7.1.1) as it seeks to create a stronger and wider network of local institutions throughout highland Bolivia. By allowing individuals at the village level to choose to join a center and/or a committee (or neither organization), involvement has been based on a genuine desire to participate.

GUATEMALA: The Penny Foundation

The Penny Foundation (Fundación del Centavo) is a private voluntary organization that began in 1963 by soliciting contributions from prominent citizens for use as a source of credit for marginal farmers. Since 1970 it has had some funding from USAID to expand its operations. Unlike other programs, the Foundation has insisted that all services, e.g. credit, fertilizer, and land purchases, be arranged through producers groups, some with as few as twenty members. The principle of group responsibility has guided the whole effort with some good but uneven results.

Sometimes the Foundation works in a facilitation role, encouraging the formation of groups, and in other instances it gives assistance to groups that have emerged without Foundation involvement such as from the government's Rural Development Agency programs. Operating concurrently in both the assistance and facilitation modes is unusual and appears to be effective.

The Foundation's efforts to stimulate and support local organizations may be more valuable than the limited financial resources it can make available (Rusch et al., 1976). This is because the program's focus is on provision of group credit, and without repayment it cannot continue. By emphasizing group responsibility and self-reliance, the record of repayment has been better than in more conventional government programs.

To some extent, the Penny Foundation has been operating as an alternative to the government program of cooperatives in Guatemala. It does not require the organizations it supports to become very formal. The government program has certain criteria for graduating organizations from "pre-cooperative" to "cooperative" status. Many of the Penny Foundation groups never qualify for the transition. This has been seen by some evaluators as a deficiency in the program, but formalization should not be equated with institutionalization. To the extent that people's needs are being met through these organizations, they will become and remain institutions even if not legally constituted.

The Foundation does not try to ensure that all of the base-level groups survive. It tries to limit its support in the form of loans and technical assistance to no more than four years though exceptions are made. "About one-third of the groups do not request further assistance; some groups become recognized as cooperatives; others find alternative funding sources; and some disband. The Fundación does not have the resources to encourage dependency and thus allows the dissolution of weak local organizations" (Peterson, 1982a:133).

Since the Foundation works in various locations in the country, its program varies in certain respects. In some regions, for example, it is able to collaborate closely with the Ministry of Agriculture on extension activities. In other areas, credit allocated for land purchases is not available. What does not vary, however, is the focus on producer groups with shared responsibility for loan repayments and self-reliance through social learning (Gow et al., 1979:127-139). This resembles the SFDP approach in Nepal presented in Annex Five.

LESSONS: One of the most interesting aspects of this experience is the "nonpaternalistic" approach. On the surface it appears not to support LID because the Foundation accepts, even expects, the disappearance of some, even many, of its affiliated groups. On the other hand, by stressing its own limited financial resources and by setting limits on the credit a group can get from the Foundation, it discourages the kind of expectations that could build up a relation of "dependency."

There is little possessiveness toward the groups it supports. If they get absorbed into the regular cooperative system, good; if they find other sources of support, fine; if they can become fully self-sufficient, so much the better; if they disappear, that is unfortunate but that is their responsibility. This attitude may seem like indifference, but it is the kind of detachment that may in some situations be necessary to encourage independence. (The approach is similar to that reported in the Malawi self-help water supply scheme in Annex Three.) It is more likely to elicit acceptance of local responsibility than an attitude which is more protective and anxious about groups' survival.

It is interesting that many of the groups that declined to enter the formal cooperative system and formal federations nevertheless have moved to create their own "informal federations akin to cooperatives" (Rusch et al. 1976:78). This suggests that autonomous rural organizations find benefit in having horizontal and vertical linkages. That these are not formal-legal structures is not necessarily detrimental. The question for outside agencies is how to work with structures that rural people find intelligible and useful.

INDIA: *Kottar Social Service Society*

This supra-local service organization in the Kanyakumari District of Tamil Nadu State is an exceptionally interesting example for its support of multi-sectoral LID. KSSS is affiliated with the Catholic Church in the Diocese of Kottar, though its work is carried out on a nonsectarian basis. Through the use of P.L. 480 (Title II) food aid, together with human and other material resources, a wide variety of emerging local institutions have been fostered.

The district has a population of 1.3 million people within 645 square miles. Despite the high density there is only one major town in the district (so this makes it somewhat like a locality despite the large size). While KSSS is able to draw on the institutional infrastructure associated with ninety church parishes and 120 priests, the actual managerial cadre works out of two offices with a staff of less than twenty persons, three of whom are long-term residents of European origin.

The largest KSSS undertaking is the Community Health Development Project (CHDP), which began in 1972. Initially mobile teams traveled from village to village visiting each once a fortnight with highly original, practical, and interesting nutrition education lessons for mothers. As an incentive for the mothers to bring their children to the programs, P.L. 480 food and basic health care were provided after the lessons given in health and nutrition and after weighing the children each time.

Over five years, more than 550 young women were recruited and trained so that by July 1978 all mobile teams were converted into stationary teams working in village health cooperatives established under the CHDP. These gradually evolved, local organizations could provide more sustained attention to health problems and could cover all members of the participating families. By 1980 the program covered more than 38,000 preschool children in 124 villages.

In order to participate in the program, each village had to make a request to the KSSS to be included, had to provide space for the clinic, and had to permit some of its young women to be trained to function as part of the delivery system. Each family joining the cooperative is charged less than $3 a year for a broad range of health and nutrition services. This has allowed the CHDP to become self-supporting in its recurrent costs.

KSSS has undertaken to build local institutions for more than health care. Among the poorest individuals in the district are local coastal fishermen. Most had to pay a large share of their catch as rent for the catamarans they borrowed for going out to sea. Most were also in debt to moneylenders, who were commonly the same persons who bought their catch at a low price.

In an effort to alter these circumstances, KSSS helped organize *sangams* (cooperatives) of young fishermen. Collective sales of fish by the sangams helped to raise the price they received. Setting aside in the bank a portion of their proceeds from each catch helped buy less fortunate members out of debt and also led to each member having some personal savings. In addition several sangams with KSSS support took out loans to purchase mechanized fiberglass boats, which enabled them to fish farther away from shore. Unfortunately the boats became targets for sabotage and vandalism. The fishermen took to using smaller boats without motors but continued to rely on fiberglass (instead of wood) to have lighter, more durable crafts. Despite threats by fish merchants to withhold financial contributions to the church in retaliation for KSSS support of the sangams, support was not curtailed.

As a spinoff of this activity, KSSS organized net-making centers in thirteen coastal villages. With food aid serving as an enabling resource, over a thousand young women produce nets with newly introduced cotton and nylon materials. The higher quality nets are a boon to fishermen and the women earn needed income.

Another major effort involved organizing almost 10,000 small farmers (60 percent of whom had less than one-quarter of an acre) to improve irrigation. They constructed forty kilometers of channels serving 1,600 acres. A large cooperative for potters was established so that they could have both a larger demand and better price for their wares than when selling individually. Other activities included organization for community water supply and for road and bridge repair using food aid. Of the twelve community development organizers employed by KSSS, half work in the sangam movement and half in agriculture and community health (Field, 1980; Field et al, 1981; and personal communication).

LESSONS: Certain features of the Kottar experience may not be replicable (e.g. staff working in the same region over four decades), but something can be learned about modes of operation for LID. Getting this network of local institutions launched has not required large numbers of people but rather a small core of very dedicated and culturally sophisticated workers. Rather than seek outside advice from short-term consultants, the staff in the field have improvised and experimented. The KSSS community organizers are experienced and committed, with a small number effectively working among a huge population. Their effectiveness is seen in their ability to recruit and train local people to take responsibility for administering village projects such as CHDP.

Outside financial and material resources have been solicited but only when they can be used to create or further develop capacities for collective advancement. Resources are never used as a substitute for local commitment, as seen by the CHDP's charging fees to cover all recurrent costs, requiring compulsory savings of sangam members, and insisting on attendance and quality work in infrastructure projects. This "disciplined" approach was found to be an important feature of membership organizations in the analysis by Esman and Uphoff (1984:155-158).

KSSS has appeared to be guided by the "hiding hand" which Hirschman (1967) wrote about. It has engaged in action without a preconceived plan and even without full appreciation of the problems it would confront. But once engaged, it has been able to summon problem-solving capabilities it did not know it had, drawing on the talents of its organizers and the communities in addition to those of the core staff.

INDONESIA: Aceh Community-Based Institutional Development

In 1979 Save the Children Federation (SCF) undertook a $2 million program in the Special Territory of Aceh, following a flexible approach stressing beneficiary participation in decision making and local institutional development. The Tangse sub-district had little previous experience with outside development agencies. There was a strong tradition of community cooperation among the predominantly smallholder farmers though there was also a tradition of centralized, relatively authoritarian village leadership.

SCF began in eight villages seeking to foster collective action capabilities rather than emphasizing any particular issue. It believed that whatever local organization emerged would be able to choose successful project activities. Community Development Committees (CDCs) were organized at the locality level. However these were dominated by more well-to-do members of the communities who did not think less educated members were competent to plan activities.

To involve a broader spectrum of the population, Village-Level Community Development Committees (VCDCs) were formed around groups working on projects such as coffee grinding, orange tree planting, and hat making. (Note that these organizations correspond respectively to the *community* and *group* levels of activity.) VCDCs gradually assumed greater operational authority and the role of the elite-dominated CDCs changed from decision maker to that of coordinator and guide. Thus, the traditional leadership was not excluded but a significant number of previously by-passed individuals were now included in responsible initiating roles.

In the initial stages, gaining broad local participation was stressed over project quality or cost-effectiveness. Rather than attempting to get villages to concentrate on one or two activities, a diverse range of projects emerged with the expectation that a certain number of them would not be successful. Nonetheless, there was an incentive for VCDCs to be effective in what they undertook since performance on previous projects was a major criterion for continuing SCF funding.

Investments by SCF were small and diverse with the CDC playing an important role in screening projects. Activities encompassed all three modes of agency intervention. Undertakings such as chicken raising involved assistance where the activity was one in which many individuals were already engaged on a small scale. A coffee grinding project was facilitated by the provision of new equipment. Family planning activities, especially at the outset, tended to be promotional in nature.

Training activities were used for much more than imparting knowledge. Practical skills to increase the capabilities of the poor were given strong emphasis. Training was also designed to spread the project's underlying philosophy through discussion of participatory approaches to management. Further, training was used to develop linkages with local government and local administration by inviting middle-level government employees to attend. Their number was kept small enough that they did not dominate the workshops.

Strong efforts were made to spread project-related information. Written correspondence, for example, was widely distributed as evidenced by the number of ccs marked on letters and memoranda. More important, information about all expenditures, income receipts, and accounts was routinely published, posted, and made available to everyone.

"A major result of this openness was the willingness of the community to isolate and even remove corrupt leaders. The availability of information made clear what was not clear before — that the community was being victimized by some of its leaders and representatives" (VanSant and Weisel, 1979:18). Whereas previously the majority accepted what their social superiors did, in this case an accountant, one village chief, and several committee members were removed for malpractice.

When it appeared that existing local institutions were suitable, i.e., benefits were not monopolized by local elites, SCF worked with these institutions rather than organize new ones. One such women's group emerged as the most promising in terms of effectively managing a broad range of projects including health and nutrition and cottage industry.

LESSONS: Providing skills and information as well as opportunities to participate in decision making produced significant benefits. "That there has been a significant effect on the attitudes and behavior of the poor is widely acknowledged by both participants in and observers of the CBIRD (Community-Based Integrated Rural Development) process in Aceh" (Van Sant and Weisel, 1979:19).

The initial approach, which was basically one of facilitation, worked quite well as a variety of specific community-supported activities were spun off as local organizational capacity grew. The early problem of elite domination was overcome in an evolutionary manner as lower-level organizational capacity was developed around activities of interest to poorer members of the communities.

The approach to government employees facilitated vertical linkages to the various departments that could help the community-based groups. The strategy of supporting a wide variety of groups and activities with the assumption that some would be winnowed out as unviable is similar to that of the Penny Foundation in Guatemala discussed previously. The remaining groups and activities were strengthened by horizontal linkages among the VCDCs themselves and vertical linkages to the CDCs.

JAPAN: Yachiho Village Institutions

The experience of Yachiho provides a good understanding of what is possible with a strategy we call "assisted self-reliance." Yachiho is a village of just over 5,000 population in central Japan. That it is less densely settled than average reflects its somewhat lesser resource endowment. Sharma's study (1984) has documented a remarkable case of LID, which we include though Japan obviously is not a less-developed country.

Beginning in 1959, with stimulation from a doctor posted in the subdistrict hospital some miles away, a program was launched that evolved into a comprehensive health care system with support from the sub-district hospital. This included school health and was largely managed by voluntary workers. A council of public health supervises all activities. It is made up of three representatives of villagers at-large, three representatives of village organizations (two from the village assembly and one from the agricultural cooperative), and three doctors (one local and two from the sub-district hospital). This structure formalizes horizontal and vertical linkages.

There are thirteen voluntary health instructors nominated from the different hamlets (neighborhoods) within the village. They are trained for simple treatment and preventive care and maintain health records on all persons in each hamlet. They monitor health conditions generally and for individual patients and provide feedback to the local health unit. Individuals are appointed for four years and given a modest stipend.

In addition each hamlet elects one or more health officers, depending on the size of its population, to maintain close liaison with the health instructor and carry out activities regarding public health and environmental sanitation with the help of hamlet residents. Each officer receives a stipend as a "conveyance allowance." Medical personnel maintain close contact with the health officers and instructors. Health standards are higher in Yachiho than most neighboring communities though expenditure per person on health services is only about two-thirds as much as elsewhere.

With the emergence of this health system, the village assembly, provided for in tradition and law, became more active. It is now engaged constantly in solving problems of the community and adopting programs for development. Its executive board and committees manage a wide range of activities from revenue collection to social services.

"The village assembly has sufficient functional and financial autonomy within the national and prefectural system to manage its functions at the local level almost independently. For this it receives grants-in-aid from the national and prefectural governments to the extent of about 55 percent of its annual expenditure; the remaining amount is mobilized through taxes, village bonds, interest from loans, economic development projects, etc." (Sharma, 1984:79).

The budget is now nearly 2 billion yen a year. One-quarter goes for public education and another quarter for support of agriculture, forestry, fishing, and industry. (This is an exception to the observation in Chapter Five that local governments are seldom extensively engaged in supporting agriculture.) Only about 13 percent goes to administration. Public services include water supply, sanitation, fire protection, a trunk dialing telephone system, and a well-maintained road network with automatic signals.

"With a view to involving the maximum number of people in community functions, it has developed an elaborate system by establishing twenty-nine committees in which as many as 300 persons, which include non-assembly members, participate on a regular basis. This has helped the village assembly in carrying out its functions efficiently through voluntary action," according to Sharma. The older ("veteran") members of the assembly who played significant roles in organizing the community after 1959 are grooming younger members to continue the tradition of self-government.

Through the community's own efforts, two nursery schools, a primary and middle school have been built and equipped with modern facilities, despite financial constraints. "A number of cultural events and extracurricular activities are organized through active support of the community, including the Parent-Teachers' Association." The village has constructed a community hall for various social and educational functions, and since 1968 has organized a regular free education program open to the whole community under the name of Yachiho Summer College (Sharma, 1984:53).

There is also an active agricultural cooperative society, which "has been instrumental in bringing to an end the long history of subordination of farmers to other occupational interests. It has been able to develop a democratic force among farmers with strong bargaining capability." (Sharma, 1984:78). The main productive activity centers on rice, which the co-op assists through inputs and marketing services, but it also "has separate branches to look after the interests of different farmers who engage in floriculture, vegetable farming, dairying, and other subsidiary activities. It helps promote savings and loans for starting other activities and embarks on its own projects like the establishment of cold storage, provision of large-scale farming machinery, etc. which cater to the collective needs." (Sharma, 1984:81).

A good example of the community's capacity to identify and act on collective interests is the recent decision of the village, which is in a location with the potential for development of tourism, to *lease* its buildable land to the residents of a particular town who wanted to construct summer resorts in the village. "As an easy alternative the assembly could have sold the land to a large company to develop the area and received an income from it. But then the village would have lost ownership and permanent interest in the land, and income would have accrued to the company. Therefore, the present decision shows the prudence and foresightedness of the village community growing out of a social capacity for development." (Sharma, 1984:55).

LESSONS: Sharma analyzes this case in terms of the significance of "social capability," which he traces in part to historical and cultural influences. At the same time the "catalytic" role of the doctor from Saku and the remarkably strong and civic-minded village leadership deserve credit for working out a variety of organizations and structural arrangements that are mutually supportive.

The local institutional system that has evolved over a twenty-year period is remarkably effective, combining volunteer and professional roles at the local level, involving a wide cross-section of the community—old and young—in responsible positions. Social and productive activities have been mutually reinforcing rather than competitive with the village assembly balancing the various needs and interests. Government agencies have worked cooperatively and supportively with local institutions, but the relationship has been more beneficial to the extent that these local institutions have had a substantial degree of autonomy, legally and financially.

The major problem for the community, as for many others in Japan, is out-migration and potential dissolution. This "threat" is being dealt with through active efforts to develop inns, hotels, etc. to attract tourists and generate income for the community. Only about 106 households depend solely on agriculture now (compared to 838 about twenty-five years ago). A wide variety of subsidiary agricultural (nonrice) plus nonagricultural activities have changed the economic structure of the village. A number of the village youth who have gone away for higher education have returned and the village assembly has a keen interest in developing local culture and opportunities, bringing young persons actively into the management of village affairs so that the community will survive and prosper.

KENYA: Kenya Tea Development Authority

KTDA has come to be recognized as a rather successful national institution, bringing smallholder tea production from zero before 1960 to one-third of Kenya's exports within fifteen years. Many lessons can be learned from it as a case of institutional development at the national level (Lamb and Mueller, 1982). However, lower level institutions are critical to this national success.

The basic forums for farmer participation are the Divisional Tea Committees, made up of elected farmer representatives who oversee production and buying in their area. Farmer committees have been formed at locality level in many locations but these are not uniform in their activity. The Divisional Committees elect representatives to District Tea Committees, which are probably the best functioning of the organizations partly because they make crucial decisions about allocating tea quotas and all producers have a stake in their operation.

The District Committees in turn send representatives to the Provincial Tea Boards. About one-third of the national KTDA Board is made up of farmer representatives. Farmers are also represented in increasing numbers on the boards that oversee the operation of tea factories through farmers' purchase of equity shares in the factories. Presently farmers hold about 10 percent of factory shares in what has become a means of mobilizing savings for capital formation in the agricultural sector.

From the outset, the KTDA leadership sought to provide for active farmer participation. Since smallholder tea growing was to be fitted into the existing farming systems not to replace them, KTDA recognized the need to have institutions that could work with peasant households as very complex units (Lamb and Mueller, 1982:2–3). KTDA was willing to invest some of its financial resources to encourage participation, for example, by organizing farmer visits to Nairobi and by paying "sitting allowances" to farmer representatives for time they spent on KTDA business. It was recognized that close linkage between KTDA and growers was crucial for maintaining quality control. Accordingly the structure of farmers' committees was made one of the four operational divisions of the Authority. (The others were extension, buying and quality control, and factory production.)

Most of the initiative for this structure came from "above." Indeed, Steeves (1975:10) has characterized the organization initially as "autocratic."

But over time, grower initiative has increased with KTDA approval. The technical sophistication of farmers has also increased. One "breakthrough" for expanding tea growing with quality control was to introduce vegetative propagation in place of earlier nursery techniques. Farmers learned this technique rather quickly and before long were able to do it better than many KTDA staff. In 1980 about half the demand for new tea bushes was met from growers' own stock. (This has placed some strains on the policy of limiting individual holdings to one acre maximum.)

Interestingly the KTDA staff have continued to champion the acreage ceiling on egalitarian grounds despite political pressure from somewhat larger growers (Steeves, 1984). One consideration is that smaller holdings are generally more intensively cared for and more carefully plucked, keeping quality of the final product high.

The incentive system worked out is ingenious. Once a month growers are paid a fixed rate (per kilogram) for the greenleaf delivered to buying points operated by the factory they sell to. At the end of each season, when the processed tea has been sold at the London auction where most KTDA tea fetches a premium price, the growers get a "bonus," which usually amounts to about 150 percent of the "base" income. The better the quality of the tea leaf delivered to the factory, as well as the better the processing there, the more the factory's tea sells for and the higher is the bonus growers receive.

LESSONS: One important element of KTDA institutional strategy has been its considerable decentralization to the factories and to the provincial, district, and divisional levels. The fact that the tea price is rather precisely pegged to some independent measure of "quality" gives all within the system—growers, buyers, transporters, factory workers, and managers— good measures of success and makes decentralized management more feasible. Everyone gets clear feedback on the quality of their collective performance, which is reinforced by material incentives.

For many years it was said that tea was too demanding a crop for "peasants" to grow, and all investment and technical assistance was reserved for the tea plantations in Kenya. The performance of KTDA has shown that a system of organization with farmer participation from the field to the factory and beyond that to the national level can achieve superior quality and efficiency compared to the more administratively managed plantation operations.

NIGERIA: Tiv Farmers' Association

In the early 1950s Tiv tribal leadership in the southern part of what is now Benue-Plateau State designed a rotating credit and savings system based on a traditional method of saving yams to make larger amounts of credit available to farm families. The groups worked through elected leaders, had a strict policy of loan repayment, and were "reorganized" on an annual basis. The last element was designed to avoid the impression that a permanent membership commitment was required.

After over a decade of impressive performance by these organizations (called *bams*), a local agricultural extension officer who was well acquainted with the region suggested to the senior tribal leadership that a farmers' association be developed to work closely with the extension service (LA). Initially a "senior council" was organized with sixty representatives from various Tiv areas. Following the growth of the association to some 1,000 members by 1968, it was decided to organize at the village level, drawing on the experience gained by the bams. Benefitting from strong traditional social structure and low stratification among the Tiv, village branches were established. Both agricultural extension officers and Farmers' Association leaders assisted in this effort to organize "permanent" membership associations.

Although considerable informal communication facilitated the process of organizing credit branches, the initiative for forming organizations usually came from the extension officer who would meet with the village chief and farmers to discuss the details of the Farmers' Association, including the system of representation at district and division levels. Once operating, village associations met on a monthly basis with the extension worker in the area. In addition, the extension officer made subsequent visits usually three or four times per year. Within six years the Tiv Farmers' Association had more than 33,000 members and a yearly operating budget from dues of $65,000. The average on-farm income over a decade showed a 72 percent increase (Morss et al., 1976:F32-F41).

LESSONS: This case offers an impressive example of using traditional structures of authority and locally tested principles of organization, albeit with some modification, to initiate a new form of organization. By being sensitive to what already existed and without any donor funding, local administration was able to make extension efforts aimed at encouraging innovation more effective. Even though LA provided much of the impetus for getting activities started, farmer control over decision making was not lost. Despite the fact that adult functional literacy was only around 10 percent, the program does not appear to have been adversely affected by lack of "educated" leadership.

PERU: Comas Women's Academy

This is one of the most impressive cases of grassroots development reported by Hirschman (1984) based on the program's rapid devolution of responsibility to local women. This devolution came about because of the unfolding of activities that served to make the incipient institution more grounded in local needs, and because of the development of horizontal linkages with other women's organizations, which led to an informal federation having supportive vertical linkages to promote members' interests.

Comas is a large squatter settlement outside Lima with the usual lack of social facilities. The Catholic Church provides much of the rather limited civic core to this amorphous community. A group of women wishing to raise their families' incomes by making clothes got together and wanted instruction in sewing and working with patterns. They came into contact with a private service organization in Lima, the Centro de Estudios Sociales y Publicaciones, which was assisting educational projects in slum areas with some financial support from Dutch and German agencies.

The Centro, according to Hirschman,

> provided the requested assistance for clothesmaking, but quite soon other topics of instruction were developed in collaboration with the Comas women: classes on literacy, the history of Peru, female health and sexuality and so on—until a whole curriculum took shape. After two years of instruction by personnel supplied by the Centro, some topics of instruction were taken over by the Comas women who had graduated from the course and felt they could handle the materials themselves. Today the administration of the Academy and most of the teaching is handled by these women. Gradually the women have developed contacts with other women's groups in Comas and a Comas-wide women's group which discusses feminist issues has been started (1984:17).

One problem the program encountered was hostility from husbands, many of whom did not like their wives being away from home one evening a week during the academic year (April to December). "The Academy has attempted to assuage the husbands by drawing them into the activities—organizing, for example, fiestas and common educational events." (1984:19). The community women have now begun to work on getting improvements in the water supply for the municipality through petitions and demonstrations.

LESSONS: An important change occurred in outside support from the Centro, from what we have called assistance in the first stage, to facilitation helping the "Academy" develop, and back to assistance as the Academy's capacity for initiating new activities grew. This is a good example of how an intermediary organization can work. The fact that the staff of the Centro took the women seriously helped them to take themselves seriously and to move from a very limited objective and capacity to an expanding and more effective institutional base. Nonmembers (men) have also been carried along by the energy channeled through the Academy.

SOUTH KOREA: Saemaul Undong Movement

Saemaul Undong (SU), meaning New Community Movement, was initiated by President Park in the early 1970s, reflecting his interest both in a strong agricultural base and rural political support. It was overseen by the Office of the President with a special secretary in charge and with consultative councils at each governmental tier representing the various ministries involved in supporting SU.

The structure was conceived and operated in a top-down manner, but it was matched by a vast spread of community organizations whose leaders (chosen by the members) were invested with authority to bargain for resources from the government to complement those of their communities. These leaders operated both as agents of the state and as partisans on behalf of local interests. They were usually not the village headmen who occupied quasi-hereditary roles. The informal competition between elected SU leaders and village headmen who were often older and less dynamic was one of the elements energizing Saemaul (Goldsmith, 1981).

Among the most impressive aspects of this national program is the degree to which formerly listless local bureaucracies (LA) have been "reoriented" into agencies working more seriously on rural development issues, frequently working closely with farmers for the first time (Yoon, 1985:151). Bureaucrats and technicians who used to resort to coercive measures find they cannot rely on these any more. Pressure from above to show results means that balking communities can make officials look bad in superiors' eyes. Local leaders can also make complaints against government staff at their regular public meetings with higher officials (Aqua, 1981).

Pressure for performance also falls on Saemaul leaders, who can less easily blame "the government" for problems when it is actively trying to support community improvement. Also, there are tangible rewards for their communities and themselves from active effort.

The figures on infrastructure built or improved are almost staggering. By 1979 for example, 43,000 kilometers of village roads had been built and an equal length of farm feeder roads, 73,000 bridges, 37,000 water supply systems, and almost 11,000 irrigation systems (Lee, 1981:318–322). A great variety of income-producing activities on a group or community basis have been instigated—mushroom growing, machine repair, etc. The sense of urgency that pervaded the movement from the start caused communities undertaking projects such as bridge construction or manufacturing enterprises to learn quickly what they needed to know through "hands-on" experimentation.

The way in which government support was channeled is also instructive. After two years of giving 35,000 villages the same level of material assistance (in the form of cement and steel reinforcing rods for construction), villages were classified into three categories: most responsive (self-standing), typical (self-helping), and least responsive (basic). The greatest assistance per village was given to the middle category, with enough to the first and third to provide some encouragement. The message to the latter category was to become more self-helping.

In 1973 about one-third of the villages were in the "basic" category, but before long this number was negligible and two-thirds had "graduated" into the top (self-standing) category, needing only assistance according to our classification of support modes. Villages accepted reclassification partly because of pride and partly because there were still benefits to be received from the program (Lee, 1981:151–153).

According to Yoon (1985:152), the period from 1975 to 1978 was "the most flourishing period" for Saemaul, and popular participation in decision making and resource mobilization was at its peak. After 1978 this has waned because the bureaucracy has taken back much control over planning and because "Saemaul had already changed the lives of those living in South Korea's 35,000 villages."

> More communities had advanced to the level of "self-sufficiency" with targets met in all indicators of success—hectares planted in new varieties of rice, length of piped water supply, paved roads, numbers of tiled roofs (to replace thatched), latrines, and public buildings. More than half of the country had electricity and village telephones and most villagers owned radios . . . .By the 1980s, almost one-third of small-farm incomes were from non-farm sources such as sericulture, viticulture, handicrafts, cattle and small-manufactured goods produced in "Saemaul factories" (Yoon, 1985:152-153).

LESSONS: Some very impressive changes in the economic and social status of villages could be achieved by government investment through a well-conceived, evolving program with strong support from the highest echelons. Communities responded with major contributions of materials, labor, and management skills. The ability to plan and carry out infrastructure produced the most visible results, but the many thousands of agricultural and nonagricultural enterprises established under SU auspices have also made a significant contribution to rural well-being. The cost to government of getting these enterprises started has been a small part of the total expenditure.

A great deal of "bureaucratic reorientation" was accomplished in a relatively short period of time with clear political signals from above and with organized pressure from below. Although the program began with a "blueprint" conception (one might say a "blueprint" mentality), it moved fairly quickly into a learning process mode as the first efforts were too uniform and mismatched to village needs and capabilities. Where the public sector and communities lacked certain technical skills, responsibilities were given to private firms, bringing in that "channel" for LID. The movement showed what a multichannel, multitier undertaking could achieve by encouraging a great deal of initiative and responsibility from rural communities and groups. When the policy environment in South Korea shifted somewhat after 1978 with less government investment channeled to rural areas and less emphasis on preserving or promoting income equality, the vitality of Saemaul declined.

THAILAND: Khorat Rural Development Program

While Thailand has registered some satisfactory economic growth overall, there has been dissatisfaction in some quarters with persisting income disparities, maldistribution of basic social services, and social blights such as pollution, drug abuse, increasing crime rate, and degradation of culture and morale, even in rural communities. The governor of Khorat province decided to promote more broad-based development within his area of responsibility and established a system of organization that reaches down to the village and group levels. It has been impressive enough in the changes it has introduced into rural areas that the National Economic and Social Development Board has taken it as an example for the country's rural development program.

The process was begun by "reorienting" government officers first at the province level then working down through the *amphoe* (district) to the *tambon* (locality) level. Officers were expected to stop acting as "donors" giving benefits to a passive, receiving community. They were to learn how to work with rural people in a participatory mode and also how to work with each other on an inter-ministerial, collaborative basis. Various meetings, conferences, and seminars were held at the provincial level at the governor's instigation until provincial officers were ready to serve as "A" Trainers. They then undertook to reorient their district-level staff who in turn became "B" Trainers.

These district officials in turn worked with tambon field staff, mostly from the departments of community development, agriculture, health, and education. These four officials were constituted as a working group for supporting community development at the tambon level. This WCT, as it was called, was responsible for about ten villages. Each WCT was to begin by working in a single "pilot" village and gradually to expand activities to other communities within the tambon, all the time working with the Tambon Council, which was the main existing unit for local government.

Each village participated through a Village Council made up of the village headman and some elected members. Village Councils had usually been moribund and needed resuscitation by the WCTs. This was done initially by working with the Council to prepare a village development plan. This was conceived so as to mobilize local resources for remedial action so that work did not depend wholly or even mostly on funds coming from above. The WCT introduced a "problem-solving approach" which classified problems as solvable (a) by the people themselves, (b) by the people with government assistance, or (c) only by the government. Proposals dealing with (b) and (c) were forwarded to the Tambon Council while local efforts were focused on problems in category (a).

Within each village, clusters of ten to fifteen households were formed to take stock of their development problems, needs, and capabilities. These small groups surveyed annually the extent to which "basic minimum needs" (BMN) were not being met on an individual or collective basis within their cluster. The data gathered were reported to the Village Council as a basis for its planning, and village information was passed, in turn, up to local, district, and provincial levels for their planning processes. While this data gathering was not perfect, it has improved year to year and has provided a persistent stimulus for development action at all levels.

LESSONS: "Bureaucratic reorientation" (as discussed in Section 7.5.4) can be initiated from above by a combination of education, incentives, and personal appeals. While BRO is needed for getting officials to help build up local institutional capacities, improvements in LID can themselves promote BRO by putting pressure on the bureaucracy from below for more responsive and effective performance. Once there were more active and informed institutions at lower levels in Khorat, officials became more enthusiastic and energetic—partly because they now had better channels to work with and through, partly because they were made more aware of the problems and deficiencies at community and household levels, but also because they developed closer personal links with villagers, which motivated them to make further improvements.

The administrative capacity of the Thai government had stopped practically at the tambon level where seldom more than four ministries would be represented by regular personnel. The Tambon Councils that existed had potential for accomplishing more development work if enlisted in constructive ways (Annex Eight), but they were seldom effective. To establish a far-reaching capacity for rural development, the Tambon Councils had to be strengthened, and below them Village Councils were activated.

Undergirding these were the cluster organizations, which were set up on an informal basis. This created capacity for planning, implementation, monitoring, and evaluation all the way down to the group level and it gave a more solid foundation to the whole system, putting pressure on higher levels for better performance. Planning from below became more feasible once monitoring and evaluation were possible at the group level.

Information is used as an instrument not only for planning but also for getting change in officials' orientation and behavior. When they know the extent and location of poverty, it is easier to get them to tackle these deficiencies. Such information also affects villagers' attitudes and activities. The "basic minimum needs" approach focused attention on problems and unmet needs. For example, a "shortfall" is reported if more than half the babies born in a cluster weigh less than 3000 grams at birth. (Public health nurses already had simple scales for weighing newborns, but there had not been much interest in using them previously—there is now much interest.) This indicator of basic minimum needs directs the attention of all the households in a cluster to the nutritional status of pregnant mothers among them. It subtly encourages them to contribute to better maternal nutrition since the group as a whole is reported to have fallen below the minimum acceptable standard if newborns in their group are undernourished.

Fifty-two "measures" of BMN have been worked out with communities' involvement over four years' time. These are culturally well understood and accepted, being legitimated with reference to the Buddha's teaching about the Four Necessities of Life. About 80 percent of the "needs" monitored can be mitigated if not fully met by local efforts. So the system promotes self-reliant efforts. It also directs the attention and investments of government staff toward improving the situation of the worst-off households and communities within their areas of responsibility.

KRDP strategy and techniques were evolved in a learning process mode. Instead of launching the effort on a provincewide basis, it started with one pilot village in each tambon. The BRO at provincial level itself started slowly and took about two years. The "basic minimum needs" criteria and the forms and methods for reporting them were developed experimentally with participation of both villagers and lower-level officials. Information was used very skillfully to mobilize resources and change expectations about what is possible and desirable in rural areas. The multitiered structure of organization created problem-solving capacity where little existed before. (From unpublished reports and conversations with the former governor of Khorat province, Suwai Prammanee; the National Economic and Social Development Board's director for rural development, Pairoj Suchinda; and UNDP advisor, Richard Sandler.)

Resource Mobilization and Management

BANGLADESH: The Grameen Bank

The Grameen Rural Bank project was started by a university-based economist in 1976. After a promising organizational methodology was developed by trial and error during a three-year experimental period the project was expanded, and by 1984 it had disbursed loans to 70,000 landless men and women. The repayment rate is close to 100 percent, much higher than achieved in previous rural credit programs. It represents substantial resource mobilization and management on the part of the rural poor by working through a simple institutional arrangement.

In a manner similar to other examples of small-group collective action to be found in the literature such as the Dominican Republic case, which follows, and the Small Farmer Development Program in Nepal (Annex Five), prospective borrowers must form a group to apply for loans. The Grameen Bank deals only with groups of five borrowers. Since landless families, who represent approximately 50 percent of the population, do not have physical collateral, one or two of the members will be allowed to borrow some $30 to $50 from the Bank with the other members assuming joint responsibility for repayment.

In order for the nonborrowing members of the group to become eligible for loans, the first borrowers must faithfully repay. No restrictions are placed on what the loans may be used for, so long as the activity is legal and provides a weekly income. The latter requirement is adhered to so that borrowers can make weekly payments into a mandatory savings fund and can repay the loan in small installments. The borrowing groups serve to provide both confidence and structure. Nonpayment by one member will affect the others. If one member becomes ill or unable to handle his finances, the others have reason to pull together and cover his or her payments.

Having started with small groups, the project encourages five to ten groups in an area to federate into "centers" of twenty-five to fifty members. These are now established in most of the villages where the project operates. The group chairmen elect a center chairman who screens and approves loan requests from the groups. The centers can encourage joint ventures of groups and can tackle social issues like ending dowries and child marriage, reducing ceremonial expenditures (e.g. for weddings, which burden the poor with debt), improving diet and sanitation, and encouraging family planning. They also sponsor self-help activities for schooling, drinking water, and latrines.

The Grameen approach began without any financial support from the government. Once the government accepted this approach, it was operated through the nationalized banks which employed the Grameen village workers as regular staff, but now it has been incorporated with its own bank. Outside assistance has come from the Ford Foundation and the International Fund for Agricultural Development. There was some initial resistance on the part of the nationalized banks, which were not at ease with this outreach approach. Similarly wealthier farmers resisted the prospect that their cheap labor would increasingly move into Grameen-supported projects. There is some evidence that wage rates have gone up in areas of Grameen Bank activity, and average borrower incomes have been increased by 50 to 75 percent (IFAD, 1984a:3).

Many of the day-to-day problems are handled by dedicated young bank workers responsible for making loans and collecting payments. These workers play both a motivating and service role being a special kind of "catalyst" (Section 7.3.2). Since nearly 50 percent of the borrowers are women, women bank workers handle their accounts to minimize the social distance (Ford Foundation, 1983). The program has expanded rapidly with external funding and with little loss of effectiveness, according to an evaluation of the International Fund for Agricultural Development (1984a). It used the funds planned for four years productively within three years and reached a loan volume of $1 million a month by 1984 (doubling the rate every year). Savings by members, some of the poorest of the poor, have also been doubling each year with some studies showing a marginal savings rate of 50 percent among beneficiaries.

LESSONS: This effort began slowly and faced skepticism in many quarters, but by relying on group capacities buttressed by certain requirements from above, the project has achieved an impressive record, especially in regard to the social changes associated with the involvement of women; e.g., dowryless marriages are increasing, and men are accepting changes in the sexual division of labor (IFAD, 1984a:45–46).

The entrepreneurial spirit and creativity of landless individuals has been demonstrated thanks in large part to the work of young, energetic employees who go out to the service areas as "bankers on bikes" to gain a close understanding of people's needs and capabilities and to keep a reliable flow of information moving in several directions. The recent IFAD evaluation noted the "exceptional human qualities" of the field staff and their people-oriented approach. It also documented how this experience benefited from a "learning process" approach as described in Section 7.1.2.

CAMEROON: Credit Union League

The rotating credit associations known as *njangi* in Cameroon have a long tradition in this part of Africa that may have its genesis in cooperative land-clearing groups. The monetized njangi have been documented from the 1930s though their savings and loan function probably goes back to an earlier date.

In 1963 two Roman Catholic priests undertook to establish more formal credit unions. With assistance from the Department of Cooperatives, independent primary credit unions formed the Cameroon Credit Union League which was given official recognition by the government. Financial assistance received from a variety of agencies facilitated training, equipment purchases, and supervision. A strong desire among people to participate in savings and loan activities coupled with a common knowledge of the procedures and operations allowed the League to expand rather quickly.

The njangi and the primary credit unions follow almost identical operating procedures. The credit unions, however, are more advantageous for those who need or want to borrow money since the interest rate they charge is substantially lower. Since the Credit Union League has external auditors, savings and loans do not have to be returned annually, a practice that the traditional groups must normally follow to retain their legitimacy.

Credit unions have not attempted to eliminate traditional group savings and loan mechanisms. In fact, they often thrive side by side with linkages beginning to appear. "In one location a group has become a 'member' of a credit union, and regularly deposits its savings there in a single account. Elsewhere all the members of a group have joined a credit union" (DeLancey 1977:321).

An interesting and important part of the expansion involved using existing organizations including church congregations, police detachments, agricultural cooperatives, and large firms. By drawing on all the capacities of these organizations and devising a check-off system whereby savings could be automatically deducted from wages, the credit unions were able to increase their efficiency. Between 1965 and 1979 membership rose from 4,000 to 26,000 with savings rising from 16 to 400 million CFA francs over the same period. The success of the expansion effort is reported to be in large part a result of relevant services of government and the Credit Union League's "ability to foresee problems and experiment with solutions" (DeLancey 1977:317).

LESSONS: The credit unions have wisely chosen to adopt practices that are familiar to local residents. Rather than trying to eliminate the traditional groups they have allowed households to decide for themselves which institutional form best meets their needs for social and economic purposes. Outside funding has been put to use in a way that results in a positive-sum situation. Loans and savings options are available through more "modern" channels to the same people as before, only now a larger number of households are able to borrow over longer periods of time. Sensible modification of popular existing practices appears to have resulted in successful LID though it should be noted that the Credit Union League has not yet become fully self-supporting in covering all administrative costs.

DOMINICAN REPUBLIC: The Triciclero Association

As in many other urban centers and smaller market towns, there are a large number of individuals who support themselves and their families as *tricicleros* (tricycle drivers), providing cheap and flexible transportation of people and goods in the capital of the Dominican Republic, Santo Domingo. This case is reported for its evidence of resource mobilization and management capacity among some of the poorest of the poor.

Most of the tricicleros did not own their own vehicles and therefore had to pay about 20 percent of their meager average daily earnings as rent. Recognizing that these persons would be greatly helped economically if they could own their own vehicles, the *Fundación para el Desarrollo Dominicano, Acción Internacional* and the Inter-American Foundation worked out a financial plan.

To reduce the level of risk associated with making loans, five to seven drivers were expected to form groups (*grupos solidarios*) which were jointly responsible for everyone's payment. It is likely that many of the members initially saw their involvement in the group as a temporary expedient through which to gain a personal benefit, i.e. ownership of a tricycle. There are now over 200 groups, and many members have indeed been able to acquire individual ownership of their means of production.

However, rather than disband once the vehicles have been purchased and paid for, most groups have acquired a strong sense of solidarity in the process of repaying the loans. Instead of going their separate ways, an Association of Tricicleros was formed which brought together the smaller *grupos solidarios*. This in turn led to new forms of resource mobilization never anticipated when the program began in 1980.

Among the activities organized by the Association is a rudimentary health insurance scheme and a program for covering the funeral expenses of members and their immediate families through regular contributions. It is expected that a tricycle repair shop with tools and spare parts to be used by members will be operating in the near future. Ironically the Association has also worked to deter certain resource mobilization efforts by the local government (i.e. payment of various taxes and fines) when these measures were not considered justified (Hirschman, 1984:13–16).

LESSONS: The organization of small solidarity groups to manage financial matters proved quite effective, based in large part on the very personal nature of the groups. Not making a payment could lead to a loss of valued friendships and more recently to loss of other more tangible benefits such as health insurance. Where members in good standing are genuinely in difficulty, others have been willing to help them out with interest-free loans.

The agencies that helped to get this program started did not attempt to chart the groups' path for them. As new ideas, activities, and capacities emerged, they were encouraged. Though the program originally focused only on economic needs, the members have been able to develop some political influence to make their lives less hard at the hands of municipal authorities by organizing "trike-ins" to protest what they think is unfair treatment by police or other officials.

"In this manner, a financial mechanism originally designated to do no more than protect a lending agency against default by individual borrowers is having powerful and largely unanticipated social, economic and human effects, enhancing group solidarity and stimulating collective action" (Hirschman, 1984:16).

INDIA: Sananeri Tank Irrigators' Organization

Agriculture in the Indian state of Tamil Nadu has depended for many centuries on irrigation water stored and distributed from small reservoirs that dam up rivers and streams or capture surface run-off. These reservoirs, locally referred to as "tanks," are now formally under the control of the Public Works Department (LA) or the Panchayats (LG). But there is a strong historical tradition of autonomous local management, and irrigators' associations (membership organizations) continue to be very active in the operation and maintenance of many tanks, on which they depend for their livelihood.

The level of resource mobilization in such organizations can be quite high. The tank association for Sananeri tank mobilizes about three times more resources per hectare for operating and maintaining its system than the Public Works Department allocates for tank maintenance (Meinzen-Dick, 1984). Farmers' contributions take the form of cash, grain, and labor. While some of the work is done directly, the association also hires and pays "common irrigators" who handle routine operation and maintenance tasks within designated sub-areas of the tank's command area.

The means by which the grain is mobilized for payment of the salaries of the common irrigators is particularly noteworthy. At the end of the season, these employees of the association go to each farmer they serve to collect a certain amount of grain per unit of land. This face-to-face collection provides a mechanism for holding the common irrigators accountable for their performance during the season because farmers not well served can express their dissatisfaction and can even threaten to reduce their contribution. The association president is expected to keep a detailed account of all the monetary income and expenses of the tank association fund.

Farmers' contributions to the association are supplemented from another source for mobilizing cash. The rights to fish in the tank have been auctioned off annually to the highest bidders, with the funds raised from this used for tank management expenses. This occurs in other communities having tanks, including some where the panchayat now handles the auction. Where higher level government bodies have taken over the control and sale of this source of income, it is reported that a well-organized association will send one representative to the official auction to make a low bid, which nobody else (under threat of social sanctions) will raise. The fishing rights are then informally re-auctioned with more competitive bidding, with the association taking the difference to use for tank management (Palanasami and Easter, 1983). Village associations in canal-irrigated areas of Andhra Pradesh State obtain funds from a similar re-auctioning of the license to sell toddy (liquor) in the village (Wade, 1979).

LESSONS: Where an activity is clearly important to rural people, such as access to adequate and reliable water for irrigation, they can be quite innovative and serious in their efforts to sustain resource mobilization and management activities. The strength of social solidarity is an important factor both for mobilizing resources and for protecting revenue sources, as seen from the re-auctioning strategem reported here.

Local organizations, like the Sananeri organization described here or the Chattis Mauja scheme reported next, can operate without official recognition or sanction. They may devise fairly complex structures, including paid employees who handle tasks where technical skill or impartial performance are most needed. In both these Indian and Nepal cases, "accountability" of LO officers and staff is important for keeping membership enthusiasm and support. Persons in these roles must be responsive and efficient to retain their position. Although there are exceptions, government employees rarely perform these responsibilities so satisfactorily.

NEPAL: Chattis Mauja Irrigation Organization

About 80 percent of the irrigation in Nepal is provided through systems designed, built, and operated by farmers at their own initiative with minimal government involvement. Often the construction is carried out by a few wealthy individuals who then recoup their expenses by collecting funds from farmers of the newly irrigated land who then own and operate the system.

The Chattis Mauja system described by Pradhan (1983) is an example of the extent and sophistication, both technically and organizationally, of such irrigator-managed systems. Constructed about 150 years ago, it irrigates over 7,500 acres of land cultivated by farmers in fifty-four villages. It is managed by them through a three-tiered organizational structure with fifty-four village committees at the base, nine area committees, and a central committee. There is even an informal fourth tier of organization in that the Chattis Mauja central committee consults with representatives of three other user-managed systems which also draw water from the Tinau river.

Because the river coming out of the mountains during the monsoon season carries so much silt, large amounts of labor are required to desilt the channels, rebuild the structures, and accomplish other maintenance tasks. There are two categories of regular labor mobilization for which villages must contribute work in proportion to their share of the total irrigated area. Records for 1981 show 3,000 to 4,000 men working during each of seventeen days scheduled to desilt the main canal, a total of 60,520 man-days. The village committees mobilize additional labor for work on the channels within their respective areas. In emergency situations, such as repairing a breach in the canal wall, the rule is that all able-bodied men may be required to work with no consideration of proportionality. Farmers take turns patrolling the canals to prevent water theft, to do minor maintenance jobs, and to alert the committees of need for major repairs.

Another type of resource mobilized is for the materials and tools required to repair the system. Although many structures are made of leaves, sticks, wood, and stone, these are becoming difficult to obtain locally. Thus, these items represent a considerable investment of resources. In order to construct more permanent canal walls and save on labor for maintenance, the central committee raised over 100,000 rupees for cement. Fines are used to ensure that villages and individuals contribute their proper share of resources. Other contributions of cash or grain are collected in proportion to irrigated area to pay the salaries and expenses of committee officials.

The committee members helping to manage these resources at the village level are not paid, but their chairman is. He represents the village on the area committee, and each area committee is in turn represented on the central committee. The president and secretary of the central committee are directly elected by farmer-members at an annual meeting and paid modest salaries. The committee hires two persons as technicians to oversee and supervise the maintenance work throughout the year. "Messengers" are also appointed and paid by the central committee (and given bicycles) to handle communication between it and the village and area committees.

LESSONS: This case demonstrates the extent of technical and organizational capability of rural people for dealing with a function which they regard as critical to their well-being. Although the literacy rate in the area is very low, the committees are able to find enough persons who can read and write to be able to keep adequate records.

The entire operation and maintenance is handled by farmers themselves without government involvement or interference. Several years ago the government tried to intervene in management decisions, and the organization said it would turn all responsibility over to officials if they were going to interfere in its management. The government decided (wisely) to let this well-run system continue under farmer control.

NIGERIA: Kwara State Local Governments

Although Nigeria is one of the developing countries blessed with petroleum supplies and revenue, it cannot finance all of the local development efforts needed to raise the living conditions of its people. It inherited a colonial structure of government which, though a nominal federation, was quite centralized. The structure brought authority down only one level, to the region, as district administration carried out regional and federal policies and programs. In 1967 the Northern Region encompassed almost 40 million people, more than in most nations. At that time, with the threat of civil war breaking out, the government in Lagos divided the country into nineteen states, and powers were then further devolved to district and local (locality) authorities.

A thesis by Atteh (1980) details some of the statistics of what was accomplished by local governments in Kwara State, one of the poorest in Nigeria.

With the inability of government to provide all the social and infrastructural amenities which people yearn for, villagers have taken the initiative of planning and executing development projects in their areas. This became so widespread that government created a Department of Community Development which became part of the Ministry of Local Government and Community Development, to coordinate these activities.

Highlights of data obtained from this Ministry show that in 1978, [of the] 100 approved post-primary schools and colleges in Kwara State, only forty-three . . . were built and are being run by government. The other fifty-seven were built by communities and are run with help from the State Schools Board.

In the 1976-77 financial year, 197 projects worth N2,789,100 were (completed in) all the twelve local government areas by people themselves, while 454 (additional) projects valued at N10,638,306 were registered with the Ministry. To aid these efforts, government gave a paltry sum of N400,000 as grants to all the communities combined (1980:421-422).

Atteh reports that the Ministry's figures show community projects from 1967 to 1977 totalling N20,430,742 in value. Even if this value is somewhat inflated, it represents a huge mobilization of resources for things that rural people judged necessary to improve their productivity and well-being. The value of government-built facilities in Nigeria and elsewhere is often even more inflated.

LESSONS: Although this decentralization effort has often worked quite imperfectly, it has elicited a great outpouring of resources from the local level, including management abilities to carry out the varied development investments. Legislation formally transferring authority to these lower and local levels was necessary, together with some technical back-up. Probably if the technical capacity of the state government staffs had been greater, still more could have been accomplished, certainly to a higher technical standard. The state government contributed only a small fraction of the total resources invested as localities found ways to mobilize relatively huge amounts of money.

THAILAND: Tambon Councils

During the early 1970s, Thailand's Department of Community Development sent community development workers to rural villages where they would stay for several days, encouraging residents to undertake various public works projects. Without benefit of a firm institutional base, few of these projects had any long-term impact.

Fortunately a number of changes subsequently occurred. In 1975 the central government initiated a program of block grants to Tambon Councils (LG), modeled somewhat along the lines of the *subsidi desa* in Indonesia (Annex Four). The program began rather quickly, with each participating council receiving $25,000 for selected kinds of infrastructure projects. With contributions of local labor, roads, irrigation systems, and ponds were constructed.

The projects proved very popular in the villages, but central bureaucrats were not happy with them, pointing to various examples of corruption and inefficiency. They managed to get the program stopped but it was reinstated within a year because of the demand from below.

The new program, renamed the Rural Employment Generation Program, no longer gave standard grants to each Tambon Council but rather granted funds based on the size of population and the extent of rural poverty in a locality. (Tambon Councils operate at the locality not the village level.) Many residents for the first time are able to find employment during the slack season. A most important feature of the new program is that the annual allocations are fairly predictable, allowing the community development staff (LA) to collaborate with the Councils (LG) in working through longer-term community plans.

In some tambons all or part of the funds are reallocated for village-level projects. In other localities local political forces create situations where small "sub-projects" are negotiated to gain support for larger undertakings. Annual decisions are reviewed at higher levels of administration, which also provide technical assistance when necessary for carrying out the project.

In localities where literacy in Thai is low, CD workers play a more active role such as filling out project data sheets. Some projects use small-to-medium sized contractors to provide heavy equipment and skilled operators. This is supplemented by local laborers who usually work for the one to three months it takes to complete a typical project. In keeping with a central government directive, all funds are spent during this period and cannot be carried over. However, each Tambon Council decides what criteria will be followed for local hiring (Calavan, 1984:236–239).

LESSONS: The central government has found it useful to develop local government capacity of the Councils while also bolstering its own position through LA personnel at local levels making for a positive-sum situation in terms of power and capacity. Some oversight by LA was provided without undermining the autonomy and legitimacy of local government.

Where private firms were employed, both local businesses and local governments were strengthened without making the projects extremely capital-intensive as happened in East Pakistan, now Bangladesh (Thomas, 1971). Forward planning was encouraged by making the funding predictable from year to year. The role of the CD workers evolved from pushing physical project completion to assisting local institutions when local skills were deficient.

YEMEN ARAB REPUBLIC: Local Development Associations

What came to constitute the LDA "movement" in North Yemen did not arise from central government initiative. Rather it emerged from various scattered examples of local initiative responding to particular needs and conditions. Many were originally welfare organizations formed in response to local catastrophes, using Islamic notions of community and of alms-giving for the poor as a means of mobilizing public contributions. One of the earliest LDAs, for example, was formed when a fire destroyed much of the shanty-town in Hodeidah. That welfare society not only tried to help those who had been devastated by the fire but went on to organize fire-fighting capabilities, garbage disposal, drainage of areas of standing water, etc. Some associations were also formed to take care of widows and orphans left destitute by the civil war between 1962 and 1969 (Carapico, 1984).

The government began to take an interest in the LDAs in 1973, and their number grew from 28 in that year to 189 six years later. A Confederation of Yemen Development Associations (CYDA) was organized to channel funds from the central government to the member LDAs, which were expected to be mobilizing at least equivalent amounts. According to Islamic law, producers are expected to pay a tax known as *zakat* (approximately 10 percent of earnings), and 75 percent of this was to be assigned to the LDA for the area where the tax was paid. Also, LDAs were to receive the proceeds from a 2 percent tax on all imports (which skyrocketed in value after Yemeni males began working in the Persian Gulf states following world oil price hikes in 1973). Other sources of finance authorized under CYDA regulations are municipality taxes, internal transport taxes, cinema taxes, and rentals of equipment, but most were inapplicable to LDAs in rural areas (Hebert, 1981:13).

Substantial expansion of rural and township infrastructure was made through LDA activity, thousands of kilometers of roads built or improved, hundreds of schools, clinics and water systems constructed. A World Bank study hailed the LDAs as "a rare example of successful local development initiative. Notwithstanding serious constraints, they mobilize substantial local resources, both human and financial; they encourage active participation of the main beneficiaries; and they help develop community spirit and local leadership. The program deserves the full support of the Central Government and of foreign aid donors" (1979:84). A more cautious but nevertheless positive assessment of the LDAs had been made in an earlier report based on four village studies (Green, 1975).

It appears that the rapid expansion of LDAs was not accompanied by substantial "institutionalization" as new roles, procedures, and norms did not become widely understood and accepted within the population. Most LDAs were able to function because they essentially represented the traditional socio-political structure. The LDA head was usually the *shaykh* of the area and other officers and board members were likely to be clan or kindred leaders. The LDAs set up at government instigation formally operated at the district level (above what we consider "local") and this remoteness could be a drawback. In practice LDAs were likely to cover a locality or sometimes just a large community where the leader was based. Participation occurred within the prevailing social norms and a mix of hierarchical and egalitarian relationships which among other things drastically limited women's role in decision making (though even this could be modified in practice, as noted in Section 5.6.2).

In one of the LDAs studied for the Cornell Rural Development Committee, conflict and competition made the organization quite unstable. Charges of corruption and ineffectiveness were frequently made by opposing groups. Such inter-group rivalry, however, was part of the social and political life in the region and carried over into LDA affairs (Swanson and Hebert, 1982:102–104). In spite of turmoil and turnover of leadership, this

LDA constructed over 100 miles of road in difficult terrain and had mobilized almost a million Yemeni rials from its members to nearly match the 1.1 million rials received from the government through CYDA. LDA members more than matched the 52,000 rials received from CYDA for local water projects (Swanson, 1981).

Province-level figures in Hodeidah suggest that the government contributed only about 20 percent and communities about 80 percent of the cost of road, school, water and health projects built by LDAs there (Hebert, 1983:27). This represents substantial local resource mobilization despite various grounds for complaint — decision making was highly personalized; meetings were irregular; projects were often begun without adequate technical assessment and planning; financial management was haphazard and subject to many suspicions. Nevertheless, LDAs demonstrated considerable grassroots capacity for self-help under very difficult physical conditions of desert or mountainous terrain and under social conditions of high illiteracy and traditional status and gender dominance (Hebert, 1983; Carapico, 1984).

LESSONS: Instituting modern forms of organization will not easily supersede traditional social roles and relationships. It is difficult to escape the constraints of a social system as ingrained as that in North Yemen. At the same time, this offers certain capacities which can be built upon. There are substantial human capabilities to be tapped, as seen from the many accomplishments of the LDAs, reflecting also material resources that could be mobilized through appropriate organizational channels.

The level of participation in planning and evaluation was not as great as might have been desired (or as was sometimes claimed for the LDAs). Yet there was a degree of accountability in the LDAs' operation. The shaykhs while very influential were seldom so powerful that they could ignore the needs and wishes of local residents. Moreover, projects undertaken without public support usually stalled for lack of contributions of money and labor. Probably both participation and accountability could have been greater if the organizations had been structured to operate at locality and community levels instead of remaining formally district-level entities.

The government's attempt to take over and control the LDA "movement" through CYDA did little to improve the performance of LDAs. (The President of the Republic was also president of CYDA.) Because of the large cash incomes being earned by Yemenis from employment in the Gulf States, there were large amounts of money available locally, and CYDA's granting procedures, cumbersome and unpredictable, sapped rather than stimulated self-help efforts. More valuable than money to LDAs was technical know-how and heavy equipment, which rural communities did not have.

USAID undertook a project to "test" what levels of capital and/or technical assistance would produce the best LDA results. But the experimental thrust of the project was displaced by an effort to achieve certain planned "output" targets (much as seen with the Botswana range management project reported in Annex Two). Donor agencies seem to find it difficult to invest in "learning" that leads to institutional capacity building. They became easily preoccupied instead (literally) with "concrete" results. The project had the potential to be quite innovative but in the course of implementation it became a conventional project focused mostly on construction targets. Ultimately it contributed very little to rural development in North Yemen, even in "concrete" terms. Having abandoned its original goal of experimenting with LID alternatives, it added nothing to local capacities for resource mobilization and management.

ZIMBABWE: Savings Development Movement

In 1963 a savings club was started by a missionary at a mission near Harare with a membership composed of twenty men and women. This initiative was supported by a small number of voluntary workers who founded the Savings Development Movement (SDM). As a small central organization, SDM has worked in both promotion and assistance modes with Savings Clubs scattered throughout Zimbabwe.

Savings Clubs have been supported in communities that have few material advantages, low financial resources and little chance of obtaining other sources of credit. Men and women who have a common bond such as church membership, residence, or work were encouraged to form groups of ten to twenty people. In time a voluntary Management Committee of at least five persons would be elected. Many Clubs also may have additional "standby" officers to broaden the leadership base and ensure continuity. The recommendation is that groups not exceed thirty members, but the average is now thirty-five, with a range of ten to one hundred (Chimedza, 1985:165).

Individuals who are not charter members and want to join must be recommended as a suitable person by a Club member. At the regular weekly meetings, all members must contribute a minimum amount (usually twenty cents). If a deposit is not made, a fine of one cent for each week missed is levied. Money collected at the weekly meeting is deposited in a traveling bank, post office, etc. as soon as possible after the close of business. In some cases Clubs pay the bus fare of a member because of the distances involved. The Management Committee inspects the Club passbook weekly to ensure that the banking has been done correctly. Three members of the Management Committee must sign one week in advance of any withdrawals. To simplify bookkeeping procedures, special stamps of ten cents value (printed as a donation by local commercial firms) are affixed to members' savings cards. This has helped eliminate errors that were prevalent in the original system.

As the viability of the Clubs has become apparent to members, their activities have expanded. Programs include a subsistence agricultural program package for the rural groups and a housing improvement program in the more urban areas. The Clubs sometimes form a basis for agricultural associations in rural Zimbabwe, reported on in Annex Five.

The central SDM office, made up of only ten volunteers, serves a coordinating role at the national level and has established linkages with agencies such as the Salvation Army, Methodist Church, Adult Literacy Organization of Zimbabwe and fertilizer companies. During the war between 1976 and 1980, almost all of the Savings Clubs activities ceased.

However, by 1981 over 400 Clubs with approximately 16,000 members had "reopened" (Smith and Dock, 1983). By January 1984 the movement had 5,700 Clubs with 200,000 members holding deposits over $2 million. (For a detailed analysis of the history and organization of the movement, see Chimedza, 1985).

LESSONS: The amount of assistance needed to get a national program going can be very small. What the CDM central office lacked in size, it made up for in quality, being blessed with highly committed and creative leadership. No subsidies were given or needed, though external assistance (e.g. donations for the stamp system) was a very helpful contribution. One of the best indicators of institutionalization is the way so many Savings Clubs rebounded after the war.

Although the credibility of the supporting agency was good, and it could have played a more directive role, its actual intervention and control were intentionally minimal. Each Club succeeded or failed by its own efforts. The organizational structure and techniques worked out through a "learning process" approach minimized the possibility of financial misuse and ultimately led to much more than accumulated savings, contributing to infrastructure, agriculture, and nonagricultural enterprises. The movement currently is faced with government pressures to become more formalized and more centralized. Whether it can be as effective in such a mode if forced to work in that way remains to be seen.

Postscript

As this book goes to press, we have received a paper by Jan Breman, prepared for a Social Science Research Council workshop, which reviews the results of "local-level" field research in the Indian state of Gujerat. Its conclusions clarify the importance of dealing with what we have treated here as *local* institutions.

Breman is an experienced Dutch researcher who was dissatisfied with the preoccupation of others with either the national level of decision making and action or the "village" or "locality"—"the small world which contained the mass of the population as well as the boundary of their social horizon." Accordingly he focused on the *district* level and its institutional frameworks, e.g. bureaucratic machinery, political setting, trade and industry, elite clubs, migration, labor market, agrarian policy, education, etc. "These, it was thought, would provide ways to observe changes at the local level in their more specific context." Breman uses precisely our distinctions when he says the district was considered a strategic middle level, describing this as the "supra-local level of analysis."

This perspective differed from "modernization" theory that saw all change as emanating from the national level, but he says

> both notions emphasized the hierarchical insertion of local-level phenomena into larger social settings, pointing to the region as the integrative mechanism in this process of expansion.

In fact, "the results of the investigation did not confirm this premise."

> It was only to an extremely limited degree, for example, that the district center functioned as the locus of power and activities in the region, initiating processes of change and channeling them to lower levels. Further, the usual stereotype of mobilization and accommodation from above, with its suggestion of the base of society as the controlled, essentially passive element in an expanding system, seemed to rest on a misconception. Different partial studies showed the dynamic of forces "from below," as appears not only from the active use of new possibilities at the local level and the entryway to a wider social network but also from the subjection of external institutions to local interests.

Economic, social, and political relationships in practice "are not constructed according to a simple pattern of hierarchic or concentric stratification." His conclusion is that "no institutional condensation arises within a territorially demarcated zone which links the top and the base of society." Rather, relationships are based more on personal and group affiliations which modify a strictly spatial concept of organization. The "region" as a unit of action is empirically ambiguous as being all that is subnational and supralocal.

Breman is rightfully skeptical of "village studies," where "social complexity is reduced to the bottom segment—the lowest link of a chain whose length is not fixed and whose connecting points remain indistinct."

Rather one needs to look at the range of institutions and channels that permit or even enforce certain relationships among people, "to observe social processes, mechanisms and networks over a greater distance." In particular, Breman found class relationships helping to track the linkages (or obstructions) for individual cooperation and collective action. Those levels between the individual and the household on one hand and the district or region on the other provided the arena for self-help and protective maneuver. The village as a geographically bounded unit is one arena, but it in no way encompasses all or even most of the significant capacities for initiative. Group action and also supra-village cooperation represent major avenues for improvement.

Thus, an expanded but rigorous conception of what is "local" is needed, embracing all three levels identified as "local" in Chapter One. Institutions are likewise to be understood as defined in that chapter. In this sourcebook, we have dealt only with "organizational" forms of institutions. Breman's work includes those that elude such classification, in particular labor markets and informal institutions for accumulation and loaning of capital. These have substantial impacts on the lives of rural people in Gujerat as in other localities around the world.

We do not regret having focused exclusively on "organizational" forms of local institutions, as extensive analysis and exposition has been required to cover this subject in a basic way. With any elaboration of our observations and conclusions, this book would have been several times longer. To have included "nonorganizational" local institutions would have made the task unmanageable and the book unreadable. But in closing it is necessary to restate that there is an even more pervasive and elusive domain of local institutional development to be studied—that concerning the informal, culturally based, extra-legal, evolved or psychologically embedded relationships that can inhibit or accelerate people's achievement of material, social, political, cultural, and other satisfactions. Common property, marriage and family institutions, patron-client relationships, ethnic identities, respect for education are different from but no less important than economic enterprises, charities, local branches of political parties, tribal or caste associations, or schools. While we would encourage practitioners and students of development to work on problems of formal local institutional development as addressed in this book, we would also like to see systematic attention given to their less formal counterpart institutions in the future.

Bibliography

Abedin, Md. Zainul
    1979 *Two Case Studies from the Village of Ballovpur under the Comilla Sub-Project of the Small Farmer Development Project.* Bangkok: FAO Regional Office for Asia and the Far East.

Abeyratne, Shyamala
    1982 *The Impact of Second Generation Settlers on Land and Water Resource Use in Gal Oya, Sri Lanka.* Ithaca: Rural Development Committee, Cornell University.

Abha, Sirivongs na Ayutthaya
    1979 *A Comparative Study of Traditional Irrigation Systems in Two Communities of Northern Thailand.* Bangkok: Social Research Institute, Chulalongkorn University.

Acharya, Harihar
    1984 *Management of Forest Resources in Nepal: A Case Study of Madan Pokhara.* M.P.S. thesis, Cornell University.

Adams, Dale W. et al.
    1984 *Undermining Rural Development with Cheap Credit.* Boulder: Westview Press.

Agrawal, Anil and Anita Anand
    1982 "Ask the Women Who Do the Work." *New Scientist,* 96:13–30.

Ahmed, Manzoor
    1980 "BRAC: Building Human Infrastructure to Serve the Rural Poor." In Coombs (1980:362–468).

Ahn, Bong Won
    1978 "Village Forestry in Korea." Paper prepared for the Eighth World Forestry Congress, Jakarta, October 16–28.

AIR
    1973 *Village-Level Disposing Conditions for Development Impact.* Bangkok: Asia/Pacific Office, American Institutes for Research.

Akande, Jadesola O.
    1984 "Participation of Women in Rural Development." In ILO (1984:129–136).

APHA
   1981 *Community Participation in Primary Health Care Projects: An Empirical Review.* Washington: American Public Health Association.
   1982 *Progress and Problems: An Analysis of 52 AID-Assisted Projects in Primary Health Care.* Washington: American Public Health Association.
   1982a *Community Financing of Primary Health Care.* Washington: American Public Health Association.

Aqua, Ronald
   1981 "Role of Government in the Saemaul Management." In Lee (1981:409–424).
   1983 "Local Institutions and Rural Development in Japan." In Uphoff, ed. (1983:328–393).

Ashe, Jeffrey
   1983 *Assisting the Survival Economy: The Microenterprise and Solidarity Group Projects of the Dominican Development Foundation.* Cambridge, Massachusetts: ACCION International/AITEC.
   1985 *The PISCES II Experience: Local Efforts in Micro-Enterprise Development,* Vol. 1. Washington: Office of Rural and Institutional Development, Agency for International Development.

Assaad, Marie and Samiha El Katsha
   1981 "Formal and Informal Health Care in an Egyptian Delta Village." *Contact,* 65. Geneva: Christian Medical Commission.

Atteh, D.
   1980 *Resources and Decisions: Peasant Farmer Agricultural Management and Its Relevance for Rural Development Planning in Kwara State, Nigeria.* Ph.D. thesis. University of London.

Axelrod, Robert
   1984 *The Evolution of Cooperation.* New York: Basic Books.

Ba, Fama Hane et al.
   1984 "The Impact of Territorial Administration Reform on the Situation of Women in Senegal." In ILO (1984:107–116).

Bagadion, Benjamin and Frances F. Korten
   1985 "Developing Irrigator's Associations: A Learning Process Approach." In Cernea (1985:52–90).

Bahl, Roy
   1982 *Urban Government Financial Structure and Management in Developing Countries.* Metropolitan Studies Program, Monograph No. 11. Syracuse: Maxwell School of Citizenship and Public Affairs, Syracuse University.

Barnes, Douglas F.; Julia C. Allen and William Ramsay
   1980 *Social Forestry in Developing Nations.* Washington: Resources for the Future.

Basu, N. G.

    1983 "Community Forestry and the Local Community." Paper for International Symposium on Strategies and Designs for Afforestation, Reforestation and Tree Planting, Wageningen, September 19–23.

Bates, Robert

    1981 *Markets and States in Tropical Africa: The Political Basis of Agricultural Policies.* Berkeley: University of California Press.

Bear, Marshall and Michael Tiller

    1982 "The Micro-Industries Development Center of the Philippines." In Bear et al. (1982:95–167).

Bear, Marshall; H. Jackelen and M. Tiller, eds.

    1982 *Microenterprise Development in the Urban Informal Sector.* Washington: Appropriate Technology International.

Beckman, Bjorn

    1976 *Organizing the Farmers: Cocoa Politics and National Development in Ghana.* Uppsala: Scandinavian Institute of African Studies.

Beenhakker, H. L.; C. Cook and R. Hartwig

    1984 "Institutional Aspects of Rural Roads Projects: A Research Report." Washington: World Bank, Transportation Department, mimeo.

Bendix, Reinhard

    1967 "Tradition and Modernity Reconsidered." *Comparative Studies in Society and History,* 9(3), 292–346.

Bennett, John W.

    1983 "Agricultural Cooperatives in the Development Process: Perspectives from Social Science." *Studies in Comparative International Development,* 18(1–2), 3–68.

Benor, Daniel and James Harrison

    1977 *Agricultural Extension: The Training and Visit System.* Washington: World Bank.

Berger, Peter and Richard John Neuhaus

    1977 *To Empower People: The Role of Mediating Structures in Public Policy.* Washington: American Enterprise Institute.

Berrigan, Frances J.

    1979 *Community Communications: The Role of Community Media in Development.* Paris: UNESCO.

Bhatt, C. P.
    1980 *Ecosystems of the Central Himalayas and Chipko Movement: Determination of Hill People to Save Their Forests.* Gopeshwar, U.P.: Dashauli Gram Swarajya Sangh.

Bhatty, K. M.
    1979 *Social Determinants of Water Management in Daudzai.* Peshawar: Pakistan Academy for Rural Development.

Bigelow, Ross E. and Lisa Chiles
    1980 *Tunisia: CARE Water Projects.* Project Impact Evaluation No. 10. Washington: USAID.

Binswanger, Hans P.
    1983 "Agricultural Growth and Rural Nonfarm Activities." *Finance and Development,* 20(2), 38–40.

Binswanger, Hans P. and Vernon W. Ruttan
    1978 *Induced Innovation: Technology, Institutions and Development.* Baltimore: Johns Hopkins University Press.

Birkelbach, Aubrey
    1973 "The Subak Association," *Indonesia,* 153–169. Ithaca: Southeast Asia Program, Cornell University.

Bjorkman, James Warner
    1979 *Politics of Administrative Alienation in India's Rural Development Programs.* New Delhi: Ajanta Publications.

Blair, Harry W.
    1978 "Rural Development, Class Structure and Bureaucracy in Bangladesh." *World Development* 6(1), 65–82.
    1982 *The Political Economy of Participation in Local Development Programs: Short-Term Impasse and Long-Term Change in South Asia and the United States from the 1950s to the 1970s.* Ithaca: Rural Development Committee, Cornell University.
    1982a "The Elusiveness of Equity: Institutional Approaches to Rural Development in Bangladesh." In Uphoff, ed. (1982a:387–478).
    1985 "Reorienting Development Administration." *Journal of Development Studies,* 21(3), 449–457.

Blomquist, William and Elinor Ostrom
    1986 "Institutional Capacity and the Resolution of a Commons Dilemma." *Policy Studies Review,* forthcoming.

Bloom, Abby
    1984 "Swift Action Saves Rural Health Care Project in Senegal." *Horizons,* 3(4), 14–17.
    1984a *Prospects for Primary Care in Africa: Another Look at the Sine Saloum Rural Health Project in Senegal.* Evaluation Special Study No. 20. Washington: USAID.

Blue, Richard N. and Yashwant N. Junghare

1975 "Political and Social Factors Associated with the Public Allocation of Agricultural Inputs in Northwest India." In *Problems of
Rural Development*, Raymond Dumett and Lawrence Brainard,
eds., 112–130. Leiden: E. J. Brill.

Blustain, Harvey

1982 *Resource Management and Agricultural Development in Jamaica:
Lessons for Participatory Development*. Ithaca: Rural Development
Committee, Cornell University.

1982a "Clientelism and Local Organizations." In Blustain and
LeFranc (1982:192–210).

1983 "Social Issues in Technology Choice: Soil Conservation in Jamaica." *Journal of Soil and Water Conservation*, 37(6), 323–325.

Blustain, Harvey and Elsie La Franc, eds.

1982 *Strategies for Organization of Small Farm Agriculture in Jamaica*.
Ithaca: Rural Development Committee, Cornell University; and
Mona: Institute of Social and Economic Research, University of
the West Indies.

Bossert, Thomas J. and David Parker

1982 *The Politics and Administration of Primary Health Care: A Literature Review and Research Strategy*. Hanover: Department of
Community and Family Medicine, Dartmouth College.

Bower, Blair T. and Maynard M. Hufschmidt

1984 "A Conceptual Framework for Analysis of Water Resources
Management in Asia." *Natural Resources Forum*, 8(4), 343–356.
New York: United Nations.

Bratton, Michael

1980 *The Local Politics of Rural Development: Peasantry and Party-State
in Zambia*. Hanover: University Press of New England.

1983 "Farmer Organizations in the Communal Areas of Zimbabwe:
Preliminary Findings." Unpublished paper, Departments of
Land Management and Political and Administrative Studies,
University of Zimbabwe, Harare.

1986 "Farmer Organization and Food Production in Zimbabwe."
World Development, 14(3), 367–384.

Brechin, Steven and Patrick West

1982 "Social Barriers in Implementing Appropriate Technology: The
Case of Community Forestry in Niger, West Africa." *Humboldt
Journal of Social Relations*, 9(2), 81–94.

Bremer, Jennifer et al.
  1985 *Fragile Lands: Problems, Issues and Approaches for Development of Humid Tropical Lowlands and Steep Slopes in the Latin American Region.* Washington: Development Alternatives, Inc.

Breslin, Patrick
  1982 "The Technology of Self-Respect: Cultural Projects Among the Aymara and Quechua Indians." *Grassroots Development,* 6(1), 33–37.

Brown, Alex K.
  1984 *Meeting the Needs of Voltaic Micro-Entrepreneurs: A Manual for Credit Training, Credit Administration and Management Assistance.* Ougadougou: Partnership for Productivity. Available from Partnership for Productivity, Washington, D.C.

Brown, Chris
  1982 "Locally-Initiated Voluntary Organizations: The Burial Societies in Botswana." *Rural Development Participation Review,* 3(3), 11–15.
  1983 *Local Institutions and Resource Management in the Communal Areas of Kweneng District.* Gabarone: Applied Research Unit, Ministry of Local Government and Lands.

Brown, Chris et al.
  1982 *Rural Local Institutions in Botswana: Four Village Surveys and Analysis for Kgatleng District.* Ithaca: Rural Development Committee, Cornell University.

Bruce, Judith
  1980 *Market Women's Cooperatives: Giving Women Credit.* SEEDS Pamphlet Series. New York: Population Council, Carnegie Corporation and Ford Foundation.

Bruns, Bryan
  1981 "Problems of Growth and Innovation in a Development Conglommerate: The Population and Community Development Association," Unpublished paper, Department of Rural Sociology, Cornell University.

Brush, Stephen
  1983 "Traditional Agricultural Strategies in the Hill Lands of Tropical America." *Culture and Agriculture,* 18, 9–16.

Bryant, Coralie and Louise G. White
  1984 *Managing Rural Development With Small Farmer Participation.* West Hartford, Conn.: Kumarian Press.

Bryant, John
  1969 *Health and the Developing World.* Ithaca: Cornell University Press.

Buchanan, James
   1968 *The Demand and Supply of Public Goods.* Chicago: University of Chicago Press.

Buijs, Dieke
   1982 "The Participation Process: When It Starts." In Galjart and Buijs (1982:50–75).

Caiden, Naomi and Aaron Wildavsky
   1974 *Planning and Budgeting in Poor Countries.* New York: J. W. Wiley.

Calavan, Michael
   1984 "Appropriate Administration: Creating a 'Space' Where Local Initiative and Voluntarism Can Grow." In Gorman (1984:211–249).

Campbell, J. Gabriel
   1979 *Community Involvement in Conservation: Social and Organizational Aspects of the Proposed Resource Conservation and Utilization Project in Nepal.* Kathmandu: USAID.

Caplan, Lionel
   1970 *Land and Social Change in East Nepal.* Berkeley: University of California Press.

Carapico, Sheila
   1984 *The Political Economy of Self-Help: Development Cooperation in the Yemen Arab Republic.* Ph.D. dissertation, State University of New York, Binghamton.

CEDA
   1973 *Comparative Evaluation of Road Construction Techniques in Nepal, I: Data, Results and Conclusions.* Kathmandu: Centre for Economic Development and Administration, Tribhuvan University.

Cernea, Michael
   1979 *Measuring Project Impact: Monitoring and Evaluation in the PIDER Rural Development Project—Mexico.* Staff Working Paper No. 332. Washington: World Bank.
   1980 *Land Tenure Systems and Social Implications of a Forestry Development Program: A Case Study in Azad Kasmir, Pakistan.* Staff Working Paper No. 452. Washington: World Bank.
   1982 "Modernization and Development Potential of Traditional Grassroots Peasant Organizations." In M. O. Attir et al., eds., *Directions of Change: Modernization Theory, Research and Realities,* 121–139. Boulder: Westview Press.
   1982a "Rural Cooperatives in Bank-Assisted Agriculture and Rural Development Projects." Unpublished paper. Washington: World Bank.

1983 *A Social Methodology for Community Participation in Local Invest-
      ments: The Experience of Mexico's PIDER Program.* Staff Working
      Paper No. 598. Washington: World Bank.
1984 "Can Local Participation Help Development? Mexico's
      PIDER Program Shows It Can Improve the Selection and Ex-
      ecution of Local Development Projects." *Finance and Develop-
      ment,* 21(4), 41–44.
1985 *Putting People First: Sociological Variables in Rural Development,*
      editor. New York: Oxford University Press, for the World Bank.

Cernea, Michael; John K. Coulter, and John F. A. Russell
1983 *Agricultural Extension by Training and Visit: The Asian Experience.*
      Washington: World Bank.

Chambers, Robert
1974 *Managing Rural Development: Ideas and Experience from East Afri-
      ca.* Uppsala: Scandinavian Institute of African Studies. Re-
      printed 1986. West Hartford, Conn.: Kumarian Press.
1979 *Health, Agriculture, and Rural Poverty: Why Seasons Matter.*
      Sussex: Institute of Development Studies.
1983 *Rural Development: Putting the Last First.* London: Longman.

Chambers, Robert; Richard Longhurst and Arnold Pacey, eds.
1981 *Seasonal Dimensions of Rural Poverty.* London: Allenheld Osmun.

Charlick, Robert
1984 *Animation Rurale Revisited: Participatory Techniques for Improv-
      ing Agriculture and Social Services in Five Francophone Nations.*
      Ithaca: Rural Development Committee, Cornell University.

Chauhan, Sumi Krishna et al.
1983 *Who Puts Water in the Taps?* London: International Institute for
      Environmental Development.

Chauls, Donald S.
1983 "Volunteers Who Work: The Community Health Care Project in
      Burma." *International Quarterly of Community Health Education,*
      3(3), 249–266.

Chauls, Donald S. and P. R. Rajbhandari
1980 "Nepal's Community Health Leader Project." *Rural Development
      Participation Review,* 2(1), 12–14.

Chen, Marta
1983 *The Working Women's Forum: Organizing for Credit and Change.*
      SEEDS Pamphlet Series. New York: Population Council,
      Carnegie Corporation, and Ford Foundation.

Chetwynd, Eric and Maurice Samaan
1984 "Basic Village Services: Fourth Mid-Project Evaluation."
      Cairo: USAID/Egypt.

Chimedza, Ruvimbo
  1985 "Savings Clubs: The Mobilisation of Rural Finances in Zimbabwe." In Muntemba (1984, I:161–174).

Cholden, Harvey
  1969 "The Development Project as a Natural Experiment: The Comilla, Pakistan Project." *Economic Development and Cultural Change*, 17(4), 483–500.

CIMMYT
  1974 *The Puebla Project: Seven Years of Experiments, 1967–73.* El Bataan, Mexico: CIMMYT.

Cleaves, Peter
  1980 "Implementation Amidst Scarcity and Apathy: Political Power and Policy Design." In *Politics and Policy Implementation in the Third World*, M. Grindle, ed., 281–303. Princeton: Princeton University Press.

Cohen, John M.; Mary Hebert, David B. Lewis, Jon C. Swanson
  1981 "Development from Below: Local Development Associations in the Yemen Arab Republic." *World Development*, 9(11–12), 1039–1061.

Cohen, John M. and Norman Uphoff
  1977 *Rural Development Participation: Concepts and Measures for Project Design, Implementation and Evaluation.* Ithaca: Rural Development Committee, Cornell University.

Colburn, Forrest
  1981 *Guatemala's Rural Health Paraprofessionals.* Ithaca: Rural Development Committee, Cornell University.

Compton, J. Lin
  1982 "Evaluating the Training and Visit System: A Recent Experience." Unpublished paper. Department of Extension and Adult Education, Cornell University.

Coombs, Philip H.
  1980 *Meeting the Basic Needs of the Rural Poor*, editor. London: Pergamon Press.
  1981 *New Strategies for Improving Rural Family Life.* Essex, Conn.: International Council for Educational Development.

Coppee, Evence Charles
  1980 "Four Cases of Forestry Organization at Village Level." Draft paper received from Robert Chambers, Ford Foundation, New Delhi.

Cornick, Tully R.
  1983 *The Social Organization of Production in Quimiag, Ecuador: A Case Study of Small Farmer Production Systems in the Highland Andes.* Ph.D. dissertation, Department of Rural Sociology, Cornell University.

Coser, Lewis
  1956 *The Functions of Social Conflict.* New York: Free Press.

Coward, E. Walter, Jr.
  1979 "Principles of Social Organization in an Indigenous Irrigation System." *Human Organization,* 38(1), 28–36.
  1983 "Property in Action: Alternatives in Irrigation Investment." Paper for Workshop on Water Management and Policy, Khon Kaen University, Khon Kaen, Thailand.
  1984 *Improving Policies and Programs for the Development of Small-Scale Irrigation Systems.* WMS Report No. 27. Fort Collins: Water Management Synthesis Project, Colorado State University.

Crowley, David et al.
  1981 *The Radio Learning Group Manual.* Bonn: Friedrich Ebert Stiftung.

Crozier, Michael and Erhard Friedberg
  1980 *Actors and Systems: The Politics of Collective Action.* Chicago: University of Chicago Press.

Dani, Anis A. and J. Gabriel Campbell
  1986 *Sustaining Upland Resources: People's Participation in Watershed Management.* Kathmandu: International Centre for Integrated Mountain Development.

Dekure, Solomon and Neville Dyson-Hudson
  1982 "The Operation and Viability of the Second Livestock Development Project: Selected Issues." Gaborone: Ministry of Agriculture.

Delancey, Mark W.
  1977 "Credit for the Common Man in Cameroon." *Journal of Modern African Studies,* 15(2), 316–322.

de Silva, N. G. R.
  1981 "Farmer Participation in Water Management: The Minipe Project in Sri Lanka. *Rural Development Participation Review,* 3(1), 16–19.

de Wit, Y. B.
  1973 "The Kabupaten Program." *Bulletin of Indonesian Economic Studies,* 9(1), 65–85.

Dobrin, Arthur
  1970 "The Role of Agrarian Cooperatives in the Development of Kenya." *Studies in Comparative International Development,* 5(6), 107–133.

Dodge, Cole P. and Paul D. Wiebe, editors
  1985 *Crisis in Uganda: The Breakdown of Health Services.* London: Pergamon Press.

Doherty, Deborah
  1979 "Factors Inhibiting Economic Development at Rotian Olmakongo Group Ranch." Working Paper 365. Nairobi: Institute of Development Studies.

Doherty, Victor and N. S. Jodha
  1979 "Conditions for Group Action Among Farmers." In Wong (1979:207–223).

Douglas, James
  1983 *Why Charity: The Case for a Third Sector.* Beverley Hills: Sage Publications.

Duewel, John
  1982 "Promoting Participatory Approaches to Cultivating Water Users Associations: Two Case Studies from Central Java." Technical Report No. 11. Ithaca: Departments of Rural Sociology and Agricultural Engineering, Cornell University.
  1984 "Central Java's Dharma Tirta WUA 'Model': Peasant Irrigation Organisations under Conditions of Population Pressure." *Agricultural Administration,* 17(4), 261–285.

Dulansey, Maryanne
  1980 "Dueñas de Algo: A Case Study of an Enterprise Owned and Managed by Women Artisans in Santiago, Chile." Washington: Consultants in Development, mimeo. Available at International Center for Research on Women, Washington, D.C.

Dunn, Edgar S.
  1971 *Economic and Social Development: A Process of Social Learning.* Baltimore: Johns Hopkins University Press.

Durham, Kathleen
  1977 "Expansion of Agricultural Settlement in the Peruvian Rainforest: The Role of the Market and the Role of the State." Paper presented at Latin American Studies Association meetings, Houston, November.

Dworkin, Daniel
  1980 *Rural Water Projects in Tanzania: Technical, Social and Administrative Issues.* Project Special Study No. 3. Washington: USAID.
  1980a *Kenya Rural Water Supply: Programs, Progress, Prospects.* Project Impact Evaluation No. 5. Washington: USAID.

Dyson-Hudson, Neville
  1985 "Pastoral Production Systems and Livestock Development Projects: An East African Perspective." In Cernea (1985:157–186).

Dyson-Hudson, Rada and Neville Dyson-Hudson
   1980 "Nomadic Pastoralism." *Annual Review of Anthropology*, 9, 15–61.

Early, Alan C.
   1984 "Training Consultancy Report: Irrigation Management and Training Project." New Delhi: USAID/New Delhi.

Easter, K. W. et al
   1986 *Watershed Resource Management: An Integrated Framework, with Studies from Asia and the Pacific.* Boulder,: Westview.

Eaton, Joseph, ed.
   1972 *Institution Building and Development: From Concepts to Application.* Beverley Hills: Sage Publications.

Eckholm, Erik
   1979 *Planting for the Future: Forestry for Human Needs.* World Watch Paper No. 26. Washington: Worldwatch Institute.

Edmonds, G. A.
   1980 "The 'Roads and Labour' Programme, Mexico." In *Roads and Resources: Appropriate Technology in Road Construction in Developing Countries,* 123–134. G. A. Edmonds and J. D. F. G. Howe, eds., 123–134. London: Intermediate Technology Development Group for ILO.

Esman, Milton J.
   1972 "The Elements of Institution Building." In Eaton (1972:19–39).
   1978 *Landlessness and Near-Landlessness in Developing Countries.* Ithaca: Rural Development Committee, Cornell University.
   1983 *Paraprofessionals in Rural Development: Issues in Field-Level Staffing for Agricultural Projects.* Staff Working Paper No. 573. Washington: World Bank.

Esman, Milton J.; Royal Colle, Ellen Taylor and Norman Uphoff
   1980 *Paraprofessionals in Rural Development.* Ithaca: Rural Development Committee, Cornell University.

Esman, Milton J. and Norman Uphoff
   1984 *Local Organizations: Intermediaries in Rural Development.* Ithaca: Cornell University Press.

Fals Borda, Orlando
   1976 "The Crisis in Rural Cooperatives: Problems in Africa, Asia and Latin America." In Nash (1976:439–456).

FAO
   1978–79 *Field Action for Small Farmers, Small Fishermen and Peasants. Vol. 1: The Field Workshop: A Methodology for Planning, Training and Evaluation of Programmes for Small Farmers/Fishermen and Landless Agricultural Labourers. Vol. II: Small Farmer Development Manual.* Bangkok: Food and Agriculture Organization.

1982 *Village Forestry Development in the Republic of Korea.* Rome: Food and Agriculture Organization.

1984 "The People's Programme in Africa: A Review of Implementation Experience in Seven African Countries." Report on the FAO/DSE Regional Training Workshop for the PPP Project Field Staff, Harare, November 26–December 7.

Farbman, Michael
1981 *The PISCES Studies: Assisting the Smallest Economic Activities of the Urban Poor,* editor. Washington: Office of Urban Development, USAID.

1983 "Pedal Pushing Peddlers and Other Small Businessmen." *Horizons,* 2(4), 21–24.

Farmer, B. H. et al.
1977 *Green Revolution? Technology and Change in Rice-Growing Areas of Tamil Nadu and Sri Lanka.* Boulder: Westview Press.

Favin, Michael N.
1982 *Project Esperança: An Evaluation.* Washington: American Public Health Association.

Feder, Ernest
1978 *Strawberry Capitalism: An Enquiry into the Mechanisms of Dependency in Mexican Agriculture.* Mexico City: Editorial Campesina.

Field, John O.
1980 "Development at the Grassroots: The Organizational Imperative." *Fletcher Forum,* 4(2), 145–165. Medford, Mass: Tufts University.

Field, John O.; Roy I. Miller and William D. Drake
1981 *Kottar: Malnutrition, Intervention and Development in a South Indian District,* Volume III. Project on Analysis of Community Level Nutrition Programs. Washington: Office of Nutrition, USAID.

Fife, D.
1971 "Killing the Goose." *Environment,* 13, 20–27.

Flavier, Juan
1970 *Doctor to the Barrios.* Quezon City: New Day Press.

1978 "Rural Reconstruction." In *Basic Health Care in Developing Countries,* Basil S. Hetzel, ed., 75-86. Oxford: Oxford University Press.

Fonaroff, Arlene
1982 "An Operational Strategy for Integrating Community Participation in PHN Sectors." Draft paper prepared for World Bank, Population, Health and Nutrition Division.

Ford Foundation
    1983 "Special Report: The Entrepreneurial Poor." *Ford Foundation Letter*, June 1, 1983, 2–3.

Fortmann, Louise
    1982 "Report on Strengthening the Role of Local Institutions in Rural Development." Paper for Applied Research Unit, Ministry of Local Government and Lands, Government of Botswana, Gabarone.
    1982a *Peasants, Officials and Participation in Rural Tanzania: Experience with Villagization and Decentralization.* Ithaca: Rural Development Committee, Cornell University.
    1985 "Seasonal Dimensions of Rural Social Organisation." *Journal of Development Studies*, 21(3), 377–389.

Fountain, D.E.
    1973 "Programme of Rural Public Health: Vanga Hospital, Republic of Zaire." *Contact*, 13. Geneva: Christian Medical Commission.

Fox, Karen A. and Philip Kotter
    1980 "The Marketing of Social Causes: The First Ten Years." *Journal of Marketing*, 44(1), 24–33.

Franda, Marcus
    1979 *India's Rural Development: An Assessment of Alternatives.* Bloomington: Indiana University Press.

Freeman, Orville
    1981 *The Multinational Company: Instrument for World Growth.* New York: Praeger.

Freire, Paulo
    1970 *The Pedagogy of the Oppressed.* New York: Herder and Herder.

Friedmann, John
    1976 *Innovation, Flexible Response and Social Learning: A Problem in the Theory of Meta-Planning.* London: Reading Geographical Papers, University of Reading.
    1982 "Rural Development in Haiti: The Institutional Options." Report for Consultancy, December 1981–March 1982. USAID/Haiti.

Fuerer-Haimendorf, Christoph von
    1972 *The Sherpas of Nepal: Buddhist Highlanders.* London: John Murray.

Gadgil, Mahdav
    1983 "Forestry with a Social Purpose." In *Towards a New Forest Policy: People's Rights and Environmental Needs*, Walter Fernandes and S. Kulkarni, eds., 111–134. New Delhi: Indian Social Institute.

Gaige, Frederick H.
    1975 *Regionalism and National Unity in Nepal.* Berkeley: University of California Press.

Galjart, Benno and Dieke Buijs, eds.

1982 *Participation of the Poor in Development.* Leiden: Institute of Cultural and Social Studies, University of Leiden.

Gall, Pirie M., Jack Corbett and David Padilla, Jr.

1975 *Municipal Development Institutions in Latin America—Interim Report.* Cecchi and Company, Washington, D.C.

GAO

1982 *Changes Needed in U.S. Assistance to Deter Deforestation in Developing Countries.* Report to the Congress of the United States. Washington: General Accounting Office.

Garcia-Zamor, Jean Claude, ed.

1985 *Public Participation in Development Planning.* Boulder: Westview Press.

Garzon, Jose M.

1981 "Small-Scale Public Works, Decentralization and Linkages." In D. K. Leonard et al., *Linkages to Decentralized Institutions.* Berkeley: Institute for International Studies, University of California.

Geertz, Clifford

1967 "Tihingan: A Balinese Village." In *Villages in Indonesia,* ed. Koentjaraningrat, 210–243. Ithaca: Cornell University Press.

Ghai, Dharam and Anisur Rahman

1979 *Rural Poverty and the Small Farmers' Development Programme in Nepal.* Geneva: Rural Employment Policies Branch, International Labour Office.

1981 "Small Farmers' Groups in Nepal." *Development,* 1, 23–28. Rome: Society for International Development.

Gillis, Jerry and Keith Jamtgaard

1981 "Overgrazing in Pastoral Areas: The Commons Reconsidered." *Sociologia Ruralis,* 21(2), 129–141.

Glennie, Colin E. R.

1979 *The Rural Piped Water Programme in Malawi: A Case Study in Community Participation.* M.S. thesis, Department of Civil Engineering, Imperial College of Science and Technology, University of London.

1982 *A Model for the Development of a Self-Help Water Supply Program.* Technology Advisory Group Working Paper No. 1. Washington: World Bank.

Goldmark, Susan; Timothy Mooney and Jay Rosengard

1982 *Aid to Entrepreneurs: An Evaluation of the Partnership for Productivity Project in Upper Volta.* Washington: Development Alternatives, Inc.

Goldmark, Susan, et al.

1982 *An Impact Evaluation of the Industrial Bank of Peru's Rural Development Fund.* Washington: Development Alternatives, Inc.

Goldsmith, Arthur

1980 *The Politics of Agricultural Stagnation: Rural Development and Local Organization in Jamaica.* Ph.D. thesis, Department of Government, Cornell University.

1981 "Popular Participation and Rural Leadership in the Saemaul Movement." In Lee (1981:427–457).

1982 "Commodity Associations and Agricultural Production in Jamaica." In Blustain and LaFranc (1982:166–191).

Goldsmith, Arthur and Harvey Blustain

1980 *Local Organization and Participation in Integrated Rural Development in Jamaica.* Ithaca: Rural Development Committee, Cornell University.

Golladay, Frederick

1980 "Community Health Care in Developing Countries." *Finance and Development,* 17(3), 35–39.

Gooch, Toby

1979 "An Experiment with Group Ranches in Upper Volta." Pastoral Network Paper. London: Overseas Development Institute.

Gooch, Toby and John MacDonald

1981 *Evaluation of Labour-Related Projects in Drought Relief and Development.* Gabarone: Ministry of Finance and Development.

Goodell, Grace E.

1984 "Bugs, Bunds, Banks and Bottlenecks: Organizational Contradictions in the New Rice Technology." *Economic Development and Cultural Change,* 33(1), 23-41.

Gorman, Robert F. ed.

1984 *Private Voluntary Organizations as Agents of Development.* Boulder: Westview Press.

Gow, David D. et al.

1979 *Local Organizations and Rural Development: A Comparative Reappraisal.* Washington: Development Alternatives, Inc.

Grandstaff, Terry
    1978 "The Development of Swidden Agriculture." *Development and Change*, 9, 547–597.

Green, James W.
    1975 "Local Initiatives in Yemen: Studies of Four Local Development Associations." Paper prepared for USAID/Sana'a.

Grijpstra, Bouwe
    1982 "Initiating and Supervising Agencies: Group Approaches in Rural Development." In Galjart and Buijs (1982:199–219).

Gunawardena, A. M. T. and A. Chandrasiri
    1981 *Training and Visit System of Extension.* Colombo: Agrarian Research and Training Institute.

Guppy, Nicholas
    1984 "Tropical Deforestation." *Foreign Affairs*, 62(4), 928–965.

Hadden, Susan G.
    1974 *Decentralization and Rural Electrification in Rajasthan, India.* Ithaca: Rural Development Committee, Cornell University.

Hafid, Anwar and Yujiro Hayami
    1976 "Mobilizing Local Resources for Irrigation Development: The Subsidi Desa Case of Indonesia." Agricultural Economics Department Paper 76-18. Los Baños: International Rice Research Institute.

Hall, Robert
    1981 *The Village Health Worker Approach to Rural Health Care: The Case of Senegal.* Ithaca: Rural Development Committee, Cornell University.

Hamer, John
    1976 "Prerequisites and Limitations in the Development of Voluntary Self-Help Associations: A Case Study and Comparison." *Anthropological Quarterly*, 19(2), 107–134.
    1981 "Self-Interest and Corruption in Bukusu Cooperatives." *Human Organization*, 40(3), 202–210.

Hamilton, John M. et al.
    1981 *Honduras Rural Roads: Old Directions and New.* Project Impact Evaluation Report No. 17. Washington: USAID.

Haragopal, G.
    1980 *Administrative Leadership and Rural Development in India.* New Delhi: Light and Life Publishers.

Haratani, Joseph et al.
    1981 *Peru: The CARE Water and Health Services Project.* Project Impact Evaluation No. 24. Washington: USAID.

Hardin, Garrett
  1968 "The Tragedy of the Commons." *Science,* 168, 1243–1248.

Hardin, Russell
  1971 "Collective Action as an Agreeable n-Prisoners' Dilemma." *Behavioral Science,* 16(5), 472–481.
  1982 *Collective Action.* Baltimore: Johns Hopkins University Press.

Harik, Iliya
  1974 *The Political Mobilization of Peasants: Change in an Egyptian Village.* Bloomington: Indiana University Press.

Hatch, John
  1981 "Peasants Who Write a Textbook on Subsistence Farming: Report on the Bolivian Traditional Practices Project." *Rural Development Participation Review,* 2(2), 17–20.

Healy, Kevin
  1980 "Innovative Approaches to Development Participation in Rural Bolivia." *Rural Development Participation Review,* (3), 15–18.

Hebert, Mary
  1981 "Local Organization and Development: Maghlaf, Hodeidah Governorate." Working Note No. 10. Ithaca: Rural Development Committee, Cornell University.
  1983 Community Structure and Participation: Yemen's Local Development Associations, Working Note No. 15. Ithaca: Rural Development Committee, Cornell University.

Hellinger, Douglas et al.
  1981 "Building Local Capacity for Sustainable Development." Report for Appropriate Technology International. Washington: ATI.

Hendrata, Lukas
  1976 "Community Health Care in Rural Java." *Contact,* 31. Geneva: Christian Medical Commission.

Hicks, Ursala
  1961 *Development from Below: Local Government and Finance in the Developing Countries of the Commonwealth.* Oxford: Clarendon Press.
  1976 *Intergovernmental Relations With Special Reference to the Less Developed Countries.* Syracuse: Metropolitan Studies Program, Maxwell School of Citizenship and Public Affairs, Syracuse University.

Hill, Polly
  1963 *The Migrant Cocoa Farmers of Southern Ghana: A Study of Rural Capitalism.* Cambridge: Cambridge University Press.
  1982 *Dry Grain Farming Families: Hausaland (Nigeria) and Karnataka (India) Compared.* Cambridge: Cambridge University Press.

Hindori, Djaienti and Jan van Renselaar
    1982 *The T&V Agricultural Extension Program in Matara District: An Evaluation.* Colombo: Agrarian and Research Training Institute.

Hirschman, Albert O.
    1965 "Obstacles to Development: A Classification and a Quasi-Vanishing Act." *Economic Development and Cultural Change,* 14(2), 385-389.
    1967 *Development Projects Observed.* Washington: Brookings Institution.
    1970 *Exit, Voice and Loyalty.* Cambridge: Harvard University Press.
    1984 *Getting Ahead Collectively: Grassroots Experiences in Latin America.* New York: Pergamon Press.

Hoben, Allen
    1976 *Social Soundness of the Masai Livestock and Range Management Project.* Washington: USAID.

Holdcroft, Lane E.
    1978 *The Rise and Fall of Community Development in Developing Countries: A Critical Analysis and an Annotated Bibliography.* MSU Rural Development Paper No. 2. East Lansing: Department of Agricultural Economics, Michigan State University.

Hollnsteiner, Mary R.
    1982 "The Participatory Imperative of Primary Health Care." *Assignment Children,* 59/60, 35-56. New York: UNICEF.

Hollnsteiner, Mary R. et al.
    1979 "Development from the Bottom-up: Mobilizing the Rural Poor for Self-Development." Paper for World Conference on Agrarian Reform and Rural Development. Rome: FAO.

Horowitz, Michael
    1979 *The Sociology of Pastoralism and African Livestock Projects.* Program Evaluation Discussion Paper No. 6. Washington: USAID.

Hoskins, Marilyn
    1979 *Women in Forestry for Local Community Development.* Washington: USAID.

Howell, John
    1982 "Managing Agricultural Extension: The T and V System in Practice. Paper for Agricultural Administration Unit." London: Overseas Development Institute.
    1985 *Recurrent Costs and Agricultural Development.* London: Overseas Development Institute.

Hufschmidt, Maynard M.

   1985 "A Conceptual Framework for Analysis of Watershed Management Programs." Draft. Honolulu: Environment and Policy Institute, East-West Center.

Humphrey, Caroline

   1978 "Cooperatives in Mongolia." Pastoral Network Paper. London: Overseas Development Institute.

Hunt, Robert W.

   1984 "Voluntary Agencies and the Promotion of Enterprises." In Gorman (1984:165–200).

Hunter, Guy

   1980 "The Management of Agricultural Development: Reflections on Field-Level Planning and Management from India and Sri Lanka." London: Overseas Development Institute.

   1980a "Report on Meeting on Local-Level Rural Organizations: Criteria for Assessment and Design." Mimeo. London: Overseas Development Institute.

   1981 "A Hard Look at Directing Benefits to the Rural Poor and at Participation." Agricultural Administration Unit Discussion Paper No. 6. London: Overseas Development Institute.

Hunter, Guy and Janice Jiggins

   1977 "Farmer and Community Groups." Mimeo. London: Agricultural Administration Unit, Overseas Development Institute.

Huntington, Samuel P.

   1965 "Political Development and Political Decay." *World Politics,* 17(3), 378–414.

   1968 *Political Order in Changing Societies.* New Haven: Yale University Press.

Hyden, Goran

   1981 *Beyond Ujamaa in Tanzania: Underdevelopment and an Uncaptured Peasantry.* Berkeley: University of California Press.

   1983 *No Shortcuts to Progress: African Development Management in Perspective.* Berkeley: University of California Press.

ICA

   1978 *Cooperatives and the Poor.* London: International Cooperative Alliance.

Ickis, John C.

   1975 "The Lunchrooms of La Venta." Case study prepared for Instituto Centroamericano de Administración de Empresas, Managua.

IFAD
  1984 "Kingdom of Nepal: Small Farmer Development Programme—
        Mid Term Evaluation Report." Rome: International Fund for
        Agricultural Development.
  1984a "People's Republic of Bangladesh: Small Farmer Agricultural
        Credit Project—Mid-Term Evaluation Report (Grameen Bank
        Component Only)." Rome: International Fund for Agricultur-
        al Development.

ILO
  1972 *Employment, Income and Equity: A Strategy for Increasing Employ-
        ment in Kenya.* Geneva: International Labour Organisation.
  1984 *Rural Development and Women in Africa.* Geneva: World Employ-
        ment Programme, International Labour Organisation.
  1985 *Resources, Power and Women: Proceedings of Inter-regional Work-
        shop on Strategies for Improving the Employment Conditions of
        Rural Women, Arusha, 20–25 August, 1984.* Geneva: ILO.

Imboden, Nicholas
  1977 *Planning and Design of Rural Drinking Water Projects.* Paris: De-
        velopment Centre, OECD.

Ingram, Helen and Lawrence Scaff
  1984 "Politics, Policy and Public Choice: A Critique and a Proposal."
        Paper presented to Western Political Science Association,
        Sacramento, April.

Isbell, Billie Jean
  1978 *To Defend Ourselves: Ecology and Ritual in an Andean Village.*
        Austin: University of Texas Press.

Isely, Raymond B.
  1979 "Reflections on an Experiment in Community Participation in
        Cameroon." *Ann. Soc. Belge Med. Trop.,* 59, Supplement, 103–115.

Isely, Raymond B. and Jean F. Martin
  1977 "The Village Health Committee: Starting Point for Rural Devel-
        opment." *WHO Chronicle,* 31, 307–315.

Jackelen, Henry
  1982 "The UNO Program of Assistance to Microenterprises in
        Caruaru, Brazil." In Bear et al. (1982:19–93).

Jaiswal, N. K. et al.
  1985 "People's Participation in Watershed Management: A Case
        Study of DVC." *Journal of Rural Development,* 4(4), 409–440.

Jancloes, M. et al.
  1981 "Balancing Community and Government Financial Responsibili-
        ties for Urban Primary Health Services, Pikine-Senegal,
        1975–1981." Draft Paper.

Jayaraman, T. K.

    1980 "People's Participation in the Implementation of Watershed Management Projects: An Empirical Study from Gujerat." *Indian Journal of Public Administration*, 26(4), 1009–1016.

Johnson, E. A. G.

    1970 *The Organization of Space in Developing Countries*. Cambridge: Harvard University Press.

Johnston, Bruce F. and William Clark

    1983 *Redesigning Rural Development: A Strategic Perspective*. Baltimore: John Hopkins University Press.

Joshi, J. P.

    1983 "Working Paper on Participation, Small Farmers, and the Role of Participatory Evaluations in SFDP/Nepal." Paper for FAO/RAPA, SSA/RAPA 81/83. Kathmandu: Agricultural Development Bank of Nepal.

Jules-Rosette, Bernadette

    1982 "Women and Technological Change in the Urban Informal Sector." *Resources for Feminist Research*, 11(1), March.

Kafumba, Charles

    1983 *Increasing Farmer Participation in a Smallholder-Oriented Forestry Project: Analysis of the Wood Energy Project in Malawi*. M.P.S. thesis, Cornell University.

Kent, Robert B.

    1980 *Local Revenue Generation: Property Taxes, Land Registration and Cadastral Mapping*. Syracuse: Local Revenue Administration Project, Maxwell School Syracuse University.

Kessler, Judd et al.

    1981 *Ecuador Rural Electrification*. Project Impact Evaluation Report No. 21. Washington: USAID.

Khan, Akhter Hameed

    1983 *Orangi Pilot Project: Progress Reports, April 1980–June 1983*. Karachi: Press Syndicate.

Kimber, Richard

    1981 "Collective Action and the Fallacy of the Liberal Fallacy." *World Politics*, 33(2), 178–196.

Kincaid, D. Lawrence et al.

    1976 *Mothers' Clubs and Family Planning in Rural Korea: The Case of Oryu Li*. Honolulu: East-West Communication Institute.

King, Roger

    1979 "Experiences in the Administration of Cooperative Credit and Marketing Societies in Northern Nigeria." *Agricultural Administration*, 2(2), 195–207.

    1981 "Cooperative Policy and Village Development in Northern Nigeria." In *Rural Development in Tropical Africa*, 259–280. J. Heyer et al., eds., New York: St. Martin's Press.

Kloppenburg, Jack

    1983 "Group Development in Botswana: The Principles of Collective Farmer Action." In *Research in Economic Anthropology*, Volume 5, G. Dalton, ed., Greenwich, Conn.: JAI Press.

Kneerim, Jill

    1980 *Village Women Organize: The Mraru Bus Service*. SEEDS Pamphlet Series. New York: Population Council, Carnegie Corporation, and Ford Foundation.

Korten, David C.

    1980 "Community Organization and Rural Development: A Learning Process Approach." *Public Administration Review*, 40(5), 480–511.

    1982 *The Working Group as a Mechanism for Managing Bureaucratic Reorientation*. NASPAA Working Paper No. 4. Washington: National Association of Schools of Public Affairs and Administration.

    1986 *Community Management: Asian Experience and Perspectives*, editor. West Hartford: Kumarian Press, forthcoming.

Korten, David C. and Norman Uphoff

    1982 *Bureaucratic Reorientation for Participatory Rural Development*. NASPAA Working Paper No. 1. Washington: National Association of Schools of Public Affairs and Administration.

Korten, Francis F.

    1982 *Building National Capacity to Develop Water Users' Associations: Experience from the Phillippines*. Staff Working Paper No. 528. Washington: World Bank.

Korten, Frances F. and Sarah Young

    1978 "The Mothers' Club of Korea." In *Managing Community-Based Population Programs*. Kuala Lampur: International Committee for the Management of Population Programmes.

Ladipo, Patricia

    1983 "Developing Women's Cooperatives: An Experiment in Nigeria." In Nelson (1983:123–136).

LaForgia, Gerard
    1985 *Local Organizations for Rural Health in Panama: Community Participation, Bureaucratic Reorientation and Political Will.* Ithaca: Rural Development Committee, Cornell University.

Lamb, Geoff and Linda Mueller
    1982 *Control, Accountability and Incentives in a Successful Development Institution: The Kenya Tea Development Authority.* Staff Working Paper No. 550. Washington: World Bank.

Lang, Gottfried, Warren J. Roth and Martha Lang
    1969 "Sukumaland Cooperatives as Mechanisms of Change." In *The Anthropology of Development in Sub-Saharan Africa*, D. Brokensha and M. Pearsall, eds., 48–63. Lexington, Ky.: Society for Applied Anthropology.

Lassen, Cheryl
    1980 *Reaching the Assetless Poor: Projects and Strategies for Their Self-Reliant Development.* Ithaca: Rural Development Committee, Cornell University.

Lassen, Cheryl et al.
    1985 "Credit and Enterprise Development Training That Reach the Small Producer Majority in Burkina Faso." Washington: Partnership for Productivity.

Lazaro, R. C.; Donald C. Taylor and Thomas H. Wickham
    1979 "Irrigation Policy and Management Issues." In *Irrigation Policy and the Management of Irrigation Systems in Southeast Asia*, D.C. Taylor and T. H. Wickham, eds. Bangkok: Agricultural Development Council.

Leach, E. R.
    1961 *Pul Eliya, A Village in Ceylon: A Study of Land Tenure and Kinship.* Cambridge: Cambridge University Press.

LeBaron, Allen; Larry Bond, Percy Aitken and Leon Michaelson
    1979 "An Explanation of the Bolivian Highlands Grazing-Erosion Syndrome." *Journal of Range Management*, 32(3), 201–208.

Lee, Man-Gap, ed.
    1981 *Toward a New Community: Report of an International Research Seminar on the Saemaul Movement, 1980.* Seoul: Institute of Saemaul Undong Studies, Seoul National University.

Lees, Susan H.
    1973 *Sociopolitical Aspects of Canal Irrigation in Oaxaca.* Memoirs of the Museum of Anthropology No. 6. Ann Arbor: University of Michigan.

Lele, Uma
 1971 *Food Grain Marketing in India: Private Performance and Public Policy.* Ithaca: Cornell University Press.
 1981 "Cooperatives and the Poor: A Comparative Perspective." *World Development,* 9(1), 55–72.

Leonard, David K.
 1977 *Reaching the Peasant Farmer: Organization Theory and Practice in Kenya.* Chicago: University of Chicago Press.
 1982 "Analyzing the Organizational Requirements for Serving the Rural Poor." In Leonard and Marshall (1982:1–39).
 1982a "Choosing Among Forms of Decentralization and Linkage." In Leonard and Marshall (1982:193–226).

Leonard, David K. and Dale Rogers Marshall, eds.
 1982 *Institutions of Rural Development for the Poor: Decentralization and Organizational Linkages.* Berkeley: Institute of International Studies, University of California, Berkeley.

Lerner, Richard
 1971 *A Place for Cooperative Farming.* Berkeley: Institute for International Studies, University of California.

Lewars, Gladstone
 1982 "Domestic Food Marketing: The Role of the Agricultural Marketing Corporation." In Blustain and LaFranc (1982:140–165).

Lewis, Henry T.
 1971 *Ilocano Rice Farmers.* Honolulu: University Press of Hawaii.

Liebenow, J. Gus
 1981 "Malawi: Clean Water for the Rural Poor." *American Universities Field Staff Reports,* Africa, No. 40.

Liedholm, Carl
 1985 *Small Scale Enterprise Credit Schemes: Administrative Costs and the Role of Inventory Norms.* Working Paper No. 25. East Lansing: Department of Agricultural Economics, Michigan State University.

Looye, Johanna W.
 1984 *Credit and the Small Borrower: Bridging the Gap Between Borrowers, Lending Programs, and Funding Sources.* Washington: Creative Associates, Inc.

Lynch, Barbara
 1978 *A Desert Agricultural System in a Mineral Export Enclave. Water Management and Productive Capacity in San Pedro de Atacama.* M.S. thesis, Department of Rural Sociology, Cornell University.

Maass, Arthur and Raymond L. Anderson
   1978   . . . and the Desert Shall Rejoice: Conflict, Growth and Justice in
          Arid Environments. Cambridge: Massachusetts Institute of Tech-
          nology Press.

March, Kathryn and Rachelle Taqqu
   1986   Women's Informal Associations in Developing Countries: Catalysts
          for Change? Boulder: Westview Press.

Marris, Peter and Anthony Somerset
   1972   The African Entrepreneur: A Study of Entrepreneurship and Devel-
          opment in Kenya. New York: Africana Publishing Co.

Martin, Edward and Robert Yoder
   1983   "Resource Mobilization and Benefit Allocation in Irrigation:
          Analysis of Two Community Irrigation Systems in the Hills of
          Nepal." Unpublished paper, Cornell Irrigation Studies Group,
          Cornell University.

Mayfield, James B.
   1974   Local Institutions and Egyptian Rural Development. Ithaca: Rural
          Development Committee, Cornell University.
   1985   "The Egyptian Basic Village Service Program: A New Strate-
          gy for Local Government Capacity Building." In Garcia-
          Zamor (1985:97–126).

Meehan, Eugene J.
   1978   In Partnership with People: An Alternative Development Strategy.
          Washington: Inter-American Foundation.

Meinzen-Dick, Ruth
   1984   Local Management of Tank Irrigation in South India: Organiza-
          tion and Operation. Ithaca: Cornell Irrigation Studies Papers,
          Cornell University.

Meyers, L. Richard
   1981   Organization and Administration of Integrated Rural Development
          in Semi-Arid Areas: The Machakos Integrated Rural Development
          Program. Washington: Office of Rural Development and Devel-
          opment Administration, USAID.

Millikan, Max and David Hapgood
   1967   No Easy Harvest: The Dilemma of Agriculture in Underdeveloped
          Countries. Boston: Little Brown.

Miracle, Marvin and Ann Seidman
   1968   State Farms in Ghana. LTC Paper No. 43. Madison: Land Tenure
          Center, University of Wisconsin.

Misch, Marion Ruth and Joseph B. Margolin
1975 *Rural Women's Groups as Potential Change Agents: A Study of Colombia, Korea and the Philippines.* Washington: Program of Policy Studies in Science and Technology, George Washington University.

Misra, K. K.
1975 "Safe Water in Rural Areas: An Experiment in Promoting Community Participation in India." *International Journal of Health Education,* 28, 53–59.

Mitchell, William P.
1976 "Irrigation and Community in the Central Peruvian Highlands." *American Anthropologist,* 78(1), 25–44.

Mohamed, Khair Haji
1981 Agricultural Cooperatives in Malaysia. *Agricultural Information Development Bulletin,* 3(1), 29–38.

Montgomery, John D.
1972 "The Allocation of Authority in Land Reform Programs: A Comparative Study of Administrative Process and Outputs." *Administrative Science Quarterly,* 17(1), 62–75.
1977 "Food for Thought: On Appraising Nutrition Programs." *Policy Science,* 8, 303–321.
1984 "Testing a Model of Institutional Development." Research note submitted to Office of Rural and Institutional Development, USAID, March 19, 1984.

Moock, Peter
1976 "The Efficiency of Women as Farm Managers: Kenya." *American Journal of Agricultural Economics,* 58(5), 831–835.

Moore, Cynthia
1981 *Paraprofessionals in Village-Level Development in Sri Lanka: The Sarvodaya Shramadana Movement.* Ithaca: Rural Development Committee, Cornell University.

Moore, M. P.
1979 "Social Structure and Institutional Performance: Local Farmers' Organizations in Sri Lanka." *Journal of Administration Overseas,* 18(4), 240–249.

Moore, M. P. and Gamini Wickramasinghe
1978 *Managing the Village Environment.* Colombo. Agrarian Research and Training Institute.

Morgan, Robert J.
1965 *Governing Soil Conservation: Thirty Years of the New Decentralization.* Baltimore: Johns Hopkins University Press.

Morss, Elliott R. et al.
   1976 *Strategies for Small Farmer Development,* Two volumes, Boulder:
         Westview Press.

Mosher, Arthur
   1969 *Creating a Progressive Rural Structure to Serve A Modern Agricul-
         ture.* New York: Agricultural Development Council.

Münkner, Hans
   1976 *Cooperatives for the Rich or for the Poor?* Marburg am Lahn: Insti-
         tute for Cooperation in Developing Countries.

Muntemba, Shimwaayi, ed.
   1985 *Rural Development and Women: Lessons from the Field,* two vol-
         umes. Geneva. World Employment Programme, International
         Labour Organisation.

Murray, Gerald F.
   1986 "Seeing the Forest while Planting the Trees: An Anthropological
         Approach to Agroforestry in Rural Haiti." In *Politics, Projects, and
         People: Institutional Development in Haiti.* D. W. Brinkerhoff and
         J. C. Garcia-Zamor, eds. New York: Praeger Publishers.

Nash, June; Jorge Dandler, and Nicholas Hopkins, eds.
   1976 *Popular Participation in Social Change: Cooperatives, Collectives
         and Nationalized Industry.* Chicago: Aldine.

Nellis, John
   1981 *Decentralization in North Africa: Problems of Policy Implementa-
         tion.* Syracuse: Maxwell School, Syracuse University.

Nelson, Nici, ed.
   1983 *African Women in the Development Process.* London: G. K. Hall.

Nemec, Jeanne
   1980 "Rediscovering an Ancient Resource: A New Look at Traditional
         Medicine." *Contact,* 58. Geneva: Christian Medical Commission.

Netting, R. M.
   1976 "What Alpine Peasants Have in Common: Observations on Com-
         munal Tenure in a Swiss Village." *Human Ecology,* 4, 135–146.

Nicholson, Norman K.
   1973 *Panchayati Raj, Rural Development and the Political Economy
         of Village India.* Ithaca: Rural Development Committee,
         Cornell University.
   1975 "Differential Responses to Technical Change in Gujerat and
         Punjab: An Analysis of Economic and Political Differentiation in
         India." Paper presented to American Political Science Associa-
         tion meetings, San Francisco.
   1984 "Landholding, Agricultural Modernization, and Local Institu-
         tions in India." *Economic Development and Cultural Change,*
         32(3), 569–592.

Noronha, Raymond and Francis Lethem
1983 *Traditional Land Tenure and Land Use Systems in the Design of Agricultural Projects.* Staff Working Paper No. 561. Washington: World Bank.

Nyerere, Julius K.
1984 Interview, *Third World Quarterly,* 6(4), October, 815–834.

Odell, Malcolm
1982 *Participation, Decentralization and Village-Based Information Systems for the Basic Village Services Project.* Washington: Chemonics International.

Odell, Marcia and Malcolm Odell
1980 "Pastoralism and Planning in a Semi-Arid Environment." Pastoral Network Paper. London: Overseas Development Institute.

Oldfield, Margery
1981 "Tropical Deforestation and Genetic Resources." In *Blowing in the Wind: Deforestation and Long-Range Implications,* V. H. Sutliff, et al., eds. Williamsburg: Department of Anthropology, College of William and Mary.

Olson, Craig et al.
1984 *Private Voluntary Organizations and Institutional Development: Lessons from International Voluntary Services, Inc. and the Institute for International Development, Inc.* Washington: Development Alternatives, Inc.

Olson, Mancur
1965 *The Logic of Collective Action: Public Goods and the Theory of Groups.* Cambridge: Harvard University Press.

Ostrom, Elinor
1986 "An Agenda for the Study of Institutions." *Public Choice,* forthcoming.

Ostrom, Vincent and Elinor Ostrom
1977 Public Goods and Public Choices. In *Alternatives for Delivering Public Services: Toward Improved Performance,* E. S. Savas, ed., 7–49. Boulder: Westview Press.

Owens, Edgar and Robert Shaw
1972 *Development Reconsidered: Bridging the Gap between Government and People.* Lexington: D. C. Heath.

Oxby, Clare
1983 "'Farmer Groups' in Rural Areas of the Third World." *Community Development Journal,* 18(1), 50–59.

Palanasami, K. and William Easter
1983 *The Tanks of South India: A Potential for Future Expansion and Irrigation.* Department of Agricultural and Applied Economics Report ER83-4, University of Minnesota.

Palin, David

    1983 "Institutional Arrangements for Afforestation." Paper for International Symposium on Strategy and Design for Afforestation, Reforestation and Tree Planting, Wageningen, September 19–23.

Paul, James C. N. and C. J. Dias

    1980 *Law and Legal Resources in the Mobilization of the Poor for Their Self-Reliant Development.* New York: International Center for Law in Development.

Paul, Samuel

    1982 *Managing Development Programs: The Lesson of Success.* Boulder: Westview Press.

Peters, Thomas J. and Robert H. Waterman, Jr.

    1982 *In Search of Excellence: Lessons from America's Best-Run Companies.* New York: Warner Books.

Peterson, Stephen B.

    1982 "Government, Cooperatives and the Private Sector in Peasant Agriculture." In Leonard and Marshall (1982:73–124).

    1982a "Alternative Local Organizations Supporting the Agricultural Development of the Poor." In Leonard and Marshall (1982:125–150).

PfP

    1984 "Working Group Meets on Small Enterprise Evaluation." *PfP Newsletter,* 5(1), Spring, 6. Washington: Partnership for Productivity.

Pillsbury, Barbara

    1979 *Reaching the Rural Poor: Indigenous Health Practitioners Are There Already.* Evaluation Report PN–AAG–685. Washington: USAID.

Popkin, Samuel

    1981 "Public Choice and Rural Development: Free Riders, Lemons, and Institutional Design." In Russell and Nicholson (1981:43–80).

Portes, Alejandro

    1973 "Modernity and Development: A Critique." *Studies in Comparative International Development,* 13(4), 247–273.

Prabowo, Dibyo

    1973 *The Impact of Government Subsidy Upon Villages.* Yogyakarta: BIPEMAS, Gadjah Mada University.

Pradhan, Prachandra P.

    1980 *Local Institutions and People's Participation in Rural Public Works in Nepal.* Ithaca: Rural Development Committee, Cornell University.

1983 "Chattis Mauja." In *Water Management in Nepal: Proceedings of a Seminar on Water Management Issues,* 218–242. Kathmandu: Agricultural Projects Service Centre.

Prosser, A. R. G.
1982 "Community Development: The British Experience." In *Progress in Rural Extension and Community Development,* G. E. Jones and M. J. Rolls, eds., 233–247. London: Wiley

Rabibhadana, Akin
1983 "The Transformation of Tambon Yokkrabat, Changwat Samut Sakorn." *Thai Journal of Development Administration,* 22(1), 73–104.

Rahman, Md. Anisur
1984 "The Small Farmer Development Programme of Nepal." In Rahman (1984a: 121–151).

1984a *Grass-Roots Participation and Self-Reliance: Experiences in South and South East Asia,* editor. New Delhi: Oxford University Press.

Ralston, Lenore; James Anderson and Elizabeth Colson
1983 *Voluntary Efforts in Decentralized Management: Opportunities and Constraints in Rural Development.* Berkeley: Institute of International Studies, University of California, Berkeley.

Range Management Center
1981 *Management of Communal Grazing in Botswana.* Gabarone: Range Management Center, Ministry of Agriculture.

Raper, Arthur
1970 *Rural Development in Action: The Comprehensive Experiment at Comilla, East Pakistan.* Ithaca: Cornell University Press.

Ray, Jayanta Kumar
1983 *Organising Villagers for Self-Reliance: A Study of Deedar in Bangladesh.* Comilla, Bangladesh: Bangladesh Academy for Rural Development.

RDC
1974 *Training and Research for Extended Rural Development.* Ithaca: Rural Development Committee, Cornell University.

Reddy, G. Ram
1982 "Local Government and Agricultural Development in Andhra Pradesh, India." In Uphoff, ed. (1982a:45–133).

Republic of Indonesia
1978 *Primary Health Care: Some Experiences from Indonesia.* Jakarta: Department of Health.

Republic of Kenya
1983 *District Focus for Rural Development.* Nairobi: Government Printer, for Office of the President.

Robertson, Lindsey
    1978 *The Development of Self-Help Gravity Piped Water Projects in Malawi.* Lilongwe: Ministry of Community Development.

Robinson, David M.
    1982 *Water Users' Associations in Two Large Philippine Irrigation Systems: Constraints and Benefits of a Participatory Approach to Water Management.* Ph.D. dissertation, Department of Government, Cornell University.

Roe, Emery and Louise Fortmann
    1982 *Season and Strategy: The Changing Organization of the Rural Water Sector in Botswana.* Ithaca: Rural Development Committee, Cornell University.

Roling, Niels and Janice Jiggins
    1982 *The Role of Extension in People's Participation in Rural Development.* Rome: Food and Agriculture Organization.

Rondinelli, Dennis
    1982 "The Dilemma of Development Administration: Complexity and Uncertainty in Control-Oriented Bureaucracies." *World Politics,* 35(1), 43–72.
    1983 *Development Projects as Policy Experiments: An Adaptive Approach to Development Administration.* New York: Methuen.

Ross, David
    1979 "The Serabu Hospital Village Health Program." *Contact,* 49. Geneva: Christian Medical Commission.

Ruddle, Kenneth and Dennis Rondinelli
    1983 *Transforming Natural Resources for Human Development: A Resource Systems Framework for Development Policy.* Tokyo: United Nations University.

Runge, C. Ford
    1981 "Common Property Externalities: Isolation, Assurance, and Resource Depletion in a Traditional Grazing Context." *American Journal of Agricultural Economics,* 63(4), 595–606.
    1983 *Sources of Institutional Innovation: An Interpretive Essay.* Discussion Paper No. 176. Minneapolis: Department of Economics, University of Minnesota.
    1984 "Institutions and the Free Rider: The Assurance Problem in Collective Action." *Journal of Politics,* 46(1), 154–181.

Rusch, William H. et al.
    1976 *Rural Cooperative in Guatemala: A Study of their Development and Evaluation of AID Programs in their Support.* Washington: USAID.

Russell, Clifford, ed.
    1979 *Collective Decision Making: Applications from Public Choice Theory.* Baltimore: Johns Hopkins University Press.

Russell, Clifford and Norman Nicholson, eds.
  1981 *Public Choice and Rural Development.* Baltimore: Johns Hopkins University Press.

Ruttan, Vernon W.
  1978 "Induced Institutional Change." In Binswanger and Ruttan (1978:327–357).

Sainju, Mohan Man et al.
  1973 *Revisit to Budhbare.* Kathmandu: Centre for Economic Development and Administration.

Sandford, Dick
  1981 "Turkana District Livestock Development Plan." Unpublished paper. OXFAM, Nairobi.

Sandford, Stephen
  1983 *Management of Pastoral Development in the Third World.* London: John Wiley, for Overseas Development Institute.

Sasaki, Takashi
  1985 "The Role of Village Collective Management Traditions in the Formation of Group Farming: Case Studies in Japan." *Regional Development Dialogue,* 6(1), 66–103.

Saunders, Robert J. and Jeremy J. Warford
  1976 *Village Water Supply: Economics and Policy in the Developing World.* Baltimore: Johns Hopkins University Press.

Savino, Margaret
  1984 "Community Development Paraprofessionals in Bolivia: The NCDS Promotores in the Field." Unpublished manuscript, Rural Development Committee, Cornell University.

Sebstad, Jennifer
  1982 "Struggle and Development Among Self Employed Women: A Report on the Self Employed Women's Association, Ahmedabad, India." Washington: USAID.

Seibel, Hans Dieter and Andreas Massing
  1974 *Traditional Organizations and Economic Development: Studies of Indigenous Cooperatives in Liberia.* New York: Praeger.

Selznick, Philip
  1957 *Leadership in Administration.* Evanston: Northwestern University Press.

Sharma, Kamud et al.
  1985 "The Chipko Movement in the Uttakhand Region, Uttar Pradesh, India." In Muntemba (1984: II:173–194).

Sharma, P. N.
  1984 "Social Capability for Development: Learning from Japanese Experience." *Regional Development Dialogue,* 5(1), 41–98.

1985 "Community Receiving Mechanisms and the Village Panchayat System: Case Studies in India." *Regional Development Dialogue,* 6(1), 24–65.

Sharpe, Kenneth
1977 *Peasant Politics: Struggle in a Dominican Village.* Baltimore: Johns Hopkins University Press.

Shepherd, Andrew W.
1982 *India's District Industries Centres: An Experiment in the Decentralisation of Small-Scale Industries.* Occasional Papers in Development Administration No. 16. Birmingham, U.K.: Development Administration Group, University of Birmingham.

Sheppard, Jim
1981 "Liberia: A Tale of Patience." *Salubritas,* 5(1). Washington: American Public Health Association.

Sheridan, Mary
1981 *Peasant Innovation and Diffusion of Agricultural Technology in China.* Ithaca: Rural Development Committee, Cornell University.

Shrestha, Bihari K.
1980 "Nuwakot District (Nepal)." In *The Practice of Local-Level Planning: Case Studies in Selected Rural Areas of India, Nepal and Malaysia.* Bangkok: U.N. Economic and Social Commission for Asia and the Pacific.

Singh, K. K.
1984 "Farmer's Associations in Large Irrigation Projects: The Pochampad Experience," Paper for SSRC/IIM Conference on Community Response to Irrigation, Bangalore, January.

Sisler, Daniel G. and David Colman
1979 *Poor Rural Households, Technological Change, and Income Distribution in Developing Countries: Insights from Asia.* Ithaca: Department of Agricultural Economics, Cornell University.

Siy, Robert
1982 *Community Resource Management: Lessons from the Zanjera.* Quezon City: University of the Philippines Press.

Smith, G. A. and S. J. Dock
1981 "The Savings Development Movement in Rural Areas: A Popular People's Program." In *Case Studies in Nonformal Education,* B1–15. Harare: Institute of Adult Education, University of Zimbabwe.

Smith, Robert J. et al.
1982 "Indian Colonization in Paraguay: What is Success?" *Grassroots Development,* 6(1), 19–22.

Soares, K. C.
1983 "Development of the Informal Sector Through Participation." Paper for meeting on Productivity, Participation and Ownership

sponsored by Department of Labor and Agency for International Development, May, Washington, D.C.

Solon, Florentino et al.

1979 "An Evaluation of Strategies to Control Vitamin A Deficiency in the Philippines." *American Journal of Clinical Nutrition,* 32, 1145–1453.

Spears, John

1982 "Rehabilitating Watersheds." *Finance and Development,* 19(1), 30–33.

Staudt, Kathleen

1978 "Agricultural Productivity Gaps: A Case Study of Male Preference in Government Policy Implementation." *Development and Change,* 9(3), 439–457.

1980 "The Umoja Federation: Women's Cooptation into a Local Power Structure." *Western Political Quarterly,* 33(2), 278–290.

Stavis, Benedict

1983 "Rural Local Governance and Agricultural Development in Taiwan." In Uphoff (1983:166–271).

Stearns, Katherine E.

1985 *Assisting Informal-Sector Microenterprises in Developing Countries.* Paper No. AE 85–16, Ithaca, N.Y.: Department of Agricultural Economics, Cornell University.

Steeves, Jeffrey

1975 *The Politics and Administration of Agricultural Development in Kenya: The Kenya Tea Development Authority.* Ph.D. thesis, Department of Political Economy, University of Toronto.

1984 "Creative Leadership and Development: Case Study of Agricultural Change in Kenya." Unpublished paper, Department of Economics and Political Science, University of Saskatchewan, Saskatoon.

Steinmo, Sven

1982 "Linking the Village to Modern Health Systems." In Leonard and Marshall (1982:151–189).

Stockley, Dick

1985 "Primary Health Care in Teso, 1980–1984." In Dodge and Wiebe (1985:221–225).

Swanberg, Kenneth G.

1982 "Institutional Evolution: From Pilot Project to National Development Program—Puebla and Caqueza." Development Discussion Paper No. 132. Cambridge: Harvard Institute for International Development, Harvard University.

Swanson, Jon C.
    1981   "Local Government and Development: Bani 'Awwam, Hajja
           Province." Working Note No. 11. Ithaca: Rural Development
           Committee, Cornell University.
    1982   "Migration and Development in North Yemen." Paper presented
           to Seminar on Gulf States, University of Exeter, April.

Swanson, Jon C. and Mary Hebert
    1982   "Rural Society and Participatory Development: Case Studies of
           Two Villages in the Yemen Arab Republic." Ithaca: Rural Devel-
           opment Committee, Cornell University.

Sweet, Charles and Peter Weisel
    1979   "Process versus Blueprint Models for Designing Rural Develop-
           ment Projects." In *International Development Administration:
           Implementation Analysis for Development Projects*, G. Honadle
           and R. Klauss, eds., 127–145. New York: Praeger.

Tadesse, Zenebeworke
    1984   "Studies on Rural Women in Africa: An Overview." In ILO
           (1984:65–74).

Tandon, Rajesh and David Brown
    1981   "Organization Building for Rural Development: An Experiment in
           India." *Journal of Applied Behavioral Science*, 17(2), 172–189.

Taylor, Ellen
    1981   *Women Paraprofessionals in Upper Volta's Rural Development*.
           Ithaca: Rural Development Committee, Cornell University.

Temple, Paul
    1972   "Soil and Water Conservation Policies in the Uluguru Moun-
           tains, Tanzania." *Geografiska Annaler*, 54, 110–23.

Tendler, Judith
    1976   *Inter-Country Evaluation of Small Farmer Organizations in Ecuador
           and Honduras: Final Report*. Washington: USAID.
    1979   *New Directions: Rural Roads*. Program Evaluation Discussion
           Paper No. 2. Washington: USAID.
    1980   *Rural Electrification: Linkages and Justifications*. Program Evalua-
           tion Discussion Paper No. 3. Washington: USAID.
    1981   *Fitting the Foundation Style: The Case of Rural Credit*. Washington:
           Inter-American Foundation.
    1982   *Rural Projects Through Urban Eyes: An Interpretation of the World
           Bank's New-Style Rural Development Projects*. Staff Working
           Paper No. 532. Washington: World Bank.
    1982a *Turning Private Voluntary Organizations Into Development Agen-
           cies: Questions for Evaluation*. Evaluation Discussion Paper No.
           12. Washington: Agency for International Development.
    1983   *What to Think About Cooperatives: A Guide from Bolivia*, with
           Kevin Healy and Carol M. O'Laughlin. Washington: Inter-
           American Foundation.
    1983a *Ventures in the Informal Sector, and How They Worked Out in Bra-
           zil*. Evaluation Special Study No. 12. Washington: USAID.

Thomas, Barbara
    1980 "The *Harambee* Self-Help Experience in Kenya." *Rural Development Participation Review*, 1(3), 1–5.

Thomas, John W.
    1971 "East Pakistan's Rural Works Program." In *Development Policy II—The Pakistan Experience*, 187–236. W. F. Falcon and G. F. Papanek, eds., Cambridge: Harvard University Press.

Thompson, James
    1982 "Peasants, Rules and Woodstock Management in Zinder Department, Niger." Paper presented at African Studies Association meetings, Washington, D.C.

Tiffen, Mary
    1980 *The Enterprising Peasant: Economic Development in Gombe Emirate, North Eastern State, Nigeria, 1900–1968*. Overseas Research Publication No. 21. London: Ministry of Overseas Development.
    1983 "Peasant Participation in District Water Planning: An Example from Machakos District, Kenya." Paper for Agricultural Administration Unit. London: Overseas Development Institute.
    1985 *Les Politiques de l'Eau en Afrique. Developpement agricole et participation paysanne*. Paris: Economica.

Tilakaratne, S.
    1984 "Grass-Roots Self-Reliance in Sri Lanka: Organisations of Betel and Coir Yarn Producers." In Rahman (1984a:152–183).

TKRI
    1980 *A Self-Help Organization in Rural Thailand: The Question of Appropriate Policy Inputs*. Bangkok: Thai Khadi Research Institute, Thammasat University.

Turtianen, Turto and J. D. Von Pischke
    1982 "The Financing of Agricultural Cooperatives." *Finance and Development*, 19(3), 18–21.

Uphoff, Norman
    1979 "Assessing the Possibilities for Organized 'Development from Below' in Sri Lanka." Paper for Ceylon Studies Seminar, 1978–79 Series, University of Peradeniya, Sri Lanka.
    1980 "Political Considerations in Human Development." In *Implementing Programs of Human Development*, Peter Knight, ed., 3–108. Staff Working Paper No. 403. Washington: World Bank.
    1982 "Contrasting Approaches to Water Management Development in Sri Lanka." In *Third World Legal Studies: Law in Alternative Strategies of Rural Development*, 202–249. New York: International Center for Law in Development.
    1982a *Rural Development and Local Organization in Asia, Volume I: Introduction and South Asia*, editor. New Delhi: Macmillan.
    1983 *Rural Development and Local Organization in Asia, Volume II: East Asia*, editor. New Delhi: Macmillan.

1984 "Rural Development Strategy: The Central Role of Local Organizations and Changing Supply-Side Bureaucracy." In *Studies in Agrarian Reform and Rural Poverty*, 59–84. Rome: Food and Agriculture Organization.

1985 "People's Participation in Water Management: Gal Oya, Sri Lanka." In Garcia-Zamor (1985:131–178).

1985a "Fitting Projects to People." In Cernea (1985: 359-395).

1986 "Activating Community Capacity for Water Management: Experience from Gal Oya, Sri Lanka." In Korten (1986), forthcoming.

1986a *Getting the Process Right: Improving Irrigation Water Management with Farmer Participation.* Boulder: Westview Press, forthcoming.

Uphoff, Norman; John M. Cohen and Arthur Goldsmith

1979 *Feasibility and Application of Rural Development Participation: A State-of-the-Art Paper.* Ithaca: Rural Development Committee, Cornell University.

Uphoff, Norman and Milton Esman

1974 *Local Organization for Rural Development: Analysis of Asian Experience.* Ithaca: Rural Development Committee, Cornell University.

Uphoff, Norman and Warren Ilchman

1972 "The Time Dimension in Institution Building." In Eaton (1972:111–135).

Uphoff, Norman; Ruth Meinzen-Dick and Nancy St. Julien

1985 *Improving Policies and Programs for Farmer Organization and Participation for Irrigation Water Management.* Ithaca: Water Management Synthesis Project, Cornell University.

U.S. Agency for International Development (USAID)

1979 *Policy Directions for Rural Water Supply in Developing Countries.* Program Evaluation Discussion Paper No. 4. Washington: USAID.

1980 *Central America: Small Farmer Cropping Systems.* Project Impact Evaluation Report No. 14. Washington: USAID.

1980a *Rural Roads in Thailand.* Project Impact Evaluation Report No. 13. Washington: USAID.

1980b *Water Supply and Diarrhea: Guatemala Revisited.* Special Evaluation Studies. Washington: USAID.

1982 *Community Water Supplies in Developing Countries: Lessons from Experience.* Project Evaluation Report No. 7. Washington: USAID.

1982a *Rural Roads Evaluation: Summary Report.* Program Evaluation Report No. 5. Washington: USAID.

1983 *Institutional Development: A. I. D. Policy Paper.* Washington: Bureau of Program and Policy Coordination, USAID.

1983a *A.I.D. Health Sector Strategy.* Washington: USAID.

1984 *Local Organizations in Development: A. I. D. Policy Paper.* Washington: Bureau of Program and Policy Coordination, USAID.

van Raalte, G. R.
1979 *Colombia: Small Farmer Market Access.* Project Impact Evaluation No. 1. Washington: USAID.

VanSant, Jerry and Peter F. Wiesel
1979 *Community Based Integrated Rural Development (CBIRD) in the Special Territory of Aceh, Indonesia.* Washington: Development Alternatives, Inc.

Vincent, Joan
1971 *African Elite: The Big Men of a Small Town.* New York: Columbia University Press.

Visaya, Benito P.
1982 "The Palsiguan Multi-Purpose Project and the Zanjeras." Paper presented to Conference on Organization as a Strategic Resource in Irrigation Development, Asian Institute of Management, Manila, November 15–19.

Vyas, V. S.; A. P. Bhatt and S. M. Shah
1983 *Basic Needs and Employment: Decentralized Planning In India.* World Employment Programme Research Working Paper 52. Geneva: ILO.

Wade, Robert
1979 "The Social Response to Irrigated Agriculture: An Indian Case Study." *Journal of Development Studies*, 16(1), 3–26.

1982 "Group Action for Irrigation." *Economic and Political Weekly*, 17(39), September 25, A103–106.

1984 "The Community Response to Irrigation: Management of the Water Commons in Upland South India." Paper for SSRC/Indian Institute of Management, Bangalore seminar, January 4–7.

Wall, Roger
1983 "Niger's Herders: Figuring Them Into the Development Formula." *Horizons*, April, 25–29.

Warren, Dennis M. et al.
1981 "Ghanaian National Policy towards Indigenous Healers: The Case of the Primary Health Training for Indigenous Healers Program." Paper prepared for Society for Applied Anthropology, April 12–17, Edinburgh.

Weber, Fred
1981 "End of Project Evaluation: AFRICARE Reforestation in Five Rural Villages." Project AID–AFG–G–1655. Paper prepared for USAID/Senegal.

Weitz, Raanan
    1971 *From Peasant to Farmer: A Revolutionary Strategy for Development.*
    New York: Colombia University Press.

Werner, David and Bill Bower
    1982 *Helping Health Workers Learn: A Book of Methods, Aids and Ideas for
    Instructors at the Village Level.* Palo Alto: Hesparian Foundation.

West, Patrick C.
    1983 "Collective Adoption of Natural Resource Practices in Develop-
    ing Nations." *Rural Sociology,* 48(1), 44–59.

Westerguard, Kirsten
    1986 *People's Participation, Local Government and Rural Development:
    The Case of West Bengal, India.* Copenhagen: Centre for Develop-
    ment Research.

WHO
    1978 *Primary Health Care.* Report of the International Conference on Pri-
    mary Health Care, Alma-Ata, USSR, September 2–6, 1978. Health
    for All Series No. 1. Geneva: World Health Organization.
    1981 *Global Strategy for Health for All by the Year 2000.* Health for All
    Series No. 3. Geneva: World Health Organization.

Whyte, William F. and Damon Boynton
    1983 *Higher Yielding Human Systems for Agriculture.* Ithaca: Cornell
    University Press.

Willett, A. B. J
    1981 *Agricultural Group Development in Botswana,* Four volumes.
    Gabarone: USAID.

Williamson, John R.
    1983 "Towards Community-Managed Drinking Water Schemes in
    Nepal." *Waterlines,* 2(2), 8–13.

Wittfogel, Karl
    1957 *Oriental Despotism.* New Haven: Yale University Press.

Womack, John
    1968 *Zapata and the Mexican Revolution.* New York: Vintage.

Wong, John, ed.
    1979 *Group Farming in Asia.* Singapore: Singapore University Press.

World Bank
    1976 *Village Water Supply: A World Bank Paper.* Washington: World Bank.
    1978 *Yemen Arab Republic: Development of a Traditional Economy.*
    Washington: World Bank.
    1978a *Rural Enterprise and Nonfarm Employment.* Sector Policy Paper.
    Washington: World Bank.

1980 "The World Bank and Institutional Development: Experience and Directions for Future Work." Report prepared by Project Advisory Staff. Washington: World Bank.

1981 *Health Sector Policy Paper.* Washington: World Bank.

Wynne, Susan
1981 "Thinking about Redesigning Resource Management Institutions in Botswana: Some Suggestions from Alexis de Tocqueville." Paper presented to the Midwestern Political Science Association, Cincinnati, April.

Yeasin, Mohammad
1984 "Organising Villagers for Self-Reliance: The Story of Deedar Comprehensive Cooperative Society, Comilla Bangladesh." Kashinathpur (Comilla), Bangladesh: Deedar Comprehensive Village Development Cooperative Society, mimeo.

Yoon, S. Y.
1983 "Women's Garden Groups in Casamance, Senegal." *Assignment Children,* 63/64, 133–153.

1985 "Women and Collective Self-Reliance: South Korea's New Community Movement." In Muntemba (1985, II:147–172).

Young, Oran R.
1982 *Resource Regimes: Natural Resources and Social Institutions.* Berkeley: University of California Press.

Country/Case Index

Page numbers in boldface refer to case studies in the Annexes

Subject Index

Author Index